INGREDIENTS FOR REVOLUTION

Ingredients for Revolution

A HISTORY OF AMERICAN FEMINIST RESTAURANTS, CAFES, AND COFFEEHOUSES

Alex D. Ketchum

Concordia University Press
Montreal

Cover illustration: tetiana_u/Shutterstock
Cover design, book design, and typesetting: Garet Markvoort, zijn digital
Proof reading: Saelan Twerdy
Index: J. Naomi Linzer

Printed and bound in Canada by Imprimerie Gauvin, Gatineau, Quebec

This book is printed on Forest Stewardship Council certified paper and meets the permanence of paper requirements of ANSI/NISO Z39.48-1992.

Concordia University Press's books are available for free on several digital platforms. Visit www.concordia.ca/press

First English edition published in 2022
10 9 8 7 6 5 4 3 2 1

978-1-988111-41-4 | Paper
978-1-988111-42-1 | E-book

Library and Archives Canada Cataloguing in Publication

Title: Ingredients for revolution : a history of American feminist restaurants, cafes, and coffeehouses / Alex D. Ketchum.
Names: Ketchum, Alex D., author.
Description: Includes index.
Identifiers: Canadiana (print) 20220400318 | Canadiana (ebook) 20220400377 | ISBN 9781988111414 (softcover) | ISBN 9781988111421 (HTML)
Subjects: LCSH: Restaurants—United States—History. | LCSH: Restaurateurs—United States—History. | LCSH: Women in the food industry—United States—History. | LCSH: Women food service employees—United States—History.
Classification: LCC TX909 .K48 2022 | DDC 647.95082/0973—dc23

Concordia University Press
1455 de Maisonneuve Blvd. W.
Montreal, Quebec H3G 1M8
CANADA

Concordia University Press gratefully acknowledges the generous support of the Birks Family Foundation, the Estate of Linda Kay, and the Estate of Tanneke De Zwart.

This book has been published with the help of a grant from the Federation for the Humanities and Social Sciences, through the Awards to Scholarly Publications Program, using funds provided by the Social Sciences and Humanities Research Council of Canada.

CONTENTS

INGREDIENTS FOR REVOLUTION

CHAPTER 1

Introduction

Food for Thought

In March 2017, Bloodroot Feminist Vegetarian Restaurant of Bridgeport, Connecticut, celebrated its fortieth anniversary. Three nights of official dinners, from the 21st to 23rd, marked the event. Over the course of six weeks, Bloodroot also hosted meals cooked by guest vegetarian chefs from around Connecticut, six different art exhibits, feminist guest speakers, a book fair, and four cooking classes.[1] These anniversary events reflected the same commitment to community building that contributed to Bloodroot's initial success. Commenting on their longevity, founder Selma Miriam remarked, "We just stuck with what we believe in," adding, "We have scraped and struggled, but we have always had devoted customers."[2] In the year of its founding, Bloodroot was one among hundreds of feminist restaurants, cafes, and coffeehouses in North America. In 2022, more than forty-five years later, however, Bloodroot is the only remaining feminist restaurant founded during the 1970s in the United States. The apex of American feminist restaurants was from 1976 to 1985. Most feminist restaurants, cafes, and coffeehouses closed after only a few years of operation; however, this does not mean that they were failures.

The history of feminist restaurants, cafes, and coffeehouses in the United States is a history of business practices, political activism, and food politics. *Ingredients for Revolution: A History of American Feminist Restaurants, Cafes, and Coffeehouses* is the first book to

1.1a and b These two images show Bloodroot Feminist Vegetarian Restaurant of Bridgeport, Connecticut's Selma Miriam (left in the foreground of both images) and Noel Furie (right in the foreground in both images), forty years apart, in 1977 or 1978 and 2017 respectively. The second image was taken as part of the restaurant's 40th anniversary celebrations. (Image 1.1a is courtesy of the Bloodroot Collective. Image 1.1b was taken by Ned Gerard of Hearst Connecticut Media)

study the more than 230 feminist and lesbian-feminist restaurants, cafes, and coffeehouses that existed in the United States, beginning in 1972. Utilizing business records, advertisements, feminist and lesbian periodicals, cookbooks, and more than a dozen original interviews, I examine the ways in which all feminist restaurants, cafes, and coffeehouses fostered non-capitalist and non-hierarchal business practices and models. Feminist restaurant history reveals the importance of physical space for socializing, activism, economics, and community building. By including a study of feminist coffeehouses, this book also highlights the contributions made by women with less access to capital than the restaurant owners. These feminist businesses were not isolated but instead were part of a larger economy and society that was not always amenable to their desires. The creation of women's spaces required innovative financial strategies. Balancing economic needs with philosophy required compromises. This book re-centres feminist entrepreneurialism and challenges narratives of postwar feminism.

Feminist restaurants, cafes, and coffeehouses merit our attention because they provide a model for creating businesses that challenge workplace inequity. Studying these spaces combats the erasure of feminist and lesbian feminist culture and underscores the contributions founders of feminist restaurants, cafes, and coffeehouses made to debates around food politics, community organizing, and labour rights, which continue today. Furthermore, this project contributes methodologically to the literature on the history of American feminist activism through an innovative consultation of lesbian and women's travel guides as sources for map building.

Feminist restaurants and cafes employed alternative business practices. These eateries were part of a larger nexus of feminist businesses. In addition to providing direct economic opportunities for the women who were employed by the restaurant, feminist restaurants and cafes promoted women-owned businesses, women artists, professionals, and craftswomen. As a result, the economic impact of these restaurants expanded beyond their single brick and mortar locations. Feminist restaurants and cafes of the 1970s and 1980s in the United States acted as spaces that challenged the status quo around cooking and consumption through the creation of feminist food. Each restaurant and cafe defined "feminist food" differently, based on the particular feminist ethics of the restaurant owners and operators. Depending on the restaurant, making food feminist required decision making around vegetarian ethics, labour issues, cost, and the sourcing of products. By analyzing what was included on or banned from restaurant menus, this book shows the ways that food could have been labelled as feminist.

In addition to including narratives about feminists from differing identity backgrounds, this book historically contextualizes the separatist strategies of certain feminist restaurants and coffeehouses within the larger story of feminist movements. The development of feminist restaurants was deeply interconnected with feminist literary culture. Written materials promoted their existence through guidebooks, periodicals, flyers, or business cards. Feminist restaurants also sold and distributed texts, hosted authors, and produced their own newsletters, cookbooks, advertisements, and ephemera. As much as feminist restaurants, cafes, and coffeehouses were about food, these spaces also were places where attendees could be exposed to feminist cultural productions: brain food.

In examining the history of feminist restaurants and the important role they served as spaces, this project also makes a methodological contribution to the field through my development of large databases of such spaces comprised from lesbian and women's travel guides, from which I then created maps using Geographic Information System (GIS) mapping technology. Bolstered by the creation of mapping interfaces, this project provides a new way to understand feminist activism during the second half of the twentieth century by prioritizing the role of space. Women studies scholar Bonnie J. Morris, in *The Disappearing L: Erasure of Lesbian Spaces and Culture*, expresses her "concern that as we advance further into the twenty-first century, we are witnessing the almost flippant dismissal of recent, late twentieth-century lesbian culture, particularly the loss of physical sites such as women's bookstores and women's music festivals and their material legacies (books, journals, albums, tapes, magazine interviews with artists)."[3] Likewise, scholar and lesbian activist Maxine Wolfe argues that one of the most persistent political struggles for lesbians has been their societal, historical, and spatial "invisibility."[4] In response, geographers such as Julie Podmore and

Line Chamberland have challenged this lack of visibility for the lesbian community.[5] Yielding to Wolfe, Podmore, Chamberland, and Morris's calls to re-centre lesbian and feminist culture, this book takes seriously the contributions of feminist restaurants, cafés, and coffeehouses, the literary culture that supported them, and the feminist nexus of the businesses that they were able to create. By including restaurants, cafes, and coffeehouses—businesses that required different initial capital investment—this book looks at feminist community spaces both created and frequented by women across lines of class, race, age, and sexual orientations.

Feminist restaurants prompt plenty of questions. One query raised is the relationship between the creation of feminist restaurants and the feminist discourse that searched for a solution to the "cooking problem": the societal expectations that burdened women with the responsibility of domestic food production. Solutions proposed by feminist authors during the era included buying pre-made foods rather than cooking, sharing housework responsibilities with male partners, requesting wages for housework, joining communes including but not limited to separatist lesbian farming communities, and founding food co-operatives to share cooking responsibilities amongst groups of families. At the start of this project, I assumed that feminists during the 1970s and 1980s had founded these restaurants when they saw that, like previous women liberationists such as Charlotte Perkins Gilman in the early twentieth century, communal cooking could lift them from the drudgery of the kitchen.[6] However, these restaurants challenged the common contemporary view of cooking as antithetical to women's liberation and instead showed that the kitchen could in fact be a space for women's empowerment rather than an oppressive sphere.

Consciousness-raising (CR) groups from the early 1970s did in fact discuss issues of housework and, specifically, cooking. Entire sections of CR pamphlets, such as Harriet Perl and Gay Abarbanell's *Guidelines to Feminist Consciousness Raising*, were devoted to gendered divisions of household labour. Feminist periodicals from the late 1960s through the mid-1970s published numerous pieces about the burden of cooking. Despite this, the motivation for creating these restaurants was far less about drudgery. Their formation was not entirely divorced from the kinds of dialogue happening in CR groups, but was instead focused on creating a new model, rather than just altering an exploitative one. Unsurprisingly, radical feminists who were invested in overturning the system found this approach appealing. In addition, these restaurants played an important role in incubating, shaping, and disseminating ideas within the feminist activist community. Feminist restaurant, cafe, and coffeehouse history thus demonstrates the necessity of access to spaces for socializing, activism, economics, and community building.

Terminology

FEMINIST RESTAURANTS AND CAFES

Feminist restaurants and cafes in the 1970s and 1980s were unique spaces that have received little academic attention. Indeed, few texts mention feminist restaurants specifically. Historian A. Finn Enke in *Finding the Movement* wrote about feminist restaurants as part of a larger study about feminist activism in the Midwestern United States. Warren J. Belasco's *Appetite for Change* chronicles the 1960s counterculture food movement in the United States. Although he is mostly interested in the ways that corporations co-opted the movement, he highlights the ways that the food movement intersected with ideas of the New Left, the sexual revolution, and women's liberation. His book has two paragraphs about Mother Courage, the feminist restaurant founded in New York City in 1972. Neither text is specifically about feminist restaurants.

More historiographical emphasis, however, has been put on the history of gay and lesbian bar culture. While histories of bars and restaurants both deal with the role of consumption in public spaces and in creating community, histories of bar culture differ from restaurant and cafe history due to their emphasis on criminalized behaviour.[7] Still, studies of bar culture provide important models for how to understand the impact of feminist restaurants. Researchers have investigated the ways that lesbian and gay restaurants were important for activism. George Chauncey's work on gay male culture in New York from 1890 to 1940 looks at restaurants, cafes, and bars.[8] His book is especially pertinent as he credits the creation of bars as central to the formation of a larger gay male world. Women's studies scholar Trisha Franzen's writings about lesbians in Albuquerque, New Mexico, show the important role played by restaurants and bars in the formation of the local lesbian community. Most importantly, the places where Albuquerque lesbians chose to congregate from 1965 to 1980 said much about their social position, emphasizing class differences.[9] Historian Nan Alamilla Boyd has looked at gay, lesbian, and queer bar culture in San Francisco until 1965.[10] Boyd emphasizes the importance of spaces that centered on food and drink for simultaneously prompting political organization and forging a sense of community. The canonical work *Boots of Leather, Slippers of Gold*, which traces the evolution of the working-class lesbian community in Buffalo, New York, from the mid-1930s to the early 1960s, provides a model for how to utilize oral histories when dealing with lesbian spaces, specifically bars.[11] Although these studies evoke space as a methodological tool, this book differs due to the larger scale of my focus.

Part of the paucity of research on feminist restaurants arises from the difficulty of defining these spaces. The feminist restaurants of the 1970s and 1980s were not a continuation of the women's restaurants from the start of the twentieth century. While there were some similarities between them, as restaurant historian Jan Whitaker notes, the women's or feminist restaurants of these two periods were quite different even though "they shared a dedication to furthering women's causes and giving women spaces of their own in which to eat meals, hold meetings, and in the 1970s, to enjoy music and poetry by women."[12] However, the women's restaurants of the 1910s that were invested in furthering women's political, social, and economic causes were, in fact, suffrage restaurants, tearooms, or lunchrooms sponsored by organizations such as the National American Woman Suffrage Association (NAWSA). NAWSA established these restaurants with the intent to lure men in with a cheap lunch, which would then provide them the opportunity to lobby these men and give them literature about women's suffrage.[13] While feminist restaurants of the second half of the twentieth century also were involved in politics, the goals tended to focus on creating spaces for those already allied to the cause rather than recruitment and conversion.

For the purposes of this book, to avoid policing who can call themselves feminist and to make the project the most manageable, I decided that a restaurant must be identified as feminist in either its title, in flyers, in interviews, or in descriptions in restaurant reviews, magazines, or periodicals. Within these parameters, a central tenet of the restaurant owners and operators' philosophy was a focus on the needs of women and feminists above all other goals. This book examines intentional feminist spaces and is interested in why owners would choose to call their restaurant "feminist."

Self-identified feminist restaurants and cafes acted as spaces that challenged the status quo of cooking and consumption. These businesses fulfilled the desire for geographies separate from men to escape the oppressive formal restraints that regulated female socializing in male-dominated establishments. Feminist restaurants and cafes also provided spaces for political organizing, recreational activity, and commerce. While the owners of restaurants such as Bloodroot Feminist Vegetarian Restaurant of Bridgeport, Connecticut, self-identified their business as feminist in their title, others were not so overt. Feminist restaurants such as Artemis (San Francisco, California) or Moonrise Café (Santa Rosa, California) relied on environmental and mystical imagery. These restaurants spoke to a connection between women and the earth, nature, mythology, and empowerment. The word "moon" was particularly common, with five restaurants in the United States using it in their title. Another common trend in naming was to use the word "women" as well as its alternative spellings of "womyn" and "wimmin." When including the coffeehouses, twenty-three of the restaurants used "woman" in the title, eighty-seven used "women," three used "womyn," and one used "wimmin." In a similar vein, five restaurants were named "mother," four used the variant "mama," and fourteen "sister." In Milwaukee, Wisconsin, Sister Moon used both the nature imagery of "moon" and the familial "sister" for both of its locations. Thirty-nine of these businesses explicitly used the word "feminist" in their title.

Feminist restaurant owners produced advertisements, business cards, and flyers for special events like concerts, poetry presentations, lectures, and guest talks by feminists, as well as other forms of entertainment. In addition, restaurant owners wrote menus and cookbooks. Owners would also identify their space as feminist in these documents, which could be important if the title was not explicit. Apart from self-definition, it can be more difficult to categorize these businesses. Many, but not all of them, were either women-only spaces or had women-only hours at some point during their operation. Collectives ran many of the spaces and radical lesbian-separatist, socialist-feminist, or ecofeminist ideologies influenced many of the owners. Most restaurants held events with feminist and lesbian poets, musicians, artists, and political speakers because creating a community space was important to many of the owners. However, the most important factor for inclusion in this study is whether the restaurant was an intentional feminist space.

For the purposes of this study, restaurants and cafes are grouped together. The word "cafe" can denote a kind of diner, coffee shop, or bistro space with a full breakfast, lunch, or dinner menu; it can refer to a business that exclusively serves a breakfast menu; or it can describe a space that just served coffee. Furthermore, if a feminist bookstore sold coffee, tea, or snacks, it was included in this category, as having refreshments created a space to linger. Coffeehouses were different from cafés and coffee shops, however.

FEMINIST COFFEEHOUSES

Coffeehouses in this book will primarily refer to temporary public spaces that served refreshments and whose emphasis was on providing entertainment. Coffeehouses could be one-time benefit shows, such as the benefit for *Hera's Journal* hosted by Judy's Café of Philadelphia in 1975.[14] Other coffeehouses, such as Mountain Moving Coffeehouse of the Chicago area, existed from 1974 until 2005, changing venues throughout their history but usually renting out local church basements for Saturday night lesbian-feminist music entertainment. Coffeehouses could also be special events or recurring events in typically non-explicitly feminist spaces, such as church basements, thus creating a temporary feminist space. In part two of this book, which focuses on these temporary spaces, I primarily discuss the recurring coffeehouses. Confusion arises because some cafes called themselves coffeehouses despite being permanent spaces. Also, feminist cafes and restaurants would hold events that they would call coffeehouse hours. To add even further confusion, feminist coffeehouses typically were not too original in their titles. Sixteen establishments within my research were entitled "The Women's Coffeehouse." Three were called "Everywoman's Coffeehouse" and one, "Anywoman." To avoid confusion, I will specify locations of the coffeehouse even when the location was not part of their formal title such as the Women's Coffeehouse, Denver, Colorado, and the Women's Coffeehouse, Iowa City, Iowa.

WOMEN'S SPACE

A consistent trend within feminist restaurants, cafes, and coffeehouses during the 1970s and 1980s in the United States was the constant questioning and renegotiation of the meaning of women-only and women-centred spaces, and whether such goals remained important. Throughout this period, women's space provided social, cultural, and political geographies for women. By the late 1970s, however, the term "women's space" generally became, in most circumstances, code for lesbian-separatist space.[15] For the purpose of this book, when referring to a particular feminist restaurant, cafe, or coffeehouse, the terms the owners used will be the ones I will employ, when available. When I speak about the spaces more broadly, however, I have created a set of terms to help make the distinction between women-only and women-friendly spaces.

Woman-space/women's spaces and women-centred spaces refer to woman-owned and -operated spaces, whether at a permanent location or run by a group at multiple venues. Women's spaces sought to create a community for social, economic, and political organization. These spaces were inherently political as they came out of discussions in the consciousness-raising groups of the late 1960s and early 1970s and the need for geographies apart from men. When, at the end of the 1970s and into the early 1980s, the word "woman" in woman-space began to be code for lesbian in many establishments, lesbian spaces entitled "woman-space" still upheld the tenets of woman-space. Although these businesses targeted lesbian participation, they were not the same as exclusively lesbian spaces. Woman-centred spaces were places whose mission statements were about women, but most allowed men to visit as long as they were respectful of the space. Finally, a woman-friendly space did not have to be owned or operated by women nor did it require any political activist principles, although it could. Woman-friendly spaces could be restaurants and cafes that did not specifically cater to women but fostered an environment that was welcoming and safe for them. To clarify, if a business described itself as a woman's space, a feminist space, a lesbian space, or some other term, I use that term to speak about the place. The labels of woman-centred and woman-friendly are categories that I have created as useful organizational concepts.

WOMEN/WOMYN/WIMMIN/WOMBAN/LESBIAN/FEMINIST

Another definitional problem comes from the use of the terms "women," "lesbian," and "feminist," and how these words do not allow for all the multiplicity of identities within those categories. Intersecting factors like race, class, age, religion, and geographic region impacted whether women chose to identify themselves and their business establishments as "women," "lesbian," "feminist," "womyn," "wimmen," "womin," "womban," "women-loving-women," "wom*n," and other terms such as "real woman," and later "cis-women," "womxn,"[16] and "trans women." The creation of alternative spellings of the word "woman/women" was a political project of redefinition: to state that women were spiritually, socially, and physically defined by their own terms and did not exist only in relation to men. To remove the "e" and thus the word "men" meant that these alternative spellings were an expression of female independence and a refutation of traditions that defined women in reference to the male norm.[17] The term "real woman" emerged when feminist and lesbian spaces were deciding who was allowed to use the space and whether transsexual or transgender women could participate in the women's community. Cisgender refers to individuals who identify with the gender that they were assigned at birth whereas transgender individuals identify with a different gender than the one they were assigned at birth. The politics of trans-exclusion and trans-inclusion was especially pertinent for women-only spaces and women-only hours. "Women-loving-women" and "lesbian" referred to similar individuals, but "women-loving-women" placed more emphasis on the emotional connection between women, whereas as the term "lesbian" emphasized sexual orientation. During the 1970s and 1980s, the word "queer" was primarily used as a slur and the political project of reclaiming the term for self-identification and empowerment did not happen until the late 1980s.[18] Calling the feminist restaurants founded during the 1970s through mid-1980s "queer spaces" would therefore be anachronistic.

The problem of terminology is not unique to this book. Historian Alice Echols, author of *Daring to Be Bad*, argues that these terminological changes have to do with shifts from radical feminism to cultural feminism. Likewise, historian Benita Roth, in *Separate Roads to Feminism*, notes that charting these changes is not so simple due to the ways in which feminism developed in various regions, within different identity groups, and on different timelines. Some scholars, however, have tried to reconcile this problem by ignoring it. Social scientist Nancy Stoller's article on lesbian activism confirms this trend when she notes that

> In many cases, the language of the movement itself conflated women and lesbians. For example, during the mid-1970s, as lesbian culture went public, it was labeled "women's culture" by its promoters; for example, "women's music", which was really lesbian music, of course, and music for a predominately white, college-educated audience at that. That this conflation still exists is shown by the fact that Olivia Records, the primary vector for lesbian/women's music, now sells "women's cruises" (no pun acknowledged), which are designed for lesbians, not for "feminists" or women in general. The feminist movement and the lesbian movement were parallel and interconnecting; they were also linked to other movements and had considerable diversity within them.[19]

But Stoller, like many other scholars, generally just accepts this confusion. Professor of women's studies Janet Jakobsen also points to this conflation and challenges its essentialism, but ultimately does not provide much of a pragmatic scheme of how to deal with it.[20]

As this book likewise covers the broad geographic range of the United States over multiple decades, these differences are complicated; activists invested themselves in the liberatory potential of language and term reclamation. During the 1970s and 1980s, activists particularly conflated the terms "lesbian" and "feminist" and would sometimes employ a simultaneous meaning by using "woman/women" as coded terms. Especially in literature and cultural artifacts that the public might have been exposed to and potentially hostile towards—such as musical records, periodicals, and books—authors and artists would employ the term "woman" so that the intended audience would know the material was for lesbians, but the general public would not see the materials as a threat to heteronormative culture.[21] Furthermore, in certain radical feminist communities, such as those inhabited by the owners of Bloodroot Feminist Vegetarian Restaurant in Bridgeport, Connecticut, the idea of lesbianism was integral to being a feminist.[22] This perspective was reflected in the motto, "Feminism is the theory and lesbianism is the practice."[23]

While current cultural discussions of gay, lesbian, and queer identities centre on debates of self-identification and the idea of a genetic rationale for sexual orientation, during the early 1970s a serious debate occurred within feminist literature and communities of whether one could have sexual relationships with men and still self-identify as a feminist.[24] As a result of these debates, some women spoke of "choosing to be lesbian," such as Selma Miriam, co-founder of Bloodroot Feminist Vegetarian Restaurant.[25] Other feminists, however, wrote about how they found living out their politics by only having sexual and emotional relationships with women as incredibly difficult because they missed having relationships with men, thus making political lesbianism untenable.[26] Flavia Rando, who cooked at The Women's Coffeehouse in New York City, said the coffeehouse's clientele consisted of mostly lesbians and youth.[27] However, the management used the word "women" so it would be flexible and open for women who were questioning.[28] Julie Podmore also believes that the term "women" allowed for openness.[29] On the other hand, homophobic activists feared what Betty Friedan termed in 1969 "the lavender menace," referring to the public's perception of lesbian feminists, and saw lesbians as a threat to the politics of respectability that was being advocated for by straight feminist activists.[30] The fear of the "lavender menace" became associated with liberal branches of feminism that sought women's empowerment through legislative change and women reaching positions of power rather than an overhauling of society and all power models, which was key to radical feminist politics. These homophobic feminists obviously did not use "women" as code for lesbian. Depending on what terms businesses used, different groups of people would either be included or excluded from feminist restaurants, cafes, and coffeehouses. For the purposes of this book, when known, I use the terms that people used for themselves.

Though I do not conflate feminists and lesbians within my project, lesbian feminists owned and operated the majority of feminist restaurants. As a result, my project also speaks to the history of lesbians within the United States. Sociologist Becki Ross has shown the way that spaces have been influential in forming lesbian cultural identity.[31] Stewart Van Cleve's *Land of 10,000 Loves* also pays attention to the importance of space. Van Cleve showcases the ways in which geographies and places have influenced activism, education, and community building by and for lesbian, gay, bisexual, transgender, and queer peoples in the American Midwest. This project follows suit. Depending on the terms the owners of the spaces used, the communities within the feminist restaurants, cafes, and coffeehouses, in turn, looked different.

The term "feminist" is likewise complicated, as there are numerous kinds of feminism, including but not limited to: socialist, liberal, Marxist, radical, separatist, radical lesbian-separatist, and ecofeminist, as well as groups that challenged racist histories in feminist movements, such as "womanist." Due to the variety of feminist ideologies, within feminist historiography authors often treat the work done by liberal feminists, socialist feminists, and radical feminists separately and do not focus on the ways in which feminists with varying ideologies also worked together. Feminist restaurants were not the only spaces to draw feminists of different political leanings together. In fact, feminist bookstores and brick and mortar businesses, like feminist gift shops, had to appeal to a broader understanding of feminism to maintain a large enough clientele to stay in business. So, while I specify particular branches of feminism when these distinctions are necessary, by keeping the term "feminism" somewhat open, as the restaurants and coffeehouses did, this book is able to discuss broader groups.

Likewise, this book employs an expanded understanding of what feminist activism is. Historian Benita Roth's book *Separate Roads to Feminism* challenges other historians' definitions of activism by claiming that work done by women of different races, whether labelled as feminist or not, contributed to the women's liberation movement. She is particularly attentive to the different pressures that women faced within their smaller, more local communities, as well as their larger regional and racial communities. This expanded understanding of activism is particularly useful for us to understand the political and social contributions feminist restaurants, cafes, and coffeehouses made.

The issue of terminology has no easy solution and is constantly evolving, as evidenced by my discussions of contemporary businesses in chapter 8. While at points in this book the term "women" may appear too broad, I have been as specific as possible. The "sisterhood" may have been powerful, but it was always diverse and meant different things to different groups.

FEMINIST/WOMEN'S MOVEMENTS VS. WAVE METAPHOR

According to the authors of "Is It Time to Jump Ship? Historians Rethink the Waves Metaphor," the metaphor of feminism's waves (first, second, and third) "highlights periods when middle-class white women were most active in the public sphere." They argue that "the multi-dimensional aspects of feminism are too often excluded." In this interpretation, "women of color, working-class women, women with disabilities, lesbians, and older women who engaged in activism that responded to overlapping forms of oppression, including sexism, have rarely been incorporated into waves narratives in their own right."[32] Likewise, the edited volume *Not June Cleaver* shows that wave theory erases the feminist activism that was happening throughout the twentieth century.[33] In fact, understanding feminist activism as a history of women's movements—emphasis on the plural—represents the historical conditions better than a monolithic singular movement.

Individual activists were often involved with more than one movement and communicated or transferred organizational strategies and epistemologies between groups, which often resulted in allied community organizations. Single-issue causes are, in fact, not truly about a single issue. A growing body of literature has developed regarding how actors in social movements could be involved in multiple, overlapping, and intersecting movements. Books such as Sara Evan's *Personal Politics*, Harriet Alonso's *Peace as a Women's Issue*, and Barbara Epstein's *Political Protest and Cultural Revolution: Non-violent Direct Action in the 1970s* demonstrate the way that feminism was so greatly influenced by other social movements of the 1960s and 1970s. They place feminism within the historical context of a politically charged time and portray activists as complex individuals who were engaged in multiple, often changing, political causes. Still, there is a gap in the literature on feminism during this period. While historians have shown the relationship between feminism and the sexual liberation movement, gay liberation, civil rights, Black power, Chicano liberation, the anti-nuclear movements, the peace movements, the food movements, and the environmental movements, no one has yet to speak of the intersections between all these movements. A spatial approach to feminist restaurants allows for an analysis that incorporates all of them while still acknowledging change over time. This technique thus enables a history of women's liberation that treats these activists as full humans with multiple commitments, inspirations, and the ability to change.

Archival Sources and Oral Histories

This book relies on archival sources, literature from the period, and oral history. To complete this project, I assembled materials from nineteen archives around the United States and Canada. I worked with English, French, and Spanish sources. At these archives I sourced textual sources such as periodicals, diaries, day planners, notebooks, and newspaper and magazine articles, as well as posters, event promotional flyers, surveys, audiotapes, buttons, t-shirts, menus, photographs, napkins, travel guides, advertisements, ephemera, and other paraphernalia. The Bloodroot records at Yale University, the Bread and Roses records at the Schlesinger Library on the History of Women in America of the Radcliffe Institute at Harvard University, A Woman's Coffeehouse records at the University of Minnesota Archives, and the Las Hermanas Coffeehouse records at the San Diego LAMBDA Archives were quite comprehensive. They housed an assortment of business records, meeting minutes, newspaper and magazine clippings with publicity, legal documents, menus, and personal papers of the owners. However, such complete records were rare. For most of the feminist restaurants, cafes, and coffeehouses presented in this book, scant traces remained in the archives. A business card, an event poster, or a mention in a musician's liner notes was sometimes the only remaining trace of a feminist restaurant's existence. Therefore, this project would not have been possible if archival materials were the only available source. I also relied on feminist literary materials such as feminist and lesbian periodicals, magazines, and travel guides (including every available edition of *Gaia's Guide*).

Oral histories were what truly made this project possible, however. The difficulty of writing a social history of marginalized peoples is that their records are less likely to be preserved in archives.[34] I conducted

1.2 These are the 1977 and 1981 editions of Gaia's Guide. *These travel guides provided travellers with information about lesbian and feminist businesses. Travel guides acted as a valuable resource for locating feminist restaurants, cafes, and coffeehouses as they noted locations and short descriptions of different businesses. (Photo by the author)*

a series of interviews with the founders, staff, and customers of feminist restaurants, cafes, and coffeehouses in the United States. While being able to conduct interviews with people who worked for or visited feminist restaurants, cafes, and coffeehouses could not have replaced the physical documents from the archives, these oral testimonies often answered the questions that business records and event flyers could not. Inspired by Ann Cvetkovich's drive to document oral histories in *An Archive of Feelings*, "In forging a collective knowledge built on memory, I hope to produce not only a version of history but also an archive of the emotions."[35] Even if gender historian Joan Scott rejects the notion that historians can capture experience in the sense of "lived reality" or "raw events," she concedes, "experience is not a word we can do without."[36] The women I interviewed spoke about their individual experiences in a particular space. That level of personal reflection is missing in a box of receipts, diagrams of floor plans, and even photographs documenting events that happened at these feminist restaurants, cafes, and coffeehouses.

The process of locating interviewees grew organically. This entire project, in fact, stemmed from a first, informal interview. While completing my undergraduate studies at Wesleyan University in Middletown, Connecticut, a friend suggested I visit Bloodroot Feminist Vegetarian Restaurant, located forty minutes away in Bridgeport, Connecticut. An initial five-minute chat with the owners Selma Miriam and Noel Furie in 2011 led to more than a dozen formal interviews with feminist restaurant, cafe, and coffeehouse founders, staff, and customers around the United States. Locating the interviewees was made possible in two ways. The first method consisted of finding the name of a feminist business owner in a feminist periodical, advertisement, or in an archive. I would then conduct internet searches, scour old phone books, and use my connections to feminist Facebook groups directed at lesbian feminists in their sixties, seventies, and eighties, where I posted to ask for help connecting with the women I wanted to interview. Occasionally, people would find me. After presenting my work in academic and non-academic settings and through sharing information about this research on the website The Feminist Restaurant Project (thefeministrestaurantproject.com), people would offer to be interviewed or connect me with their personal network of friends and former co-workers who had worked in these establishments.

Part three of this book, which focuses on feminist restaurants and cafes founded after 1989, benefits from internet resources. In the twenty-first century, it has become more commonplace for American businesses to create websites to share information with their customers. Furthermore, the rise of businesses using social media networks for publicity and community building has provided a trove of resources. Parts 1 and 2 of this book utilize more analogue research methods, while part 3 employs more digital methods.

Quantitative Methods: Maps and Digital Display

While the combined archival work, literary analysis, and interviews yielded useful case studies, additionally I have incorporated a quantitative aspect to my research. I built original databases, which showcase the locations and years of these feminist restaurants, cafes, and coffeehouses' operation. From these databases it was then possible to create a series of maps that are useful for both visualization and for analytical purposes. For a detailed description of how I built my databases and maps, refer to the appendix.

With a commitment to open access and public dissemination, in 2013 I created the Feminist Restaurant Project to showcase my findings and gather new data. On this website there is a simplified version of my database, which is also available in the appendix. The Feminist Restaurant Project website also serves as a useful interface with the public, where former patrons and owners of feminist restaurants, cafes, and coffeehouses can contact me and suggest other locations for research. From the collated information from the guidebooks, periodicals, advertisements, interviews, and the website interface, I was able to update my database and create colour-coded maps that showed confirmed feminist restaurants in magenta and possible, but not confirmed, feminist restaurants in teal. For the larger, international map showcasing the locations of all the restaurants, cafes, and coffeehouses, Google Maps was the most pragmatic application. In addition to being able to email about their own experiences, visitors to the site had the opportunity to add to their own contribution to a public map made with Story Map Crowdsource (beta), an ArcGIS web application designed to collect photos and captions from anyone and displayed them on a map until 2016.[37] As the editors of *Queers in Space* Gordon Brent Ingram, Anne Bouthillette, and

Yolanda Retter note, temporary geographies were important to queer activist organizing and community building.[38] Digital representations like maps and user forums have thus helped to maintain and create new digitally based communities.

The first step of finding feminists, especially an expanded group of women that could be categorized as feminists, is to find where they gathered. The technique of analyzing spaces to find a broadened definition of historical actors is not unique to my research. A. Finn Enke, in *Finding the Movement*, is interested in locating feminists in the Midwest and looks at a variety of places, including bookstores, cafes, parks, health clinics, and credit unions, to find them. Furthermore, feminist geographers such as Lise Nelson, Joni Seager, and Madge Clare have made great developments on ideas about how women use space. In the most basic sense, feminist geographers have unsettled assumptions about what are women and men's spaces by crafting nuanced descriptions of the public and private spheres.[39] They have shown how space is gendered and that there is spatial variation between communities.[40] Most importantly, feminist geographers have raised important questions about how spaces change the ways that people relate with ideas, their surroundings, and each other.[41] My own employment of the spatial approach is somewhat different.

Qualitative Methods: Case Studies

Mapping enabled me to notice patterns and analyze differences between the various feminist restaurants more readily. Of course, the maps do not stand on their own. To supplement this quantitative methodology, the rest of the book focuses on qualitative research methods. Each chapter relies on a few sample restaurants as case studies to explore the contributions of feminist restaurants, cafes, and coffeehouses to debates around cooking and feminist businesses in greater detail. The case studies were chosen based on several factors: I wanted to represent geographical diversity, focus on longevity and impact, showcase the histories of founders from diverse identity backgrounds, and illustrate the major themes in the book.

Prioritizing geographic diversity was important as this project challenges the historiographical concentration on feminist movements during the 1970s and 1980s in New York City, the Eastern Seaboard, and San Francisco. Indeed, these cities contributed to the history of feminist restaurants, cafes, and coffeehouses and are not overlooked in this book. However, Iowa City, Portland, and Tampa had thriving feminist business communities (as can be seen in the maps of their feminist business nexus in 1981 in the appendix). In fact, as is apparent on the major map, feminist restaurants, cafes, and coffeehouses were spread all over the United States. Every state at some point during the 1970s and 1980s had a feminist restaurant, cafe, or coffeehouse, with the exceptions of Alaska, Arkansas, North Dakota, West Virginia, and Wyoming.[42] The common factor of these regions was that, except for West Virginia, most had small or sparsely distributed populations that made supporting a feminist restaurant more difficult. By 1989, however, Fargo, North Dakota, had a lesbian bar and Anchorage, Alaska, had a women's centre beginning in 1979.[43] Women's studies scholar Barbara Ryan's work on feminism in the Midwest shows that by looking at feminist activism outside of these few urban centres, we can see the ways in which certain ideas of the women's movements came to different regions at different times, sometimes after more than one or two years of circulating in an urban centre.[44] As is evident from both the timeline concluding this chapter and the directory in the appendix, it was not so much that feminist restaurants started on the coasts and spread inwards but rather that feminist restaurants, cafes, and coffeehouses began earlier in larger cities and then were founded in smaller cities. This happened because those regions had large enough populations of women who identified as feminists to support a specifically feminist business earlier on. In smaller cities and towns that did not have large enough populations to support numerous feminist businesses, the feminist bookstore served as a meeting point and space of congregation, eating, and socializing, as was the case of the Community Café and Women's Bookstore in Bethesda, Maryland, in 1983. In even smaller towns, a single business would serve as a multi-functioning space for various marginalized communities, such as Alan Gold's of Chattanooga, Tennessee, which was frequented both by gay men and lesbians. As the comment about Alan Gold's from the 1984 edition of *Gaia's Guide* states, "we basically all stick together as a group."[45] In the directory, italics mark these women-friendly spaces like Alan Gold's. These spaces were women-owned (but not identified as feminist) or advertised as being spaces where women and lesbians were welcomed to eat alone or as a couple. The italic list is incomplete but provides a sample of the kinds of spaces women would use for socializing, and that were advertised to women for socializing but were not explicitly women's spaces/feminist spaces/lesbian spaces.

I was initially interested in regional differences and the role that feminist spaces had in shaping and being shaped by those differences. What I found, however, was that while federal, state, and municipal laws created conditions that feminist restaurant founders had to contend with (such as how to file their taxes, deal with zoning laws, food safety laws, and alcohol licencing), the geographic difference between states were not as significant as linguistic, racial, and class differences. American feminist restaurants were generally founded due to the same motivational drive: the owners sought to create space where they could socialize, work as "out" lesbians, and make money in a manner that reflected their political values.

Despite geographical differences, feminist restaurant owners in the 1970s and 1980s were primarily white, lesbian, working and middle class, with some external way to access capital or utilize intense sweat equity. They were also between the ages of twenty-five to forty at time of starting the business, English speaking, and a disproportionately large percentage, relative to the general population, were Jewish.[46] There were a few notable exceptions to this description, for example, the owners of the Black women's restaurant the Philadelphia Mahogany Black Women's Club (1984).[47] The linguistic difference exemplifies the privilege held by English-speaking business owners in most American states, and also the importance of a shared feminist anglophone literary culture that promoted the creation of these feminist restaurants, cafes, and coffeehouses. Feminist restaurants, coffeehouses, and cafes' connection to feminist literary culture in the 1970s and 1980s in the United States was vital for the dissemination of their ideas and the creation of feelings of community. Written materials promoted their existence, be they guidebooks, periodicals, flyers, or business cards. Feminist restaurants sold and distributed texts, hosted authors, and produced their own newsletters, advertisements, and ephemera. As much as feminist restaurants, cafes, and coffeehouses were about food, these spaces were also places where attendees would devour their words. This ability to access print culture is key to understanding how women found these feminist restaurants, cafes, and coffeehouses.[48]

Coffeehouses had a greater diversity of founders, especially regarding race and class. In Minneapolis, Minnesota, A Woman's Coffeehouse was frequented by primarily white working-class lesbians, and San Diego's Las Hermanas coffeehouse was founded by working-class Latina women. Chapters 2 and 6 delve deeper into the identities of the founders of feminist restaurants and coffeehouses and chapters 3 and 7 deal explicitly with class issues and financing. Chapter 8 discusses how twenty-first century feminist restaurants and cafe owners and operators represent a greater diversity of identities.

As this study covers the entire United States, a level of precision regarding laws and regulations that impacted feminist restaurant owners' decisions regarding business operations is impossible in the way that a micro-study of a singular region could attend to. Similarly, a scaling up of this project to the level of a global history of feminist restaurants would require too vast a literature and would make claims about laws even more difficult than dealing with municipal, state, and national differences. To analyze restaurants, cafes, bookstores, health centres, women's shelters, and galleries throughout the United States would be impossible. Thus, I have decided to narrow my research to feminist restaurants, cafes, and coffeehouses. Chapters 4 and 7 show the relationships between feminist restaurants and coffeehouses and other feminist businesses in a particular town or city. I have used the term "feminist nexus" after the 1976 *Boston Herald* feature which called the conglomeration of feminist businesses in Cambridge, Massachusetts, a "nexus."[49] The maps in this book's appendix marking feminist businesses in Portland, Oregon, Tampa, Florida, and Madison, Wisconsin, from 1981 illustrate some of these dynamics.

Case studies were also based on the availability of source materials. As previously mentioned, for restaurants such as Womonspace in Lawrence, Kansas (1977), The Sunshine Inn in St. Louis, Missouri (1983–84), and A Place of One's Own in South River, New Jersey (1979–81), all I had was a listing in a *Gaia's Guide*.[50] For other restaurants, I only had a single business card or a single event flyer. As Bloodroot Feminist Vegetarian Restaurant's owners continue to operate their business and were interested in participating in the research, I was able to interview them on multiple occasions. These women have also produced six cookbooks as of 2018, have donated their personal papers to Yale University Archives, and have been the subject of documentaries and interviewed for dozens of newspaper and magazine articles since 1977. Patricia Hynes of Bread and Roses Feminist Restaurant of Cambridge, Massachusetts, donated her personal papers to the Schlesinger Library of Harvard University and was willing to be interviewed. Businesses that have operated for a longer period generated a greater paper trail. Restaurants that went out of business after a few months of operation were less likely to retain their files and the owners were less likely to donate their files to an archive. Furthermore, despite having gathered materials from nineteen archives and collections, I was still very dependent on just a few women's recollections. For most of my case studies, even if the information came from flyers, meeting minutes, and interviews, oftentimes the narrative of a restaurant's history came from a single perspective without corroboration. Just as there are challenges in piecing together a restaurant's history from a few scraps of text, it is also challenging to reconstruct a restaurant's entire history from the recollections of a single individual.

Combined Methods

The combination of quantitative and qualitative methods broadens the scales of analysis that are possible. The time has come to take space seriously in researching the past, not just intellectually but methodologically. Giving more attention to lesbian and women's travel guides enables this pursuit. Utilizing these geographic methodologies presents a new perspective through which to view activism of the past. By analyzing spaces in this way, we can locate a broadened definition of historical actors. Building databases and creating maps with GIS software complicates our understandings of the developments of social movements and challenges our assumptions about where activism happened. To navigate these issues of scale, the methodological choice to bring together case studies and maps

1.3 (OVERLEAF) *When available in archives, the day planners and notebooks of feminist restaurant founders helped provide a sense of the day-to-day work of operating these establishments. This day planner of Patricia Hynes, the founder of Bread and Roses of Cambridge, Massachusetts, includes her notes for different tasks, such as when to make orders from suppliers, the dates of special events, and more. The planner itself is also an interesting historical artifact as it is a feminist day planner that includes women's history facts for each day. (Schlesinger Library, Harvard Radcliffe Institute, Papers of H. Patricia Hynes, 1974–2004, Box 1, Folder 6)*

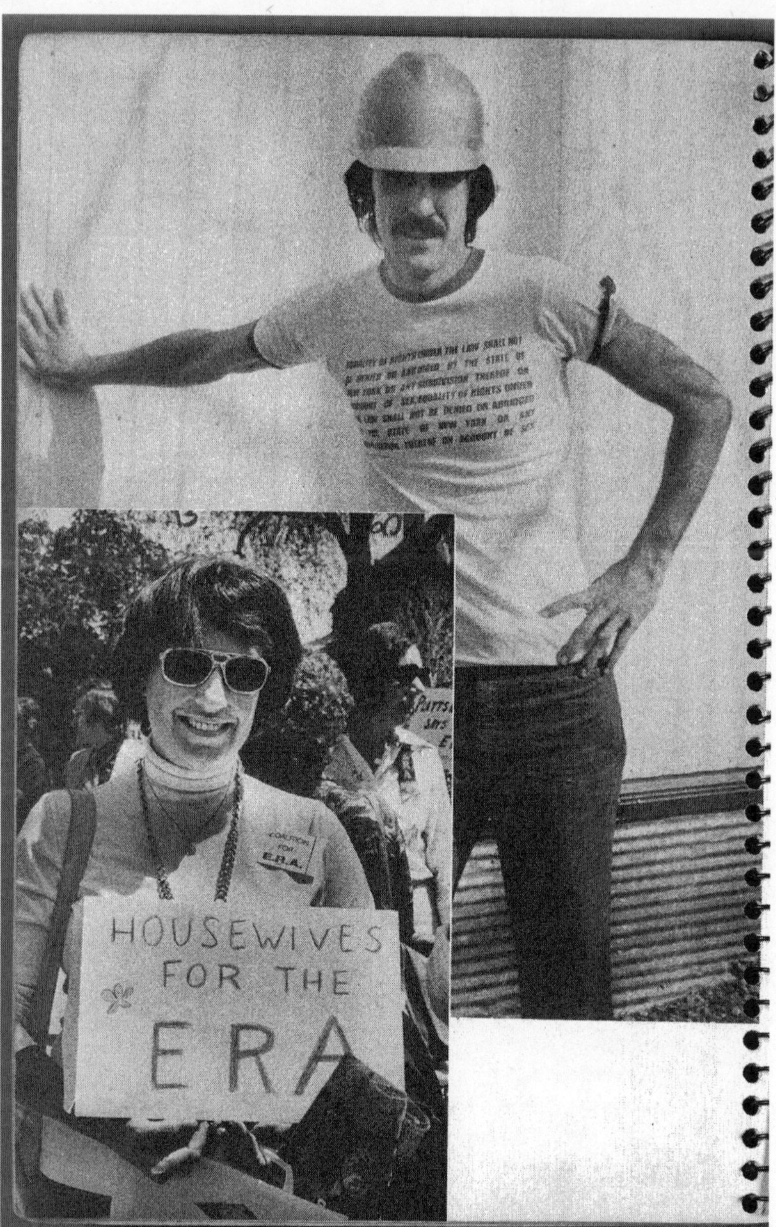
COALITION FOR E.R.A.
HOUSEWIVES FOR THE ERA

FEBRUARY

sun 20

Dinner 6:30 Italian $4.25
presentation to be announced
Ann Tyson 628-2808 N. Cambridge

Angelina Grimké, Southern suffragist and abolitionist, born, 1805.

mon 21

~~Lexington Now~~ - ~~Dinner + Talk~~ $5.00
~~Will contact HPH~~

Washington's Birthday celebrated

Susan Estrich is elected the first female president in the 89-year publishing history of the **Harvard Law Review**, 1976.

tues 22

Josephine Kirby Williamson Henry, the first woman in the South to run for a state office (in Kentucky) and author of more than 300 articles on the subject of "Married Women's Property Rights," born, 1846.

wed 23

Ash Wednesday

U.S. Supreme Court agrees to decide whether it is illegal to discriminate against widowers on the basis of sex by making it easier for widowed women than men to get Social Security survivor's benefits, 1976.

thurs 24

Acting on a suit brought by Stephanie Crawford, a federal appeals court rules that it was unconstitutional for the Marine Corps to discharge women marines automatically because they became pregnant, 1976.

fri 25

Backers of the ERA in Washington pledge a political battle to win ratification in the last four states needed to make it part of the Constitution, 1976. □ A bill outlawing employment discrimination in Colorado because of marital status, sex, or physical handicaps is unanimously approved in the Judiciary Committee of the House of Representatives, 1976.

sat 26

A special government committee in Stockholm suggests that the word "homosexual" be banned from legislation dealing with sex and that homosexuals be treated in the same manner as heterosexuals, 1976.

of international business history was made to try and capture both intimate histories as well as larger trends in feminist business and social movement history in the United States.

The combination of quantitative and qualitative methods enabled me to identify some major trends. Most of the restaurants and cafes of the 1970s and 1980s were begun by white, lesbian, English-speaking, radical or socialist feminists who were working class or middle class, and that had some way to access capital outside of bank loans. Cooking was not the primary motivation, but creating a woman-centred, feminist space where staff could live as out lesbians and financially support themselves in an environment that reflected their values was. General trends in the restaurants revealed that most were built with sweat equity, and even for restaurants that lasted past their first two years—when most restaurants (feminist and not-feminist) fail—finances were always tight. The longer-lasting restaurants were either initially, or adapted quickly to become, highly organized, had a set idea of how the work would be structured, did not over-extend their programming, and had a plan to deal with emotional conflict, especially if a collective operated the restaurant. Having a liquor license provided greater economic stability but alcohol was not always desired, as creating substance-free space was a factor that motivated some of the restaurant and coffeehouse founders (as is explored in greater detail in chapter 7). Restaurants that employed accountants and professional legal counsel saved themselves from costly mistakes. As Jill Ward, cofounder of Mother Courage explained, "When we started, we were financially timid." She continued, "If I had it to do over again, I would have bought out an existing operation with all the fixtures, fixes, and all conveniences close at hand." Her other recommendations for women interested in starting a feminist restaurant were that they should know how to buy and produce food efficiently and in accordance with current economic conditions; that they should obtain adequate financing from the start; that they should get a liquor license early; that they should get an accountant; and that they should have trustworthy, reliable, and professional legal counsel. Ward also advised that, "as in any form of enterprise, careful planning is essential. Going into business does not mean leaping in. Developing good management and acquiring adequate resources (both personal and financial) takes time at the beginning but they save money and heartache later on."[51] Most feminist restaurants and cafes founded in the 1970s and 1980s closed by the 1990s. As is evident by looking at the timeline and directory in the appendix, the highpoint of feminist restaurants in the United States was from around 1976 to 1985. However, a new generation on feminist restaurants and cafes have since emerged.

Organization

Ingredients for Revolution is organized thematically and chronologically. The historical case studies of this book elucidate important lessons for contemporary feminist organizations and businesses. Due to the thematic and intersectional approach of this book, some key details may appear more than once. Given the important function of these businesses as places of convergence, it should not be surprising that there will be some overlap between the key themes and the case studies. Parts 1 and 2 of this book primarily focus on the period of 1972 until 1989 to add historical context and framing.

Part 1 focuses on how feminist restaurants and cafes founded between 1972 and 1989 challenged existing power structures and constructed new communities. Self-identified feminist restaurants and cafes were part of a larger movement in which feminist activists created women-only and women-centred spaces for political organizing, recreational activity, and commerce. While each restaurant and cafe embodied its feminist ideals uniquely, these businesses challenged the status quo of the food service industry, cooking, and consumption.

Owning their own businesses also afforded the feminists, lesbians, and feminist lesbians who created these establishments the opportunity to financially support themselves while being out as lesbian or feminist, and to do so while contributing to their vision of the kind of world that they wanted to see. They used these restaurants and spaces to challenge oppressive patriarchal capitalism. Feminist restaurants and cafes functioned as spaces to build community but were also businesses—a fact that created a tension felt by certain feminists who were engaged with Marxism and/or socialism. Even radical lesbian feminists felt uncomfortable with the links to business. Capitalism was the economic model of the United States during the 1970s and 1980s, and thus the restaurant owners were confined by the boundaries of capitalism, to a degree. Nevertheless, they used these spaces as ways to challenge some of these economic models. Their goals were not strictly commercial, but were, rather, to create spaces for their communities. Feminist restaurants thus challenged capitalism. The chapters in Part 1 are organized thematically to reflect the progression of designing and operating feminist restaurants and cafes: establishing the business; networking and building a clientele; and operating the business, including menu design.

Rampant sexism plagued typical restaurants and cafes in the 1970s and 1980s. Chapter 2 examines how feminist restaurants challenged management hierarchies, serving practices, and typical restaurant structure. While feminist restaurants and cafes challenged capitalism, they still had to be part of the economy. Balancing economic needs with philosophy necessitated compromises. The third chapter shows that these feminist restaurants and cafes were not isolated but part of a larger economy and society that was not always amenable to their desires. The creation of woman-space required innovative financial manoeuvrings.

In chapter 4, feminist restaurants and cafes were part of a larger nexus of feminist businesses. In addition to providing direct economic opportunities for the women employed at the restaurants, feminist restaurants and cafes promoted other women-owned businesses, women artists, and women craftspeople, tradeswomen, and feminist lawyers. Feminist restaurants and cafes helped support and were supported by feminist credit unions, feminist bookstores, artists, musicians, writers, performers, real estate agents, plumbers, carpenters, and lawyers. As a result, the economic impact of these restaurants was felt beyond the single brick and mortar location. These changes were also reflected in the dishes themselves.

Feminist restaurants and cafes of the 1970s and 1980s in the United States acted as spaces that challenged the status quo around cooking and consumption through their creation of feminist food. Each restaurant and cafe defined "feminist food" differently based on the particular feminist ethics of the restaurant owners and operators. Depending on the restaurant, choice about how to make their food feminist revolved around vegetarian ethics, labour issues, cost, and sourcing of products. By examining what was included on and banned from these restaurant menus, chapter 5 shows the different parameters through which food could be labeled as feminist. Furthermore, this chapter demonstrates how one could assert feminism within a business dedicated to food and centred on the kitchen—a space often labeled as a "traditional" place for women—and the complex relationships that emerge therein. Choices surrounding which food to serve, how to serve it, and where to source it from either reaffirmed the financial and organizational choices founders made in designing and operating their restaurants or risked undermining the mission of the restaurant.

Part 2 looks at the temporary spaces of coffeehouses founded in the 1970s and 1980s. There is some irony in the fact some coffeehouses lasted longer than restaurants, as their space itself was borrowed space/temporary space. As theorized by philosopher Michel de Certeau, marginalized individuals and communities rely on tactics to claim space for themselves. De Certeau writes, "The place of the tactic belongs to the other. A tactic insinuates itself into the other's place, fragmentarily, without taking it over in its entirety … It has at its disposal no base where it can capitalize on its advantages, prepare its expansions, and secure independence with respect to its circumstances … Whatever it wins it does not keep."[52] Professor of women's studies Agatha Beins adds that people, "without a proper place—without a place that is secured in some way—are thus relegated to a position in which they temporarily take a space (e.g., a street, a living room, a place owned by someone else) and use it as best they can to meet their needs."[53] Coffeehouses expanded participation. Owning a feminist restaurant or cafe required significant capital. As most coffeehouses operated without the high fixed costs of monthly rents and utilities, coffeehouses thus enabled women with less privilege due to class, race, or sexual orientation to create women's spaces within feminist communities. They were constantly self-reflective and always soliciting advice. These temporary spaces also allowed for other forms of women's space. Chapter 6 focuses on who managed and who used feminist coffeehouses. The next chapter discusses the challenges that coffeehouses faced and the contributions they made to the larger feminist community.

Part 3 explores feminist restaurants, cafes, and food businesses from 1989 to 2022. Chapter 8 meditates on how the legacy of the feminist restaurants, cafes, and coffeehouses of the 1970s and 1980s has impacted more contemporary feminist food businesses. Feminism has evolved since the 1970s and 1980s and the needs of feminist restaurants have likewise transformed. In addition to wrapping up arguments expressed throughout the project, the conclusion elucidates important lessons for contemporary feminist businesses. Although this book focuses primarily on historical case studies within the United States from 1972 to 1989, the findings of this book elucidate important lessons for contemporary feminist organizations and businesses.

Since 1972 feminists have asked, can a business actually be feminist? This book answers affirmatively, yes! Ultimately, this project is not just the history of feminist restaurants, cafes, and coffeehouses. This book is, rather, the story of different groups of women, men, and gender non-conforming people, straight, lesbian, and queer, all trying to live a life that truly represented their values.

1.4 (OVERLEAF) *Timeline of the years of operation of the feminist restaurants, cafes, and coffeehouses used as the primary case studies in this book.*

Timeline of Case Studies

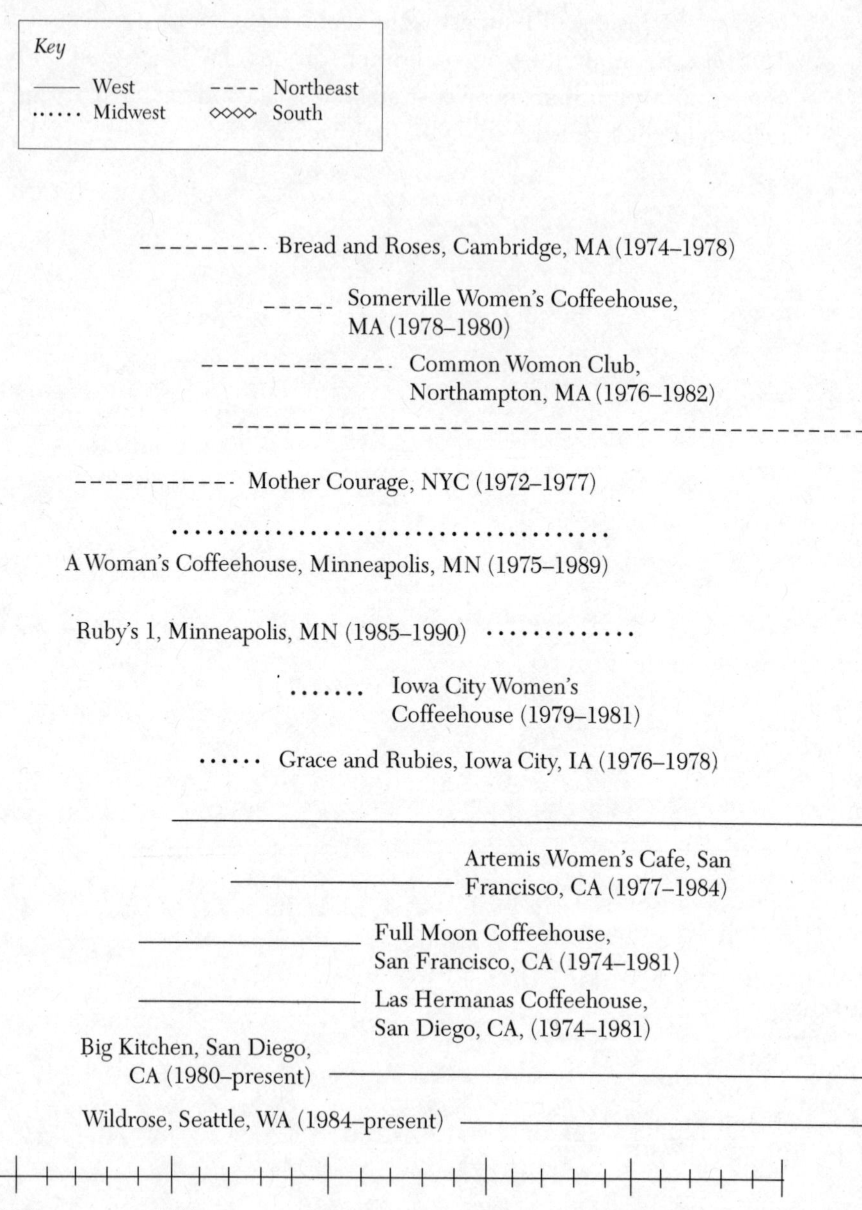

Key
West
Northeast
Midwest
South
Bread and Roses, Cambridge, MA (1974–1978)
Somerville Women's Coffeehouse, MA (1978–1980)
Common Womon Club, Northampton, MA (1976–1982)
Mother Courage, NYC (1972–1977)
A Woman's Coffeehouse, Minneapolis, MN (1975–1989)
Ruby's 1, Minneapolis, MN (1985–1990)
Iowa City Women's Coffeehouse (1979–1981)
Grace and Rubies, Iowa City, IA (1976–1978)
Artemis Women's Cafe, San Francisco, CA (1977–1984)
Full Moon Coffeehouse, San Francisco, CA (1974–1981)
Las Hermanas Coffeehouse, San Diego, CA, (1974–1981)
Big Kitchen, San Diego, CA (1980–present)
Wildrose, Seattle, WA (1984–present)
1970
1975
1980
1985
1990
1995

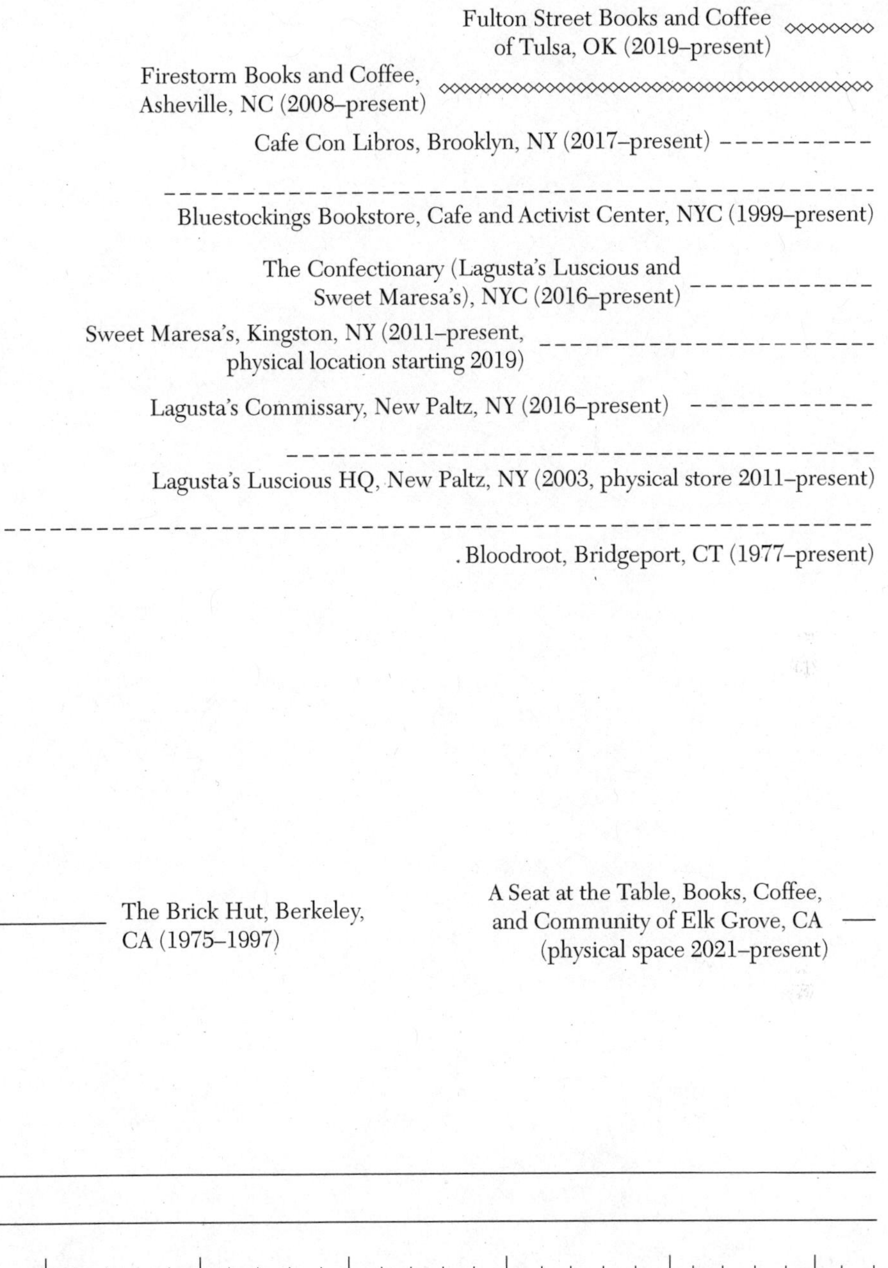
Fulton Street Books and Coffee of Tulsa, OK (2019–present)
Firestorm Books and Coffee, Asheville, NC (2008–present)
Cafe Con Libros, Brooklyn, NY (2017–present)
Bluestockings Bookstore, Cafe and Activist Center, NYC (1999–present)
The Confectionary (Lagusta's Luscious and Sweet Maresa's), NYC (2016–present)
Sweet Maresa's, Kingston, NY (2011–present, physical location starting 2019)
Lagusta's Commissary, New Paltz, NY (2016–present)
Lagusta's Luscious HQ, New Paltz, NY (2003, physical store 2011–present)
Bloodroot, Bridgeport, CT (1977–present)
The Brick Hut, Berkeley, CA (1975–1997)
A Seat at the Table, Books, Coffee, and Community of Elk Grove, CA (physical space 2021–present)
1995
2000
2005
2010
2015
2020

PART ONE

Feminist Restaurants/Permanent Space, 1972–1989

CHAPTER 2

Cooking Up Alternatives

The Creation of Feminist Businesses

As feminists, we are naturally opposed to capitalism. Though we cannot work outside the realities of American economic life, we hope as far as possible to operate as an alternative to business institutions as we have known them. Our main goal is not commercial; structurally we see the enterprise as a co-operative venture and one responsive to the needs of our community.[1]

Bread and Roses Restaurant Business Proposal

Rampant sexism plagued typical restaurants and cafes in the 1970s and 1980s. Feminist restaurants challenged capitalism, mainstream restaurant management hierarchies, serving practices, and tipping. The women who founded these restaurants and cafes felt that they needed spaces separate from male-dominated establishments to escape the oppressive formal restraints that regulated both female socializing and female economic activities. While each restaurant and cafe embodied its feminist ideals uniquely, all feminist restaurants and cafes challenged the status quo of the food service industry, cooking, and consumption. Feminist restaurants and cafes simultaneously functioned as businesses and as spaces in which to build community, a combination which could create tension. As the above quote from the business proposal of Bread and Roses feminist restaurant of

Cambridge, Massachusetts, suggests, while the restaurant's creators were partially confined to the boundaries of the greater economy, the owners were not powerless. Founders of feminist restaurants and cafes used their spaces to challenge oppressive patriarchal capitalism within both the food industry and American society at large. Feminist restaurants provided new kinds of economic opportunities for women. This chapter will explain how feminist restaurants and cafes functioned as businesses: they ran counter to capitalism while operating within a capitalist system. Feminist restaurants and cafes reconceptualized the meanings of the kitchen for women from domesticity to productivity.

New Economic Models

> What is work? Is it scheduled physical labor; is it producing a product; is it creative activity; is it spiritual development of the self? Is childcare work? Is practicing an instrument work? Rarely have we felt so perplexed as we did this time about the meaning of the words that will adorn our cover: "Women Working" ... We realized that once you stop equating work with jobs, trying to define it is like trying to define love. No definition is inclusive. In talking about work, we discovered how much emotion, how much guilt, pride, anger, resentment, anxiety, and attraction we feel towards it. We found that our own options and choices affected what we felt qualified as work, and we never transcended the fragmented perspectives on work that had arisen from our individual experiences ... On the whole, our feelings towards the work we've done for money were pretty bleak ... With jobs being as unappealing as they are, many women have opted to find a way to work around them. But we've become aware that many of our alternatives to holding a job still keep us basically dependent on men.[2]
>
> *Country Women Magazine*

In June 1975, when trying to organize its forthcoming issue on "Women Working," the editorial collective of the Mendocino,

California–based, *Country Women Magazine* (1973–80), realized that the idea of "work" was not as simple as its members had first thought. The editorial board, which also functioned as a women's agricultural collective, struggled to decide if by "work" the members meant solely remunerated tasks, or whether work included reproductive labours such as cooking, cleaning, and childbearing. These debates reflected significant questions that emerge when deciding upon feminist values. American feminists during the 1970s and 1980s—especially Marxist and socialist feminists—frequently returned to questions over what work "was" and what work "should be." Feminist discussions around the meaning of work were embedded within greater conversations about economics. The New Left countercultural movements of the 1960s and 1970s were deeply invested in a critique of capitalism. Within American countercultural movements such as the back-to-the-land movements, Marxist critiques of capitalism's oppression of working-class people dominated discussions. However, this class analysis was lacking an understanding of the role of gender and race, especially the ways that class was gendered and racialized.

By 1972, when America's first feminist restaurant, Mother Courage of New York, had opened, these discussions over the meaning of work were alive and well. Feminists had been questioning the idea of what work was within periodicals such as *Country Women* and *Ms. Magazine*. Much of the discussion centred on trying to make sense of the way that work was valued. Consciousness raising pamphlets encouraged conversations about the implications of women doing the majority of domestic labour.[3] Scholars such as Michele Barrett in *Women's Oppression Today: Problems in Marxist-Feminist Analysis* and Heidi Hartmann in "The Unhappy Marriage of Marxism and Feminism: Towards a More Progressive Union" detailed the manner in which feminists proposed changes during the 1970s and 1980s to the existing issues in the American workplaces. A full analysis of all of these changes is beyond the scope of this book. However, I am interested in the ways that feminists challenged ideas of work related to food preparation.

Change within the System: Making Feminist Businesses

When moving "back to the land" was an undesirable or untenable option for combating capitalism and patriarchy, other feminists explored the possibility of creating feminist businesses.[4] Reporter Karen Lindsey of the *Boston Phoenix* newspaper explored questions about what it meant to be a feminist business and to work within capitalism as a feminist in her 1974 article, "Feminist Capitalism—Banks and Eateries." Lindsey worried that feminist capitalism was a contradiction, particularly regarding feminist banking, stating, "The whole idea of a women's bank is an immediate source of political confusion to me. Feminist capitalism? Isn't that like feminist racism—a contradiction in terms? After several hours talking with Alice Heyman, one of the founders and a member of the advisory committee of the The First Women's Bank and Trust Co., I decided that it isn't such a contradiction after all."[5] As Lindsey realized, these businesses supported women. The feminist banks and credit unions served to fulfill financial needs unmet by mainstream financial institutions for women interested in beginning businesses. Not until 1974 did the United States Congress pass the Equal Credit Opportunity Act (ECOA), which enabled a woman to get a line of credit in her own name and prohibited lending discrimination on the basis of race, gender, colour, religion, national origin, marital status, or age. Prior to the passage of the act, the inability to establish individual credit proved especially difficult for single heterosexual women and lesbians trying to start women-centric spaces.[6] The creation of businesses in a capitalist system, which was viewed as inherently anti-feminist by Marxist feminists and socialist feminists in particular, led to ideological debates that feminist business owners navigated.

The women who saw benefits in being actively involved in the capitalist system rather than moving away from it wrote materials instructing other women in methods to build these kinds of businesses. Not all founders of feminist restaurants and cafes had previous business experience, however. As a result of limited educational opportunities due to barriers on the basis of race, class, gender, and sexual identity statuses, quite a few women were barred from entering business realms prior to the feminist business movement. Difficulties in procuring loans to start businesses were particularly significant.[7] Feminists who had managed to overcome these barriers tried to create services to foster other women's involvement in business.

Part of increasing women's participation in business required research on the statistics of women's involvement in business, and this meant collaborating with governmental bodies. A committee to form an association of women entrepreneurs, called Women Who Are In Business for Themselves, had launched an extensive research program aimed at developing an American national organization for self-employed women to begin in 1974 or 1975. This committee also requested that the American Senate and House Committees on Small Business determine discriminatory practices in the programs and expenditures of federal tax monies for small business purposes. Calling women business owners "invisible," committee chairperson N. Jeanne Wertz noted that in its ongoing statistical studies of private enterprise, the group, which alone had access to the necessary data, had not yet done the basic statistical and qualitative studies about women business owners.[8] This call for statistical data and analysis was necessary to develop more effective strategies to encourage women to start small businesses.

Besides gathering statistics, feminists created how-to guides that encouraged women to begin their own businesses. As business laws were specifically localized to the city or county level, as well as affected by state or federal legislation, women would create guides on how to open local businesses with information specific to their regions. For example, the Women's Action Alliance in New York City created comprehensive guidebooks such as "How to Make the Media Work for You" and "How to Organize a Multiservice Women's Center."[9] These pamphlets had advice as specific as incorporation and tax structure as well as broader business and organizational advice. Similar guides, but with more general advice directed towards national audiences, were published in feminist periodicals after feminists had been engaged in trying to start businesses for a few years since the early 1970s. In April 1976, *Ms. Magazine*, a feminist periodical founded by renowned feminists Gloria Steinem and Dorothy Pitman Hughes, released a special edition of *Ms. Handbook*, which consisted of a sixteen-page insert about "How to Start Your Own Business." As the journalists Heidi Fiske and Karen Zehring describe,

> More and more women are starting their own businesses—to find work in a tight job market, to find freer expression of their creative and management abilities, and to put into practice their own ideas of how the business world should operate. Whatever the motives, or combination of them, the self-employed woman is an idea whose time has come. According to the Census Bureau, in 1972 there were 402,025 women-owned businesses generating $8.1 million in receipts, that's only 3.1 percent of all businesses, but that number is growing.

The purpose of this guide was to inspire women readers to create businesses. The sections they included are "Making a Business Plan"; "Professional Services: Who You Need and What to Expect"; "Inexpensive Business Advice and Where to Get It"; "How to Raise Money"; "Cash Flow—the Make or Break Item"; "How to Sell Yourself: Graphics and Publicity"; "The First Year in Numbers"; "How Not to Blow It"; and "Another View: Toward a Feminist Business Ethic."[10] While the guide encourages women to create all kinds of businesses, the final section on feminist business ethics particularly expresses why feminist businesses were different than mainstream businesses.

The section on feminist business ethics in the *Ms. Handbook* both highlights the tension feminists encountered when they wanted to start businesses and offers advice on navigating these conflicts. Women faced guilt and conflict as they tried to challenge capitalist structures from within. For example, the handbook includes advice like "the product or service should fulfill a feminist need, advance a feminist cause, or improve the quality of feminist life"; "the product of service should not be overpriced by market standards and the highest possible quality should be delivered for the money"; and "the margin of profit should be large enough to ensure the survival of the enterprise but not so large that one becomes a guilt-ridden profiteer."[11] This final line is especially poignant. According to the *Ms. Handbook*, part of the ethics of a feminist business was not to get rich but rather to be able to support itself. Within this view of feminist businesses, founders were not trying to create multinational corporate empires but rather were trying to find a way to live ethically and support their feminist values. The authors of this particular section, feminist jewellers Toni Carabillo and Judith Meuli, go on to state, "If something costs us $0.70 to make we charge about $1.50 wholesale or $3.00 retail."[12] They explain that commercial jewellers in their area work on double their profit margin. Carabillo and Meuli emphasized that "Making a reasonable profit isn't inherently a corrupt act. It can be ploughed back into the business or used for expansion or donated to other Movement projects."[13] For them the profit was not to be used just to increase one's personal wealth. They continue, "Co-workers' wages and benefits and working conditions and profits shared with a collective should be as generous as the enterprise can afford" and advise that

> All transactions with employees, customers, and suppliers should be performed in good faith. This is supposedly the controlling ethic in American business, but we think that employees seem more willing to give a fair day's work for a fair day's pay when you work as associates, not boss and hired hand. We've found, though, that a true collective spells doom for a business. When we ran "women's heritage series" as a seventeen member collective, it turned out that three people did all the work but we had to divide the profits among seventeen. It's better to keep the business ownership small and limited to those with a real interest in it ... We don't hesitate to extend credit within the feminist community ... we extend credit and give wholesale discounts to feminist groups that use our products for fund-raising ... offering professional services to other feminists may create a special problem: the client may feel she's entitled to a break on the fee simply because feminists should help feminists. Unfortunately, this attitude suggests to the worker that her services are not worth the full market price commanded by men in the same field.[14]

This entire section speaks to the dilemma of what fees to charge and evokes greater questions about the value of one's work. These queries about value were embedded within larger discussions about how labour was given value through payment within a masculine capitalist model, and whether or not money was equated with value within the feminist model.[15] As if these tensions were not enough for the feminist businesswoman to balance, the authors continue, "The entrepreneurs should in some way be involved in the Movement beyond the contact provided by the business."[16] An important tenet of these feminist businesses, at least in the opinion of the authors, is that their business is not just about the owner but also about supporting an entire community of other businesses and the people that lived within their cities and towns. They may have been independent businesses, but they were embedded within a larger community nexus. Despite these businesses being part of a feminist nexus, this feminist capitalism took on specific forms within the restaurant industry.

Comparison with Traditional Restaurants

The modern restaurant developed in late eighteenth-century France. Boulanger is often credited as being the first restaurant founder in 1765, although food historian Rebecca Spang has challenged this claim.[17] Since then, restaurant management has changed dramatically, most notably through the development of traditions regarding the expected service and the creation of a wider variety of named positions. The role of restaurant manager gained a new level of professionalization in the twentieth century with the introduction of educational programs. While the stratification of roles, division of tasks, and the expected level of service differs between, for example, colonial taverns, family-owned pizza palaces, and upscale French bistros in downtown Manhattan, all restaurants over the past two and a half centuries require the management of finances, staff, food and beverage ordering, and food preparation. Restaurants in the 1970s and 1980s were predominately male-owned, with male chefs receiving praise for their skills. As in other industries, when tasks previously performed by women moved outside of the home and were remunerated, they became dominated by men. As feminist food historian Sherrie Inness argues, the professional kitchen was viewed as a male space.[18] In popular culture during the 1970s and 1980s, however, the act of cooking and the space of the home kitchen were portrayed as being within the domestic and feminine realm. As a result, changing cooking from an unpaid labour to a paid task was described as a feminist act, although even this depiction was debated by various feminists of the period.

Most restaurants were managed hierarchically in the 1970s and 1980s; feminist restaurants, however, challenged this structure. The restaurant management profession consists of administration responsibilities, front-of-the-house management, and back-of-the-house management. Although some form of restaurant management has existed since the creation of the first restaurants, the practices and responsibilities of restaurant management have become increasingly standardized over the past two and a half centuries. Despite the differences between restaurants in their expectations of restaurant management, most restaurants retain a hierarchical relationship between their management and their staff. Feminists and anarchists have questioned this power relationship and have opened restaurants with a collective form of restaurant management. Depending on the size of the restaurant, the responsibilities of restaurant management may be performed by one manager or by a team of managers. Larger restaurants or chains typically have a greater level of stratification between management roles and responsibilities, and those of the employees working on the floor or in the kitchen. Furthermore, the operating hours of a restaurant may determine if the restaurant has a day manager and a night manager, or some other configuration. For the smallest businesses, one person may do all these duties. The golden rule of traditional restaurant management focuses on customer satisfaction: "The customer is always right." Within the industry, remarkable service is thought of as courteous, friendly, and welcoming.[19]

In the 1970s, feminists began to critique gender inequity in a variety of workplaces, including restaurants. Particularly, they believed that the relationships between restaurant managers and waitresses, and between waitresses and customers, systematically disempowered women.[20] Men owned and operated most restaurants, whether they specialized in fast food or fine dining. In the 1970s and 1980s, according to the US Bureau of Labor Statistics, far fewer women managed restaurants than in 2017 (ownership was not studied). In 1972, only 32.4 percent of restaurant, cafeteria, and bar managers were women and 8.9 percent were Black men and women.[21] In 2017, 46.3 percent of food-service managers (the category that has replaced "restaurant, cafeteria, and bar managers") were women, 9.5 percent were Black, 11.7 percent were Asian, and 16.9 percent were Latino or Hispanic.[22] The gender imbalance between who owns restaurants, who are the head chefs, and who gets the praise continues to present times. Although women were traditionally cooks and waitresses, they have also been underrepresented in management and ownership positions.

Feminist restaurants challenged the patriarchal capitalism of the typical business structure. Feminist critiques highlighted the demeaning aspects of waiting on tables, servicing the patron, the low salaries, and the heavy reliance on tips, and demonstrated how there was little place for advancement in this arrangement. The owners of Bread and Roses feminist restaurant of Cambridge, Massachusetts, thought seriously about these ideas. Writing in 1976 about how the restaurant was different than others, interviewer Gale Goldberg remarks, "The women at Bread and Roses and the physical space help create an easy, supportive atmosphere for women and their women friends. In urbanized America, other types of restaurants, including both inexpensive fast-food establishments and high-priced restaurants, are mostly owned and operated by men."[23] In the 1974 Bread and Roses business prospectus the owners speak about how,

> in contrast, the male tone of a restaurant business venture is aimed more directly at profit making, commercialism, and a hierarchical structure of organization. Traditionally, women have been noticeably absent from places at the decision-making level. The harried long hours on foot are more familiar to women. The often demeaning and thankless job of waiting on tables, servicing the patron, has fallen to women who receive low salaries and rely heavily on tips. There is little place for advancement in this arrangement. Rewards perhaps come in getting better hours—peak times—when the turnover is

> greater and the pace is quicker. Currently, the waitress must work harder for her gratuity … The ideas of feminism encourage recirculation of profits into the women's community by supporting other women's energies.[24]

These feminists were challenging the ideas of what it meant to run a restaurant in the process of creating one. Feminist restaurants upended mainstream restaurant management by making changes to the organizational structure, spatial arrangement and decor, layout and design, menus, atmosphere, community service, and sex-role behaviour. Bread and Roses "expanded the concept of restauranting from the feminist perspective" by building upon the typical three factors for customer satisfaction: "1. Good food that is well-prepared and attractively served, 2. Good service that is courteous, skillful, and prompt, and 3. An attractive environment."[25] Feminist restaurant owners wanted to redefine who could own and operate restaurants and who could enjoy them.

Feminist restaurants and cafes were not alone in advocating for more involvement by women within the food industry. After feminist restaurants had begun to change conversations around women, gender, feminism, and restaurants, organizations such as the Women's Culinary Alliance, founded in New York City in 1981, encouraged women to enter the restaurant industry.[26] The organization fostered networking, education, and cooperation for women in the culinary and beverage fields in the New York metropolitan area. The alliance also provided members with continuing education opportunities by sponsoring ongoing food and wine tastings, hands-on workshops, field trips, and business-related seminars. It also supported the preservation and sharing of culinary information through member-generated programs. According to its records, the alliance organized outreach programs and fundraising for women's health and nutrition issues. It acted as a forum for dozens of women whose careers centred on food and beverages, encouraging them to meet, share expertise, and drive new directions in the food world. Early founders included chefs Sara Moulton and Maria Reuge, and from the start its members included well-known authors, caterers, chefs, cooking schoolteachers, editors, food writers, marketers, photographers, and stylists. Members of the alliance produced dozens of bestselling cookbooks, hosted nationally televised cooking shows, and produced or edited content for the country's leading magazines and newspapers.[27] This organization tracked women's involvement in restaurants in New York City. Rather than encourage women to create their own kinds of businesses, this organization took a more liberal approach; their idea was to integrate more women into the already existing system so that they would eventually become chefs, restaurant owners, or managers.

While the solution of changing the system from within was popular amongst such organizations as the Women's Culinary Alliance, feminist restaurants sought to break away from the mainstream restaurant industry and do something different. Feminist restaurants still had to function within the same economic system but functioned on the periphery, set apart. The owners' goal was not just to challenge the restaurant industry itself but to challenge capitalism and male-run spaces more generally. Feminist restaurants and cafes were founded out of the desire to create different kinds of spaces. To be clear, there were differences between the feminist restaurants themselves. Even within a single restaurant, employees and collectives could have different goals. As Marjorie Parsons reflected on the Common Womon Club of Northampton, Massachusetts: "For some women this was a political project, for others this was a livelihood."[28] Despite these differences, there were similarities between the spaces that set them apart. What did they look like, though?

Political Aesthetics

Feminist restaurants embodied an aesthetic that emulated their founders' politics. Grace and Rubies of Iowa City (1976–1978) was located in an older, two-storey house. University of Iowa journalism student Lynne Cherry described the restaurant for her college paper:

> Plants are located throughout the building and any wall can be used to display members' artwork. Downstairs are a kitchen, two dining rooms connected by a small chamber lined with bulletin boards. On the boards hang handwritten notices for such things as a club meeting, a costume party, inter-mural flag football, and a women's clinic. The dining rooms are crowded with tables, dimly lit and rather drafty, yet they are made cozy by the feeling of comradeship among the members and the cheerful wisecracks issuing from the kitchen. Another dining room, a bathroom, and a reading room housing a small library are upstairs. The library consists of two bookcases of donated books, mostly by and/or about women, and some feminist newspapers.[29]

This cozy and eclectic home aesthetic was not unique to Grace and Rubies. In 1977, when Selma Miriam and the rest of the Bloodroot Collective decided to begin Bloodroot Feminist Vegetarian Restaurant in Bridgeport, Connecticut, they were expanding upon a previous project. Miriam had been serving meals at her home and decided to fully commit to the endeavour by founding a restaurant. When Miriam began to design Bloodroot, the restaurant retained the cozy, homey feeling. Restaurant reviewers describe the decor as featuring "photographs of women offering, as [Miriam] puts it, 'another concept of beauty' women's art and the background music [was] women's music."[30] Another reviewer, this time from the *Hartford Advocate*, focuses on how when "patrons sit they can see through a wide window into the Julia Child–like kitchen where … Selma, Betsy, Sam, and the additional help they've recently hired … are busy at work."[31] Rather than have printed menus, a chalkboard listed the dishes of the day, which changed with the seasons. The walls of the dining area were covered with photographs of women found at tag sales and donated by customers and the bookstore was adorned with women's art. A large quilt made by Miriam hung overhead. Through the exterior windows it was possible to see Long Island Sound and swans swimming by. The space was filled with feelings of warmth and comfort. Miriam and the Bloodroot Collective founded this restaurant not only to serve excellent food but also to be a feminist community space. Unlike most kitchens, which are secluded from the dining area, a large pass-through window and doorway passage enabled the customer to see working women preparing the meals in Bloodroot. The same open-kitchen concept existed at Bread and Roses of Cambridge, Massachusetts.[32] This arrangement minimized the difference between the customer and those working in the establishment. Breaking down these literal walls encouraged feelings of familiarity between customers and staff. By having open-kitchen models these restaurants not only challenged the power dynamics inherent between the two groups in mainstream restaurants but also added to the home-like aesthetic. These restaurants, containing feminist books, women's art, women's music (as will be discussed in detail in chapter 4), and open-kitchen designs, promoted an image that marked their difference from other establishments the moment a customer entered, signalling a feminist space.

While this eclectic-home aesthetic could create warm and welcoming environments for socializing, feminist restaurants looked different from other restaurants in part due to financial circumstances. In the next chapter I will discuss the financial situations of most of these restaurants and cafes. Suffice it to say, most of the restaurants' owners did not have a large budget for decorating their spaces. Many of the women did the construction themselves, relying on either collective effort, the effort of their community, or in some cases, family members. These were mostly do-it-yourself jobs. For example, the creators of Mother Courage took five months of tedious labour to renovate their low-rent location, an old, squalid luncheonette, called Benny's (or Bennie's), in Greenwich Village.[33] In founder Dolores

2.1 Sweat equity was key to the creation of feminist restaurants. To save money, feminist restaurant founders did many renovations and repairs themselves. The above photo depicts some of the demolition work that Jill Ward, Dolores Alexander, Ward's father, and six other feminists completed between December 1971 and May 1972 before opening Mother Courage of New York City. (Smith College Archive. Dolores Alexander Unprocessed Papers, Box 21 of 21. Folder, 1971–1975 Photos and Stats.)

Alexander's own words, "the renovation, impressive job when you see the 'before' photographs, was done entirely by women: Jill, myself, and friends who were mostly volunteers. We literally gutted the place, tore down the ceiling, ripped up the floor, stripped plaster and paneling from the brick walls then totally rebuilt it."[34] After the initial repairs, little money was invested into the decor. Two thousand of the $10,000 that Mother Courage founders raised went into buying used kitchen equipment and little money was spared for furnishings.[35] In fact, decor at Mother Courage was a last-minute thought. As Dolores Alexander's day planner suggests in her entry on September 3, 1973, a year after Mother Courage had opened, she still needed to "decorate the walls."[36] As one restaurant reviewer states: "The décor is determinedly un-affected. One medium sized room with tables relatively close together make it easy for feminists to meet, greet, and gossip during courses. The unclothed, plainly varnished tables, lit overhead by New Jersey surplus street lamps, are an interesting contrast to the profusion of lush plants in the windows and the original art displayed on the brick walls."[37] While this aesthetic originated primarily from a lack of budget, the decor did not subtract from the ambiance.

Mother Courage's owners were not the only feminist restaurateurs who rebuilt their space. The original group of women who began Wildrose in Seattle, Washington, did their own remodeling. The space previously had a fake wood-cabin aesthetic. The women got rid of the logs on the wall and drywalled. Everything had to be redone, and owner Bryher Herak regretted that she could never afford to do the floors.[38] The group was able to cover the walls with women's art, and switched the pieces every two months, or when people bought pieces on display. In the back room there were two pool tables and folding chairs for performances, which would draw crowds of three or four hundred people on the weekends.[39] At the Common Womon Club, Marjorie Parsons built the tables of the restaurant in somebody's basement. She reflected: "That kind of energy to put into one project was incredible." They were saving money on the front-end but using their energy to subsidize it. It was a lot of unpaid labour. The owners had little liquid capital, but in Marjorie Parsons's words, they had immense "woman power."[40]

In addition to amateur repairs, part of the eclectic aesthetic originated from that fact that most of the supplies were second hand and mismatched. In the newly refurbished space, the Bloodroot Collective filled the room with a hodgepodge of furniture. Selma Miriam and her partners Betsey Beaven and Sam Stickwell outfitted the former machine shop and office building with finds from tag and garage sales, picking up high-end china and lamps. They described their choices to *Fairpress* paper in 1977: "We decided never to pay more than $10.00 for a table or $5 for a chair. You can get some very nice chairs for two dollars and some lovely dishes for $0.15 and $0.25."[41] Miriam's Westport garage overflowed with furniture. The refinishing began when some of Miriam's carpenter friends began "turning the office building into the warm, atmospheric and charming restaurant."[42] A 1975 review in the *New England Business Journal* mentions that the plates and glasses at Bread and Roses of Cambridge, Massachusetts, did not match.[43] Although a mixture of need and desire drove these choices, the aesthetics of feminist restaurants signalled to their customers that these spaces reflected a different set of values.

Location

A contributing factor to feminist restaurants' unique aesthetic was that these restaurants were often in unusual locations due to financial constraints. Bloodroot of Bridgeport, Connecticut, began in a repurposed machine shop.[44] The Common Womon Club of Northampton's founding collective members first considered buying the rundown former food stand, Kenny's. However, Marjorie Parsons noted, "It was an ugly spit that would have taken two years to clean."[45] Their intentionally chosen female real estate agent also showed the women in the collective a small house, near the fire station in Northampton, which had seven rooms. Adjacent was a storefront like a garage but with a glass front. The United States Navy had been renting the storefront at the time and the State of Massachusetts used the house as a living facility for men with mental disabilities. Neither part of the property had been maintained and Parsons remarked that the stench of the building was "terrible."[46] The property cost them $38,000. The collective members viewed the two rooms upstairs as potential income as rentals: for the Valley Women's Union, the karate club, a bookstore, therapists, and masseuses. They also used the garage in the back of the storefront to have tag sales. The Common Womon Club members creatively used their space to raise income.

Many of the restaurants were located in run-down buildings or in poorer neighbourhoods. When Bryher Herak and a collective of four other women decided to open The Wildrose in 1984, the women knew that they wanted to find a space with windows, "a place with light."[47] In Seattle, Washington, in 1984, most gay and lesbian hangouts were secretive, dark places out of necessity for safety and financial concerns. Herak wanted The Wildrose to be a place where lesbians could bring their friends and families without feelings of shame. As Herak said of Wildrose, "At that time it was very closeted … it was mostly going into alleys, knowing about it word-of-mouth, because of the culture."[48] Feminist restaurant owners wanted to create beauty and promote community building in their spaces.

The choice to lease or buy property in lower income neighbourhoods was in part due to the limited capital that women had to invest in making a restaurant, as well as the ghettoization of the lesbian community. While gay male communities are known for their gentrifying effect, lesbians, and especially lesbian mothers, in the 1970s and 1980s, tended to be poorer.[49] Women faced lower wages and lesbian and single mothers also were saddled with childcare costs. Fewer educational and work opportunities combined with hiring practices that discriminated against women and lesbians meant that the women and lesbians who opened these restaurants had small initial budgets and needed to build their businesses in areas with lower rents. The Brick Hut Café of Berkeley, California, switched locations three times over its fifteen years in business. The first location was small and only had nine counter seats, three booths, and a menu on a board attached to the hood. Here, as owner Joan Antonuccio remembered, the weekend crowds spilled out into the street even after the owners built a backyard patio where they served a limited menu of blueberry muffins, coffee, and tea.[50] The second Brick Hut had fifty seats, including the three booths, and an open kitchen. Finally, the third version had seventy-five seats inside; twenty-five on the patio; an open kitchen; an espresso, beer, and wine counter in the front; and a banquet room for meetings and events. The moves were not always made by choice; the first move was due to an eviction. The owners had thirty days to find a new place, and fortunately a neighbour had a restaurant space he wanted to sell. The restaurant staff rolled its equipment down the street on flatbed carts, made a few improvements, and opened for business. On the first day, there was a line down the block, in part due to the owners' philosophy. Antonuccio said that, "We welcomed everyone who was an ally in our common cause of social justice and inclusion."[51] On the second day, however, the windows were smashed. The Brick Hut was not the only feminist restaurant that dealt with crime.

Neighbourhood crime was a problem for the restaurants, but not a restrictive problem.[52] Berkeley's Brick Hut remained at its second location until the neighbourhood fell to the crack epidemic and staying became untenable.[53] At that location the staff were robbed and held at gunpoint, and the building was burgled and vandalized seventeen times over the years. At the Brick Hut, "We were targeted by vandals many times: broken windows, anti-gay graffiti, threatening letters. [However,] mostly, we were appreciated and everybody ate there because our food was really good."[54] At The Wildrose of Seattle, the patrons faced occasional threats from drunken men on their way home from straight bars. Around midnight these drunken men would come in and harass the women. The Wildrose staff had to call the police a few times, but usually these incidents consisted of people shouting, "you fucking queers or fucking dykes" and running.[55] Across the country in Connecticut, Selma Miriam's mother tried to discourage her from putting the word "feminist" in the title of Bloodroot Feminist Vegetarian Restaurant because she assumed there would be a brick through its window on the first day, but there was not.[56]

The owners and collectives that ran these restaurants and cafes were at risk of gentrifying neighbourhoods; but rather than be anonymous storefronts, feminist restaurant owners often worked with members of the neighbourhood to create open community events centred on food and socializing. These restaurants played important roles in their communities. While customers would drive from miles around to eat at Bloodroot, and appreciated the camaraderie of like-minded women, anyone who was willing to be respectful in the environment was welcome.[57] Even though the space was intentionally woman-centred, Bloodroot never sought to ban men. The owners "wanted this to be a feminist community, but [they] didn't want to exclude men. After [they] opened up Bloodroot [Selma] was really surprised at the number of men who came in and did not find the word feminist threatening or disparaging."[58] They also sought to have good relations with their greater community. One example of their community building in their Black Rock neighbourhood of Bridgeport, Connecticut, was holding block parties because "it is important to get to know each other and respect our differences. Food is one delicious vehicle for that."[59] They wanted to use their restaurant as a community space to make alliances and build coalitions. In an interview with the *Connecticut Post*, the owners expressed that "we want to be available to the Spanish speaking community and to Black women in Fairfield County. We want to make those political connections where we can."[60] Likewise, the Brick Hut Café was an important resource in its community. Sharon Davenport remembered that the

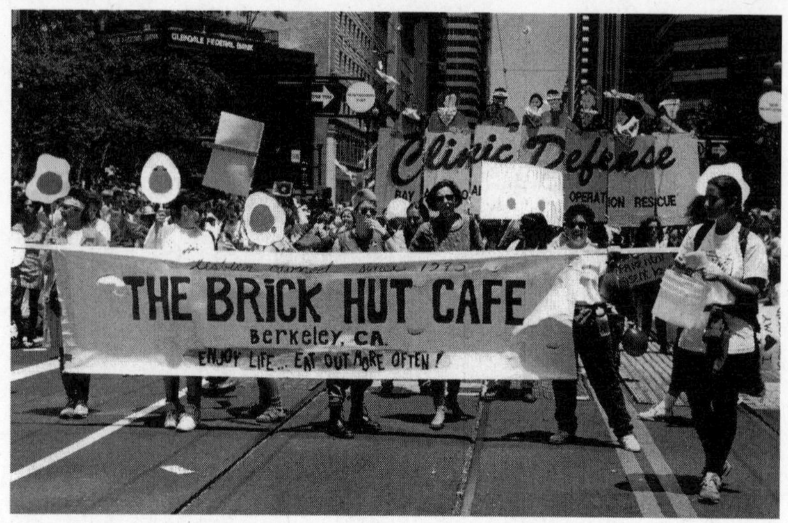

2.2 The Brick Hut Café participated in community events. Some of the staff marched at San Francisco's 1984 LGBT Pride March. (Photo shared by Wendy Goodfriend)

Berkeley city council, mayors, community figures, political counter-culture figures were regulars at the Hut. In addition to the above response, she added that,

> The customers changed as the times changed. We stopped seeming alien to the mainstream, so more mainstream people visited us. More articles about us appeared in more print media. We catered backstage at the Bank of the West tennis classic for three years, so there were programs and banners at the matches. We were a haven for lesbians and gay men, an information center for LGBT activists, an anchor for a diverse community that included working girls, bad-boys, suburban queens, transmen and transwomen. We maintained our welcome mat for the queer community and all their allies. We served all genders, races, classes, and sexual identities. The

> only ones we didn't serve were those who showed disrespect or hostility to others—they had to go.[61]

Food connected diverse groups of people living in the nearby neighbourhoods and visitors alike. Both Bloodroot's and the Brick Hut's owners worked on being integrally involved in their neighbourhood communities on opposite sides of the United States, aiming to not be a gentrifying force that would displace the original habitants of the neighbourhoods in which their restaurants were located. They were not alone in these efforts.

Judy Forman of The Big Kitchen in the Golden Hill neighbourhood of San Diego, California, used her restaurant as a resource to serve the community beginning in 1980, and customers noticed. In speaking to the *San Diego Free Press*, when Forman bought the restaurant The Big Kitchen in 1979–80, she described Golden Hill as being "a neighborhood in transition. It was the first "suburb" of downtown San Diego at the turn of the last century. The white population had fled to the suburbs leaving multiethnic families and all of the most talented people of San Diego living in Golden Hill for the same reason—the rent was reasonable."[62] She wanted her restaurant to employ people from the neighbourhood and thus she hired "all the gang members" to come and work at the restaurant.[63] She also helped organize the Golden Hill Community Development Corporation, a nonprofit group that worked on obtaining grants to improve the neighbourhood. The GHCDC secured a grant that resulted in an after-school program at Brooklyn Elementary run by Forman, a new playground at Brooklyn, and a leash-free dog park. Forman stated that her "focus was on making a nourishing, multi-ethnic community of different economic levels," continuing that "There was a faction in the community that didn't want to be identified as multi-ethnic because it brought down their property values. I'm sorry I ruffle feathers when I tell this story, but you know, we rode the backs of poor people to improve this community and we didn't do it so people in real estate could make more money on their houses. That wasn't the function of those grants!"[64]

Forman was aware of the gentrifying effects of community improvement projects. She wanted her restaurant to be beneficial to the community of people who already lived there, not to change the neighbourhood so that the original inhabitants would be priced out of the housing market. Forman's goal with her restaurant was to be part of the community. In an interview with *The San Diego Free Press*, she remarked that "We were all poor together: the artists, the musicians, the theater people, the activists, the healers, the thinkers. I used to refer to them as the 'colorful' characters of Golden Hill. We live in a culture that honors the military industrial complex, based on destruction, instead of the healing world of creativity and peace. The Big Kitchen was a space where the latter could thrive."[65] As the *San Diego Troubadour* noted, Forman had been at the vanguard of civil rights, women's rights, and gay rights and involved in after-school programs, rehab programs for drug abusers, shelters for homeless folks, and care for those who are HIV positive. In appreciation of Forman's work, a San Diego local wrote *Big Kitchen: A Counter Cultural Musical*, a production with twenty-two original songs based on interviews with thirty people including current and former employees, regulars, and neighbours.[66] The musical, as described by its author, focuses on "Forman's work in building a truly equitable world, all the while serving some hash browns on the side."[67]

An emphasis on community building is not part of the mandate of traditional restaurant management, however for feminist restaurant owners such as Forman, these actions were pivotal to their work. The Big Kitchen had meaningful effects in people's lives beyond serving food.[68] In 2005, the California State Legislature honoured Judy Forman as Woman of the Year.[69] Forman was actively involved in supporting the LGBTQ community and San Diego Pride since 1981, leading the parade twice; once as its marshal and the other time as "Friend of the Community." She also offered space, support, and fundraisers for numerous LGBTQ+ organizations including the Frontrunners, the Women's Chorus, and the Gay Youth Alliance.[70] Forman's past education as a social worker is often cited in the articles about her and The Big Kitchen as a way to explain how she knew how to listen, care, and help everyone she came into contact with—customer or employee. Forman used her restaurant not as a space apart but as a part of the community.

Feminist restaurants and cafes' relationships with their local communities would change over time. At Ruby's in Minneapolis, Minnesota, owner Mary Bahneman explained in an interview that she tried to make the restaurant a place where it would be okay if you came in by yourself. A person would not be harassed, regardless of gender, race, or sexual orientation. Rather, she wanted the restaurant to be a place where people could meet new friends. In both locations, Bahneman recounts that she had regulars and customers who would work on a crossword puzzle together. At other moments, the whole place would be singing "Edelweiss" from the *Sound of Music*.[71] They noted that local politicians would come to Ruby's to eat, and not as a campaign picture stop, but rather to talk strategy. Despite an earlier reviewer homophobically noting that "he liked his breakfast 'straighter,'" according to Bahneman, Ruby's had the reputation of good food, good people.[72] Similarly, the relationship between Wildrose of Seattle and their local community changed over time. Initially no one from the outside community would enter, and there was zero street traffic. Bryher Herak, the owner, later found out that apparently there was a rumour that they did not serve men and if a man wanted a burger it would be served raw. Herak found these stories, motivated by fear, sad, when the intent of the founders was to create a welcoming place. It took four to five years to get the neighbourhood to come in, but eventually the eleven-to-three lunch crowd took off.[73] By 1989, Ruby's began to serve espresso, which made a difference because it had wide appeal in the community. Herak then hired Lori Potter, a great cook, and her cuisine attracted a broader clientele. Even at Mother Courage, the customer base widened. As recounted by reporters, "The originally heavily feminist clientele has been somewhat diluted, particularly after a very favorable notice in *New York Magazine* brought in more men dining out with their wives and women friends. Jill and Dolores point out that the publicity has also brought in more Movement women from suburbs outside of the city, from New Jersey, Westchester, Long Island. The balance is still very much on the side of the feminists who constitute a good 60 percent of the diners on any given evening."[74]

These restaurants' locations affected their customer base and reputations. While feminist restaurants could be welcoming to members of the entire neighbourhood, the focus was still primarily on women. The owners of Bloodroot focused on promoting women and women's community, stating to a journalist that "although men are welcome, and, indeed, do come, Bloodroot is clearly out to support and promote women."[75] If businesses were for-profit, by law they had to allow people of all genders to attend, and as explained above, there was a genuine interest in doing so by promoting social justice principles in their neighborhoods. However, the next chapter will explain how the restaurant owners of establishments that wanted to create completely women-only separatist spaces, such as the Common Woman of Northampton, Massachusetts, and Grace and Rubies of Iowa City, had to structure their businesses as nonprofit corporations. Even non-separatist restaurants, such as Bloodroot, had women-only nights. Making women-only hours did not preclude the desire to positively connect with their larger communities. Precisely what "community" meant, and who was included, was subject to the discretion of the owners.

Different Owners and Operators

Feminist restaurants were owned and operated by a different kind of person than the ones who ran mainstream restaurants. As previously discussed, in the 1970s, men, particularly cisgender heterosexual white men, owned the majority of restaurants in the United States due to their ability to secure financial and educational opportunities. The women who began feminist restaurants were not a uniform group. Working- and middle-class lesbians who identified as radical feminists, radical lesbian-separatist feminists, or socialist feminists owned most of the restaurants, although there were exceptions. Of the restaurants where details about the owners are known, most of the owners were white. At the Brick Hut Café of Berkeley, the entire collective of lesbians were white except for Sharon Davenport, who was the only woman of colour, identifying as half-Filipina, though often passing as white.[76] In email correspondence Joan Antonuccio of the Brick Hut also added that a few of the collective were middle class and a few members were working class and that "race and class were regular discussions among ourselves and in the broader community."[77] Bryher Herak of Wildrose of Seattle was a white working-class lesbian. Patricia Hynes was a white radical lesbian. Marjorie Parsons and her colleagues of Northampton's the Common Womon were white working- and middle-class lesbians, many of them still students.[78] The women who started these restaurants were typically between twenty-five to forty years old.

Jewish owners were prominent. Selma Miriam of Bloodroot has spoken about how she has brought together her knowledge of Jewish cooking from her culture with different cooking methods.[79] Mary Bahneman, after selling Ruby's Café, worked with Jewish Children's Services for eight years.[80] Sara Lewinstein, founder of San Francisco's Artemis Society Women's Café (1977–1984), is Jewish. Big Kitchen of San Diego's owner Judy Forman has talked about how her Jewish roots influenced her desire to open a restaurant. As *The San Diego Troubadour* noted, Forman has made a career out of "serving great nosh with a side of tikkun olam" (a Jewish concept defined by acts of kindness performed to perfect or repair the world). Since she began running the restaurant in 1980, Forman's activist philosophy

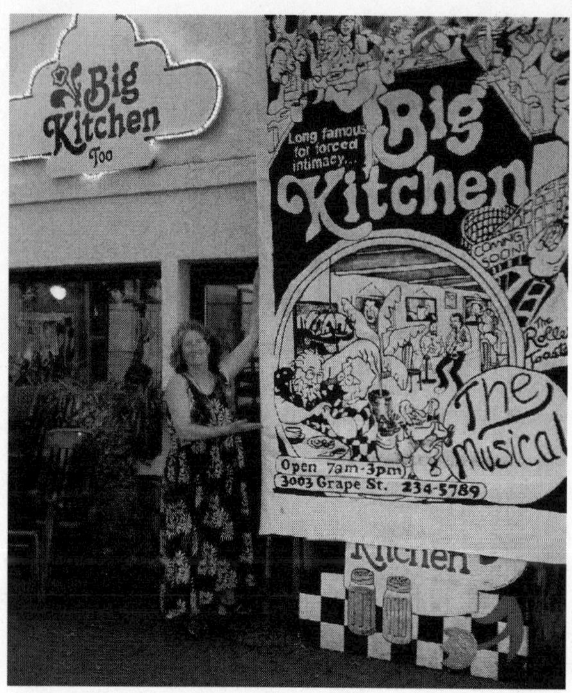

2.3 Judy "the Beauty on Duty" Forman stands in front of the poster advertising Big Kitchen: A Counter Culture Musical *in 2014. The musical launched at the San Diego, California Fringe Festival. The original songs celebrate the restaurant's long-standing commitment to the community. (Photo courtesy of and by Robert Schleeter)*

has extended far beyond the walls of her eatery, which she attributes to her Jewish roots. She proclaimed that, "as a Jew and a minority, I don't feel safe unless everyone is safe,"[81] continuing,

> I came to San Diego in October 1979 after working for the state of Michigan as a social worker for ten years. I had graduated from Michigan State University but found that my real education took place on the streets of Detroit, working with gangs. Politically speaking I have been a civil rights activist since the sixth grade when I realized the plight of migrant workers in my county. But what really activated me early on was the realization that I could be discriminated against

> merely because of my religious beliefs and/or ethnicity. My grandparents left Russia because of the pogroms of Stalin and my grandmother was the only survivor of her large family after the Holocaust in Germany. After reading *The Diary of Anne Frank* I realized the only way I could be safe was to ensure that everyone was safe. To me that meant being a civil rights activist. I marched in the streets for racial equality, for ending the Vietnam War, for Gay Rights, and for Women's Rights. There is an incredible adrenaline rush that occurs for me when I am in the street screaming against injustice. I feel empowered linking arms with brave activists and watching the police aim their guns and rifles at us from the rooftops because we believe in changing the culture to include everyone, not just rich white men.[82]

Judaism was not the only religion held by feminist restaurant owners, but it is notable in interviews and articles how often Jewish restaurant founders cited their Jewish roots as being integral to their motivation behind creating feminist restaurants, using food to bring people together and create positive change.

As will be discussed in greater detail in chapters 3 and 6, feminist restaurant owners were less privileged than middle-class, upper middle-class, and rich white men who dominated the restaurant industry during the 1970s and 1980s. However, the ability to access capital, particularly loans, meant that the women who started feminist restaurants were often white, free from the double bind of racial and gender oppression. White working-class and middle-class lesbians founded the majority of feminist restaurants and cafes. Coffeehouses with lower overhead costs had a greater diversity at the level of management.

One aspect that allowed the owners to think creatively about how they would organize their restaurants was that few had previous experience in the restaurant business. While restaurant managers of typical restaurants do not need to have a degree in restaurant management, food industry experience is typical; some restaurant managers begin their careers as waiters or hostesses and work their way up within the hierarchy of a particular restaurant. However, colleges and universities in the United States offered training programs at the associate, bachelor, and graduate level in restaurant management. Since most of the owners had never started a restaurant, they had to learn everything by trial and error. Selma Miriam recounted her initial naïveté when she described Bloodroot's origins to a reporter, stating that, "this piece of property was for sale and my parents said they'd give us the down payment for it, but nobody would lend us money for the mortgage because we had no history."[83] They finally acquired the property, but they had to get a building permit. "I went to city hall" and said "tell me what you want me to do and I'll do it. I didn't know how."[84] Marjorie Parsons of Common Womon Club repeatedly said, "we were doing it by the seat of our pants."[85] Likewise, Joan Antonuccio remarked that Brick Hut was done "totally seat of the pants. Sometimes that worked to our advantage—we weren't aware that much of what we did was considered impossible. We just did it."[86] Bryher Herak wrote of getting her start in the food industry by working with a lesbian bread collective in Seattle. Despite having no prior experience working in the restaurant business she had known bars her whole life, so she built up the skills within the lesbian feminist community and felt okay about opening Wildrose.[87]

Women with former restaurant experience did begin some of the feminist restaurants. Ruby's owner Mary Bahneman had worked in quite a few restaurants previously and had a home economics degree. Even though Brick Hut's collective felt like they were operating "totally seat of the pants," some of their collective members had worked in the restaurant business, such as Joan Antonuccio, who had been working in the food industry since age fourteen.[88] Wania of La Fronde in New York City was a trained chef. What is important to note is that women who already had worked in the restaurant industry founded the restaurants that functioned most similarly to mainstream restaurants. By comparison, Marjorie Parsons was working as a head resident at the University of Massachusetts. Mother Courage's owners had no previous restaurant experience: Jill Ward was in management and Dolores Alexander was a newspaperwoman.[89] Most of the founders were motivated by the desire to create community spaces and food served as the vehicle to realize their goals. The owners' lack of industry experience led to problems, as will be discussed below. More importantly, however, it also encouraged creativity, which enabled feminist restaurants to challenge work structures and relationships with customers.

Changing Work Structures and Relationships

> Many feminists have talked about changing their workplace but few have done so, explained Miss McKay. By eliminating the hierarchy implicit in most businesses and by giving women employees the opportunity to be themselves, we think we have gone a long way toward making it possible for them to be feminists on the job.[90]
>
> *McKay, Los Angeles Women's Saloon*

Feminist restaurants transformed the relationship between staff and customer. Changing the relationship between the customer, their money, and the establishment was also important. For instance, most feminist restaurants did not allow tipping. Bread and Roses had a jar on the counter, which was used to raise money for local feminist causes instead of tipping the staff.[91] Unlike other low-wage restaurants in 1976, which encouraged their waitresses to smile, flirt, and ingratiate themselves with customers in hopes of getting larger tips, the *Lakeland Ledger* noted that the Los Angeles Women's Saloon and Parlor paid all its employees a high wage of $3 an hour.[92] In 1976, the minimum wage in California was $2 an hour for non-tipping jobs (jobs with tips had a lower minimum wage), so the $3 an hour wages were far above the norm.[93] Poly Molina, who had worked as a waitress at other restaurants in Los Angeles before taking a job at the Women's Saloon, remarked to the journalist, "I don't feel like I'm an automaton here." She continued: "Other restaurants make you wear ridiculous costumes or walk with a silly grin on your face. Male managers permit and sometimes even encourage customers to insult or mistreat waitresses. Here no matter what job we do we are treated with respect."[94] At the Common Womon Club of Northampton, Massachusetts, there was also no tipping. Eliminating tipping practices was an important factor in changing the relationship between staff and customers and thus was common in feminist restaurant business dynamics.

In another example of changing the work structure, the restaurants would often request that each table of people clear their soiled dishes. In fact, there were no waitresses at Bread and Roses of Cambridge or Bloodroot of Bridgeport. When the food was ready, customers were called upon to serve themselves.[95] Clients were to pick up their own food from the counter and clear their plates at the end. Patricia Hynes of Bread and Roses explained to an interviewer that "We don't feel comfortable with women waiting on other people."[96] Although self-service was a concept that more traditional restaurants have employed with buffet tables, salad bars, and cafeterias, to save money by requiring a smaller staff, these feminist restaurants used this technique additionally for political reasons; to challenge the hierarchical, patriarchal standards of the regular service industry. According to the *Lakeland Ledger*, at the Los Angeles Women's Saloon and Parlor most customers were sympathetic to the needs of the staff. If the waitresses were busy, the customers were encouraged to get their own silverware or help themselves to a second cup of coffee. One night a group of regular customers did all the cooking and cleaning so that the staff could have a night off.[97] For the most part, customers seemed to be okay with this arrangement.

Not everyone was amenable to this different kind of service, however. As Marjorie Parsons noted, when the original collective ran the

Common Womon Club, women self-served. Customers went to a counter to order and pick up their food. This allowed the restaurant to have a smaller staff of about two people working per shift, which facilitated its being open six days a week.[98] In a later version of the Common Womon Club, when a second collective took over operations, it moved to having a wait staff. Parsons noticed that richer customers preferred this change, as the women with more money preferred to be waited on.[99] She saw that even within this purported egalitarian space, class differences mattered. Parsons reflected, "One of the saddest things was that the restaurant … was like creating a monster that perpetuated keeping women down instead of giving them a place to raise them up."[100] Certain customers felt emboldened when there was class stratification. The second collective realized that richer customers were willing to spend more if they were waited upon. This discrepancy indicates that power structures from the outside world, despite the staff's efforts to challenge them, were replicated within the restaurant. Race, class, and gender did not disappear at the door just because the space was called feminist. Customers' desire to keep purchasing cheap food despite the Common Womon Club not having the purchasing power of a chain like McDonald's meant lower wages for the women working there.

Feminist restaurants often had different staff procedures than mainstream restaurants. In the case of the Los Angeles Women's Saloon and the Common Womon of Northampton, each woman working at the restaurant shared the different management roles by taking turns planning the meals, doing the cooking, organizing the finances, washing the dishes, and doing maintenance. By rotating positions, these feminist restaurants subverted traditional restaurant management hierarchy. At the Los Angeles Women's Saloon and Parlor, all fourteen of the employees participated in the major decisions, although those who were experts in cooking or marketing made day-to-day decisions in these areas. For instance, the "dirty work" was divided, so nobody was stuck scrubbing the floor every day.[101]

Collective structures tended to encourage people to share the work. The Common Womon Club began during a February 1976 meeting for women who wanted to get into business. The initial meeting brought in fourteen women: seven or eight women wanted a restaurant, four or five wanted a bookstore, and a few just wanted to be involved. At their second meeting, they limited the group's membership to the nine people who showed up and called themselves the Women's Restaurant Project.[102] From the first day, the fundraising began and never stopped. The group's money issues, which will be discussed further in the next chapter, caused a lot of the problems. All nine members worked in the kitchen, cooked, and cleaned. The collective also changed sizes—lowering to seven. Interest in being involved in the collective impeded its efficiency. There was a limit to how many people could make a living wage. Marjorie Parsons, reflected:

> Theoretically if we had three or four people working forty hours a week with the food service—we could have given them a living wage. Then we had lots of women working twenty hours. Then we had people doing fundraising which wasn't paid. This was all collective people. We did not open the collective up—because we couldn't possibly afford it—we needed a stable body of people—if we were going to move or something we needed a stable group to stay with it. It's interesting because in some ways that commitment level was very high … One of our important issues was that especially doing shift-work, women should be paid.[103]

Different ideas about work and expectations led to problems.

Despite having a vision of challenging the hierarchy, collective models were not the easiest to maintain. When asked if there were tensions within the collective, Brick Hut owner Joan Antonnucio replied, "Hahaha. Always. It was a collective. With people." Then more seriously she added, "We usually tried for consensus, later a two-thirds quorum, then just majority rule."[104] By creating a procedure to deal with conflicts, the Brick Hut Café was able to mitigate tensions. Personal conflicts and different expectations tore other restaurant collectives apart. Nevertheless, Marjorie Parsons of the Common Womon Club emphasized repeatedly how committed the collective was to the project. The downside to that level of emotional investment meant that "also the anger and the resentment built up because some people did more work."[105] In order to compensate for this problem, the collective held processing meetings in addition to their organizational meetings. Business meetings were held to work out scheduling, fundraising, event planning, discuss money matters, and write the tasks lists for jobs ranging from cleaning the bathrooms to writing the menu. These business meetings showed why the process meetings, when the group would take time to discuss emotions, were important. Parsons remarked, "There were times in the group when people didn't get along—had a really hard time with each other."[106] Over time tensions built within the collective; sometimes the conflict would be over former lovers and co-collective members fighting, and sometimes it would be over something as simple as a debate about whether to use butter or margarine.[107] Poor communication skills could result in businesses imploding over something as simple as butter.

Part of the tension at Common Womon Club resulted from frustrations regarding the menu and workload. Even if the collective had planned to share all the tasks, there was a "natural division of labor. Certain people had to do certain things. Certain people had certain interests or hobbies" and these "obvious power dynamics [existed] between the person who knew how to cook and who didn't and if someone needs more eggs because [she] felt like making custard that wasn't on the menu plan and now it's brunch day and we have no eggs."[108] These power discrepancies led to further conflicts. There was a collective member who loved making desserts and was very talented at it, but she would not follow the menu plan. The other collective members wanted to follow a menu plan that made sense and that was balanced because they worked with co-ops that only delivered once a week.[109] The members were also quite territorial over the kitchen, but the real source of conflict was poor communication.

Apart from the menu and food ordering, a lack of open communication was a constant source of tension. Marjorie Parsons had taken over the books, "and there was an issue around that because people would harass me about the money and people wouldn't listen to me about the money issue and I wasn't feeling supported—and people doing the menu planning weren't feeling supported—undermined."[110] Furthermore, there was little communication about setting up cultural events. One time a miscommunication resulted in printing the wrong information on publicity flyers. Parsons even admits that

> I remember dealing with an issue that wasn't in my area at all—basically I laid her out—was letting my mouth go—and was sarcastic. And the whole collective—there had to be a collective response. Fuck her and the woman who was dealing with the leasing and rental stuff felt so undermined that I had mouthed up. So these are all process things—you can imagine what comes out of valuing the different kinds of politics and goals and different amounts of time you could put in. There were times in the collective when there were women who couldn't work—who couldn't cook in the kitchen together.

Lots of anger built up. Growing frustrations impacted by working under constant stress meant that collective members ceased to be empathetic to one another. Rather than expressing their frustrations in a constructive manner, the collective members would tear each other apart. To put it simply, Parsons said it best when she stated, "It was a big failing as a collective—our process."[111]

Parsons was able to learn from her collective's mistakes, and while her collective was unable to resolve these issues, she passed on these lessons to other feminist collectives. Part of challenging mainstream restaurant hierarchy meant experimentation, and experiments sometimes failed. Initially, the women would compartmentalize their emotional needs to deal with business issues, but these tensions simmered under the surface and would be released in explosions. Collectives were dependent on members being able to trust that the other women would follow through on their tasks and commitments to the restaurant.[112] At the Common Womon Club, the constant infighting resulted in burnout. Marjorie Parsons recommended that future collectives "get a good facilitator to come in once a month to come in and talk with the group."[113] With a group therapy session once a month the anger could get released and people could move on. She also advised against overextending oneself. These businesses, especially in smaller towns, often served as the community centre/women's centre or LGB centre. As a result, the business owners were often trying to organize so many events that they became spread too thin. The Common Womon Club aimed to do care work for the entire women's community of Northampton, but the collective members forgot to care for themselves in the process. While Parsons's collective was unable to implement these techniques in time to save the Common Womon Club, she wanted to share this advice with other women interested in beginning feminist businesses.

Collectives rarely lasted: for the restaurants that lasted for more than three years, even if the businesses began with collective management, they would usually transition to private ownership. Initially, Wildrose of Seattle was collectively managed. Two of the women were management and the other three would work two to three nights a week as bartenders, waitresses, and sous chefs. Additionally, the collective hired three or four other part-time staff.[114] At the Wildrose's start, Bryher Herak kept her day job and the capital from it was often used to support the restaurant. Eventually she took over managing the entire restaurant herself. She only hired women. In an interview she stressed that it was not that she would not have hired men, but at the time she had so many women who wanted to work for her and politically she liked the idea of women working there.[115] Bloodroot of Bridgeport also began as a collective that, over its forty years of operation, dwindled to Selma Miriam and Noel Furie. However, the restaurant was able to function because it also employed staff. The Brick Hut of Berkeley began as a collective where all collective members did all the jobs. After eight years, the business grew and the collective dissolved. After the Brick Hut collective was evicted and moved to a new location, it incorporated and operated as a core group of five owners, with eight to thirteen employees that it hired on a short-term or revolving door basis. Antonuccio explained that if "someone was short of money (often a musician!), she would come in and work with us for a few days or weeks."[116] As partners left to pursue other interests, Davenport and Antonuccio stayed, operating the cafe for the last twelve years as co-owners. As the Brick Hut expanded and no longer operated as a collective, Antonuccio notes that she and Davenport hired more and more people to work with them. At their apex in the late 1980s they had around thirty-two employees. Collectives fulfilled a philosophical and political desire to disrupt hierarchies, but in practice the full collective model created problems that became untenable for long-term operations.

Not every feminist restaurant radically changed work structures. Bryher Herak described the Wildrose's structure as "very traditional in terms of service." The kitchen was partly hidden in the back. The bartenders and waitresses were often the same people, each table was numbered, and customers were waited on. She called it a "pretty straight by the book business model" that proved successful.[117] Likewise, Ruby's owner had a business-partner arrangement in the first location.

Through the 1970s and into the 1980s, there was a noticeable difference in how professional the restaurants became. Amateurs without previous food industry experience and with scant bookkeeping skills most often began the earliest feminist restaurants. By the late 1970s and early 1980s, feminist restaurants functioned more professionally.

In an article, "Why Women Leave the Full Moon," staff members discussed how they were upset over the way the management tried to organize the space and resolve problems. Spaces like San Francisco's Baybrick Inn (opened in 1982), which housed a restaurant, were far more regimented with a formalized staff guidebook/rulebook.[118] Part of the change in professionalism had to do with mentorship and expanded educational opportunities for women in business. The pioneers of feminist restaurants identified some of these problems and created resolutions for them.

This chapter does not argue that feminist restaurants were the only type of restaurant to challenge restaurant hierarchy. Other restaurants also tried to change the role of restaurant management. Feminists also were not the only people to attempt collective restaurant management. Moosewood Restaurant in Ithaca, New York (1973–present), is one of the most famous restaurants that utilized collective management. It is not alone, however, as a variety of restaurants have attempted non-hierarchical collective agreement, though they are still in the minority of the general restaurant population. Many of the participating restaurants have political reasons for doing so, whether they identify as anarchist, feminist, or rooted in some idea of social justice. What made feminist restaurants different was that they emphasized their feminism. For them it was important to create decidedly feminist spaces.

Reconciling Capitalist Tensions

Despite the tensions and uncertainties over whether one could have a business within capitalism and be feminist, women ultimately proceeded to open these spaces. As Wania of La Fronde, a feminist restaurant in New York City, remarked in 1974, "I don't know how far one can carry feminism."[119] Wania had been working as a translator for the State Department, at the time known as the foreign office, and was a member of the radical feminist group Redstockings. She noted in an interview with *The International Herald Tribune* that "Like Mother Courage, her restaurant was founded for ideological, not culinary reasons."[120] In the foreign office, she "worked with girls, that's what they called us and that's what we were" but at her restaurant, she "was fascinated to work with women."[121] She acknowledged that there might be limitations for feminist businesses but these restaurants were important due to their ability to empower and humanize workers. Not every woman saw a conflict between running a feminist business and her anti-capitalist ethics.

There were feminist restaurant owners who did not see these restaurants as part of capitalism, or at least as part of the problematic aspects of capitalism. In replying to remarks about Bloodroot of Bridgeport's relationship to capitalism, Selma Miriam elaborated:

> The notion of capitalism is very oversimplified in terms of lefty circles and always was. My father had a fabric store. He was a business owner. He was also a socialist. There was no [conflict]. Yea, that's no conflict. All you have to do is think about the 99 percent right now. It's the people, and I'm not blaming them, but whenever you hear talk about capitalism and they are talking about workers, they are talking about the people who are in the thousands working for GE or Google. They aren't talking about a Mom and Pop store where the people are selling burritos. So you want to call that capitalism? I don't think so. That's ridiculous … In the 70s this was not capitalism. Of course people had businesses. You had to have some way to make a living. So either you worked for the man in a very stultifying, miserable way or you're some kind of secretary or you work for the school system or you work for the government. But all of those things are great big miserable sorts of jobs. You might get off on working with kids but in terms of the people that we have things in common with are like I said, the guy who sells the burritos or the Vietnamese

> restaurant or you know what I mean. People who are selling food to their friends and they are people from their countries and make them feel at home and nourished. That's not capitalism. Never mind we're not making money and we're really in trouble with this economy. This is not capitalism. Capitalism is exploitation.[122]

For Selma Miriam and Noel Furie of Bloodroot there was no ethical conflict. In Miriam's interpretation, the socialist and Marxist critique of capitalism did not mean that people could not operate restaurants. For her, the value of Marxist rhetoric was its critique of exploitation. Feminist restaurants encouraged recirculation of profits into the women's community by supporting other women's energies. Similarly, other women viewed their work as an alternative to capitalism. As the editors of *Country Women Magazine* stated, "We are still part of a capitalist economy. But we're also beginning to build alternatives. We only work with women we really care about, who are our friends, so there is respect and love in our business."[123] These women hoped to make enough money to support themselves and their dreams. Money enabled these feminists to build the kinds of alternative communities they hoped; as they stated, "we want to make lots of money so we can buy land."[124] When these activists made money, they did not keep it for individual use but for the community; sharing the profits made their money-making ventures justifiable to themselves.

Lessons Learned and Conclusion

Feminist restaurants worked and looked differently from mainstream restaurants during the 1970s and 1980s. Bloodroot Feminist Vegetarian Restaurant began as a woman-centred space that reflected the owners' values. As Selma Miriam explained to the *Fairfield County Advocate*, "We wanted to start a woman's center, but we needed a way to support it. So we decided on a restaurant and bookstore; mental food because feminist writings are so important to us."[125] This creation of a women's centre in the Bridgeport area, for a bookstore, and for a healthy place to eat allowed for them to "make a living for themselves without selling out."[126] Selma Miriam stated that the values she wanted to reflect "through much soul-searching, and with the support of her Bloodroot partners, [she] came to believe that her passions for orchid-growing and cooking were consistent with and spring from her relationship to Earth, and should be carried forward into her life as a radical lesbian feminist."[127] Noel Furie of Bloodroot agreed, stating to *The Black Rock News* that starting Bloodroot "was a matter of doing something political ... Political in the sense of being able to have full control over our own lives and have our work in concert with our beliefs."[128] Sam Stickwell of the original Bloodroot Collective commented that "the joy of serving women from all walks of life is its own reward."[129] Women from all over the world have visited Bloodroot and the restaurant has many regular customers. Even forty-five years after its founding, some of the original customers from the first year continue to return. Selma "believed strongly in the fact that "you could make a community with food" and she and the collective certainly did.[130] A similar theme follows from the reflection of the other restaurants. Feminist restaurants had an impact beyond their businesses because they were part of a nexus; they were also part of a larger conversation about how to live and live out one's values within a capitalist society.

Feminist restaurants allowed women to live openly as feminists, and to challenge both the system and the restaurant as an institution. While reflecting on Mother Courage's first year, Dolores Alexander noted,

> Thank God the first year is over. The biggest lesson we learned is that nothing—nothing good—comes easy. But we are very satisfied with the choice we have made. We really see the best chances for personal fulfillment AND revolutionary

> change in women getting going their own enterprises and institutions. In the man's world, as far as women are concerned, the trend will be tokenism for years to come. And you can bet that not many feminists are going to be among these tokens. Of course, we still have to live in and deal with that world. You know, Mother Courage is a character in a Brecht play who endures and survives the Thirty Years' War by dealing with both sides. Obviously to survive we all have to compromise to some degree. The trick is to retain one's values with minimum compromise. That's what we are trying to do.[131]

Mother Courage's founders realized that they could not fulfill every aspiration, as they were only two women constrained by the physical limitations of their bodies and time, in addition to economic and social systems. However, Dolores Alexander explained on a sign that she placed in Mother Courage that she and Jill Ward had "been working in the movement and we wanted to find a way to continue contributing to the movement and still make enough to support ourselves."[132] She stated, "neither of us wanted to compete in a man's world, a world created by men—which excludes us and yet which has taught us that it is because of our inadequacies that we don't make it."[133] A feminist restaurant was a way to have feminist-oriented work connect with their daily lives.

While feminist restaurants and cafes embodied their feminist ideals uniquely, these businesses challenged the status quo of the food service industry, cooking, capitalism, and consumption. These spaces had different aesthetics and work structures due to a mixture of need, a lack of financial resources, and feminist values that sought to overturn the sexism experienced by women in mainstream restaurant culture. Feminist restaurants experimented with challenging restaurant hierarchies. Choices to eliminate tipping, having customers serve themselves, and working in collective structures all changed the relationships between owners, staff, and clientele. The restaurants were political projects. The owners extended the meaning of restaurant management beyond an orchestration of front- and back-of-the-house functions. While questions about how to manage a business within a capitalist society continued to be debated by feminists, feminist restaurant owners sought to balance their values with practical needs. Feminist restaurants did more than serve food; their owners worked on serving the greater community, both of feminists and that of their neighbourhoods.

The next chapter explores how feminist restaurants and cafes still had to be part of the economy while they challenged capitalism. Balancing economic needs with philosophy necessitated compromises. These feminist restaurants and cafes were not isolated but were part of a larger economy and society that was not always amenable to the desires of their owners. The creation of women's space required innovative financial manoeuvrings.

CHAPTER 3

Financing Feminist Restaurants, Cafes, and Coffeehouses

The money question was central. We were working under the tension of money … And money is a very hard issue. And women get very uptight about that. And it's really painful. It's almost as bad as looking for a job. Pushing.[1]

Marjorie Parsons, Common Woman Club

Although feminist restaurants and cafes challenged capitalism, they were still part of the system. Balancing economic needs with ideology meant compromises. These feminist restaurants and cafes were not isolated but part of a larger economy and society that was not always amenable to their aspirations. The creation of woman-space required innovative financial strategies. Founders of feminist restaurants and cafes had to secure funding creatively when banks were unwilling to provide loans. Financial laws constrained feminist restaurant owners and, as a result, the owners sometimes faced pushback from the legal system. Navigating these constraints meant that the restaurants did not necessarily look how the founders originally intended; however, the restaurants' impact in individuals' lives remained meaningful. Feminist restaurants expanded economic opportunities for women. They ran counter to capitalism while operating within a capitalist system. Sometimes this process involved "cooking the books." While other chapters discuss the cultural meanings of these restaurants, this chapter will explain how they functioned as businesses.

Feminist restaurants, once operational, would provide economic opportunities for the women involved in them; however, securing the necessary start-up capital could be prohibitive. Running a restaurant or cafe required significant funding to pay for rent, equipment, decoration, and supplies. Obtaining this amount of money was difficult for most of the women interested in opening these spaces. Choices made over location, management organization, staff, and menu options could lower costs. However, as discussed in the last chapter, because most of these women had never run a food business before, the learning curve for these new business owners impacted revenue. As Selma Miriam noted, the seeds of Bloodroot Feminist Vegetarian Restaurant were planted in 1977 when Miriam began hosting women's meetings in her home in Westport, Connecticut, just after her divorce. She explained, "I did it for nine months and decided it was the only good thing I was doing in my life, short of picking up my mixer and hitching to San Francisco."[2] Betsey Beaven met Miriam at a lesbian rap group and Selma invited her to be part of the business. Reflecting on her initial desire to create the restaurant, Beaven remarked, "We had this vision which is still grounded in feminism being a resistance movement. But in resisting you also have to create something. So that's what we did."[3] Noel Furie, who separated from her husband around the same time Bloodroot was founded, knew Miriam through the National Organization for Women (NOW) chapter in Westport. Furie, who started working at Bloodroot shortly after it opened, commented, "I didn't know what I was going to do for a living but I thought it would be incredible to plan a lifetime of work around doing what I really liked with women I respected and loved."[4] The women of Bloodroot, similar to the other feminist restaurants discussed in this book, wanted to use their businesses to create positive change in the world. But the enthusiasm to start a feminist restaurant did not necessarily come with knowledge of the business world or the capital needed to create these spaces. As a result, the women who started feminist restaurants, such as Bloodroot, needed to turn to creative sources of funding.

Overcoming Funding Difficulties and "Hipping Yourself to the Government"

Women who sought traditional funding sources for their feminist restaurants were repeatedly denied access, citing sexism as the cause. As the 1974 American Senate and House Committees on Small Business stated, banks' credit policies were notoriously discriminative toward women, especially women without collateral assets. Restaurant owner after restaurant owner recounted stories in interviews and in publications about being denied loans from banks and often of facing scorn and ridicule. Speaking in 1981 as part of San Francisco KGO-TV's special news report on lesbians, Sara Lewinstein, founder of San Francisco's Artemis Society Women's Café (1977–1984) focused on the relationship between women and finances. Lewinstein stated, "I think women are struggling. There's a long way to go. There always will be, as long as women are trying to have businesses. I see it as a long struggle. Women don't have the money and the backing that men do. There is such a difference. You go to Castro Street and you see all these gay men's places. Every place you go to is a gay men's bar. On the weekend it is so packed that you can't get in. You don't have that same thing. You don't see so many women's bars."[5] The women's community of San Francisco had less capital than gay men to invest in founding restaurants, bars, and other businesses. It was not that there were no women with money. The women who started feminist restaurants and cafes tended to have some form of available capital through an inheritance, extended family, or from savings from a previous "non-movement" job (work unrelated to feminist activism). The owners' ability to secure traditional funding sources like bank loans depended on being able to pass as straight, white, middle class, and not politically radical, even if they were not. One's marital status, or more specifically the lack of having a husband, still created difficulties due to legal discrimination in lending practices. Whether or not the owners were able to secure traditional funding sources, these restaurants depended primarily on sweat equity.

Relying on hard work and facing sexism as women business owners was not unique to feminist restaurants. However, the historical conditions in which the feminist restaurant owners operated, the founders' political motivations, and the important role that self-identifying as feminist played in their business models is what made feminist restaurants different.[6] Feminist restaurants were not the only restaurants to exist as a result of "sweat equity," referring to the increased value in property earned from labour toward upkeep or restoration. As the historiography of ethnic restaurants in the United States shows, new immigrants created restaurants as a way to establish an economic foothold in their new homeland and improve their family's economic status for future generations.[7] Feminist restaurant owners were not the only women to own restaurants.[8] However, women owning and managing a restaurant were still less common than men. The percentage of women who were restaurant owners and managers in the United States hovered around 33 percent in the United States between 1972 to 1989 and people of colour were underrepresented.[9] Feminist restaurant owners did not necessarily see themselves represented in all women restaurant owners due to different political leanings and because not all women restaurant owners were interested in assisting out lesbians and aspiring founders of feminist businesses. This matter is complicated. On the one hand, there were situations like when Bloodroot's owners contacted the only woman they knew in Connecticut who owned a restaurant and she was not interested in mentoring them. At the same time, women's travel guides such as *Gaia's Guide* noted if restaurants were women-owned-and-operated, even if the owners did not identify the space as feminist. These guides promoted women's businesses, reflecting the philosophy of the subset of lesbian feminists that believed it was important to support women's endeavours.[10]

Despite the relative privileges of feminist restaurant founders, as they were able to access some form of capital to begin their businesses, it is also important to note how often feminist restaurant owners represented their own stories as a narrative of struggle. This is not to say that the owners of feminist restaurants did not actually struggle. They were operating with small starting budgets and with a small available margin of error, having to buy everything second hand or build it themselves, all while facing sexism and homophobia. However, as will be discussed later in this chapter, they were able to access unique sources of funding made available through their employment of the term "feminist" and by being embedded in an already established feminist community. As chapters 6 and 7 discuss, for the women who were rich in enthusiasm but poor in capital, feminist coffeehouses were another option.

Securing Bank Financing

Some owners persisted and eventually found a banker to finance their enterprise, but most of the women interviewed for this book abandoned the idea of creating their restaurants solely through traditional funding avenues and instead utilized alternative sources. Selma Miriam recounted in an interview with *Fairpress* that when she was trying to raise the initial capital for Bloodroot, "We had the down payment and money for renovations and a few commitments from investors, but it was still a hassle because banks don't want to give money to restaurants and some banks gave me a hard time because I'm a woman."[11] Nevertheless, she persisted. Miriam believed that Bloodroot was an especially hard pitch: "whether it was because it was women or a restaurant, nobody wanted anything to do with it. One day in great desperation, I called Harvey Koizim, the president of County General Savings and Loan. When I told him I wanted to start a women's center [the restaurant and bookstore], he started laughing, but he came to see it two hours later and gave us the mortgage."[12] Selma Miriam was able to secure a traditional loan after multiple rejections. Also, unlike the other restaurants in the chapter, as she revealed in an interview with *Gay City News*, she had recently secured an inheritance that she decided to fully invest into the restaurant because she had just received a medical diagnosis suggesting she would not live for longer than three years.[13] Knowing of her breast cancer, she had the incentive to devote all her resources into creating her dream, unlike other feminist restaurant founders.

The feminist restaurant owners that were able to secure bank loans found success when they could pass as white, straight, femme, and middle or upper middle class, even when those attributes did not describe their actual identities. Collective members of the Common Womon Club of Northampton, Massachusetts, went to a few banks before finally finding a bank that would support them. Marjorie Parsons of the collective attributes part of the collective's success to the fact that it had finally found a woman banker who was more amenable to its pitch. However, securing the loan still required a degree of performance. The collective needed to appear to be a culturally legible group worthy of investing in rather than appearing too radical and presenting themselves as what they were: a countercultural radical lesbian-separatist feminist collective that wanted to start a women-only restaurant. Parsons took pleasure in explaining how her collective had "played the system."[14] According to her, the oldest member of the collective was forty years old and used her age and clothing to perform respectability. This elder member dressed in her most formal clothing and "acted grown up" when she went into the bank. Additionally, the oldest member of the collective got her mother to co-sign the loan to guarantee financial stability. The only other woman in the group that had a full-time job was the second co-signer, so in Parson's words, "they looked relatively clean."[15] Although most of the collective members were lesbian students or former students in their early twenties with little personal wealth, they could lean on their whiteness and education to perform in a way that visible women of colour and non-femme women could not.

Despite its success in securing a loan, the Common Womon collective still had to contend with a sexist society and deal with bank managers undermining its abilities. The bank that finally supported the collective charged a higher interest rate than the other banks that it had approached. Furthermore, the bank also lied to the women, saying that they had to use the bank's lawyer for the closing and title search, which was not legally true, so they "got taken for several hundred dollars by the lawyer at the bank."[16] Marjorie Parsons remarked that the collective's mistake was embarrassing but that such incidents were a result of being naïve and new to business. The collective's lack of experience, matched with what Parsons perceived to be the bank's sexism, meant that the bank required a large down payment. The members put down $10,000 on the $38,000, which included real estate tax. The benefit of their large down payment was that it brought their monthly payments on the building down to $350 a month.

Finance Laws

Time played an important role. Although the social and cultural historical conditions in which these restaurants were operating changed throughout the 1970s and 1980s, the differences between the earliest and the latest feminist restaurants in this period seem most stark when it came to financing. As discussed in chapter 2, the passage of legislation such as the Equal Credit Opportunity Act in the United States in 1974 helped women get credit in their own names, which was previously not a guaranteed right. This is not to say that unlawful discrimination on non-mortgage loans did not later occur but the passage of these acts on paper gave single, heterosexual women and lesbians trying to begin women-centred spaces legal protection.[17] The changes between 1972 and the late 1980s are evident in Ruby's Café owner Mary Bahneman's account. Bahneman opened her first cafe at the end of the 1980s and her second in the early 1990s, when she claims that she did not face the same extremely overt sexism as the restaurant founders did in the early 1970s. However, as Bahneman remarked in an interview, while a woman owning a cafe did not seem odd to lenders, her being a lesbian still created difficulties.[18] For her first cafe she did not require a loan because she rented a fully equipped and furnished space. However, for the second cafe she had to write a business plan and sought external funding. The first bank "wouldn't give [her] a loan since their clientele would be mostly gay."[19] Even though these restaurants were founded less than fifteen years apart, the owners still faced discrimination; however, the issues shifted over time, and women who founded their restaurants later in the period benefitted from the earlier battles fought by their foremothers.

Credit Unions

Later-founded feminist restaurants and cafes had the benefit of potentially receiving funding from feminist credit unions, which began in reaction to the institutionalized sexism of mainstream banks. Feminist credit unions, credit unions oriented towards more social justice projects, and feminist moneylenders allowed feminists to obtain funding outside of banks. In California's Bay Area, the Cheese Board Collective, which had started as a small cheese store, served as an informal moneylender for other local businesses.[20] In 1983, with the financial help of the Cheese Board Collective, in addition to the efforts of customers and friends, the Brick Hut Café of Berkeley, California, moved to a new location.[21] Ever the adaptable group, the Common Woman Club also received a $1,000 loan from the Massachusetts

Credit Union. Parsons claimed that the union was very supportive of the collective and the members never missed a payment.[22] The collective bought supplies from Western Massachusetts food cooperatives, some of which were operations as small as the Common Womon Club. The members also needed more capital to establish credit with people and organizations such as Flagstaff, a big restaurant supplier and a sub-core service organization. Only for a month or two was the restaurant able to operate "in the black," but it tended to run at a loss.[23] However, with little start-up capital the collective was beholden to lenders and alternative fundraising.

Personal Finance Networks: Friends, Community, and Self-financing

Due to the difficulties of accessing both traditional funding sources and knowledge about corporate strategies, most restaurant owners had to secure funding outside of the banking system, primarily by relying on women in the greater feminist community. Opening a restaurant in New York City was not an inexpensive venture. In 1972, Jill Ward and Dolores Alexander of Mother Courage estimated that it would take a minimum of $10,000 to begin their restaurant, which they probably would not recover for two or three years. They already had $5,500 in personal savings and were faced with the problem of raising the rest of the money.[24] Every single restaurant case study examined in this book began with at least a portion of their initial start-up costs coming from the founders of the restaurants and cafes. As Selma Miriam told the *Boston Sunday Globe*, she used her entire life savings of $19,000.[25] At Wildrose in Seattle, Bryher Herak invested her own money and continued to hold a second job to help with finances.[26] Initially at the Common Womon Club, before approaching the bank, the collective of nine women assembled $10,000 between them. At the time of its initial formation, Marjorie Parsons was a head resident for the housing residences at the local university and made $6,000 a year. She remarked that she "was young and naïve" and invested all that she could into the restaurant.[27] In exchange, she retained a promissory note that stated if the building were ever sold, she would get paid after the bank. Not everyone in the collective gave the same amount of money.[28] The collective members wrote the promissory notes so that they could request payment at any time, but due to their commitment to the collective and "their honor as women," they made an agreement that they would never call in payment of their notes.[29] Parsons went on to further explain that she no longer considered that money as hers but as a "brick in the fireplace."[30] However it took about $30,000 to get the whole project going, and like other restaurants discussed in this book, the remaining money was raised through alternative methods such as fundraising and donation efforts.

In addition to their own $5,000 investment into Mother Courage, Jill Ward and Dolores Alexander decided to look for funding from women in their community. Because they believed in the project so wholly, they decided to share their idea of creating their restaurant with the larger feminist community of New York City. Ward and Alexander crafted a five-page business prospectus describing their concept, the reasons they felt a women's restaurant was needed, and their confidence in the financial prospects of the project. They circulated 125 copies to friends in the Women's Movement asking for loans of any amount on which they would pay 15 percent interest. Within the space of a month, thirty-seven people had given $6,500 in amounts ranging from $25 to $1,000.[31] As they explained to journalists for a spread on women in business, "women responded so well we were actually turning money away by the time we hit our number. This is an incredibly good way for women to raise capital for their own ventures. We are surprised more women in the Movement haven't tried it."[32] In fact, other feminists interested in beginning feminist restaurants implemented a similar model. Raising money by directly borrowing money from friends was not unique to Mother Courage. According to *The Daily Iowan: Iowa's Alternative Newspaper*, the founders of feminist restaurant Grace and Rubies of Iowa City gathered "loans ranging from $10 to $1500 from local women."[33] These individual loans allowed for restaurant owners to circumvent the barriers they encountered with banks. Other restaurant founders secured money from friends. The Wildrose of Seattle's owner Bryher Herak said that the collective faced inward and raised the money within its collective and community members.[34] The members of the collective gave what they could and continued to work second jobs. On reflection, Herak wondered why they did not do any more formal fundraising. At the time she remembers thinking that "if we do this, we need to have the money."[35] They went to the people that they knew had jobs and wanted a space like Wildrose. Eventually they were able to pay back every cent.[36] In each interview, recording, and magazine article, the feminists who began these restaurants emphasized that they always repaid their debts to the women in their community.

For these alternative fundraising methods to work, there had to be trust in the community. As Marjorie Parsons of the Common Womon remarked, "There were a lot of honor systems back then. Loan us five bill [$500] now—okay but you have to pay it back in six months when I pay my tuition—okay."[37] However, if the financing was done without contracts, additional problems could occur. Parsons continued, "again it was cash flow [problem] and we were always this short of falling off the edge. So, there was constant continuous low-level anxiety."[38] The women who began these restaurants already needed to be part of an established community to have the kind of trust to have these exchanges. Such exchanges built upon emotions and personal connection, implicated people even more emotionally in the business. Emotions do not disappear when dealing with banks; a human aspect remains despite the motto of "it's not personal, it's business." The formality of banking transactions, however, obfuscates the human element of the exchange. In addition, what could seem like a neutral space for some people with privilege would be a dangerous space for others. When the feminist restaurant owners were unable to trust banks, they needed to rely on their larger network of feminists to support their ventures.

Women did more than donate money. Community members donated time, which lowered operating costs for the restaurants to function. Family members and friends of the founders of Mother Courage contributed significant personal time. According to a history of Mother Courage written by Jill Ward and Dolores Alexander, between December 1971 and May 1972, Ward's father and six feminists completed the demolition work needed for their restaurant and installed the new ceiling, floor, and pipes.[39] Two days before opening, her mother loaned her $600 to buy food, and her mother, father, and sister-in-law helped make 640 meatballs the day before opening.[40] The Common Women Club, as Marjorie Parsons commented, "got lots of volunteer time and energy which was as valuable as money and then that made a difference."[41] For example, when the collective declared that the attic needed to be cleaned, local women gathered and cleaned it in an hour. The collective would make a big pot of soup to share and cleaning became a social event. After months of operating, one collective member learned about restaurant auctions: when a restaurant goes bankrupt, the bank holds an auction. It was possible to buy refrigeration units for $5 if no one else wanted them at the time. One time, a woman who was a fan of the restaurant mentioned that she was going to a big auction at the St. Regis and the collective went to get new glasses. Apparently, this unnamed woman was particularly excited about a stove at the auction. The woman donated $200 towards its purchase with an additional $400 coming from the collective. The only problem was that the group now had a stove and no way to transport it. According to Parsons, fifteen lesbians lined up and carried the stove on their backs seven blocks through downtown Northampton, stopping traffic because no one had the money to rent the truck to get it there.[42] Parsons's story illustrates how there were women who would donate their money and others who would donate their time.

Parsons's story is also a reminder that the lack of initial capital created more work. Women had to carry the oven on their backs. Since the collective initially could not afford a new oven, which could have cut its breadmaking labour in half for the first six months, the staff had to spend more time baking bread. Having more seed money makes it easier to make money. The process of producing newsletters and asking for donations was time-intensive. Establishing a stable restaurant would have been simpler with more initial funding. Parsons admitted that the entire project would have been much easier if the collective had had more capital at the start, as the constant letter campaigns, cultural events, and membership sales became a drain on the members' emotions and energy.[43] Mother Courage's owners echoed this same sentiment and wished they could have bought an already established operation so that they would not have had to do so much hard labour.[44] The lower initial capital meant that the restaurants had a harder time making ends meet. After a feminist restaurant or cafe gathered enough capital to start the restaurant either from banks or elsewhere, funding needs continued.

Fundraising Events

Some restaurants relied indirectly on friends by organizing community events to raise capital. However, when organizers wanted to raise money to begin feminist restaurants and cafes, one technique was to host coffeehouse nights and other events centred on music and dancing. The Common Women Club of Northampton, Massachusetts, fundraised by organizing dances and selling food. Before opening the restaurant, they held fundraising events every two weeks. The Common Women Club was involved in many different side fundraisers. Marjorie Parsons advised, "I think when you are entering into a project where you need a good deal of capital and are trying to go about that" it is important "to connect with your sources within the community."[45] For dances, the Common Womon Club collective would find a women's band to donate its time, the collective would ask a women's group on the college campuses to acquire the space, and the publicity would take a minimum of fifteen hours, but the collective might earn the equivalent of two hundred hours' worth of wages.[46] They would only charge $1 for entrance to the dance, but the event ticket also served the dual purpose of promoting the forthcoming restaurant.

At special events, restaurant founders had the opportunity to speak with potential donors. While at the dance, Parsons, a self-described "hustler," would walk around the event asking people to donate money to the project. She would usually also use this time to assuage potential donors' fears about "being taken."[47] Parsons perceived Northampton women as skeptical and worried about what would happen with their money and what the club would do with it. Her self-described "hustler" status was most apparent when she admitted that sometimes she would convince someone to donate money for a particular project, like painting, and then the collective would use the money for its salaries. She admitted that "on some levels it was not the truth," but the members had to prioritize where the money went, and they would eventually paint the space as they had claimed.[48] Constantly asking for money became emotionally tiresome. In addition to its intital funding, the Common Womon Club continuously asked for money in its monthly newsletter. As Parsons reflected, "I'll tell you one thing—our newsletter started to read like a begging sheet: *The Common Womon Newsletter* for Brunch. Please help us!—We need help on Tuesday cleaning the attic—and pay your dues this week and oh by the way there's a cultural event next week ... It was too much asking—too much asking all the time. And it became a drain on people and it sets up an image that you aren't making it you know—why are you asking ... it's a fine balance about the image you give people—an attitude."[49] The collective knew that its restaurant was an important resource to the community and that the community did not want to lose it, but making ends meet was difficult.

More aboveboard fundraising techniques included throwing private parties and hosting special events. As the restaurant was in a university town (part of the Five College Consortium of Western Massachusetts, which includes Smith, Hampshire, Mount Holyoke, Amherst, and the University of Massachusetts), the Common Womon was a hangout spot for female academics. One scientist greatly appreciated the space and would host specialized women-in-science dinners at the restaurant, and each woman would pay $6 or $7 for her meal, a fee greater than typical dinner fare at the Common Womon.[50] Another benefit of being located within a university town was access to a larger network of writers and scholars, allowing the club to host dinners and cultural events like poetry meetings with prominent feminist figures. Special poets and activists who would come into town receiving $5,000 as a special guest at one of the universities would then make an appearance for free at their restaurant. Lesbian theorist and poet Adrienne Rich, for example, came to brunch, and Parsons remarked that star-struck customers would just want to sit around her.[51] Patricia Hynes, who had founded Bread and Roses feminist restaurant in Cambridge, Massachusetts in 1974, came to the Common Womon and spoke on feminism and vegetarianism. These events served to promote and finance both the restaurant and intellectuals within the feminist community.

Membership Fees

Membership fees also provided money to help finance feminist restaurants. The Common Womon Club, Tuxedo Junction of San Francisco, and Grace and Rubies of Iowa City sold memberships. At Grace and Rubies, any female over the age of ten could become a lifetime member by reading and understanding the club's bylaws and paying

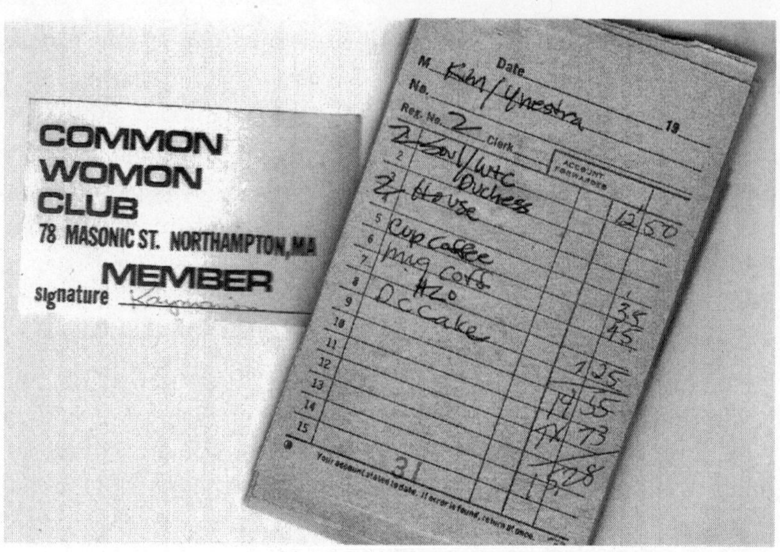

3.1 While selling memberships was a fundraising technique, these cards also enabled some feminist eateries, such as the Common Womon Club of Northampton, Massachusetts, to meet specific requirements of their 501(c)(7) status. (Photo courtesy of Kaymarion Raymond)

$0.50.[52] While the dues were a fundraising technique, they also allowed the club to meet specific requirements of their 501(c)(7) status. Tuxedo Junction was a restaurant conceived as an alternative to the bar scene and was marketed as an "elegant speakeasy" restaurant with an "exclusive atmosphere." Reservations were required except for members and their guests.[53] The restaurant club had 350 members by 1979. The club featured women musicians playing a variety of genres from swing trios for "close-dancing couples" to quartets appealing to those with the "urge to rock." The club advertised "candlelight dinners" and "romance" for its patrons. Membership dues were initially set at $120.[54] Such high fees determined the economic status of the patrons that would attend. The Common Womon Club used a sliding scale to accommodate every woman. The first dues-paying member of the club was a seven-year-old girl who put down $0.25, while in the same night someone put down $1,000. While the dues were a fundraising technique, they also allowed the club to meet specific requirements of their 501(c)(7) status. As Marjorie Parson remarked, "it is interesting that there is a certain number of women in the world who have money and needless to say because of varying politics they tend to keep it pretty quiet."[55] But when they were able to donate and support a cause they could care about discreetly, some would. Memberships helped with fundraising but also affected who could and would use the space, serving as a form of gate keeping.

Compromises Made to Secure Funding and Avoidance of Financial Rules

Even if the restaurants and cafes aimed to serve as alternative, countercultural spaces, they were still embedded within the culture at large and were still held to the same laws as the rest of society. However, rules could be bent.[56] The Common Womon Club collective demonstrated how knowledge of the law, particularly corporate status and tax structure, could benefit countercultural activities. The nine charter members of the collective incorporated as a nonprofit, tax-exempt corporation, Ceres Incorporated, under status of 501(c)(3) and later shifted to 501(c)(7) status. (This is the non-profit American tax status for social and fraternal organizations.)[57] The collective created two sets of books: one for the corporation, Ceres, and one for the club itself. The corporation would pay the mortgage, and the club collected dues and money from the restaurant and would use that to pay the corporation for the space and use of the dishes and silverware.[58] The corporation protected individuals from personal bankruptcy that could ruin their futures.

The philosophy behind this set up was that by having a mother corporation, the Common Womon established itself as a private club and could control who could enter the space, thus allowing the establishment to prevent men from being clients. If the establishment had been solely a restaurant, the collective would not have had the same control over its clientele. However, private clubs had to be nonprofit. The Common Womon Club was always in debt to Ceres Incorporated, so Ceres "appeared philanthropic" by paying off the mortgage every month.[59] Although the gross annual income of the club was between $20,000 and $30,000, after expenses the restaurant was always at a loss. Ceres Incorporated would forgive this loss and would also host fundraisers to help cover other costs. By organizing its structure and finances in this manner, the Common Womon Club collective always declared a loss, which protected its nonprofit status. Marjorie Parsons believed there was a tremendous advantage to running the business in this manner. Learning how to use the law to their advantage helped the members of the collective achieve their dreams of a women-only restaurant.

To maintain their tax status and ability to run a club, the collective members had to have a firm understanding of tax and corporate law. The collective members received legal advice to do all of this from their friend and lawyer, Nancy Brockwell, who wrote the initial incorporation papers. The collective paid her a "couple hundred dollars of legal fees but she also drank a lot of coffee and ate a lot of soup and got a lot of love and support."[60] Part of the provision of this club status necessitated having a mailing list and newsletter.[61] The government also required that clubs had a formal way of defining club membership, but the organizers were able to decide upon dues. The collective made it as easy as possible for any woman to become a member of the club. All a woman needed for membership was to provide her name and address to receive the newsletter. In speaking to a group of women interested in beginning their own feminist restaurant or coffeehouse in the Boston area, Parsons explained that "501(c)(7) the tax status the club is under is incredibly easy to get"—much easier than having to deal with the costs of being a for-profit business.[62] Legally, there was a fairly complicated requirement of monthly meetings and cultural meetings, but as the collective already hosted cultural events once a month, the members put that on the application for the club.

One of the most fortunate aspects of this tactic was that when the original collective members were burnt out and left the restaurant, the new management was able to easily take over. Ceres Incorporated remained the corporation through which everything ran, and Marjorie Parsons took a day to teach the newcomers the books.[63] However, it appeared that the new managers in 1979 were better businesswomen than the former managers. The four women of the second collective made over $90 each per week. As Parsons noted, "No one is going to the Bahamas there, but the fact that there are four women right now making a livelihood from a lesbian-owned, lesbian business brings tears to my eyes. It's all I ever wanted. It's all I ever wanted."[64] Strategic planning enabled the collective members to protect themselves as individuals and safeguard their dreams of a feminist restaurant. As Parsons explained, "hipping yourself to the government" is strategic.[65] Without knowledge of these strategies, obtaining financing from the bank would have been far less likely and the financial liability of running the business would have been greater.

Most feminist restaurants founders lived under constant stress when their restaurants struggled to survive. As a result, the founders attempted several solutions for their financial woes, including the creation of side businesses. However, the frustration and stress from financial difficulties was compounded when the restaurant owners faced harassment from government officials and individuals. These problems eventually resulted in the businesses closing.

The Experience of Running Loss-Making Enterprises

By the second year of operating, the Common Womon Club was unable to secure enough money to pay its mortgage. At that point, the collective was generating less than $50 of income per person weekly. The other collective members would be frustrated with Marjorie

Parsons as she was doing the books at the time. She remarked that people would get anxious and angry and scream at her, and she reflected, "And I would say 'I'm sorry' and then I would get enraged because I would think 'what did I do?'—I would go home with the same $50 in my pocket." In the end, she was staving off not just her co-workers but also the moneylenders. She remarked that she "would write these letters where I would compromise my English and my intelligence and my pride to say to a person we were in debt and that 'we have screwed up this, this and this' and they would hold off another two weeks."[66] For Parsons, the constant stress about finances led to immense burnout and strongly contributed to her desire to sell the restaurant. Parsons was not alone in these feelings. However, many founders believed in their projects and thus attempted solutions by creating additional revenue streams.

Feminist restaurant and cafe owners occasionally ran businesses on the side to try to support the restaurant itself. According to early issues of *Gaia's Guide*, Bloodroot was an inn at one point.[67] The Bloodroot Collective also published a series of cookbooks, selling over 5,000 copies of its first book, sold calendars, and simultaneously functioned as a bookstore.[68] Other feminist restaurants and cafes had their own bookstores, such as: Wild Seeds Feminist Bookstore and Café of Rochester, New York (1989); Sisterspirit Café and Bookstore of San Jose California; Reader's Feast Feminist Bookstore and Café of Hartford, Connecticut (1985); Three Birds Feminist Bookstore and Coffeeshop of Tampa, Florida (1989); Jane Addams Bookstore and Coffeeshop of Chicago, Illinois (1981); and Community Café and Bookstore of Bethesda, Maryland (1983).[69] Having a non-perishable good, such as books, to sell in the restaurant was a common practice.

Feminist restaurants were embedded in networks of people in alternative communities helping one another out; even in the case of the Common Women Club, a women-only separatist space, these restaurants were never isolated from men entirely, be it in their business dealings, their location, or their operation. Men still came in to do handywork occasionally when a tradeswoman was unavailable, men worked at food distribution companies and for the electrical companies, men were farmers of their food, and so forth. Men also played a role in fundraising. One of the Common Womon Club's big fundraisers was apart from the lesbian community. The collective would run booths at events like county fairs. As Parsons explained, "let me tell you how popular you can be if you are veggie" at the alternative energy fairs. They cooked soups and sandwiches, and the collective made $1,000 per fair.[70] The Common Womon collective did not have to worry about food licencing and the health code, as it operated a restaurant that already met most of the requirements, so participating required minimal effort. However, these events could be hit or miss. At one county fair, "no one came near us and it rained the whole time and we all sat with each other and were hysterical with each other but we did one of the solar ones with UMass [University of Massachusetts] and we were throwing soups over peoples' heads. We were the only coffee maker—so some years it was really good and some years it was hopeless."[71] Feminist restaurant owners used their imaginations to find funding and were dependent on larger networks within the countercultural community.

Alcohol Sales

Some restaurants tried to ease financial burdens by selling alcohol. Financially supporting a restaurant could be difficult, and alcohol is a fairly reliable source of income. Grace and Rubies of Iowa City served a variety of alcoholic beverages.[72] Mother Courage decided to start selling alcohol when food prices soared.[73] In New York State in 1975, when the owners made the decision to sell alcohol, a liquour license cost around $1,600, a beer and wine license was about half that.[74] Despite the devastating effect of inflation from the food crisis,

Mother Courage's willingness to adapt by selling alcohol, as well as its loyal clientle, helped it survive.

However, some feminist restaurants did not serve alcohol, as founders sought to be an alternative to bar culture.[75] Having a sober space was especially valuable to lesbian feminists who were recovering alcoholics, when so much lesbian socializing happened in bars.[76] For the Common Womon restaurant, having a non-alcoholic space was a priority (although that did not mean that people did not bring in their own alcohol).[77] As Marjorie Parsons remarked, "We could have done a lot better if we had alcohol."[78] In fact, at one point she was willing to go through the process of securing an alcohol permit. The collective members asked its community six times in its monthly newsletter if they should serve alcohol, but no one in the collective was interested either. The only feedback that the restaurant "ever got was an alcoholic who was sober saying don't do it."[79] Parsons knew that she "could have filled out the papers" and she continued that she was "sure women would have come in and bought and I'm sure it would have made us stable," but doing so would have undermined the Common Womon Club's mission to remain open to women of all ages.[80] The choice many of these spaces made to be dry made it even harder to fundraise. If feminist restaurants and cafes did choose to serve alcohol, this choice occasionally incurred resistance from government officials.

Harassment and Its Impacts on Financial Stability

Restaurants already operated on slim profit margins, and outside interference made the financial status of feminist restaurants even more precarious. Conflicts over liquor licences, zoning, funding, and taxes affected financial stability. Bureaucracy could provide frustrating barriers for any business owner. For example, despite the Common Womon Club collective gaining a comprehensive understanding of how to structure its business model, the collective still initially applied for the incorrect type of restaurant licence. Only after submitting its application did the collective learn that there was a licence specially for serving passersby and one for customers who were seated.[81] These kinds of mistakes were understandable, but sexism and heterosexism created additional problems for the women running these restaurants. While the restaurant owners' lack of experience sometimes meant that they did not know how to fill out the proper forms, the owners also faced sexist regulatory officials that made matters more complicated. Despite doing everything by the books, Wildrose of Seattle was audited four times while Bryher Herak managed the establishment. She always assumed homophobia was the motivating factor. Over four audits, the Internal Revenue Service only once found a discrepancy of $126.[82] When Mother Courage's owners applied for a wine and beer licence in September 1973, they were worried they would have difficulty because when they hand delivered the forms they were asked, "No men involved in the corporation? You may need the signature of a male relative."[83] They were worried that it would be another hassle like a previous one with the Securities and Exchange Commission (SEC).

To raise money for Mother Courage, as explained earlier, Jill Ward and Dolores Alexander sent out a four-page business prospectus to feminists and other friends where they asked for the small loans, totaling $5,000 at 15 percent interest. The financial editor at *Newsday*, where Dolores Alexander once worked, telephoned, asking to do a story. Despite their own apprehension about media attention so early into their venture, the owners agreed.[84] The feature piece on the "money" page, entitled "Women's Lib Takes the Plunge—Into Business," piqued the interest of a complaint officer of the New York office of the SEC.[85] The SEC officer called to tell Ward and Alexander that their fundraising methods may have broken the law by making a public offering with their prospectus, as "any piece of paper, any form of IOU, which has no intrinsic value of its own, which is essentially worthless, is a security."[86] The SEC lawyers insisted that according to

Regulation A of the 1963 Securities Act, the restaurant would need to be registered as a public offering and that it would cost them $50,000 to do so.[87] In recounting this stressful experience, Alexander and Ward remembered the roomful of men suddenly opening booklets and quoting legal passages to them and insisting that they get a copy of No. 33-4552, which they later learned was a short statement issued in November 1962, which covered certain exemptions to Regulation A.[88] After reading that section, Alexander and Ward knew that they had not broken the law. The lawyers and complaint officer then began to accost the restaurant owners asking them why they did not know about such regulations and asking if they could even cook. When asked about the location of the money from the loans, Ward replied that it was in a separate chequing account.[89] Alexander pushed back at the officer's comment that she looked depressed, responding that she was confused as to why they insisted on using jargon and buzzwords that only the four men understood. She further questioned why they needed four people to discuss $5,000. Alexander felt that the men did not respond to the question; they did however explain what the women could do to avoid penalty. One of the SEC lawyers said that Alexander and Ward could return the money or SEC could freeze the money. In addition, they could be jailed and fined up to $25,000.[90] He suggested that they close the account and put out a letter saying that they have returned the money or have their lawyer do so. Alexander responded that they would go and consult with their lawyer. She later remarked on the irony that the meeting probably cost the government more than $5,000 in salaries.

The clash with the government officials became a personal attack. After Alexander's lawyer called SEC, one of the SEC lawyers called Ward and said that their lawyer was acting like "some militant or something" and that they "had better straighten her out."[91] He then continued to threaten her. Ward responded that she had read release 33-4552 multiple times and she believed that she had complied with the requirements for a nonpublic offering under the private exemption clause of section 4-2.[92] Despite having raised money from thirty-seven people versus the originally expected number of investors being twenty, that numerical test was only to be applied under 33-4552 if people have the requisite association with and knowledge of the owners. As their investors were friends, Ward pointed out that they were still acting in accordance with the law. Even under the *Ralston-Purina* case that the SEC lawyer used to intimidate her, the decision was "based on whether a particular class of persons needed the protection of the act."[93] She continued by saying, "you mean to tell me that our friends who loaned us money, because they are mostly women, need protection—that women don't have the intellect or ability to determine whether or not" to loan their own money?[94] She also refuted his claims that they broke the law by advertising in the paper because the article in the paper was not about fundraising and the piece clearly stated that they "were only raising money from sisters and friends."[95] The founders remained confident in their own abilities to understand the law and did not bend to the intimidation tactics of the SEC, which led the SEC to eventually back down.

According to Alexander, eventually the government officials admitted that the entire incident resulted from sexist attitudes. She claimed that after all these incidents the SEC lawyer confessed: "Let me tell you what happened. Word got out that two freaks in women's liberation were coming into the office and everyone in the office wanted to see them. I was happy to find out that you two weren't freaks at all. Incidentally I think you ought to know that most of the lawyers down here are under twenty-eight [like him] and more liberal [than the other officials.] And I wouldn't want you to get a bad impression of SEC."[96]

The SEC lawyer then said that all he wanted was a letter from their lawyer saying that they had returned the money so he could stick the letter into their file. Otherwise, he claimed that he would have no choice but to hand the case over to law enforcement, and despite it only being $5,000, the federal government could still press charges. When Ward asked him to clarify if he meant that they should return the money, he responded, "That's your business. If you don't, don't tell anybody, especially your lawyer. Then I don't care how you raise the money again. But next time be more discreet. As far as I'm concerned, for this particular case, I just want the letter so I can close the case so it doesn't have to be turned over to enforcement."[97] Ward responded, "well that doesn't seem to comply with the spirit of the law. You're telling us to comply with the letter of the law. [But actually] you don't care about how we raise the money, as long as it doesn't come to your attention," to which he allegedly responded, "Look I don't want to get into a philosophical discussion. I'm working here for a few years, to make some money, get a good resume so I can go on from here."[98] Ward retorted, "I know what you mean. We're trying to survive too."

The situation ended with Ward and Alexander's lawyer sending them a letter advising them to return the money and carbon copying it to the SEC as proof that they had done so. They never heard from the SEC again. Mother Courage's owners also followed through on their promise by returning the money and the 15 percent interest promised one year later when the loans were due.[99] This entire situation illustrates how personal relationships changed the ways that the law was applied: the law was never about justice as much as it was about upholding specific power structures. Mother Courage demonstrated that feminist alternatives to traditional fundraising were possible but also that the owners and their business could face threats from politically motivated legal intimidation.

While Mother Courage was able to overcome bureaucratic resistance, selective application of regulations meant demise for other feminist restaurants. The owners of Grace and Rubies wanted to implement a simple, non-elitist, women-only membership policy, but the Iowa City Council responded by trying to determine whether the membership policy was "discriminatory." The argument was that Grace and Rubies did not charge enough to be a real private club and that the owners' goal to be accessible for all women—but still meet the requirements as private club that charged memberships (and thus could exclude men)—led to problems. In the spring of 1976, *Dyke: A Quarterly* published this response to the issue:

> Meanwhile, back in Iowa City, Grace & Rubies Restaurant is still alive, kicking and struggling to get out from under while the City's new mayor, a woman, instructs the human relations commission to investigate the legality of the restaurant's policy of refusing membership (and admittance) to men. The outcome of the investigation is unknown, but if it takes the commission as long to investigate Grace & Rubies as it does to investigate sex discrimination in employment claims, the restaurant will be around for a number of years, no matter what the outcome.[100]

Apart from the pushback Grace and Rubies' owners faced from the local city council, they also dealt with the backlash from a story about their restaurant in *Penthouse*, the pornographic men's magazine. Novelist T.C. Boyle, while still a student at the Iowa Writers' Workshop, became obsessed with *womyn's* spaces and his perceived "exclusion" from them. In May 1977, he published a short story called "The Women's Restaurant." The story explored his fixation on Grace and Rubies and his unrelenting desire to invade that space.[101] The harassment of owners by private citizens and government officials led to their eventual closure.

This is not to say that some restaurants did not skirt the law, sometimes partly a result of wanting to make a political statement. Marjorie Parson's entire explanation about the Common Womon Club's history demonstrated that when people were empowered with the knowledge of what loopholes existed within the system, they could save a lot of money. Parsons also admitted to having few qualms crossing into illegal territory, citing her disappointment with the ways that the United States government used taxpayer money for exploitation of individuals and to fund wars overseas. As Marjorie Parsons explained, "See I'm pretty hip about staying out of the government's eye as much as possible."[102] She believed that if the restaurant's nonprofit status did not hold under an audit, the Common Womon might have been liable for a state corporation fine, which according to her was only $250 and worth the risk. She argued that "the legal liabilities aren't tremendous—no one has done anything significantly illegal."[103] Her comfort level with lying to the government extended beyond how the collective structured its taxes. To survive on a $50 salary each week, the members of the Common Womon Club had various sources of income. Parsons admits that she "was on unemployment and lived fairly illegally for awhile. Other women had savings. Other women had jobs. Other women had independent sources of income."[104] With the Common Womon Club, the only restaurant in this book that admitted on record to committing a crime, legality was not the reason for the closure; the restaurant could not financially support itself.

In addition to conflict with government agencies, there was also resistance from private sources. The restaurants, even when they intended to operate as separatist spaces, still had to interact with the rest of society. For the Common Womon Club, the collective faced the "all boys network" and the idea "that [only] men go into business."[105] While the other restaurants operated by men in the area would be able to get credit, one of the Common Womon Club's food distributors, Flagstaff, never extended credit to the restaurant even though Parsons argued that the collective never missed its payments. It also took two years before their oil company would put them on an automatic fill.[106] These barriers made it even more difficult to be a successful business, as every step required more work. However, if it seemed as if lenders might be wary of the Common Womon Club based on its admittedly less-than-legal dealings, it was not the only feminist restaurant to face difficulties with the private sector. The founders of Mother Courage remarked that it was difficult to get credit and to have wholesalers make deliveries. Even when wholesalers did deliver, the men would make sexist comments or look for a man to sign the receipts and order forms, not believing that women owned the restaurant. In fact, this issue was mentioned during most interviews conducted with feminist restaurant owners. Facing the "boys club" mentality added additional strain to the regular ups and downs of restaurant management.

Closure

Regardless of the ways that the feminist restaurants raised the money, many of their owners still had a difficult time making ends meet—an issue not uncommon within the restaurant business. In 1996, the Brick Hut Café of Berkeley, California, fell into serious financial difficulties and filed for Chapter 11 status.[107] In 1997, it filed for Chapter 7 bankruptcy and closed its doors for the last time at 2:00 p.m. on March 24, 1997. (Under Chapter 7 bankruptcy, the debtor liquidates her assets to pay back the creditors.) However, as owner Joan Antonuccio remembered, "Rather than tucking their tail between their legs, they ended things with a big, crowded, raucous party."[108] Bloodroot's founders did not do any direct fundraising, as they were able to borrow money. However, as they wrote in a letter, "at this point in time [1981] we have repaid those loans and have been able to raise our draw to $700/month for each of the four of us. Since we are working over twelve hours a day, five and a half days a week we still make less than minimum wage."[109] Even more than forty-five years after the restaurant's founding, Selma Miriam and Noel Furie are not making significant money. Regardless, in 2017 Selma Miriam and Noel Furie continued to repeat to reporters at the *New York*

Times they had no intention of stopping.[110] In 2022, they continued to operate Bloodroot.

Collective Issues

The collective structure created its own problems.[111] Collectives required much more trust, and Marjorie Parsons acknowledged that despite their goals of opening an alternative space, "we are used to working within hierarchies and there is more of an inclination to divide it up, because in the collective the work roles were not defined as clearly."[112] She found that without distinct roles, people latched onto a position even more strongly to make themselves experts in that area. For Parsons, challenging patriarchal capitalism was possible without the added stresses of being in a collective, although she still understood the appeal of the collective.

When the initial collective members of Common Womon Club burnt out, another collective of four lesbians took over the space. The second collective had the benefit of learning from the former collective's mistakes. This new collective ran the Common Womon more like a business. Before the re-launch, the new collective members made repairs on the building and redecorated the restaurant with new paint and curtains. Parsons reflected that, "the community response has been terrific—absolutely terrific."[113] She saw that the new collective could thrive because "they [weren't] trying to run a social service agency with bulletin boards with referrals and selling tickets to all of the concerts or answering the phone every three minutes."[114] When Parsons worked at the Common Womon, there was no women's centre in town, so the restaurant became the hub for event coordination. Parsons seemed proud and envious because "what they are doing now is running food service. They are running a restaurant and now they are waiting tables."[115] Even though Parsons admitted that she benefitted from learning bookkeeping, setting up a basic cash-flow system, and the laws of corporate tax structure from the collective's woman lawyer and female accountant, she and the rest of the Common Womon Club's first collective members were unable to adapt to all of the changes they needed to make in order to continue operating their restaurant. This new collective was not overextending its energy. The women who began feminist restaurants could not escape the power dynamics of North America. These dynamics would often be replicated in the spaces themselves. Even when inequity was challenged inside their businesses, restaurant owners would still have to deal with the outside world. For these owners to make their feminist restaurants successful, they had to learn a lot about business quite quickly.

The restaurant owners learned many lessons from this process, and as a researcher I have benefitted immensely from their desire to share those lessons. Much of this chapter was made possible by Marjorie Parsons's willingness to speak to a group of women in Boston in 1979 who wanted to start either a feminist restaurant or a coffeehouse. Her frank honesty about how she and her collective negotiated the difficulties that they faced and the lessons that they learned helped later groups of women interested in beginning feminist restaurants. Furthermore, her agreeing to have her presentation recorded and the donation of these tapes to Northeastern University by the Somerville Women's Coffeehouse Collective, which eventually emerged after these meetings, provided important insights into the topic. Other feminist restaurant owners, such as Jill Ward of Mother Courage, shared their own insights as well in their discussions with journalists.[116] Common lessons that emerged included being braver, spending more time during the planning stage, having a set idea of how the work would be structured, not allowing workers to overextend themselves, and having a plan to deal with emotional conflict. Passing on these lessons could help women trying to begin their own restaurants then and now.

While starting a feminist restaurant was an emotional experience, Parsons viewed her time at the Common Womon as a valuable and important time in her life. Apart from hiring a lawyer and an accountant, having more initial funding, and scheduling group-therapy sessions for the collective to air their grievances, she also recommended that restaurants keep copious records of everyone who donated money, noting how much, when, and what the money went towards. She further advised that workers keep track of the number of hours that they put into the restaurant with the hope that at some point they would be able to reimburse themselves for their time. Parsons further remarked that if she were ever to have a second restaurant, she would run her own restaurant differently than the Common Womon. She said that her next restaurant would be for-profit and she would potentially work with one or two other people with a clear division of work, such that either someone else would run the kitchen and the floor while she managed the business, or she would run the floor and manage the business while someone else would run the kitchen. She would not run the next one with a collective because, "I think I just have different needs … I still know every brick—I cleaned it all at least once. It's that kind of emotion. And I left it because I needed to get back to myself. I think it's a very, very good commitment. Something you should think really serious about because it takes a lot of your life energy. Especially if you do it collectively. [However] if you are boss man you can go any direction that you want."[117]

Can a Restaurant Be a Fitting Place for Feminists?

The women who ran feminist restaurants made their money from cooking. When feminist rhetoric drew attention to issues surrounding the postwar image of the housewife relegated to the kitchen, the idea of investing one's time into creating a restaurant where feminists would be cooking food seemed counterintuitive for some. Indeed, the founders of Mother Courage of New York City were asked about this frequently. A reporter for *The Capital Times* in 1975 asked one of the waitresses and cooks at Mother Courage, who self-identified as an aspiring songwriter, "How can a liberated woman be so enthusiastic about cooking?"[118] "I get paid well," said Ms. Gaffney, while arranging a pie. She added, "And the minute you get paid, it's not woman's work anymore."[119] Furthermore, Gaffney remarked that "she found her job challenging—almost a mystical experience."[120] For Gaffney, the issues feminists had with women cooking were not actually about cooking but unremunerated domestic labour. In another article, a reporter from the *International Herald Tribune* commented, "Not all feminist groups, however, are supportive of feminist restaurants, arguing that women should get out from in front of the stove and become doctors, lawyers" and other white-collar professionals.[121] This was a recurring theme, as another reporter wrote:

> It is possible that the dearth of feminist restaurants result from women avoiding work associated with one of the more oppressive roles into which they have been traditionally locked. Even for Jilly Ward, a management consultant, and Dolores Alexander, a journalist, it was not so much food and cooking which lured them into starting MOTHER COURAGE in April 1972, as the idea of creating a social mileu where women could get together over good food, where THEY would set the tone, not the male waiters, owners, customers—a place badly needed by the New York feminist community. Both women were also looking for ways of making a living outside the male-dominated business world, which, as committed feminists, they were finding increasingly intolerable and oppressive. They have succeeded in both respects.[122]

Most notably, the concern about what running a feminist restaurant meant in terms of women's relationships with food seemed to be coming from outsiders rather than from within feminist movements.

Even if there were debates in the feminist movement, as seen in feminist publications from the period, the 1970s was an era of great exploration and feminist questioning and debate; there was never consensus on anything, as everyone had a different approach to enacting their feminist principles. Feminist restaurants provided one avenue for feminists to make money and live by their values. Owners were able to create a feminist community built around food. It was a way to bring new businesses opportunities for women in the community, while also challenging ideas of unremunerated labour.

Conclusion

Despite frequent discussions on creating alternatives to capitalism, the realities of the structural violence of greater society would often seep into these women's spaces. Parsons discussed how she and the collective attempted "consciousness raising and [discussed] what it means to be a white person waiting tables and the race, class, and gender aspects of that positionality."[123] However, as shown in the last two chapters, guests of the restaurant also brought in their own expectations. She admitted, "this might sound a little rough to you but I think there's a certain level of violence that happens in the community in the sense that lots of women are tight about money and lots of women are affected by politics outside of them."[124] Parsons was frustrated that women in their own community, as products of the sexist environments in which they had been raised, also undermined the workers at the Common Womon. She remarked that customers would have unfair expectations when they entered a feminist restaurant because "women are supposed to be different."[125] Most frustrating were customers' comments about money, like when a woman would say that they could buy cheaper food at a place like McDonald's. However, unlike McDonald's, "we were small-time," and basic products would cost them more because they were not able to buy at bulk rates. Parsons would grow particularly frustrated because "women would come in with their own attitudes about money but they did not have a business sense and they would come in expecting a product better than theirs at less money and then they would get angry and I used to do the same thing until I started doing books and saw the money and saw ... [*exasperated sigh*]."[126] In her frustration describing the past difficulties around money, she spoke quickly and her sentences broke into half thoughts, describing the various pressures that she faced from different directions. In sum, capitalism is powerful. While these restaurants and cafes owners challenged capitalist structures and traditional financing practices, in part due to their politics and in part since it was the only way they could make these spaces exist, they still were forced to reconcile with the greater world and capitalism more generally.

On top of all these economic difficulties and hurdles and the need to be creative and resilient, there was little direct economic benefit in being a women-only or women-centred space. As Wania, founder of La Fronde feminist restaurant in New York City, put it bluntly, "women don't have the money to spend in restaurants."[127] When La Fronde opened, Wania only had $4.68 left in the bank.[128] Women did not open feminist restaurants to get rich, and the restaurants were not about individualistic capitalism. The founders of feminist restaurants faced several barriers: capitalist values, sexism, homophobia, and the general difficulties in learning how to manage a restaurant. Of course, these businesses wanted to survive and, as mentioned before, they were trying to support women working, but ultimately they were about supporting a larger feminist network. This larger network included other feminist and women-owned-and-operated businesses, independent workers, artists, and teams.

Some people never really understood why feminist restaurants and cafes were so valuable. The greatest irony was a man who wanted to start a chain of feminist cafes due to the success of Mother Courage. Allegedly, "the success of Mother Courage has inspired feminist restaurants in other cities and a man is rumored to be thinking of a feminist restaurant chain."[129] Talk about missing the point! The reason for the success of Mother Courage and other feminist restaurants was the support for women-run and women-supported businesses. Not everyone would be able to raise the financial capital to support a woman-run restaurant or cafe due to various economic, racial, and class factors. However, feminist restaurants did provide a larger network of economic support for other feminist businesses, as will be discussed in the next chapter.

CHAPTER 4

Nourishing Communities

Feminist restaurants and cafes differed from their mainstream equivalents during the 1970s and 1980s due to their role within the feminist business nexus. These businesses enabled other feminist businesses to exist by providing other business owners, independent contractors, and artists with spaces to operate, audiences, and cross-promotional opportunities. When Selma Miriam spoke of her initial vision of Bloodroot, it was for "a place to warm the belly and warm the mind, a meeting place for people who have a particular point of view."[1] This view meant people who shared their ideas of feminism. For the Bloodroot Collective, "'feminist' means we're interested in Black equality, the problems of Spanish-speaking people, and we do feel that the largest number of people who are discriminated against are women."[2] As a result, they wanted to amplify the work of other women. Joan Antonuccio of the Brick Hut likewise remarked that from 1975 to 1997

> We were completely unique. Not so much for our food, at first, though that came later, but for our openness, our participation in the community, and our obvious respect for ourselves and each other. At the Brick Hut, I believe we celebrated difference. We were visibly different, we forefronted difference, we encouraged difference, we hosted difference. We did not try to assimilate, disappear into conformity, or become mainstream. We did not build the Brick Hut Café so

> we could have jobs, although that was good. We did not build it to have careers, or support career-moves, although that was a possibility. We did not build it only to make money for ourselves, although we wanted to maintain a viable business that supported our friends, our fellow workers, our causes, and ourselves. We built it to create the possibility of a workplace and a community where no one's politics or cultural affiliations were left at the front door.[3]

The owners enabled women and community members to have a special kind of space in which to connect. Likewise, Seattle's Wildrose was a safer place where women could gather. In its founding, owner Bryher Herak thought that "we need a place that is a restaurant where we can serve good food to the lesbian feminist community, where we can have windows, and where our families can come and feel good about it."[4] She wanted a space where people could be out but, unlike the lesbian bars of the period that were dark, served no food, and were just for cruising, people could bring their families and friends of all sexual orientations. While each feminist restaurant and cafe had its unique qualities, these businesses fostered community. In addition to providing direct economic opportunities for the women employed at the eatery, feminist restaurants and cafes promoted and enabled other feminist and women-owned-and-operated businesses, independent workers, artists, and teams. The economic, social, and cultural impacts of these efforts nourished American feminist communities.

The role of feminist restaurants and cafes within feminist business networks is largely absent in the existing scholarly literature. Additionally, while historians have done less research on feminist business networks in the late twentieth century, researchers from other fields have looked at how feminist businesses, organizations, and collectives connected to their communities. Although most of the existing research focuses on nonprofit organizations, some work does focus on for-profit feminist organizations and businesses. Author Susanna Sturgis writes about Ladyslipper, the company devoted to the distribution of women's music and women's culture based in North Carolina in the 1970s and 1980s.[5] Her article looks at the success of Ladyslipper, how it embodied feminist principles, and was also attractive to the lesbian community. Ladyslipper connected women across the United States through shared art and cultural experiences. Another case study is sociologist Meika Loe's article about a woman-owned-and-operated sexual products business, Toy Box, established in 1977. This study reveals the complexities of running an alternative business during the late 1970s through 1990s and of balancing political ideals with profit needs.[6] Meika Loe reveals that when feminist businesses could navigate the moral and ethical difficulties of creating a business, their own success could not only be measured by profits but also in their ability to influence patrons and their communities. Gender studies scholar Kristen Amber Hogan has looked at the way that feminist bookstores built communities around literature, the influence of feminist bookstores in the publishing world, and the importance of these spaces for the feminist community.[7] Geographer Linda McDowell has emphasized that geography is very important to feminism.[8] In her argument, the actual interior space of the feminist business was very important, as was its location. There is a gap in the literature regarding the connections formed between American feminist businesses. Furthermore, while attention has been given to the women's bookstore, feminist restaurant history has fallen into obscurity. This means that the ways in which different kinds of feminist businesses interacted with one another has largely gone unacknowledged.

Larger Business Networks

Feminist restaurants were part of a larger network of feminist businesses in their local, national, and international communities; the owners were aware of these connections. In 1976, the *Boston Herald* ran a feature article on Boston and Cambridge, Massachusetts's feminist businesses.[9] The article declares that Bread and Roses feminist restaurant was part of a nexus of nearby feminist institutions, including the Feminist Health Center, New Words Bookstore, and the Women's Credit Union, and details how the restaurant worked in conjunction with these other feminist institutions to sponsor women-focused events. Furthermore, the businesses were all economically linked as the credit union supplied funding, the bookstore provided intellectual stimulation and community events, the health centre kept the customers healthy, and Bread and Roses provided food, space for socializing, and hosted art shows, musical performers, and guest speakers. The article failed to mention how the feminist business network extended beyond the storefronts. Bread and Roses employed feminist women to work in the restaurant, craftswomen, and women technicians for plumbing, lighting, and carpentry. Bread and Roses was not alone in its promotion of other women-owned businesses and independent women contractors.

The practice of being linked to the other feminist businesses in the community and promoting women-owned businesses happened at feminist restaurants founded across the United States in the 1970s and 1980s. Ruby's Café of Minneapolis was located next door to Amazon Bookstore.[10] Occasionally there would be over an hour wait to get in the door to the cafe for brunch so customers would browse in Amazon while they were waiting. As Mary Bahneman, founder of Ruby's, remarked in an interview, it was a kind of nexus of women-owned businesses on that part of the street. The businesses all supported each other and brought other feminists to the area and even though at the time she did not think of that support network as being inherently feminist, Bahneman later remarked that she thought it was.[11] There was not a single interview conducted for this research in which a former feminist cafe, restaurant, or coffeehouse founder did not mention her relationship to the other feminist businesses in her local areas. Most of the founders deliberately thought about how

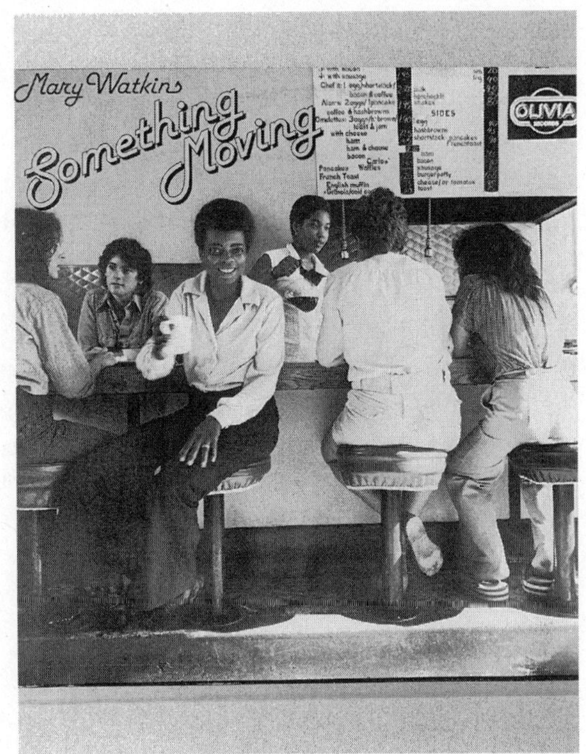

4.1 Musician Mary Watkins is pictured sitting at the counter of the first location of the Brick Hut Café in Berkeley, California, on the cover of her album Something Moving, *produced by Olivia Records. The Brick Hut's menu was small, painted by Peggy Mitchell of the band BeBe K'Roche, on a board attached to the hood above the stove. Watkins's album includes the song "Brick Hut," about the inclusivity of the restaurant.*

they were part of a feminist nexus. In an interview, owners of the Brick Hut Café of Berkeley, California, remarked that they were part of a greater community network. Located nearby were A Woman's Place Bookstore and the Women's Press Collective. These businesses served as access points for books, publishing, and networking with artists and writers like Judy Grahn, Wendy Cadden, Willyce Kim, and Pat Parker. These figures then frequented the cafe. There were also local bars that functioned as part of the network: Ollie's Bar, the Bacchanal, and the Jubilee, and across the street from Mama Bears Bookstore, Thursday nights at the White Horse.[12] Marjorie Parsons, a member of the lesbian collective that founded the Common Womon Café of Northampton, Massachusetts, recalled during a taped appearance that the collective saw its suppliers as part of its feminist network as well. The collective intentionally bought supplies from women-operated, leftist cooperatives. For their food, Parsons remarked that "it's good healthy vegetarian food that's bought through cooperatives and it's an alternative economy that is an example to a whole lot of [what] we were trying to do."[13] Bloodroot Feminist Vegetarian Restaurant of Bridgeport, Connecticut, founded in 1977, also functioned as a bookstore. Within the restaurant and bookstore, the owners supported the feminist writers who penned the theories that inspired the creation of the business. Additionally, Bloodroot has consistently supported women's business ventures. Like Bread and Roses' founder Patricia Hynes, the managing Bloodroot Collective adorned its walls with the work of women artists and played women's music. The collective also hired and sponsored women performers, lesbian feminist poets, academics, authors, and musicians. These restaurants intentionally used their positions in the community to support other feminist businesses in both their local areas and beyond.[14]

Chefs and Restaurant Workers

Feminist restaurants and cafes created spaces where women could be paid to cook and live openly as feminists and, oftentimes, as lesbians. It may seem obvious, but these feminist restaurants could provide welcome support for women chefs due to the challenges they faced in the male-dominated cooking environment, particularly in fine dining. Although women in the United States during the 1970s and 1980s, as today, were the primary cooks in the domestic realm, the restaurant industry was and is dominated by men.[15] Guest spots at feminist restaurants highlighting women chefs provided needed resources and exposure for their work. At the Brick Hut Café, there was a brief appearance of the Night Hut, with Chef Amy Shaw making her culinary debut cooking and serving dinner.[16] The Brick Hut was not the only space during the period that led to women chefs developing their cooking talents. After the Brick Hut closed in 1997, owner Joan Antonuccio worked in two restaurants. She moved on to work as executive chef at Bon Appetit and worked as a personal chef.[17] Despite the reality that most of these restaurants had kitchens that were operated by women without professional training, they were also a useful resource for women with professional chef training.

Feminist restaurants and cafes acted as important financial resources to the women in their communities and provided women with a form of income where they could be out and feminist and lesbian and that was powerful. Regarding the Common Womon of Northampton, Marjorie Parsons asserted, "I would say that there were a lot of women we hired that wouldn't have an income without the [restaurant]."[18] While they were in business, it was a way to make money in a way that supported their ideals. In a letter reflecting on their intentions, a member of the Bloodroot Collective wrote that "when we opened Bloodroot, three and a half years ago, we needed a way to make a living consistent with our politics. We hoped that by making a women's space, playing feminist music and having a bookstore, we would be a connecting point for many different kinds of women, and possibly an example of a successful women's business as well."[19] For Wildrose, "all the women were happy to have found each other and have community—very cooperative—magical" and as a result "people were very generous."[20] Reflecting on Mother Courage of New York City, Lucy Komisar, author of *Down and Out in the USA*, a study of welfare, reflected that it was "more than a restaurant, this is part of a social movement."[21] Novelist Alix Kates Shulman remarked, "This is the one place I can walk into and feel I don't have to be someone else's appendage. Just knowing the restaurant is here makes me feel that we can prevail."[22] Women usually join the crew at Grace and Rubies because they "feel at home" there and have a "sense of belonging, of having something in common," Blair said. When asked what Marjorie

Parsons meant when she said that the Common Womon Club was reaching out to "all women," Parsons replied, that they in fact did mean *all* women, remarking that her "fantasy was to always make the place handicap accessible. I wanted to add a ramp to the backdoor so bad I also ripped up the whole backyard myself because somehow at that time there was something symbolic for me. I wanted a multi-racial, multi-ethnic and a much wider range in terms of ages. I wanted to see my mother comfortable there and, you know, and I wanted to see her mother there, and the seven-year-old come in and feel like a person instead of a child. And that was my vision."[23]

However, she said she never fully succeeded, as outreach was very tiring. Some "third world women wouldn't come near us for a time," fearing xenophobic and/or racial discrimination and others were mad that it wasn't a wholly lesbian separatist space.[24] All of the goals were hampered by the realities of life in that the collective "had limited energy and so much energy went into running the food service and the kinds of outreach and work we wanted to do were very hard."[25] She continued that "it was hard for the women in the collective that were trying to do something political and it was hard for the women trying to make a living wage."[26] Likewise, Bread and Roses of Cambridge was about providing more than bread. The roses symbolized that the restaurant would nourish women beyond their material needs by also fulfilling their souls.[27]

The women involved with these ventures also encouraged other women to create their own restaurants. Jill Ward of Mother Courage was interviewed for an article called "How to Start Your Own Business: A Restaurant" in the *Ms. Magazine Handbook*, where she encouraged women to follow their dreams and gave tips for running a restaurant.[28] However, she was also realistic about the difficulties of such work, citing the long hours and low pay. Mother Courage, in the article, was also attributed to inspiring at least three other feminist restaurants.[29] The Brick Hut's owners mentioned in an interview that they knew about Mother Courage.[30] Bloodroot's owners also remarked that knew about Mother Courage and Beetle's Lunch in Allston, Massachusetts.[31] Bryher Herak of Wildrose remarked that she knew of Maude's in San Francisco and had visited the space, but it "wasn't like 'let's be Maude's.' Instead, it was 'we need our own place.' We wanted to have a place where we could be out."[32] Many of the restaurants opened due to an independent need of their local communities rather than modelling themselves upon others. These restaurants inspired other women and acted as spaces of support. Joan Antonuccio of the Brick Hut remarked that "A couple other places tried but failed; I actually mentored a proprietor of one of them. Some thought that was crazy. I was asked if I felt nervous or threatened by new women-owned businesses. Really? I said there is always more room for them."[33] Feminist restaurants and cafes were part of building up other women in their community and supporting others, while paying attention to the specific needs of the local feminist communities.

Independent Workers

Feminist restaurants and cafes did more than support other feminist established businesses; they also provided business opportunities for independent contractors, artists, musicians, writers, and athletes. Feminist restaurant and cafe owners made the intentional effort to hire women to help with the business. In an interview, Wildrose owner Bryher Herak noted how important independent women contractors were to make her business a reality. Herak had worked in an official capacity with the tradeswomen community in Seattle, Washington, before opening Wildrose and knew the women involved well. These connections allowed her to then support women in her community, while establishing informal trade networks. Furthermore, these connections gave her the economic flexibility to create Wildrose at a time when she had very little financial flexibility. Herak would offer women carpenters cards for free food and free beer.[34] Owners remarked in interviews that the ability to barter made creating these restaurants possible. Since the craftswomen appreciated the intention behind creating these restaurants and cafes and wanted these businesses to exist, tradeswomen would discount, donate, or trade their skills both to enable the creation of the business and to be able to enjoy the fare of the restaurant once it was established.

These intentional hiring choices regarding labourers, suppliers, and tradeswomen pervaded the daily conduct of business at restaurants like Wildrose. For example, Herak also hired a female plumber who was grateful for a job in which her employer would not sexually and verbally harass her.[35] Female tradeswomen during the period in feminist periodicals lamented their working conditions and the biases they faced.[36] As discussed in chapters 2 and 3, women faced systematic barriers that prevented women, particularly unmarried women, working-class women, lesbians, women of colour, and those at the intersection of these identities from accessing the capital necessary to start a restaurant. As a result, they sought alternative routes to accomplish their aims. This process often involved mutual support systems of like-minded craftswomen and tradeswomen, who might in turn accept lower pay because of their belief in the cause. They could also benefit from publicity, recommendations, and word-of-mouth to become established as the plumber, electrician, or carpenter to hire in the feminist community. Working on a feminist restaurant could aid craftswomen in the long run as they could expect to find more employment through lesbians and feminists who also frequented the venue, as was the case for the craftswomen who helped repair the Wildrose.[37] Being paid in "exposure," however, furthered the issue of women getting paid less than their male peers and the continual undervaluing of female labour. Nonetheless, the ability to support the creation of women's spaces made the sacrifice worthwhile for women labourers who did provide discounts.

The choice to hire women as independent contractors was commonplace amongst feminist restaurants. Wildrose had a female accountant "set up the books."[38] The Brick Hut was able to get carpentry help from Seven Sisters Construction. This feminist construction collective would help with carpentry projects—sometimes in exchange for breakfast.[39] The Brick Hut also hired an outside bookkeeper.[40] The Common Womon Club of Northampton decided to hire as many women as they possibly could. It was one of the first decisions that they made as a collective.[41] However, they found this decision quite difficult to enact as locating local tradeswomen in Northampton, Massachusetts, in the early 1970s could be difficult. Men dominated the trades in the 1970s and this occupational segregation has continued to this day.[42] The Common Womon collective was eventually able to hire two women carpenters who did major renovations on the side of the building. The collective members found that oftentimes they were significantly undercharged because the carpenters were trying to support the restaurant. These women wanted to help without the pressure of making a formal commitment of financially supporting the club but would offer a donation by lowering their prices. The Common Womon Club also found a female real estate agent who showed them multiple properties. Eventually they also hired a female accountant. The owners of Bloodroot likewise discussed how difficult it could sometimes be to hire tradeswomen and at times they would have to hire men but only after looking for a woman to fill the role first. As Selma Miriam told the *Bridgeport Sunday Post* in 1977, "We try to use women wherever we can: we have a woman attorney, a woman accountant, and a woman carpenter. I understand that there are women plumbers and electricians, but not in this area because we really looked for them. I know how hard it is for a woman to get a job in a field where women are unusual. We plan to have a bulletin board at Bloodroot for this purpose especially."[43] These testimonies make evident the concerted effort made to prioritize investing and circulating commerce within the women's community. This was done out of a conviction about the importance of supporting those women—particularly the out lesbians—to find work while facing gender and sexual-orientation discrimination.

Regional factors influenced the ease feminist restaurants encountered in finding tradeswomen and women professionals to do necessary services. In places like San Francisco, it was possible for the women to advertise themselves as lesbian carpenters in existing gay publications and because they lived in an area with a substantial out-lesbian population, they could advertise to this specific community.[44] However, in other regions of the United States in the 1970s and 1980s, it would be more pragmatic for independent contractors to not advertise either their sexual orientation or their feminist identity.

The founders of Mother Courage feminist restaurant responded to the question "What advice would the owners of Mother Courage give other women who are thinking of starting a restaurant?" with, "Count on at least three years before you can make a profit. Don't start undercapitalized. Before going into business get as much advice as possible: talk to other women who have restaurants; go to city agencies like the Small Business Association. Get a feminist laywer, accountant, and insurance agent. But, above all, DO IT!"[45] Feminists who started restaurants and cafes in the later period of this study were able to learn from the feminist entrepeneurs who had come before. These informal women-centred business networks were instrumental to supporting feminist businesses. Being able to depend on other women in the community allowed them to create community that also financially supported itself. Although sometimes they were not paying with money but with subcultural capital.

Artists and Musicians

In addition to feminist tradeswomen and professionals, feminist restaurants and cafes engaged independent artists and musicians, which encouraged customers to frequent their establishments. This decision brought money to both the space and to the artists themselves, as well as adding value to the businesses by endowing subcultural capital. Sociologist Sarah Thornton's book *Club Cultures: Music, Media, and Subcultural Capital* highlights the way that cultural values such as authenticity and hipness within subcultures create a kind of cultural capital in the way that Pierre Bourdieu understood cultural capital. However, this subcultural capital does not hinge on approval from the dominant or "mainstream" culture but rather gains value from its juxtaposition against and disparagement of the mainstream the subgroup uses to measure its alternative cultural worth.[46] The decision to support feminist artists and musicians was a necessary decision for the economic wellbeing of the restaurants and cafes as well as the artists and musicians. Both business and artist were able to receive literal capital from this exchange, while the choice to perform at these spaces, as well as the decision made in bringing lesbian and feminist performers and artists within them, rewarded the restaurant and the performer with the subcultural capital of the feminist culture and community. The attainment of subcultural capital does not undermine the intention of artists and musicians and feminist restaurants and cafes to support one another, it rather highlights the integral nature of this relationship. The economic, cultural, and social relationships between feminist restaurants and cafes with feminist and lesbian artists and musicians was mutualistic.

The network of support branched beyond the formalized businesses and the construction of the space and occurred in the creation of the atmosphere as well. These spaces fostered and held together a feminist artistic community that linked these restaurants across the continent, especially as touring musicians and artists would hop between them. It was similarly common for feminist restaurants and cafes to feature the work of local female artists. The Brick Hut featured the work of community artists such as Amana Johnson, Grace

Harwood, Barbara Sandidge, Kyos Featherdancing, Cathy Cade, and Wendy Cadden. Once a year, the Brick Hut exhibited the artwork of the children of Berkwood-Hedge School.[47]

Furthermore, the Brick Hut was located around the corner from Olivia Records, the feminist record company that was responsible for producing most of the "women's music" during the 1970s and 1980s.[48] The Brick Hut was so closely linked to the Bay Area's lesbian and feminist women's music scene that lesbian poet and Black Panther Pat Parker co-wrote with Mary Watkins "The Brick Hut Song" as part of Watkins's first album with Olivia Records, *Something Moving*.[49] Stars Vicki Randle and Linda Tillery are also featured on this album and they frequented the cafe. As Parker and Watkins's lyrics explain, "It's always crowded, got to wait for a seat / but watching the people is some kind of dream."[50] Other musicians and cultural activists would eat at the cafe, which would sometimes be repaid with a song. As Joan Antonuccio remembers, "customers still remember the day Linda T. spontaneously sang a cappella for the masses. The women of BeBe K'Roche, an all-woman electric rock band worked at the Brick Hut from time to time."[51] They held a Third Thursday Open Mike started by popular lesbian musician, Alix Dobkin, to encourage women to perform. Furthermore, one of the owners, Sharon Davenport, was a published poet and she organized salons and hosted readings. At the Brick Hut, performances and author readings were free, or pay-by-donation. No tickets were ever sold, with the exception of their tenth-anniversary party celebration that had music and comedy and was hosted at another local venue.

In 1982, Wild Sisters Café, located on the south side of Pittsburgh, Pennsylvania, featured feminist artistic performances and exhibitions.[52] Wild Sisters had a space where women could display artwork or perform talent on an open stage. That year the *Pittsburgh Post-Gazette* remarked that "Wild Sisters is in shambles now as the erstwhile Wobblie Joe's undergoes remodeling, but soon it will be the first feminist restaurant, bar and cabaret in Pittsburgh. When it opens, women artists will perform and exhibit, and freshly baked breads, soups, quiche, and sandwiches will be served."[53] This kind of entertainment was commonplace at feminist restaurants and cafes.

Feminist restaurants would often be gathering spaces for local artists. Alison Bechdel, renowned lesbian feminist cartoonist, most famous for her *Dykes to Watch Out For* comics and *Fun Home* graphic memoir, got her start in Minneapolis and often frequented Ruby's Café.[54] Some of Bechdel's inspiration for Café Topaz in the comics, where the characters frequently eat, may have come from Ruby's as it was located close to the feminist bookstore Amazon Books, which Bechdel has stated inspired the Madwimmin Books depicted in the comics.[55] In Bechdel's comics "The Option" and "The Blow," behind the seated characters the menu board declares "wheat free, dairy-free pizza w/ no tomatoes!" and "vegetarian meatloaf with steamed french fries," pointing to the vegetarian menus that were common at eateries that targeted feminist and lesbian communities.[56] Ruby's also had one staff member who was a curator and would put on different shows. Mary Bahneman, the owner of Ruby's, only ever requested that one picture be taken down because it was gory and would have been unappetizing to have in a restaurant. Local gay and lesbian artists created most of the art at Ruby's.[57]

The Wildrose Restaurant and Bar of Seattle, Washington, supported and brought jazz musicians to the area. Its owner, Bryher Herak, fondly remembers how much joy she had in bringing international jazz performers to the Wildrose, commenting that those performances were "some of the most exciting times of [her] life."[58] She tried to keep the cover between $5 and $10 and the performers received 80 percent of the take after the performers helped with promoting the event. De Laria, Alix Dobkin, and other women's music musicians would also play. A regular Thursday night event featured jazz musicians from the local music school. The Wildrose also hosted guitar music, talent shows, comedy shows, open mics, and drag shows.[59]

The practice of welcoming feminist artists and musicians was integral to these spaces, giving them a unique platform in a safe environment that simultaneously bolstered the spaces themselves. Mountain Moving Café, the self-declared feminist coffee shop located in Portland, Oregon, was known for its women's nights, "nice atmosphere, live music and assorted types of entertainment."[60] Guests could dine on vegetarian fare while enjoying dancing, films, speakers, and poetry.[61] Amaranth, the feminist restaurant that moved into the space formerly occupied by Bread and Roses in Cambridge, Massachusetts, described itself as a women's restaurant that served whole foods only and pizza, with salads and fruit drinks as its specialties. The flyer described, "The atmosphere here is warm and *womonly*—we encourage women to hang out and socialize. Our large back room also serves as a gallery to show female artists' work. Sporadic entertainment too."[62] Serving the feminist and New Age community of San Diego, the women-owned-and-managed Wing Café and Gallery, was dedicated to the development and growth of women's culture and community. It hosted art shows, music, and poker games.[63] These events encouraged women to patronize the restaurants and cafes.

There were even feminist cafes located within designated art spaces; here food and art mutualistically provided sustenance. In Los Angeles, California, the Identified Woman Café, which later became Val's Café, was located on the third floor of the Women's Building—a nonprofit arts and educational space founded by artist Judy Chicago, graphic designer Sheila Levrant de Bretteville, and art historian Arlene Raven. The building was central to the development of the feminist art movement from 1973 to 1991. Feminist art activist groups such as The Waitresses gathered at the Women's Building to develop their 1978 consciousness-raising performance *Ready to Order?*, a series of guerrilla theatre pieces at various restaurants that included a number of workshops and panel discussions on the history of working women, job discrimination, and assertiveness training.[64] As Terry Wolverton describes, all of the different feminist artists

ARTEMIS CAFE

23rd & VALENCIA
SAN FRANCISCO CA
821 – 0232

☆ APRIL 1982 ☆

friday	saturday
2 WOODY SIMMONS Advance Tickets 8 pm and 10 pm $4.50 advance $5.00 at door	3 REEL WORLD STRING BAND Traditional Appalacian music On tour from Kentucky 9 pm $4.00/don.
9 DEBBIE SAUNDERS vocals, piano 9 pm $3.50 - $4.00/don.	10 TERRY GARTHWAITE and AVOTCJA poetry, music, and vocals 9 pm $4.00/don.
16 GAYLE MARIE and MIMI FOX guitar, piano, and vocals 9 pm $4.00/don.	17 JILL ROSE and guests solo piano and vocals 9 pm $3.50/don.
23 NANCY and WENDY ROBERTSON with Suzanne Shanbaum guitar, piano, vocals 9 pm $3.50 - $4.00/don.	24 LIZ BURCH and JANE HASTY flute, piano, vocals, jazz, and originals 9 pm $3.50/don.
30 ODALISQUE Belly Dancers !! 9 pm $3.50/don.	1 GAYLE MARIE vocals, piano 9 pm $3.50 - $4.00/don.

Sunday Brunch 11 am to 2pm

☆ NOW OPEN ☆

7 DAYS A WEEK

11:30am-11:30pm Sunday 11am-10pm

4.2 *One of the most common pieces of ephemera that survive from now-closed feminist restaurants and cafes are flyers advertising events. This April 1982 flyer for Artemis Café of San Francisco, California, publicizes poetry readings, concerts, and dancing. (Used with permission from the GLBT Historical Society, San Francisco. GLBT Ephemera Collection, Business Box, AM – AV, Artemis folder)*

and patrons "did not necessarily rub elbows in the small café [Val's], or chat while standing in line for the bathroom, but they did walk through a common door, and stand under the same roof."[65] By spending time in these shared cafes and studios, they developed feminist arts practices which enabled them to critique sexist labour practices and foster the creation of feminist ventures.

Each artist brought new people to the space. Artist collectives, as a result, were likely to flock to spaces that supported them and fostered creative environments. The original clientele of Mother Courage was to a great extent, from Westbeth, the artists' housing project a block away. Joseph Chaikin of the Open Theatre also came in often.[66] Visual artists could display their work on the walls, women in the community could buy art pieces, and artists could network and find collaborators. Noel Furie, co-owner of Bloodroot, was a photographer, and the two-spirit writer and activist Chrystos wrote in a letter, "Tell Noel I'm looking for a new 'publicity photo' to send out and would buy copies."[67] This letter was a response to Bloodroot's request that they use some of Chrystos's written materials in their latest cookbook that featured lyrics, poetry, and writings of feminists that they admired. In return Chrystos wanted a copy of the cookbook and to support Noel's photography. Likewise, in response to a material usage request for their Bloodroot cookbook, the musician Aleegra sent a note thanking Bloodroot for wanting to include her lyrics amongst other artists she admired and looked forward to receiving her copy of the cookbook. She also enclosed a copy of her tape of women's music for the restaurant to play. Furthermore, the owners of Bloodroot and Aleegra made plans to speak more at the East Coast Lesbian Festival.[68] Festivals acted as a temporary intermediary space, able to link some of these artists and businesses. Other women who were part of the feminist collectives that ran the restaurants or just worked at the restaurants were also using their wages from their work to support their art practices. Lesbian artist Sheila Pepe worked at the lesbian-owned-and-operated Beetle's Lunch in Allston, Massachusetts, while earning her BFA.[69]

Feminist restaurants thus served more than food: they fostered women artists as well as an entire feminist music community that also linked them to the bar culture. This micro-culture was extremely significant to those who lived in it. Women were underrepresented in media at large, yet here was a business network that fostered an artistic and music community where music could be played. As Selma Miriam explained in her choice to only play women's music at Bloodroot, "It's not that we don't have men's music at home, that we don't use men's products, that we don't like men, but this must be a place that is for women."[70] Here women's production and performance were put at the forefront. Musicians then linked these spaces together connecting the community across the continent. As the photographer Joan Biren's collection of old event posters and flyers demonstrates, it was common for lesbian and feminist musicians to travel between feminist restaurants, cafes, and coffeehouses, crisscrossing the continent and connecting women across borders.[71] These artists served as a way of transporting ideas across the communities and created greater connections between them all.

Authors and Speakers

Feminist restaurants and cafes supported and were supported by the feminist intellectual community, particularly authors and speakers, by offering event venues and retail opportunities for their publications. Feminists across the United States were reading from similar books and periodicals, but there were also more locally oriented periodicals like *Ain't I a Woman* in Iowa City (1970–1974), or local event newsletters such as *Feminist Communications: Las Hermanas Coffeehouse Newsletter* of San Diego, California (1975–1979). Many of these local periodicals would reprint popular articles such as Judy

Syfer's "I Want a Wife," which appeared in *Ms. Magazine's* December 1971 issue and was republished in numerous feminist periodicals.[72] National and international periodicals such as *Off Our Backs* (1970–2008) were popular within feminist communities across North America. These periodicals also featured reviews of feminist books such as Bloodroot's cookbook *The Political Palate.* Both books and periodicals were sold at local feminist cafes and restaurants and the feminist bookstores that had cafes such as Berkeley, California's The Old Mole, which served espresso, drip coffee, and pastries and offered books by and about women—fiction and non-fiction, cloth and paper.[73] Furthermore, in cities that did not have explicitly feminist restaurants, feminist bookstores would serve as de facto cafes that sold coffee and snacks and provided a space to linger. Feminist intellectuals would also hang out and gather at these spaces.

It was not just the poets, musicians, and artists that would travel between the cafes from city to city. They also served as venues to welcome authors on speaking tours. For example, Bridgeport's Bloodroot hosted radical anti-porn feminist Andrea Dworkin on multiple occasions. Articles about Mother Courage often highlighted the feminist intellectual community that would gather. As the *People Magazine* article about Mother Courage's anniversary party mentioned, "you are as likely to find Movement 'heavies' as you are regulars; New York Radical Feminists, as NOW women; Lesbian Feminist Liberation caucusing, as the Modern Language Association's Commission on the Status of Women dining out."[74] Under the photos were captioned,

> Melinda Schroeder, left, who is starting a feminist credit union in September, raps with overalled Marta Vivas, a founder of Redstockings, one of the oldest and most radical feminist groups. Listening is Minda Bikman, who produces video films for women … The guests, who celebrated with champagne, quiche and chocolate cake, included New York City councilwoman Carol Greitzer, writers Susan

Brownmiller, who has an upcoming book about rape, Lucy Komisar, Kate Millett (*Flying*), Alix Kates Shulman and Phyllis Chesler (*Women and Madness*). (Gloria Steinem was away at a conference).[75]

Leading feminist figures during the period, such as Jaqui Ceballos, Mryna Lamb, Lucy Komisar, and Susan Sontag, would also make appearances to more than 100 feminist attendees.[76] It is important to remember that these were sites where women could gather without interruption and discuss their ideas and socialize. Certain restaurants, such as Mother Courage, cultivated reputations as being the hot spots for the intellectual heavy hitters, but these kinds of events were not confined to New York and its elite. Roberta Achtenberg spoke on lesbian parenthood at the Brick Hut in Berkeley, California.[77] Old Wives' Tales Restaurant of Portland, Oregon, in addition to advertising their live concerts, proudly featured the works of women artists and writers.[78] In these spaces, ideas grew and thrived. Literary culture and food culture were greatly linked. Feminist restaurants were for voracious readers and eaters.

Feminist Professional and Personal Organizations

Feminist restaurants and cafes served as meeting spaces for local organizations, which expanded ideas of whom the spaces were for. Bryher Herak believed that the staff at Wildrose did their best to reach out to working-class communities, women of colour, and various LGBTQ communities. The invited performers brought crowds from various subcultures, which further diversified the space. At Wildrose, Herak worked frequently with Seattle's Lesbian Resource Center and hosted the African American lesbian support group meeting. The Wildrose publicized and organized with the local feminist bookstores, feminist health collective, feminist print shops, and the local women-centred art galleries. Furthermore, they hosted Women in the Trades, Association of Lesbian Professionals, the Seattle Women's Commissions, and tried to persuade a female Black church minister to encourage her congregation to dine there. These efforts provided networking and economic opportunities; however, feminist restaurants were not solely focused on providing financial opportunities but also social and cultural ones. The leather community would gather at Wildrose.[79] LGBTQ Alcoholics Anonymous meetings were held at the Wildrose and the Brick Hut Café.[80] As Herak explained, while the Wildrose could always have improved outreach efforts, she and her staff made a concerted effort to support local community groups focused on social justice and community building. Herak made it her mission to make the space a safe sanctuary for LGBTQ people of all races, economic backgrounds, genders, and religions.[81] Feminist restaurants' grassroots work in their communities supported a diverse array of feminist and lesbian groups and had the effect of expanding business communities. Feminist restaurants and cafes also supported the unpaid labour of their community members, including their activism.

Support of Activists in the Community

These businesses served to support activist causes in their communities and offered them spaces to gather, often for free. The San Diego Lesbian Organization met at Wing Café on Thursday evenings and the Coalition for Take Back the Night, a group focused on making women safe from sexual violence in public spaces, met on Monday evenings.[82] For Gay Pride, Wildrose would serve a big lunch and then the owners and staff would go to the parade with customers and rally. Wildrose was open on most holidays so that the many Seattle lesbians who did not have a home to go to for the holidays could have a spot to socialize and have a nice meal. Also, as the restaurant was located in an area with unhomed people, every Monday Wildrose served them soup and sandwiches for free.[83] On Wednesday nights, Bloodroot of

Bridgeport hosted the G. Knapp Historical Society—a feminist organization named for Goody Knapp, who was hung for being a witch in 1653, not far from Bloodroot. The group met to commemorate the death of all the women who were tortured before and after its namesake.[84] The Brick Hut supported many causes and issues, from feeding the anti-nuclear proliferation protesters at University of California, Berkeley's weapons research facility, Livermore Labs, to the striking students when Mills College threatened to go co-ed. ACT UP, the AIDS activist organization, held meetings after hours in the space. The Brick Hut closed on what was then called Gay Day to attend political demonstrations and rallies. The staff would place a sign on the door, "JOIN US AT …" then fill in information about a parade, rally, or demonstration. The Hut gave most of its support through contributions of food and energy to anti-nuclear demonstrations, anti-war rallies, and the feminist causes of Inez Garcia, Norma Jean Croy, Joan Little, and Yvonne Wanrow.[85] To mark the importance of the events, the Brick Hut closed and the people who worked there attended the vigil for the assassinations of Harvey Milk and George Moscone. The Hut also closed to protest the verdict of their killer, Dan White. It was important to the Brick Hut owners and staff to be involved by feeding protestors and participating in protests and using their sound system to play every minute of the Iran–Contra hearings each day they aired in 1987. Listening to each day of Anita Hill's testimony at Clarence Thomas's Supreme Court confirmation hearings in 1991 brought people in for breakfast, who then stayed through lunch. Customers had discussions with customers at other tables, playing musical chairs the whole time. According to owner Joan Antonuccio, it was "Pretty amazing. [Customers] came in because they knew we would have the radio tuned in."[86] The Brick Hut was the first cafe, at least in the East Bay area, to hang posters stating "You can't get AIDS from a glass" and the owners did their best to advocate and care for their ailing and dying brothers, men in the gay community afflicted with the disease.[87] The Brick Hut also continued to support feminist and queer causes and activities like the Lyon-Martin Clinic, Queer Nation, and East Bay ACT UP. KPFA Radio broadcasted their International Women's Day program directly from the Brick Hut.[88] As Joan Antonnucio described the Brick Hut's staff's activism, "Everything we did was a feminist issue. We were out lesbian feminists every minute of the day. Our work, our interactions with each other and our customers, the way we taught new workers was feminist. The personal really is political. Again, everything we did was activism."[89] In their cafe, they were able to support the kind of world that they wanted to see.

Athletes

Feminist restaurants and cafes would also support other efforts of community building, socializing, and women's health through the sponsorship of women's sports teams. While it is important to understand feminist restaurants and cafes' support for women's sports teams and athletes beyond economics, by providing sponsorship and fundraising feminist restaurants and cafes amplified the labour of women in their communities. As an anonymous contributor noted in a roundup article, "A Place for Us," published in *Ain't I a Woman*, "going to a women's softball tournament raised my consciousness" and provided female role models.[90] The Brick Hut sponsored the Grillfriends, a women-only team.[91] Restaurant by day, lesbian bar by night, the Hung Jury of Washington, DC, also sponsored a team.[92] Sara Lewinstein, owner of The Artemis Café, started what became a thriving women's softball league in the Bay Area.[93] She later was a co-founder of the international sporting event, the Gay Games. Bread and Roses sponsored the local women's softball, basketball, and volleyball teams. Instead of a tip jar, the restaurant had a collection can with a different cause each week. The money from the can funded the teams, as well as thirty-five different causes in their first year of operation.[94] Historian A. Finn Enke, in *Finding the Movement*, expressed the important role that these lesbian softball teams played in fostering

4.3 *Rather than tipping at Bread and Roses, customers could donate money to feminist organizations in the Cambridge, Massachusetts area. One of the organizations to benefit from the "TIP" can was the Bread and Roses Softball team. (Courtesy of Schlesinger Library, Harvard Radcliffe Institute, Papers of H. Patricia Hynes, 1974-2004, Box 1, Bread and Roses Softball Team Folder 6)*

community, particularly for lesbians in the Midwest. Wildrose sponsored a softball team, a bowling team, and a golf team. Restaurants would give the teams money, buy them t-shirts, and offer them discounts on postgame food and drinks. Bryher Herak explained that the sponsorship would cost more than the restaurant made up for, but the women would come back on the weekends.[95] The teams also provided publicity for the restaurants. The teams' uniforms would have their sponsors' names written on them and their posters would publicize their sponsoring restaurants. Although the softball teams were not technically a feminist business, encouraging this kind of social networking led to economic opportunities.

Conclusion

The more than 230 self-identified American feminist restaurants, cafes, and coffeehouses founded in the 1970s and 1980s, made an economic, social, and cultural impact that expanded beyond their single brick and mortar locations. They were part of a larger movement in which feminist activists created women-only and women-centred spaces for political organizing, recreational activity, and commerce. Together these businesses challenged the status quo of the food service industry, cooking, and consumption. Owning their own businesses allowed the feminists, lesbians, and feminist lesbians who created these establishments to financially support themselves while being out as lesbian or feminist. Controlling their workspaces also allowed the founders to contribute to their vision of the kind of world that they wanted to see. Feminist restaurants and cafes functioned as spaces in which to build community and foster a larger nexus of feminist businesses.[96] Feminist restaurants not only gave women opportunities in them but also provided inspiration and a structure for other women to be involved in the paid marketplace. Not everyone within these communities desired separatism; while there were moves towards separatism by some within the movement even these individuals advocated for building feminist business networks. The proliferation of feminist businesses made separatism more possible by expanding the options women had for work and consumption. But these spaces ultimately supported women across the continent and readers of periodicals knew about them internationally, creating the feeling of a community much larger than themselves. To sum it up best, as an article remarked on the third-anniversary celebration of Mother Courage, "No speeches were necessary. The word 'feminist' already implies an attitude."[97]

CHAPTER 5

Feminist Food and Balancing Concerns

> We consider ourselves to be a feminist restaurant and I think that we consider feminism to be much broader than simply a place for women to congregate, as desirable as that might be ... We think that the food we serve, the way we serve it, and the relationship with our customers are all very, very different from other restaurants or "cafés." It is all inspired by our feminism.[1]
>
> *Selma Miriam, co-founder of Bloodroot Feminist Vegetarian Restaurant*

American feminist restaurants, cafes, and coffeehouses served up activism with a side of feminist food. Feminist restaurants came into existence during a period when Americans dined outside the home at record-breaking numbers.[2] As discussed earlier in this book, self-identified feminist restaurants and cafés acted as spaces that challenged the status quo around cooking and consumption. "Feminist food" was usually vegetarian and represented the feminist and environmentalist values of its makers. Each restaurant and cafe defined feminist food slightly differently depending on the particular feminist ethics of the restaurant owners. While it may seem evident that the women's music these restaurants played, the women's art they displayed, and the visiting performers they hosted all promoted feminist principles, what is less obvious is how the *food itself* was also a manifestation of these restaurants' politics. Feminist bookstores sold feminist books, but it is less apparent how feminist restaurants sold feminist food. In fact, the types of foods offered on the menus of these restaurants were indeed integral to the restaurants' feminism. The kinds of dishes and drinks sold, the ingredients used, and the prices all reflected the different feminist ethics of the restaurant owners, to an extent. By looking at what was included on and banned from these restaurant menus, this chapter shows the various ways in which restaurateurs defined what is feminist food. Similarly, other feminists during the 1970s and 1980s in the United States used cookbooks to share not only a recipe for a dish but for a new world order. Thus, within the feminist restaurants and cafes in the United States that were established in the 1970s and 1980s, food was feminist. However, choices over what to serve challenged each restaurant and cafe's feminist principles. Despite best intentions and business plans, this chapter shows how food brought to the fore the difficulty of balancing responses to various social inequities within feminist restaurants.

In 1972, when two women's movement organizers, Dolores Alexander and Jill Ward, created Mother Courage in New York City, many of the activist groups within the 1960s and 1970s countercultural movements already had incorporated food as part of their political outreach. For instance, in 1969 the Black Panther Party began the Free Breakfast for School Children Program in Oakland, California, which aimed to improve students' academic success by making sure that they were properly nourished before a day of learning.[3] The Back to the Land movement, in which thousands of North Americans left cities to begin farming or start communes, was in full force.[4] Although exact numbers are unknown, there were over two thousand communes during the 1960s and early 1970s in the United States.[5] Alice Waters, the renowned founder and chef of Chez Panisse in Berkeley, California, had made the connection between the anti-war and anti-Vietnam movement and food, which inspired her to create her farm-to-table restaurant. The companies Monsanto and Dow Chemical that had manufactured Agent Orange, the defoliant used by the United States military during the Vietnam War that was linked to widespread birth defects, also produced the chemicals used in American industrial agriculture. As a result, peace and environmental activists sought food from organic producers.[6] While not everyone in each movement was interested in the ways that food intersected with their activism, these kinds of connections were made in the feminist, anti-racist, anti-classist, and anti-war movements. Thus, the idea that food would be tied to activism is not surprising given other contemporaneous movements. But what was unique for these feminist restaurants was the discourse around why the food was feminist and vital to the feminism of their owners. As will be demonstrated below, for establishments such as Bloodroot of Bridgeport, Connecticut, choosing dishes was a primary concern. For the restaurants that prioritized community building over concerns about their menus, the decisions the owners made regarding their food further upheld their political convictions.

Serving Up Activism and Vegetarianism

As there were numerous types of feminism in the 1970s—liberal, socialist, Marxist, radical, radical lesbian, and radical lesbian separatist—that had a diversity of ideas of how to implement their specific worldview, there were similarly diverse ideas about how the owners believed that their food could be feminist. While feminist restaurant owners stated that their vegetarianism, their decisions about the items on their menus, and their low prices made their food feminist, any owner or manager who did not claim feminist ideological leanings could make the same business choices, such as operating a sandwich shop serving only inexpensive vegetarian food, without being a feminist restaurant. A large variety of restaurants have had vegetarian menu items to serve the small but not insignificant percentage of the population that was vegetarian.[7] Other restaurants such as Black Cat Café of Seattle, which existed from 1993 to 1998, charged lower prices to make food more economically accessible as part of an anti-capitalist and anti-poverty stance, prioritizing social justice over profit.[8] Yet it is the ideology and symbolism surrounding the food that makes the food feminist. The discourse around the food is as much a part of the preparation of the meal as the actual cooking of the ingredients. Understanding the owners' motivations behind their choices about the dishes to serve is key to understanding what makes feminist food indeed feminist. Making food feminist depends on a grounded ideology. There were practical reasons behind these choices that supported the owners' ideological agendas. The owners reflected thoroughly about the ways they would build their menus and restaurant experiences in ways that would support their political and activist goals. The owners of feminist restaurants used food to undermine oppressive sexist structures in the United States. In a more practical sense, food was the fuel of a revolution, nourishing the bodies of the activists.

Feminist food in feminist restaurants, cafes, and coffeehouses in the 1970s and 1980s was both a physical production and a discursive production. In one sense, a variety of contradictory food philosophies were still feminist when there was feminist reasoning behind them. But these ideals were different than the material requirements of physical food production, encompassing ethics, labour conditions, and economics. Some feminist food practices could engage with both physical and discursive production in their decision making, such as by not supporting the dairy industry to protest feminized exploitation or purchasing from suppliers who heeded farm workers' rights.

Vegetarian food was not solely tied to feminism. People around the world have adopted vegetarian diets, usually due to respect for sentient life and a code of ethics motivated by various religious and spiritual beliefs, a prioritization of animal rights, reasons that are health related, political, cultural, environmental, aesthetic, economic, or personal preference, or due to poverty.[9] In the 1960s and 1970s, as part of the countercultural movements, vegetarianism experienced resurgence.[10] As historian James J. Kopp demonstrates, the new attention to vegetarianism in the 1960s and 1970s was the result of anti-war pacifist ideologies being extended beyond protests against the Vietnam War; a circulation of Eastern philosophies and belief systems that endorsed meatless diets within countercultural circles; and concerns over the system of industrial food production decried by colourful personalities like California health-food guru Gypsy Boots.[11] Vegetarianism was very popular in many activist communities and as part of the counterculture, not only due to ethical values but economic motivations. As documented by historians of vegetarianism in the United States Karen and Michel Iacobbo, counterculture, Back to the Land movement leaders, and hippie radio show hosts advocated for vegetarian lifestyles.[12] However, for feminist restaurants that decided to have vegetarian menus, the choice to be vegetarian was an integral part of their brand of feminism. The food on their menus was vegetarian for the following reasons: the ecofeminist philosophy of the owners, environmental concerns, the needs of the clientele, and for cost, which spoke to class needs through either a Marxist or socialist discourse.

Owners Selma Miriam and Noel Furie of Bloodroot Feminist Vegetarian Restaurant prioritized cooking vegetarian food when they opened their business in 1977. They stated, "We don't use meat—not only because it's not healthy, but because we equate the oppression of women with that of animals. As women, we do not want to profit from the sale of animal flesh."[13] Their vegetarian principles and activism were based on ecofeminist ethics. In their first cookbook, the *Political Palate*, they write, "Feminism is not a part-time attitude for us; it is how we live all day, everyday. Our choices in furniture, pictures, the music we play, the books we sell, and the food we cook all reflect and express our feminism."[14] Noel Furie and Selma Miriam were ecofeminists, connecting the domination of nature and the exploitation of women. Ecofeminism is entangled with anti-nuclear movements, environmentalist activism, and lesbian feminism. Professor and activist Greta Gaard has repeatedly demonstrated the ways that vegetarian ecofeminists connected the kinds of foods women prepared and ate to a larger social activist framework. Furthermore, she has shown "how vegetarian ecofeminists have developed critiques and activist strategies for responding to various situations involving the linked oppression of women, people of color, and nonhuman animals,"[15] which included not eating meat. The Bloodroot Collective explicitly put ecofeminism at the forefront of its vision for the restaurant. In the collective's third cookbook, *The Perennial Palate*, the members stated, "eating meat is wrong for its cruelty to creatures who can feel and experience pain, and wrong because it contributes to worldwide starvation, mostly of women and children."[16] In no way was their vegetarianism an accident or by-product of another specific countercultural influence. The Bloodroot Collective's members repeatedly insisted that their vegetarianism was integral to their feminism and that the food they served was feminist itself. Bloodroot's owners prioritized serving primarily local, seasonal, and organic food. In Miriam's words, "I do consider it important that we are much more than a coffeehouse or café. And as you know, I think, the food we serve is what many different peoples do, especially the poorer ones, and that perspective is very different from health food restaurants. We have always cared deeply about others' food possibilities and creativity."[17]

The changes in Bloodroot's menu offerings over the course of its existence demonstrate the evolution of Selma Miriam and Noel Furie's understanding of what made food feminist. In addition to creating a vegetarian menu, the Bloodroot Collective (the group of women who managed the restaurant), wrote and published seven vegetarian cookbooks. Ideas about feminism, lesbian identity, and vegetarianism were in flux through this period, and these changes can be traced in looking at the six vegetarian cookbooks published by Bloodroot.[18] In America during the early 1970s, a common definition of the vegetarianism that many left-leaning, predominantly white activists subscribed to usually included eating fish.[19] Bloodroot stopped serving fish in 1980 as ideas about vegetarianism began to shift. The restaurant

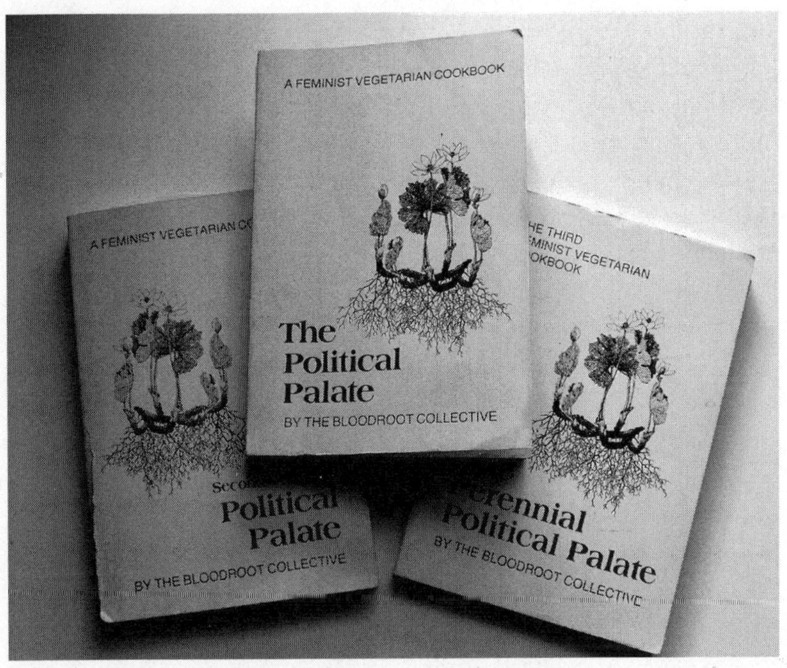

5.1 *The Bloodroot Collective of Bridgeport, Connecticut, has released seven cookbooks since its founding. These three cookbooks,* The Political Palate: A Feminist Vegetarian Cookbook *(1980),* The Second Seasonal Palate: a Feminist Vegetarian Cookbook *(1984), and* The Perennial Political Palate: The Third Feminist Vegetarian Cookbook *(1993) were the first published by the collective. They feature recipes organized by season and their pages are adorned with feminist quotes and poetry. Each cookbook includes a detailed introduction section explaining how the cookbook reflects the collective's feminism. (Photo by the author)*

also became increasingly vegan. This transition happened in part due to the owners becoming more aware of environmental concerns over the dairy industry and also the needs and desires of their customer base.[20] The collective had fifty-two vegan recipes out of 303 in its first book (published in 1980), fifty-five of 209 in its second book (1984), and 140 of 167, or 84 percent, in its third book (1993).[21] The long introductions in these cookbooks serve to educate readers about how the Bloodroot Collective connects their philosophy of feminism, lesbianism, and vegetarianism.

Meanings of what made food feminist varied from restaurant to restaurant and over time, as ideas of feminism evolved. Bloodroot was not alone in leveraging vegetarianism to promote feminist ideology. There were other feminist restaurants, cafes, and coffeehouses that were vegetarian because of their clientele's interest in this sort of diet. Vegetarianism was widespread across politically active communities during the period. Historian Sherrie A. Inness discusses how women who did not decide to open explicitly feminist restaurants during the 1970s often focused on vegetarian foods or "natural foods" as ways to engage with the politics of the period. Playing on essentialist ideas of "naturalness," these women used the socially naturalized role of the "woman in the kitchen" but subverted this role by opening small businesses that allowed them to financially support themselves while promoting their political views.[22] In this sense, the woman in the kitchen was not passive but rather active in her role. Yet, the relationship between vegetarian cooking and health-food ideologies was not in fact seamless. In a 2015 interview with *Vice Magazine*'s affiliate *Munchies*, Bloodroot's owners reflected on the countless diet fads that have come and gone since they opened, noting that "their timeless focus on global home cooking and whole foods has kept them relevant, whether people were avoiding fat, carbs, or gluten."[23] While their vegetarian and vegan menu was the result of their politics, customers' desire for meatless fare has continued to support the restaurant for over forty years.

For the restaurants that were vegetarian due to the interest from the community, even when the owners were not vegetarians themselves, the owners were still enacting their feminist principles. Their feminism relied upon community building and supporting the activism of their fellow feminists. The decision to be vegetarian was not just a marketplace analysis, fulfilling an economic need, but was also filling an emotional or activist need. Opening a feminist restaurant constituted a labour of love more than a profit-driven venture. This is not to say that decisions were never made to support the business, but the driving force behind deciding what items would be served was grounded in political decisions. The Common Womon Club of Northampton, Massachusetts, would occasionally host private dinners to fundraise, relying on the female faculty of the local universities and colleges to plan events there, and would draw specific attention to their food choices. In the words of the owners, "We offer an imaginative and nutritious vegetarian menu including fish and dairy dishes. All women are welcome!"[24] Former Common Womon Club collective member Marjorie Childers, explained

> A typical evening meal would offer a choice between two soups, salad, three entree choices and desserts. Among the most popular soups were butternut squash and cream of potato, and we also made a vegetarian chili. We always had a quiche of some sort, an Italian dish such as eggplant parmigiana, and other pasta or rice-based dishes. We often made Chinese spring rolls, and occasionally we had a fish dish. For dessert we tried to make honey-sweetened or maple fruit pies and cobblers, but we often fell back on commercial, sugar-sweetened ice cream as a topper. Tea, coffee and fruit juice were served. For brunch we had purchased bagels, but we also had eggs and omelets and pancakes made to order. We always had mixed grain bread that we made on an almost daily basis.[25]

The founders knew that many of the women in their town were vegetarian. Northampton was a very liberal community with many lesbian inhabitants who were vegetarian due to their various activist affiliations and politics.[26] The 1977 handout about Common Womon's

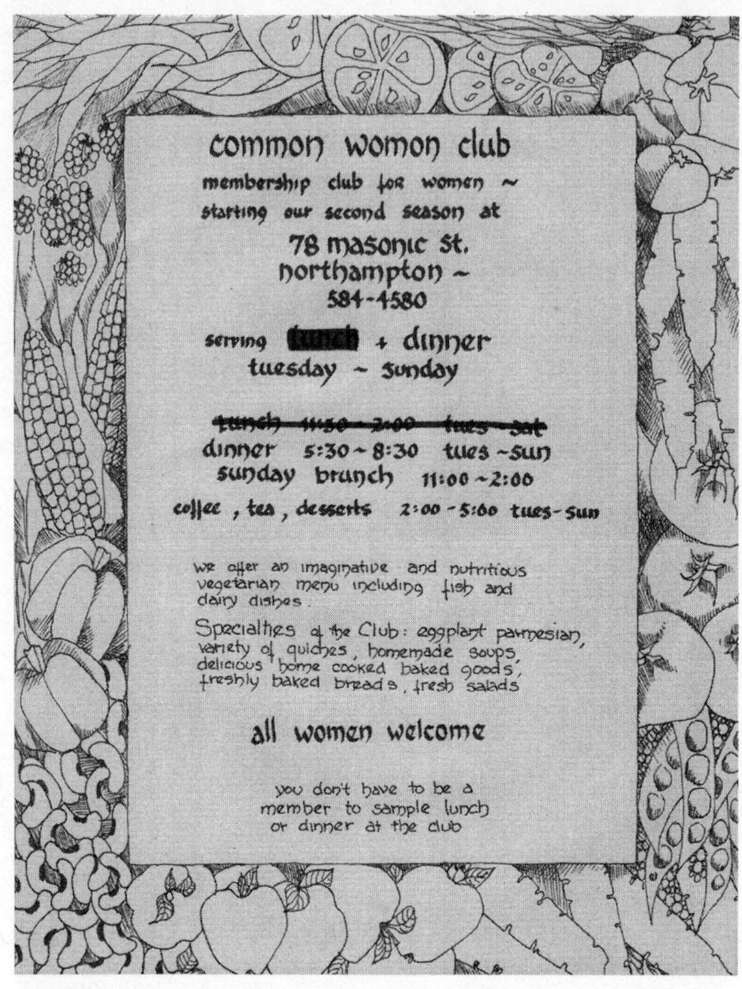

common womon club
membership club for women ~
starting our second season at
78 masonic st.
northampton ~
584-4580
serving + dinner
tuesday ~ sunday
~~lunch 11:30 - 2:00 tues-sat~~
dinner 5:30 ~ 8:30 tues ~ sun
sunday brunch 11:00 ~ 2:00
coffee, tea, desserts 2:00 - 5:00 tues-sun
we offer an imaginative and nutritious vegetarian menu including fish and dairy dishes.
Specialties of the Club: eggplant parmesian, variety of quiches, homemade soups, delicious 'home cooked baked goods', freshly baked breads, fresh salads
all women welcome
you don't have to be a member to sample lunch or dinner at the club

5.2 *The second season announcement for the Common Womon Club of Northampton, Massachusetts, emphasizes their vegetarian menu "including fish and dairy dishes." As was common in 1970s feminist restaurants, fish was accepted as part of a vegetarian diet before the widespread adoption of the distinguishing term "pescatarian." This understanding of vegetarianism shifted in most feminist restaurants by the 1980s and fish was no longer served. (Photo courtesy of Kaymarion Raymond)*

policies further explains that many of the members had a strong dislike for cooking meat while others believed that "meat-eating encourages a wasteful use of the world's resources … and that the excessive consumption of meat, particularly in the United States, is very tied to the male domination of the culture."[27] Here, the feminist principle enacted in their menu was about being supportive to the intersecting political interests of their customer base.

It was not rare for feminist restaurants to be vegetarian. Snake Sister Café of Rochester, New York, founded in 1981, was a women's collective vegetarian restaurant. The owners encouraged women in the community to come to a Sunday brunch to share great food and the *New York Times* and *New Women's Times* around their woodstove. Snake Sister's owners focused on building a community with board games, social events, a weekend coffeehouse performance, vegetarian meals, music, films, poetry, and live jazz Thursday through Sunday.[28] After it closed, Wild Seeds Feminist Bookstore and Café opened in Rochester in 1991. Like Bloodroot, it was a lesbian-owned-and-operated bookstore and vegetarian cafe. The cafe featured meatless meals, snacks, and desserts. For weekend entertainment, the cafe showed movies, hosted poetry readings, and played acoustic music. Across the country in 1978, Mountain Moving Café in Portland, Oregon, was a feminist cafe owned by a collective of lesbians, which promoted its ladies-only nights in the women's travel guide *Gaia's*. Mountain Moving Café had a vegetarian menu, dancing, films, speakers, poetry, live music, kids' night on Fridays, and was very welcoming to the gay community.[29] In 1981, Genesis of Cleveland, Ohio, was a vegetarian cafe and bar that was collectively owned and, as its advertisements stressed, inexpensive.[30] All of these establishments were vegetarian as they were part of left-leaning activist communities in which a significant portion of the clientele was vegetarian. The note about the expense of the food speaks to another important component of what made the restaurants vegetarian apart from ethics and the desires of their clientele.

Vegetarian menus at feminist restaurants often showcased international cuisines as many cultures have a long tradition of cooking without meat. In the case of restaurants like Bloodroot, which has employed women from a range of cultures who have shared their own recipes with the restaurant, these feminist restaurants exposed clientele to a wide range of fare while enabling employees to economically benefit from their own cultural knowledge. At Bloodroot, this has meant that cook Carol Graham has made her recipe for meat-free Jamaican jerk "chicken" one of the most popular dishes.[31] However, restaurants that showcased dishes from cultures other than those of their workers risked cultural appropriation. Financially benefitting from other cultures' dishes was not unique to vegetarian restaurants, yet it is worth noting as feminist restaurant founders sought to create eateries that did not perpetuate oppressive power dynamics.

Cost impacted feminist restaurants' and cafes' choices to be vegetarian. Food did not have to be vegetarian for the restaurant to be feminist but often, vegetarian food was the cheapest to make and to sell at the cheapest price. Vegetarian foods had fewer associated health risks related to refrigeration and preparation. Furthermore, meat was more expensive to store and possible spoilage was a larger economic liability. Decisions about money were vital to the feminist identities of these establishments.

Pricing and Access

Women made less money than men in the United States, especially during the late 1970s.[32] Therefore it was important to the owners that the food that they sold would be accessible to as many women as possible; the prices were not to be prohibitive. Environmental activist and engineer Patricia Hynes and writer Gill Gane created Bread and Roses Restaurant of Cambridge, Massachusetts, in 1974. In their initial business prospectus they write, "We are starting a women's restaurant, a place where women and their friends can get together and eat in a feminist atmosphere. We'll serve mainly good healthy food, much of it vegetarian. At least as important as the food is the atmosphere we hope to create. We want this to be a community center where there will be a range of entertainments and activities for the women of Boston. We want it to be a place where any women can feel comfortable, whether she comes on her own or with friends."[33] Thus, Hynes created a simple and nourishing menu. There were soups, breads, and salads, to which she gradually added more selections of soup. Eventually Hynes and her staff offered three entrees each night, two of which were vegetarian dishes and one of these was called the "Poor Women's Special."[34] Hynes and Gane wanted people in their community to be able to afford the meals. Bread and Roses was not alone in making this decision. Bloodroot had "Tightwad Tuesdays" and many of the restaurants had some lower-cost menu options. This choice spoke to the founders' intersectional awareness of gender and class.

Unlike their counterpart feminist restaurants, Hynes and Gane mention in the Bread and Roses business prospectus that they would be mindful of the needs of the women who wanted to lose weight. Feminist restaurants such as the Los Angeles Women's Saloon and feminist and lesbian publications during this period usually spoke of weight-loss programs with disdain, as they believed that diets were a way for the patriarchy to further shame women's bodies. The Women's Saloon avoided diet plates and diet sodas deeming them insulting to large-sized women.[35] Bloodroot had a sign above the counter that said, "Because all women are victims of Fat Oppression and out of respect for women of size, we would appreciate your refraining from agonizing aloud over the calorie count in our food."[36] However, Bread and Roses' initial incarnation was also trying to cater to its clientele by not making women feel judged for being interested in losing weight.

There were a handful of feminist restaurants whose owners marketed their businesses as higher class or gourmet, but these tended to be located in metropoles such as New York where there were already feminist and lesbian restaurants and cafes aimed at serving working-class lesbians and feminists.[37] Restaurants interested in being associated with elite labels were largely the exception. In the mid-1980s, La Papaya advertised itself as "New York's Newest Women's Restaurant" that served gourmet vegetarian food.[38] Calling the restaurant "gourmet" may have only been a marketing technique because playwright Sarah Schulman remembers it not as a fancy restaurant but rather as a lesbian hangout in a working-class, Irish and Latino neighbourhood without exorbitant prices.[39] The majority of feminist restaurants were operating as frugally as possible and promoting themselves as such. Tactics like Eunice Hundseth's creation of the soup restaurant Susan B's of Chicago in 1973, in which she chose to sell soup because it could be made simply and sold cheaply, were more prevalent. As chronicled by the *Chicago Magazine* in 1975, Hundseth served one meat soup and one vegetarian soup each day, later adding a salad and a dessert fruit cup.[40] Food was the medium through which feminist activism and community were enabled—making cheaper food improved the accessibility to feminism itself.

Even when the owners of feminist restaurants and cafes incorporated class consciousness into their business plans, they would often undermine their own principles while trying to enact them. On the one hand, women were embodying their feminist principles by making food and the space more readily available and accessible. Yet, on the other hand, they were compromising their feminist principles by underpaying themselves and relying on what sociologist Arlie Hochschild in 1979 would later call "emotional labor."[41] By keeping the restaurant in business through depending on inkind labour, they found themselves in a complicated situation. At the Common Womon Club in Northampton, all the employees were "super broke," at times making less than $70 a month.[42] One founder of the restaurant, Marjorie Parsons, said that she was paid in part by being able to fulfill her dream of creating a women's space, but when a woman was trying to operate a space where she was charging the least possible for her product, turning a profit was near impossible.[43] The owners of Bloodroot have repeatedly stated that they also did not make money in the endeavour.[44] These feminist principles of making the food financially accessible to the masses usually led to the restaurants' demise. Paying women to cook was an activist gesture in that it gave economic value to the typically female task of cooking. It gave monetary value by paying for a task traditionally unpaid in non-feminist spaces and kitchens, heightening the respect the task received within a capitalist framework, which awarded value with money. However, even when profits were distributed among the collective staff, most employees remained underpaid, forcing them, in turn, to live in poverty. Therefore, even though the goal was to undermine sexist traditions, this type of remuneration played directly into the same sexist, capitalist traditions it was seeking to undermine. This kind of contradictory economic dynamic was prevalent. Emotional gratification did not pay the bills. Furthermore, undercharging customers and underpaying staff made it difficult to maintain feminist ethics in the purchase of the raw food goods. Often what made the food feminist was what was behind the menu: the sourcing of the products.

Sourcing Products

The Brick Hut Café of Berkeley, California, offers an example of the difficulty of sourcing products in a feminist manner. The Brick Hut's staff served breakfast and lunch.[45] In 1977, when former beauty pageant winner and spokesperson for the Florida Citrus Commission Anita Bryant developed a media campaign against gay rights in Dade County, the Brick Hut collective discussed boycotting Florida orange juice. The one straight male in the group found this decision absurd, but the rest of the group was in favour. He asked what customers would think of a breakfast cafe that did not serve orange juice. The women replied that when their customers would ask, they would

the brick hut cafe

since 1975

we welcome the community to our magnificent new space, and look forward to serving you for the next 20 years !

5.3a and b This twentieth-anniversary menu of the Brick Hut Café of Berkeley, California, featured pretty standard breakfast fare along with a tofu scramble. Here the freshness of ingredients and the welcoming atmosphere of the cafe are emphasized. (Photo courtesy of Joan Antonuccio and Wendy Goodfriend)

pancakes . waffles . french toast

Pancakes and waffles are made with your choice of spiced, whole wheat batter or corn batter. French toast is made with your choice of bread, dipped in fresh eggs & cream. Blueberries, walnuts, cranberries or apples sauteed with cinnamon can be added to any of these dishes for $1.00 per item. Pure maple syrup available on request $1.00

PANCAKES - corn or spiced whole wheat:

full stack (3) 4.25
short stack (2) 3.75
just one 2.00

WAFFLE - corn or spiced whole wheat 3.75

FRENCH TOAST - whole wheat, sour batard, walnut raisin, or "Texas-style" (made with Challah bread):

full stack (3) 4.25
shortstack (2) 3.75
one slice 2.00

Of course we also have . . .

CEREALS

granola (served with milk or yogurt) 2.25
oatmeal (hot, with raisins, brown sugar, and milk) 2.75

specials and combinations

please, NO SUBSTITUTIONS

ALAN'S SPECIAL
two eggs, one pancake, homefries 5.50

CHEF'S SPECIAL
one egg, bacon, shortstack or waffle 5.95

HUEVOS CON CHILI
two eggs any style with chili, cheese, green chiles and sour cream on a flour tortilla 6.25

TOFU SAUTE
nigari tofu sauteed with sesame oil and a variety of fresh vegetables - served with homefries and toast 6.25

PESTO EGGS
we make our pesto with fresh basil, garlic, pure olive oil and aged parmesan cheese - served with homefries and toast 5.75

FARMER'S BREAKFAST
two eggs scrambled together with generous portions of homefries, onions, and cheddar cheese - served with toast 5.50

BAGEL PLATE
bagel of choice, cream cheese, tomato, red onion, cucumber 4.75
(with lox, add 2.25)

explain how they could not promote a product that capitalized on their oppression.[46] The man left the collective and the women placed a poster in the window announcing the boycott. This decision came at a cost when their windows were broken. Joan Antonuccio, one of the owners of the Brick Hut, said that while they expanded the menu offerings over time, the restaurant continued to serve mostly standard breakfast and lunch items. She wanted to "serve only organic, cruelty-free eggs because the chicken industry is a nightmare, but they were not available. Customers who raised chickens brought us some, but not enough; we used upwards of 3,000 eggs per week."[47] Otherwise, she noted, "We were in Berkeley; we served Berkeley food, which meant a lot of vegetarian options and we made everything from scratch."[48] Berkeley, as Antonuccio gestured towards, housed a large progressive and hippie community filled with vegetarians.[49] Antonuccio's story reflects the tension that these establishments faced between dreams and reality. Economic concerns and practical constraints, such as being unable to obtain local eggs, curtailed some of their ideals. When practical decisions limited owners' ability to enact all their goals, rhetoric and discourse around the food allowed the owners to continue to promote their feminist vision.

Feminist restaurants other than the Brick Hut also thought politically about the sourcing of their products. Selma Miriam and Noel Furie of Bloodroot Feminist Vegetarian Restaurant continuously tried to serve local and seasonal food. They wanted to buy products from local industries and would act in solidarity with growers and farms that were protesting labour conditions. As stated in their interviews, these choices were ways to show class and activist solidarity.[50] As reported in *The Lakeland Ledger Newspaper* in 1976, the Los Angeles Women's Saloon likewise supported California farm workers' protests against unfair wages and they boycotted lettuce and grapes.[51] The article emphasized how the restaurant served crab quiche and vegetarian meatloaf instead. Thinking about the source of the ingredients was not just about supporting local agriculture or acting in solidarity with boycotts. Rather, when Mary Bahneman, owner of Ruby's in Minneapolis, Minnesota, decided to use fresh rather than frozen potatoes, she was interested in making food taste good, which feminist restaurant owners saw as part of their politics.

Did feminist food taste differently? While the idea of what made food "good" was subjective, the idea that feminist restaurants needed to serve "good" food was both prevalent and political. Flavia Rando, who cooked for the Women's Coffeehouse in New York City, believed that "people deserve good food" and "it was a matter of dignity."[52] Rando, when designing the menu for the Women's Coffeehouse, took great pride in offering a delicious menu. She would source fresh ingredients at Hunts Point, the produce market for all New York City food retailers, and at the wholesale warehouses that supplied packaged goods to New York City retailers. She learned this skill set while working with the Lesbian Food Conspiracy, a project of the organization Radicalesbians, in prior years.[53] Additionally, she purchased cheese and bread at small traditional Italian stores and artisans. Preparing nourishing, affordable meals was part of an ethics of care that placed human needs above advancing a business agenda.

Selma Miriam and Noel Furie echoed the desire to serve "good" food, pushing against stereotypes that vegetarian food was bland.[54] Numerous cultures around the world have rich vegetarian traditions and tasty cuisines and Bloodroot drew upon these traditions. Bloodroot employed women from a wide range of cultural, racial, and ethnic backgrounds. In this space, the women in the kitchen had agency and

5.4 (OVERLEAF) *The Mother Courage of New York City menu contains meat, which sets it apart from many feminist restaurants of the 1970s and 1980s. Like the Common Women Club announcement and the Brick Hut Café menu, the freshness of ingredients is emphasized with the tag line "The freshest food available, simply and deliciously prepared." (Courtesy of Smith College Archives. Dolores Alexander Unprocessed Papers, Box 21 of 21)*

Mother Courage

...The freshest food available, simply and deliciously prepared.

Appetizers

- Feta Pie .... 2.—
Spinach, feta cheese, & dill in a flaky pastry.

- Homemade Soup 1.50
—See the blackboard for soup du jour.

Salads

... served with homemade bread

- Greek Salad 3.95
Crispy lettuce & fresh spinach, tomato wedges, sliced peppers, feta cheese & choice of Green Goddess or house dressing.

- Spinach Salad 3.95
Fresh spinach & raw mushrooms, garnished with crispy bacon & hard-boiled egg.

Entreés

... served with green salad

- Chicken Supreme 6.00
Whole boneless chicken breast stuffed with prosciutto & mozzarella, then simmered in Marsala wine.

- Chicken Curry 5.50
Chicken, mushrooms & onions in our creamy sauce. Please specify: mild, medium or hot. Served with chutney.

- Stuffed Sole Mornay 5.75
Fresh sole fillets stuffed with sauteed mushrooms, smothered in a creamy, rich sauce Mornay.

• Broiled Sole 5.25
Fresh filet of sole in garlic or plain butter.
Also poached, if you prefer.

• Shrimp Scampi ....
Our own style – shrimp smothered in garlic butter
with a dash of breadcrumbs, topped with mozzarella cheese.

• Eggplant Parmigiana 4.25
Served with spaghetti or spinach.

• Veal Marsala 5.50
Fresh veal cutlet simmered in Marsala wine.

• Veal Parmigiana 5.50
Fresh veal cutlet with sauce + mozzarella cheese.
Served with spaghetti or spinach.

• Broccoli Moutarde 4.50
Fresh broccoli, mushrooms + onions, smothered in our special
sauce + garnished with sesame seeds. Served on noodles.

• Spaghetti + Meatballs 4.10
For the traditionalists. Yummy!

• Spaghetti + Mushrooms 4.10
Fresh mushrooms sautéed in garlic butter. With
tomato (marinara) sauce or plain.

• Spaghetti + Garlic Butter 3.85
Simple, straightforward + strictly for garlic lovers.

Desserts

Chocolate Mousse Pie 1.25 Chef's Cheesecake 1.25
Apple Walnut Cake .... Butterscotch Pecan Pie 1.50

P.S. We can modify chicken, veal, fish or shrimp for dieters.
Please ask your waitress.

shared their own cultural food knowledge. As a result, Bloodroot had a menu with offerings as diverse as the women who have worked in the kitchen over the past four decades. Bloodroot's vegetarian fare has received high praise by restaurant reviewers for forty-five years for its satisfying flavours.[55] Another lauded feminist restaurant was Big Kitchen of San Diego, California, which *Bon Appétit* magazine named "one of the best places for breakfast in America."[56] While flavourful food was always a plus, customers came to feminist restaurants and cafes for more than the food, even at the award-winning Big Kitchen. A regular customer remarked that he usually ordered oatmeal for breakfast because he did not come for the food; he came to socialize.[57] Not every restaurant was as successful at making good food. Restaurant reviews from the 1970s recall that the food at Mother Courage was inconsistent, with *New York* magazine's writer Linda Wolfe in 1974 remarking that while Mother Courage's cooks did not "skimp on feta cheese … main dish offerings were chancy, though. Veal parmigiana ($3.75) [was] tender and well-flavored, but veal marsala ($3.90) was, on a recent visit, cloyingly sweet, while veal Garibaldi ($3.75) was too salty."[58] However, the desire to create good food that nourished bodies and feminist communities, remained important.

Marketing

Food as a raw material has its own discourse that includes the working conditions of the farmers, the distance it must travel, and the kinds of inputs into the soil. What cooks, chefs, and feminist restaurant owners decided to then do with those ingredients was also key to their feminism. Feminism, however, did not end at the plate. Sometimes it was not the type of food that was different but the name. The marketing of their products as feminist showed the owners' awareness of the importance of discourse. Mary Bahneman started Ruby's in the 1980s as a self-styled "breakfast joint." The restaurant had a simple menu of eggs, pancakes, toast, and other common breakfast foods.[59] Ruby's was, as described by the owner, a welcoming place for members of the lesbian and gay communities of the Twin Cities.[60] On Ruby's Facebook remembrance page, past customers echo this sentiment.[61] While the menu seemed typical for a breakfast or brunch spot, the main difference was that the omelets were all named after women.[62] At the Brick Hut Café there were also omelets named after women who inspired the owners: the Sister Marion omelet was named for a marathon-running nun; the Ruth Reid for an early twentieth century lesbian poet and activist; the Seven Sisters for the Berkeley feminist construction collective; and the Mendocino omelet for the herb blend that the owners ordered from a woman-owned business.[63] This technique of paying homage to women within the community or famous feminists was not exclusive to Ruby's and the Brick Hut Café. It was a common activist technique in women's spaces of the period, especially those that engaged with cultural feminism.[64] Naming products after women seems subtle but it was a way of bringing attention to women's contributions, which have long been hidden and undermined. It was a way of countering subtle but insidious sexism that continuously praised and recognized men's efforts and often erased important female figures in history.

Balancing Concerns

Feminist restaurants challenged the entire process of food production. While women were typically associated with the kitchen, they were not typically paid for this labour, which, as food scholar Barbara Haber writes, accounts for the typical perception of "feminists [who] disdained women's role in the kitchen, seeing it as a symbol of subjugation because of the persistent and repetitious demands made on women throughout history to fill the waiting maws of husbands and children."[65] With the unique structural design of feminist restaurants, women were paid for their labour and customers were reminded

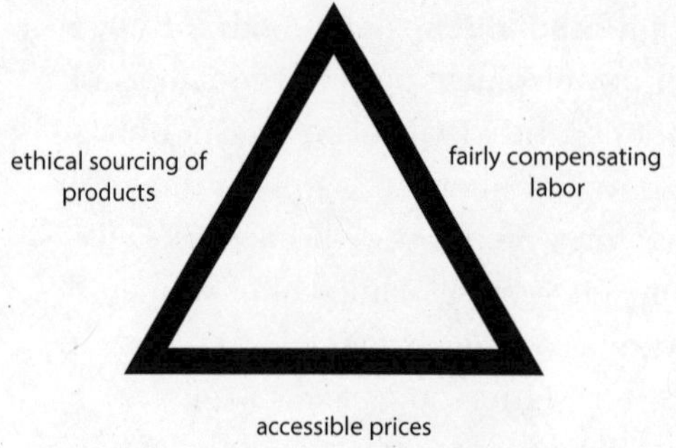

5.5 *The triangle of feminist food represents the challenge of balancing concerns surrounding sourcing products, fairly compensating labour, and offering accessible prices for customers.*

who was cooking their food. Feminist restaurant owners supported alternative farming practices, they bought raw products from their local communities, they often served vegetarian dishes, and they employed primarily women and thus paid women for a task that was, when confined to domestic spaces, unpaid. They changed the kinds of dishes served, what the items were called, the way the dishes made it to the table, and the way the space was cleaned. Similarly, as chapters 2 and 3 detailed, by disrupting labour practices in the serving of food, feminist restaurant owners discursively altered not only the meaning of the restaurant space to be feminist but also rendered the food feminist. Such tactics not only upended the problematic gendered hierarchy that existed in dominant restaurant culture but also were part of a strategy that saved money. Self-serve techniques lowered the need for hiring as much staff and could enable restaurants to sell their food at lower prices. Furthermore, they changed the way that customers interacted with the staff, challenging the typical restaurant hierarchy that promoted class differences and gendered and racialized differences as well.

Depending on the restaurant, decisions about how to make food feminist revolved around vegetarian ethics, labour issues, cost, and the sourcing of products. How could feminist restaurant owners and operators design their menus to reflect their values? As the above figure shows, balancing all these concerns was difficult. How could restaurants properly compensate farmers for ingredients, workers in the restaurant, and have a menu with prices accessible for their target clientele? This challenge extends beyond feminist restaurants into feminist businesses more broadly.

In addition, the reasons that explain why food was framed, viewed, or understood as feminist may seem disparate or jumbled. If "feminist food" meant a different thing in each place, did it really have a meaning? Such questions were discussed throughout the 1970s and 1980s, appearing in feminist and lesbian periodicals such as the 1978 "Food as a Feminist Issue" edition of *Amazon News* and *Ain't I a Woman*'s piece on food and feminism.[66] Even though the meanings of food symbols were as diverse as the feminisms of the restaurant owners themselves, it was still important that they called the food feminist because they wanted to show they had feminist intentions behind their cooking. Acknowledging the importance of this discourse was within the feminist framework that politicized the personal. Within these feminist communities then, living one's politics was intrinsically tied to creating the kind of world that these feminist restaurant owners wanted to see. Furthermore, the rhetoric about the food was grounded in feminist ideologies and the choices made in constructing the menu reflected these ideologies, whether they were about the sourcing of the products, the process of cooking, or the mode of consumption.

PART TWO

Feminist Coffeehouses/Temporary Space, 1970s and 1980s

CHAPTER 6

Creating Temporary Space

> The Women's Coffeehouse belongs to us and if it is to survive and thrive, we need to make this all women space a priority in our lives. Working and playing together in a safe space, we'll all get much more than our money's worth.[1]
>
> *Women's Coffeehouse of Iowa City Community Letter*

In the fall of 1981, the pledge committee of the Women's Coffeehouse of Iowa City released a letter to the regular users of the coffeehouse. In addition to announcing that the coffeehouse collective had found a new space for its operation, the committee used the letter as a chance to restate the goals of the coffeehouse, remind users of the history of the space, and speak to the future.[2] A group of nine women had founded the Iowa City Women's Coffeehouse collective in September 1979. In December, they began operating a women-only coffeehouse that continued for eighteen months. By the summer of 1981, few original collective members remained, and this group planned to re-launch the coffeehouse. In its 1981 letter, the pledge committee reminded readers of the coffeehouse's purpose and goals, stating, "First and foremost [we want] to provide a safe women-only space. All *women*, regardless of age, creed, sexual preference, political beliefs, race, etc. are welcome here. Our recognition and acceptance of our diversity and differences allows us as a community to share, learn, grow, and become stronger. We want this space available and accessible to all women, both physically and financially. The

Women's Coffeehouse is a space for almost any kind of event (except maybe roller-skating)."[3] The Iowa City Women's Coffeehouse held meetings, parties, potlucks, concerts, poetry readings, and brunches.[4] It was the sole women-only space in Iowa City, established after the closing of Grace and Rubies feminist restaurant in 1978. Unsurprisingly, the coffeehouse pledge committee's note ended by discussing money.

Coffeehouses retained greater financial flexibility than feminist restaurants and cafés; nonetheless material concerns dominated coffeehouse collective discussions. While the first configuration of the Iowa City Women's Coffeehouse (1979–1981) had relied solely on donations and voluntary membership dues to cover operating expenses, the pledge committee emphasized that the rent for the new, larger coffeehouse was $350, nearly double the cost of the past location and as a result, new funding sources were required.[5] Besides rent, operating costs included utilities, the phone bill, and all the sundry expenses. With the new space, the collective needed to obtain appliances such as a stove, sink, and refrigerator to accommodate cooking community breakfasts, soup dinners, and all the events listed in its newsletters and calendars.[6] To ensure the success of the new coffeehouse, the collective launched a massive pledge drive. Operating expenses were between $450 and $500 a month, so each woman was encouraged to donate $5 to $10 a month to cover costs.[7] However, the letter's writers acknowledged class differences between their members. They encouraged wealthier members to contribute more financially, while still emphasizing that pledges were not a requirement for attending events. Keeping the coffeehouse accessible was a priority for the collective. When the organizers realized that pledges would not cover all expenses, they decided to fundraise. These strategies included: soliciting donations from individuals and groups that used the coffeehouse; hosting special events; supplementing weekly breakfasts with regular soup dinners; requiring a percentage of the door sales from women who used the space for income-producing events; charging a nominal fee for the rental of kitchen facilities to cover utilities used; and installing a coin-operated pool table. The committee finished their note by reminding readers that "the Women's Coffeehouse belongs to the women who use and support it."[8] While the exact conditions of the Women's Coffeehouse of Iowa City were unique to their location, this letter indicates some of the primary concerns of American feminist coffeehouses and speaks to the themes of this chapter.

Feminist coffeehouses expanded the ability for women from a wider range of economic backgrounds to create feminist spaces without needing to make the same large capital investment required by feminist restaurants. In communities where a women's centre did not already exist and feminist coffeehouses were the first kind of feminist space in the area, coffeehouses typically took place in church basements, as churches charged little for use of the space, or in other low-cost spaces. This model of feminist organization expanded opportunities for women of different backgrounds to participate in managing an enterprise in some ways. Without high fixed costs, coffeehouses enabled women with less money, women from marginalized racial groups, and women with marginalized sexual orientations to create women's spaces centered on food, drink, and socializing. However, these spaces were not utopic; racism, ageism, trans-exclusionism, and classism created tensions within their respective communities. As coffeehouse organizers tried to address various inequalities, their approach in treating each identity category as discrete often erased women who experienced multiple forms of oppression simultaneously.

In chapters 6 and 7 of this book, I discuss recurring coffeehouses: feminist coffeehouses that happened more than once but could vary in whether they occurred daily, weekly, or monthly. These two coffeehouse chapters will discuss how feminist coffeehouses expanded participation and access to women's space. This chapter explains how coffeehouses operated, particularly how the organizers financed their endeavours, chose their spaces, and who participated. Large sections of this chapter pull from recordings of coffeehouse meetings. The Somerville Women's Coffeehouse in Massachusetts (1978–1980) met with consultant Betsy Zelchin to discuss how to establish a nonprofit structure and the organizers of A Woman's Coffeehouse in Minneapolis, Minnesota (1975–1989), recorded the open community meeting they held to discuss a series of difficulties that the coffeehouse faced. These recording are extremely useful because the meetings show a diversity of opinions and debates between attendees are highlighted. The Zelchin tapes detail the actual process for setting up the necessary legal and financial apparatus that enabled a coffeehouse to function, facts that were not available in other archival resources and were only hinted at by looking at business records. A Woman's Coffeehouse of Minneapolis's recorded meeting showcased the diverse opinions of more than fifteen participants from inside and outside of the organizing collective. The recordings reveal the variety of the struggles the coffeehouse faced and shape the thematic organization of this chapter. Apart from the responses to the questionnaires from A Woman's Coffeehouse of Minneapolis, it is rare to find such a rich resource that includes so many perspectives differing from those of an organizing committee.

This chapter draws on the works of spatial theory about temporary women's spaces and queer spaces. Gordon Brent Ingram, Anne Bouthillette, and Yolanda Retter in *Queers in Space* argue that queer space is not always a fixed location but can be temporary geographies, areas made queer by the temporary users and usages. For example, a public park becomes a queer space when gay men cruise at sunset. These temporary geographies are not bound by fixed boundaries but by temporalities. While the editors argue that certain spaces are more conducive to temporary queering if the location has fewer formal constraints (such as parks compared to private enterprises), queer individuals also transform the space. As a result, queering space is a multidirectional, give and take, relational process.[9] Geographer Julie Podmore applies this theoretical lens when discussing women's relationships and lesbian bonding. Podmore argues that when lesbian spaces have been peripheral and existed on the same plane as straight spaces, lesbians transformed spaces through performative actions such as silent exchanges and looks, creating a kind of layering of space, unnoticed by community outsiders.[10] Gay villages can be dominated by gay men who still retain their male privilege and greater access to capital and higher wages than their female and genderqueer and gender non-conforming counterparts. Within the feminist and lesbian-feminist communities, only the individuals with relatively more privilege within that group would be able to start feminist restaurants and cafes. Thus, while sociologist Ray Oldenburg shows how cafes, coffee shops, and other hangouts form the heart of a community,[11] key to the establishment of these places is that they are accessible. Fewer barriers to entry, such as low-cost food, drink, or tickets, make entrance and participation in the community more possible for a greater number of people. Lower labour inputs and operational costs, such as those at feminist coffeehouses, enabled this kind of heightened accessibility. However, feminist coffeehouses were not completely approachable or welcoming to all.

Coffeehouses began when organizers intended to create permanent feminist spaces such as a restaurant, cafe, bookstore, or women's centre, or to fill a gap after a permanent institution had closed. In 1974, the organizers of Michigan's Ann Arbor Coffeehouse proposed their coffeehouse as a means to provide a space where women could discuss opening a feminist business or a women's centre.[12] Similarly, three women began the Somerville Women's Coffeehouse in November 1980 to fill a gap not met by the Boston Women's Center.[13] The Iowa Coffeehouse opened after the feminist restaurant Grace and Rubies closed.[14] Candace Margulies of A Woman's Coffeehouse of Minneapolis explained, "I really wanted the coffeehouse to become a legitimate moneymaking business where a few people could make a living. I wanted to have a restaurant and to have a permanent venue and to not be so underground and to have some permanence."[15]

Coffeehouses were rarely imagined as the end goal but as transitional operations; in practice however, recurring coffeehouses would become community fixtures.

Feminist and lesbian organizers were not the only people to create coffeehouses. As demonstrated by a list in the countercultural publication *The Peoples' Yellow Pages of Massachusetts*, the Cambridge area had Nameless Coffeehouse (its actual name), which was "open to the community and had performers"; Off the Runway, a military coffeehouse; Rainbow Trout Teahouse, which specialized in music, poetry, and stories; The Sun, which had an arts and crafts centre in addition to music five nights a week; and Wit's End, which the publication described as "a new community coffeehouse."[16] Although the coffeehouse concept was not exclusive to feminists, feminist coffeehouses were unique because of their focus on the women's community.

Money Matters

Coffeehouses cost less to begin than feminist restaurants because they required fewer investments in infrastructure. Collectives financed coffeehouses by charging for events, gathering donations, and occasionally selling memberships. Coffeehouses required lower capital investment than feminist restaurants, yet money still mattered.

Coffeehouse collectives began fundraising efforts before opening. The Ann Arbor Women's Coffeehouse collective sold posters, t-shirts, and pottery at the local art fair.[17] As documented by its meeting minutes, the Somerville Women's Coffeehouse collective researched the potential to obtain start-up capital from the Haymarket Foundation and the Artists Foundation of Boston. In addition to applying for grant money, the Somerville collective once held a raffle for two tickets to lesbian musician Holly Near's concert, which local women's music production company Allegra donated. The collective sold raffle tickets at $0.75 each, raising approximately $150, which it deposited in its account at the Feminist Credit Union. The collective members considered holding their own benefit concert with local women artists performing. Despite compiling a list of possible venues, performers, and technicians, the collective decided to not hold the concert until after it was more established.[18] Instead, it considered other fundraising opportunities such as holding additional raffles, seeking out loans, organizing flea markets, hosting a women's dinner and evening event, finding benefactors, and selling memberships or shares.[19] The members also discussed approaching women they knew for possible donations of supplies and equipment instead of money. Similar financing efforts allowed groups like the Iowa City Women's Coffeehouse to eventually begin. In a letter reminding attendees of its simple beginnings, the Women's Coffeehouse collective recounted that the women built the coffeehouse by "begging or borrowing chairs, tables, and coffee cups."[20] Acquiring second-hand furniture reduced operating costs.

Such fundraising efforts did not end after coffeehouses commenced operations. After the Iowa City Women's Coffeehouse moved into a larger space, the collective could not pay the new rent with its former fundraising methods, so it established a fundraising committee. In August 1981, the committee released a report suggesting fundraising activities such as pledges and subsequent monthly periodic contributions; garage sales and yard parties; dances (one member volunteered to coordinate six to eight dances a year); and another member volunteered to organize a dinner open to the community.[21] These continuous fundraising events typically supported the mission statements of the coffeehouses by creating programming for women, lesbians, or feminists in their communities. Constantly asking for money could become a grating task, but when fundraising efforts were incorporated into events integral to the coffeehouse's mission, the effect was less jarring.

Common fundraising techniques included selling memberships, requesting a commitment of a monthly donation, and asking for door

A WOMAN'S COFFEEHOUSE

member pass number 26 Penny Costello

12-15-83

signature date

see terms on back

A WOMAN'S COFFEEHOUSE

member pass number 27 Lisa Johnson

12-15-83

signature date

see terms on back

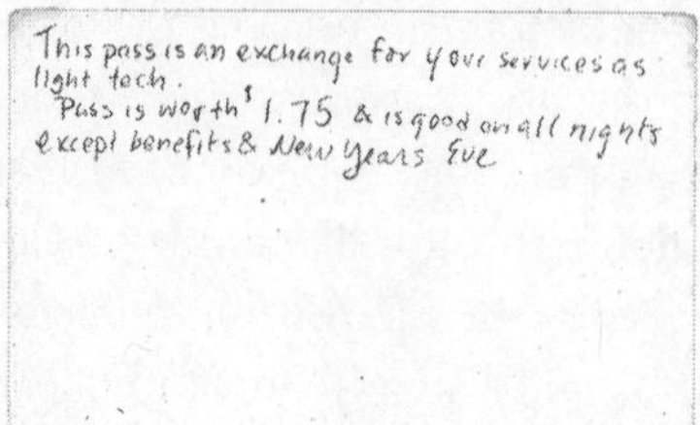
This pass is an exchange for your services as light tech.
Pass is worth $1.75 & is good on all nights except benefits & New Years Eve

This pass is an exchange for your services as light tech
Pass is worth $1.75 & is good on all nights except benefits & New Years Eve

6.1a and b These membership cards for A Women's Coffeehouse of Minneapolis state that they were given to Lisa Johnson and Penny Costello in exchange for their service as light technicians. The passes were stated as being worth $1.75 and covered entrance to the coffeehouse for every event besides the New Year's Eve event. While most coffeehouse members paid the membership fee, these passes also served to compensate women who volunteered their time to coffeehouse. (Courtesy of the Jean-Nickolaus Tretter Collection in GLBT Studies, University of Minnesota Libraries. A Woman's Coffeehouse Collective Records, 1976–1985)

donations. When the Iowa City Women's Coffeehouse collective circulated a questionnaire asking how much women were willing to contribute to the coffeehouse financially, the average member felt comfortable donating about $5 a month (responses ranging from $2 to $10).[22] If money was a barrier, there were other ways to contribute. For example, one Iowa City coffeehouse member did not have money to donate, so she donated her handywoman labour (indicated as such when she returned the donation slip).[23] Other coffeehouses, such as Massachusetts's Somerville Women's Coffeehouse, released a yearly membership donation request. The first year the collective requested $1. In their second year, it raised the request to $2 so that the collective could give the other half of the raised money to the performers at their events.[24] The remaining money covered the cost of food and publicity.

Generally, the feminist coffeehouse collectives were aware of class issues. Most coffeehouses had sliding scales for participation and did their best to keep costs low. When the Iowa City Women's Coffeehouse discussed selling memberships as a fundraising technique during a collective meeting, the members worried that memberships would promote classist attitudes. The collective eventually settled on implementing memberships but made clear that it did not want the coffeehouse to be exclusive, and any woman could attend events whether or not they were a member.[25] A Woman's Coffeehouse of Minneapolis also discussed the possibility of memberships at its open community meeting. As one participant explained, a membership did not mean that "you would have to be a member to come to the club but it would mean [the collective] would have sense of budget" in advance of the year.[26] Members could receive decreased ticket prices. Memberships would also encourage repeat attendance.[27] Instead of implementing such policies for their New Year's Eve Party in 1985, A Woman's Coffeehouse collective introduced a sliding fee scale, with cheaper entrance fees following the evening's performance.[28] Women could also volunteer their time as work in exchange for attending the event for free. Lesbians did not run every feminist coffeehouse but were actively engaged in most. As a group, lesbians in the 1970s and 1980s had few financial resources and it was common to allow pay-what-you-can or to work in trade.[29] As women, they already were paid less and they likewise would face discrimination based on their sexual orientation. Additionally, the returned questionnaires from A Woman's Coffeehouse of Minneapolis indicated many of the participants had children, sometimes making the $1 to $2 per event cost of entertainment a burden. Coffeehouse collectives also demonstrated some understanding of how class intersected with other identity factors like being a lesbian and/or a woman of colour, as will be discussed later in this chapter.

Feminist coffeehouse collective meeting minutes, whether from Iowa or Minneapolis, showed that these collectives constantly discussed financial matters. As noted in the Iowa City Women's Coffeehouse collective meeting minutes from the fall of 1980, the members were interested in re-evaluating their goals, but their main task was "to keep the joint open, to keep responsible to the community, to keep it clean, to do the long-range planning."[30] Throughout meeting minutes, their discussions focused on finances, plans for upcoming shows, changing locations, and how to train volunteers. Likewise, A Woman's Coffeehouse of Minneapolis collective's meeting minutes reflected a similar focus on money and event planning. The December 1984 meeting notes showed that even when a meeting was supposed to centre on preparations for a specific event (in this case its New Year's Eve Party) and on hiring a new collective member, money issues dominated discussions.[31]

While coffeehouse collectives prioritized fundraising, these coffeehouses were not moneymaking schemes. To demonstrate how little coffeehouse events made, Karen Voltz, the organizer of the 1978 Kitty Barber and Mary Pelc concert at Sister Moon in Milwaukee, Wisconsin, published the budget and profits from the show in *Amazon: A Midwest Journal for Women*. Voltz collected $130 in tickets and $110 went to pay the performers. With the remaining $20, $11.25 paid for rental of the sound equipment. Ultimately, Voltz showed a profit of $8.75, noting that the profit was "obviously not the reason I do things."[32]

Financial inexperience and personal insecurities surrounding money made fundraising awkward. One participant at the open community meeting for A Woman's Coffeehouse of Minneapolis raised an important point: perhaps the women running these coffeehouses were afraid of the idea of "big money." At the meeting she continued,

"Lots of people [came to the meeting] with money in their pocket even if they don't have any. And it is really scary to think about big bucks but big bucks [are] out there and we as women are trained to be terrified of big bucks and I think we need to understand that we have it together to do big moves if we want to. If we believe it, we can do it. I know we can do it."[33] While the collective proudly announced that it had just raised $1,700 and was going to be passing around a basket for more donations, this participant wanted to emphasize that as women they had been socialized to be afraid of finances. Undercharging and underestimating the collective's potential hurt everyone involved.

Even with lower overhead costs, money was the cause of constant stress for coffeehouses. After ten years in operation, A Woman's Coffeehouse of Minneapolis could not pay its quarterly $300 donation to the church that provided its space. Although a fundraising campaign yielded positive results, in the recorded open community meeting one member of the coffeehouse stated that "the coffeehouse is losing money and that's the problem."[34] She continued, "the reason why the coffeehouse is losing money is people don't come and for me that's a sign of dissatisfaction and that's why we have this meeting. I don't think we wouldn't do this if we didn't want the coffeehouse to be here."[35] Women wanted the coffeehouse because they recognized the importance of having the space, but there was constant turmoil amongst users and this lowered attendance. The following section will show how issues of money, space, and attendance were constantly interlinked.

Space

Where did coffeehouses exist? Unlike feminist restaurants and cafes that required a large enough population to support the business, feminist coffeehouses could rely on smaller populations. As evidenced by the map in the appendix, coffeehouses existed in both large cities (such as Astra Plane Feminist Coffeehouse of Philadelphia) and small towns, especially those with universities (such as the Women's Coffeehouse of Ithaca, New York).[36] Whether in a small town or large city, coffeehouses typically existed in temporary spaces and oftentimes happened in already established feminist and women's spaces like women's centres or feminist bookstores. In communities where a women's centre did not already exist and feminist coffeehouses were the first kind of feminist space in the area, coffeehouses typically took place in church basements. A Cup of Warmth Coffeehouse in the small rural town of Mankato, Minnesota, took place in a bakery after hours. This location was feasible when events drew crowds of fifteen to twenty women and organizers could use the space for free, besides the cost of the bakery's cookies.[37] A Woman's Coffeehouse of Minneapolis, which regularly drew crowds of 125 to 150 women and as many as 500 people with special events such as their New Year's Eve Party, needed larger spaces for little money.[38] Choices about space greatly affected discussions over finances and attendance.

Churches charged little for the use of space but being in a church was not always ideal. A Woman's Coffeehouse of Minneapolis donated $100 a month to use Plymouth Church's basement. When the collective wanted to use the room with better acoustics it cost an additional $65 to rent per night. While the church provided an inexpensive venue, woman after woman explained at the open community meeting how they wished the coffeehouse happened in another location.[39] The dance floor was too crowded and women complained about there not being enough space to talk. However, if the coffeehouse moved to a larger space, the collective would be in an even more difficult financial situation than the one that provoked having the meeting in the first place. One collective member responded to the suggestion of leaving by saying, "we'd love to get out of the church ... [but] the overhead would be a lot higher."[40] As the collective members explained, it cost a minimum of $200 to operate each night to cover rental space, equipment, toilet paper, and coffee.[41] It would have been nearly impossible to find a cheaper venue than a church basement. Operating out of the Minneapolis Lesbian Resource Center would not have been possible due to fire codes, which was why the coffeehouse ended up in the church in the first place.[42] The support of the church's minister, Elaine Marsh, a mostly closeted lesbian at the time, and her partner Alice, was another reason.[43] At the open community meeting, one participant suggested that the collective move the coffeehouse events to a local bar. Most coffeehouse members were opposed, as doing so would have undermined the coffeehouse's goal of creating a chemical-free space. The coffeehouse never left Plymouth Church and in November 1985 the collective sent a letter to the church saying that lack of funds meant it could not pay its quarterly donation of $300.[44] Changing spaces was also risky. When the Iowa City Women's Coffeehouse collective moved to a larger space, its doubled rent meant that the coffeehouse was under greater financial pressure and made more vulnerable. While a new space had the potential to draw new participants and motivate past coffeehouse members to return, the higher rent outweighed the benefits.

Where a coffeehouse was located impacted who attended. Churches carried specific connotations and even though feminist coffeehouses were using church basements outside of the context of Christianity, being associated with a church created a barrier to some women participating.[45] Holding coffeehouses in already established feminist spaces had drawbacks as well. In 1979, a group of women in the Boston area was interested in starting a coffeehouse with the goal of eventually becoming a feminist restaurant or cafe. The group invited feminist entrepreneurs who were knowledgeable about the law and financial matters to speak to them. One of its guest speakers was Betsy Zelchin, who explained the necessary steps for establishing a nonprofit organization. When Zelchin spoke to the group about holding its events in the Boston Women's Center, the group vehemently opposed the suggestion. The group, which would eventually start the Somerville Women's Coffeehouse, did not want to use the Boston Women's Center as that centre already had an established identity. The group wanted to create a new kind of space, "where women who might not have found the women's center welcoming might find a place to go."[46] In its meeting minutes it had noted, "ideally we would like to be located in Central Square but … we have discussed the importance of being in a safe and easily accessible location. We have a lot of women realtors to contact."[47] The Somerville Coffeehouse collective understood that location impacted clientele.

As the coffeehouses were not typically housed in fixed spaces with regular operating hours, people not already involved in the feminist community were less likely to know about them. By not attracting much notice, most coffeehouses were able to avoid conflict with antagonistic individuals, yet this concealment meant that the coffeehouses could be more difficult for interested women to locate. At its meeting on July 10, 1980, the Iowa City Women's Coffeehouse collective discussed "How do we wanna be listed at the WRAC (Women's Resource and Action Center at the University of Iowa) and bookstore? How much do we protect the address?"[48] The collective decided to tell campus information that it was not interested in being listed. The balance between making the space accessible to women of its community and protecting themselves from hostile individuals was a difficult one to strike. The coffeehouse collective ultimately did not directly advertise the space. However, once a woman knew of the space she could access it at any time because the collective hid a key on the back of the soda machine.[49] The Iowa City Women's Coffeehouse collective was especially paranoid, as it had already had an issue with one neighbour. The collective posted the sign "Attention women: Chuck, the boy who owns the house across the street, now claims he owns the whole parking lot and will call the cops if any of us park in it."[50] Striking a balance between the perception of safety and inclusivity could be difficult. Issues of safety stretched beyond relationships with neighbours to financial and legal security, as well as relationships with the government.

Legal Status—Nonprofit

The law affected feminist coffeehouses; collectives had to deal with city ordinances, fire codes, and taxation issues. Legal status affected what kinds of spaces the coffeehouses could use. At the meeting on July 10, 1980, when the Iowa City Women's Coffeehouse collective was discussing the possible expansion of the coffeehouse, the meeting minutes only recorded first names. One woman named Christie wanted the organization to take out a loan and buy a house. However, she was unanimously shouted down due to the financial risk this choice would impose. Tess, another collective member, then suggested that the coffeehouse be in people's own homes. Similarly, she was unanimously shouted down, although as the meeting minutes noted, "with slightly less energy" since the collective had used most of their energy on "shouting down Christie."[51] No space to hold the coffeehouse was completely neutral, but people's personal homes were especially charged locations and would impede attracting new membership. Once the collective established that it would continue to rent space, it needed to re-establish its legal status. Another meeting participant, Vicki, noted, "FINE, we're a club and that's legitimate. Problems would come if we a) advertised which we don't, and/or b) if we made money, which we also don't. Important to emphasize that we are organization that provides space and not a [business]."[52] Similar to the discussion around tax statuses for feminist restaurants discussed in chapter 3, the legal requirements to become a women-only space meant coffeehouses had to organize themselves as clubs. Clubs could not be for-profit and had to have nonprofit status. Part of being a nonprofit meant that the coffeehouse had restrictions on how it advertised. The collective reminded its community of that fact when it sent out its "Guidelines for Using the Coffeehouse" letter.[53]

In fact, the nonprofit model was popular amongst feminist coffeehouses and employed by every case study in this book.[54]

When Betsy Zelchin proffered advice to the future collective of the Somerville Women's Coffeehouse in 1979, she proposed different fundraising schemes, explained how to arrange capital, discussed how to work with the city for permits, and told the collective about how to establish corporate status and apply for nonprofit status. Zelchin, as Marjorie Parsons had told the same collective earlier, explained that there were various legal statuses the collective could obtain. She explained that the group either had to organize as a nonprofit or a for-profit organization.[55] Nonprofit organizations could pay employees but the group could not just be a vehicle for people to be paid; a nonprofit organization's primary purpose needed to be helping community and people could only be paid if their labour supported the nonprofit's work. Nonprofit statuses were available throughout the United States during the 1970s and 1980s and although the procedures of obtaining the status differed slightly, being a nonprofit corporation generally provided the same benefits.[56] In Massachusetts in 1979, incorporating as a nonprofit organization cost less than $35. Zelchin suggested the bylaws include language like, "Seven people need to be there to make decisions about money, etc. In a nonprofit corporation someone has to be contact person, etc."[57] Once the collective organized as nonprofit in Massachusetts it could file under federal tax laws as a 501(c)(3) organization and then people could make contributions to the collective. The contributions were tax deductible and the collective's money would not be taxed either. Zelchin highly endorsed the incorporated nonprofit model.

Nonprofit status restricted aspects of what feminist coffeehouses could do, especially concerning political lobbying and fundraising. The collective members wanted to make their space available for politically active groups and asked Zelchin if sharing their space would be considered political lobbying.[58] Zelchin emphasized the flexibility of nonprofit status came from how the group framed its activism. The coffeehouse could allow lobbying groups into the space, but the collective could not lobby under their own name. The collective could host events and shows and collect money for them. Zelchin further responded that if the collective made their bylaws specific that they were a community service organization that served a valid function, they would be fine. In this case, "bringing in local artists could be phrased in more community terms or educational terms."[59] The same was true if the collective charged money for lectures. By writing the bylaws in a particular way, the collective could be classified as a women-only club, which provided a space where women in the Boston area could learn about music. Nonprofit organizations could charge membership dues if they stipulated where the money went in their budget. Zelchin warned that the main difference between the federal 501(c)(3) forms and the state ones was that the federal forms asked for more detail.[60] Careful planning and framing of its bylaws would enable the women to create the kind of coffeehouse that they wanted and still be in line with state and federal laws.

Feminist coffeehouse collectives experienced tensions as they worked to embody their politics while simultaneously trying to do political and social work and navigate the law. In the 1970 article "Lest We Begin to Oink" from the feminist periodical *Ain't I a Woman*, the anonymous author reminded feminist organizations that

> As we grow in size—as our movement becomes older—our vision of what we want expands and the projects we commit ourselves to increase. There is so much we must do that we find ourselves looking for efficient and reliable ways to get it all done. It is not surprising that the things we choose as efficient ways of working too often reflect the bureaucratic individual business—like pigshit we have been brought up in or the male-dominated counter left some of us are refugees from. To learn to work collectively we may have to sacrifice much efficiency and that is a difficult thing to sacrifice when

> we frantically want to struggle to win. Nonetheless we must struggle in ways that enrich and spur growth in our movement, not ways that bureaucratize and stagnate us. We should be concerned about appearing as a group against the system, not a group that looks like part of it. We cannot afford to not question such actions as incorporating, applying for mailing permits that require a subscription list be supplied to the government, or hiring full-time staff people.[61]

The ways that collectives tried to embody their politics could be fraught with tension. This anonymous author wanted collectives to ask themselves if they were bolstering the patriarchal capitalist system that they purported to exist in opposition towards. Following laws, incorporating, and applying for nonprofit status, granted the coffeehouses legal protection. However, the legal protection came from a state that created sexist legislation and was integral to maintaining capitalism. Likewise, not only did collectives need to question their relationship to the state, they also needed to question how they organized themselves. As the author continued,

> For example, hiring full-time staff puts certain women in a position to know more about what's going on in the group than other women—no matter how hard the staff tries to avoid this. The staff can afford to be at the office all the time because they are paid while the other women who may be equally committed have to work full-time at jobs they hate or who have children to take care of. Staff people are generally hired at least partially for their ability to run an office or make public contacts—an ability many women don't have because they have not had the privilege to develop that ability. The staff may be willing to teach others, but those others will not be paid to learn and can often not afford the time if they have to work to earn.[62]

In her group, the women all lived collectively and pooled resources and money. She acknowledged that this solution might not be possible for everyone. Women who were married to men and/or who worked other jobs could not take advantage of the privilege of living collectively with other women dedicated to women's liberation. Mixed communes could rarely be expected to prioritize their finances or time to women's liberation work.[63] However, she suggested that there were some things that could be tried: jobs could be split into shifts done collectively so several women with little time could participate; and resources could be pooled so women who badly needed the money they received from employers they hated could work instead on women's liberation activities. After listing these options, she reminded readers "THESE ARE NOT SOLUTIONS TO THE PROBLEM—REVOLUTION IS."[64] She finished her article by stating, "We must avoid bringing about a revolution like corporate business-*men* (which could probably not be done anyway)."[65] This letter challenged collectives to question their relationship with the government and the relationship between members.

Who Ran Coffeehouses?

The typical feminist coffeehouse management arrangement was a collective of women, primarily lesbians, who ran the space as volunteers or for small stipends. A Woman's Coffeehouse of Minneapolis paid its collective from 1975 to 1985. When the collective members were seeking to add a new collective member, they wrote on the job application, "we are a collective of six lesbians who work together to produce A Woman's Coffeehouse, and we are looking for a lesbian to join us. This is not a salaried position, but collective members receive a stipend."[66] At a later community meeting, they explained how much pay each member received: $10 a week except Candace Margulies, the main manager, who made $100 a month. Relative to the time and energy required to organize the coffeehouse, this pay was low.

At the Full Moon Coffeehouse of San Francisco, California, the main collective, which called itself the "small collective," received small stipends and the larger collective worked for free.[67] Most coffeehouses did not pay the people who worked there; this influenced the makeup of the management as only women with enough financial flexibility could afford to not be paid.

The fiscal constraints of coffeehouses impacted efforts to diversify leadership. On the job application looking for a lesbian to join the organizing collective of A Woman's Coffeehouse of Minneapolis, the form stated, "We want to open the collective to women of varied cultures, backgrounds and abilities. IF you are interested and can meet the following requirements, we encourage you to apply."[68] Applicants had to live chemically free or be supportive of chemically free space, be able to make a one-year commitment, be able to work at least one night on most weekends, and be able to attend collective meetings every other Sunday afternoon.[69] Although the application stated that they were looking for diversity, the collective still wanted members to embody the coffeehouse's mission statement of creating a lesbian, chemical-free space. Furthermore, even if the collective said that it sought out diversity, as was pointed out at the open coffeehouse community meeting, the kinds of parameters for the applications meant that only certain kinds of women would be able to devote the required time, thus limiting class diversity. Also, as some participants in the meeting mentioned, racial diversity would likewise be limited because lesbian women of colour in Minneapolis in 1983 as a group typically had lower incomes.[70] To deal with these issues and to mitigate some of the difficulties of running a coffeehouse, organizers sought other work arrangements.

Managing coffeehouses was time and energy consuming, as evidenced by multiple collectives writing letters about issues of burnout. For example, in June 1982, the collective of the Iowa City Women's Coffeehouse sent a letter to the users of the space stating, "This is serious. You have been generous in your contributions and the

Women's Coffeehouse has managed to survive financially, but we are all suffering from a crisis—of energy. All but one of the women on the coffeehouse collective have served for over a year. Several have served for over two years. Some of the members are leaving the collective soon. We have lots of ideas for improvement, new programs, a better facility, but our energy is bottoming out."[71] The collective desperately needed more help in addition to financial contributions. Coffeehouses depended on a few people to make the coffeehouses continually happen. When one collective member quit, the rest of the collective would face greater burdens.

When the managing collectives sought out additional help in organizing the events, responses were mixed. At the Minneapolis A Woman's Coffeehouse open community meeting, the managers asked the women in attendance to join a set of committees: there was the survey committee; the committee of handywomen (to make physical improvements, place lights for artwork, and affix ceiling fans); the stereo committee (to buy a second turntable, update sound equipment to play the songs back to back, and to establish expertise on sound equipment); the taskforce on race issues; the music committee (tasked with buying records and continually assessing how to adapt the music for the majority's preferences); the advisory board for women who wanted to take on some smaller tasks; the mailing committee (to meet once every two months to send out the calendar); and the lights and sound committee (especially for special events). The core collective of managing members intended to retain their positions but they wanted to delegate tasks. They believed that in addition to personally needing to spread out the work, coffeehouse members who joined committees would then feel more invested in making the space better. Janice, a participant at the meeting, stated she liked "the idea of committees. People have joined the collective that have poured their life into it [with a] high level of dedication desired. Committees will allow more diversity—so more diverse types of people [could] join the collective without giving as much time."[72]

At the meeting, other participants expressed support for the idea of committees and also suggested the creation of additional committees, such as a greeting committee to deal with the fact that new women would come to the coffeehouse and sometimes feel isolated.[73] While respondents re-established that they thought the coffeehouse was important in their lives, few women were interested in or able to provide the kinds of support that the coffeehouse needed, and the responsibility to manage the coffeehouse continued to fall on a few members in the organizing collective. The collectives that organized coffeehouses faced immense pressures and committees were one way of mitigating that pressure.

Being in a feminist coffeehouse collective could feel overwhelming. At the end of the open meeting for A Woman's Coffeehouse a former collective member reacted to all the complaining that happened during the meeting and stated,

> I am not a collective member anymore but I am more willing to listen to suggestions from the people who come here all the time rather than the people who never come because they are too angry at the place or think they are too good for the place and I don't feel any love for the coffeehouse in this room and I am really hurt by that. I wanted to come here because I wanted to hear people say, "I want to participate" and "I want to pitch in" not "you did this wrong. You did this wrong. You did this wrong." Maybe I have this wrong, but I didn't think we would just complain. We can't even afford to spend more money. We can't even afford what we are doing and it is cheap.[74]

Another member of the audience remarked, "I don't think you could pay me enough to be in this collective—everyone wants a lot of different things ... We need to take responsibility." She continued by suggesting that "maybe [we can try having] different nights specializing on different things [or] one way to deal with it that is to not expect things to be always our own way. We won't all come together."[75] There was no way to be a perfect feminist, but those who actually participated in the coffeehouse's collective faced particular criticism. Another woman responded to this tension:

> I want to address something Amy said. It seems like things tend to be really polarized tonight—but the idea of losing the coffeehouse scares me … I wonder if this tendency towards hostility and to hit against each other is because it is really scary for us and I think something about this meeting was that the agenda didn't fit what I came for and that's okay but what my responsibility is towards the collective and I see that built in terms of the committees and I came here with money in my pocket and I love this place a whole lot and not everything is on the collective and I feel okay with the collective asking for suggestions, but there has been a tendency for people to choose this time for people to say what they don't like about the collective and I've been thinking this for the last half hour that these people are going to go away feeling really shitty you know, and so I just want to say that—that I am really glad this place is here and I wish there was a meeting with space in the agenda to talk about what we can do to help the committee.[76]

She wanted to thank the committee members for their work and believed that the criticism of their work originated from their fear about losing the space that had been so important to the feminist and lesbian community of the Twin Cities. Spreading work amongst committees could provide the necessary time and energy to keeping it going. Another participant remarked, "I'd [also] like to respond to what Amy said … and I'd like to validate what you said … We haven't had committees. We haven't had enough people invested—we've had a small nucleus and unfortunately we have workshops and we process but we don't honor our own, but I think we need to honor those people right here."[77] This led to a chorus of other women chanting, "I think she's right!" and "You go!"[78] The women at the meeting then gave a round of applause to the collective members. Regardless of this cheer at the end of the open community meeting, having listened to tapes, which recorded the two-hour meeting, this rally of positivity was short lived. The collective members were critiqued for over two hours with only a two-minute break when the above statements occurred.

This constant criticism that coffeehouse collectives faced also likely led to burnout. After the community meeting for A Woman's Coffeehouse of Minneapolis, the collective closed the meeting by stating that due to the responses, it would hold a future community meeting about how

> the community can get involved and I think we personally should take that away and I think that's what the next meeting should be about—the thing about the committees is not to create more unwieldy things but to get things done. And some of you threw out suggestions for other committees that I think are good—but the committees are to address things we identified in the collective that we don't get done because we can't take on any more work and those are some things we identified are important. We don't know what the structures of the committees will be. We just haven't addressed them because our meetings are too long and we are too tired and too burnt out or it's something that we need more input on. So, we would like your input.[79]

Collectives had to be realistic about what they could take on and sought help elsewhere. The methods for soliciting help could lead to other criticisms.

Disagreements over the proper division of work, music, performances, and substance use plagued coffeehouse collectives. As evidenced in the public letter distributed to the Full Moon Coffeehouse community in 1975, ten women, half of the volunteer staff, and one of the owners of the Full Moon Women's Coffeehouse/Bookstore in San Francisco, decided they could no longer be a part of the existing structure.[80] They stated that

> We, as women, acknowledge our lack of experience in handling and confronting issues of power with other women. We also admit to our lack of experience in creating alternative structures in which we could deal with those issues. We recognize our perceptions of this particular struggle may reflect some of our feelings of hurt and anger. Yet, we have attempted to state clearly the issues involved. We hope this statement will raise vital questions for women to consider and will clear up misrepresentations and rumors that have been spreading in our community.[81]

Trying to create alternative work structures required experimentation and could lead to problems. Even before opening in early 1974, the five women of the smaller collective that ran the Full Moon Coffeehouse appealed for volunteers to run the coffeehouse and its affiliated bookstore by agreeing to work shifts. They gave the following reasons to justify volunteerism, reasons which seemed sufficient and for a time remained unquestioned: that women could get satisfaction from this kind of involvement; that women would thus be donating energy to the women's community; that when profits were made there would be profit-sharing; that as time went on and volunteers proved reliable, there would be greater sharing of all responsibilities; and that this would take place by opening up and enlarging the small collective.[82] The volunteer groups came to be known as "the large collective." As the public letter stated, the owners were for the most part unwilling or unable to devote their full-time energies to the coffeehouse and bookstore and needed the work of volunteers for the

Full Moon to function. The rest of the letter then describes in detail how the owners were exploiting the volunteers by not paying wages, not sharing responsibilities, and just giving the volunteers drudgework. In addition to not paying attention to the needs of the workers, the food and sound quality of the coffeehouse had declined, and four members of the small collective were unresponsive to requests for changes. As a result, ten women left. The disagreements that happened illustrate tensions in trying to embody politics and issues over wages. When groups within a collective were paid and others were not, resentment built.

Not all disagreements were quite as dramatic as what occurred at Full Moon Coffeehouse, but typical of collectives, interpersonal relationship issues led to conflict. As evident in the minutes of the Iowa City Women's Coffeehouse collective meeting, the group bickered. Teasing and small disagreements over matters like whether to go to dinner and how to make signs were relatively minor.[83] However, some comments in meeting notes hinted at interpersonal conflict and love triangles that could lead to a collective's demise.[84] Group dynamics could be more difficult to manage when love, friendship, and sexuality would clash during a business meeting. Unlike the Full Moon letter of resignation, the women who wanted a break from the Iowa City Coffeehouse repeated that they wanted to leave due to fatigue. In all these cases, the women participating dedicated a great deal of their time and energy towards these coffeehouses, which could also be trying.

Coffeehouse collectives were not all bad experiences. In 1974, journalist Molly Reno described the process behind the creation of the Ann Arbor, Michigan, coffeehouse. In her article "Women's Coffeehouse," Reno described a group of approximately fifteen women who were meeting on Wednesday evenings to plan this type of coffeehouse, which they hoped would be open by September. As Reno noted, the "unique aspect of their planning process is that the needed organizing skills, such as publicity, writing proposals and fund raising, are taught to everyone as an integral part of the planning process. In this way the result of the group's energy will produce more experienced, skillful women organizers as well as a woman's coffeehouse."[85] Likewise, in these early stages, the coffeehouse collective functioned as a consciousness-raising group where the women would also discuss other common problems experienced by many women in the Ann Arbor area such as childcare, health education, the lack of emergency housing, and the need for a women's school to share skills. The group saw the meetings not as a step to forming a change-creating establishment but rather saw the process as political itself. Reno described the women as "optimistic that the coffeehouse will generate additional energy to meet more of the needs experienced by women in this area. Perhaps, a women's community center will be the eventual form in which these needs are met."[86] Thus, the coffeehouse and the collective was not an end in itself. The collective continued to invite others to join these meetings at the Michigan Union, the student union building of the University of Michigan. However, this piece was also written when the coffeehouse collective was in its initial stages and full of optimism and yet to be burdened by financial woes.

Coffeehouse collectives typically were comprised of dedicated groups of women who took their duties extremely seriously. Being part of these collectives meant facing criticism, hard work, and little or no pay, but occasional appreciation. On December 12, 1981, the Iowa City Women's Coffeehouse collective received a letter stating "many of us in the community wanted a C.H. [coffeehouse]. Quite a few of us did things to help make it happen. You all, the collective, hung up in there every week, shouldered most of the burden, will end up taking most of The Flack and will no doubt get little verbal or physical appreciation. This dyke is giving you this little expression of my personal appreciation ... You are beautiful!!"[87] Collectives made coffeehouses possible. These feminist coffeehouses provided a valuable resource to their local communities, becoming centres for socializing, entertainment, resource sharing, and activism.

Who Wanted to Use the Spaces?

Who were the coffeehouses for? Coffeehouse collectives constantly questioned and renegotiated issues over race, sexuality, gender, age, class, and substance use. With lower capital inputs and flexibility in location choice, unlike feminist restaurants that had to appeal to a broader clientele, coffeehouses could cater to more specific groups, either more specific in types of feminism (i.e., socialist, radical, liberal) or identity factors. Discussions over a coffeehouse's goals typically became discussions about the kinds of people coffeehouses aimed to serve. For example, at the Somerville Women's Coffeehouse collective meeting in 1979, the minutes indicate that the members resolved to exclude men. The organizers stated, "we want to reach all women, not just the feminist community" and "provide an atmosphere conducive both to being by yourself as well as sharing a time with friends."[88] They sought to act as an information network for the women's community and make the space available for other community groups. Regarding childcare, the collective members discussed the possibility of providing it for mothers and admitted that "We decided that if there is a need for this, the mothers might organize a childcare network among themselves."[89] It would be drug and alcohol free, but the collective would attempt to provide for the needs of both smokers and non-smokers and suggested dividing sections of the room. Instead of alcohol, it would serve fresh fruit, juices, healthy snacks, and hot drinks. Space and time would be made available for local performers, artists, and other events. It is notable that in its initial meetings, no notes recorded how the collective would react if trans women wanted to join the collective, as this question became a point of contention for many feminist coffeehouses.[90] Mixing discussions of food and entertainment while addressing questions about the gender, age, race, sexual orientation, and able-bodiedness of the desired participants were common at feminist coffeehouses. However, while these discussions tended to understand the relationship of refreshments and entertainment to community building, there was less awareness of how the treatment of various oppressions as discrete factors threatened that community.

The following sections of this chapter are arranged around identity categories, not to erase the lived experiences of women's intersecting identities but rather to reflect the way feminist coffeehouses approached various oppressions inside their spaces. Within meeting minutes, event programming, and recorded discussions, feminist coffeehouses approached issues of race, class, gender, age, accessibility, and sexual orientation as separate categories to be addressed one at a time. In contemporary discourses of intersectional feminism, this approach may appear inadequate or outdated, yet it reflected the way the coffeehouse organizers engaged with these conversations. This approach did not fulfill the needs of all coffeehouse attendees and potential attendees and thus could dissuade participation while the coffeehouses aimed to increase diversity. By treating these categories as distinct within this chapter, these tensions are made more apparent.

Gender (Children and Trans) and Sexuality

> I just want to say that one issue that we have not addressed tonight is that I have a lot of straight women friends that would like to come here but would not feel comfortable here. If we are going to be a lesbian coffeehouse let's call ourselves a lesbian coffeehouse. If we are going to be a women's coffeehouse we need to be receptive to other women who aren't lesbians.[91]
>
> *A Woman's Coffeehouse of Minneapolis, open meeting recording*

At A Woman's Coffeehouse of Minneapolis's open meeting, one participant wanted to know if it was a space for all women or just for lesbians. Questions over what the word "woman" meant was not restricted to this Minnesota coffeehouse. The question of gender for women's coffeehouses at first might seem readily apparent, but what was really meant by "a women's coffeehouse?" This question arose in many early organizing meetings of coffeehouses, including at the initial gatherings of Duluth, Minnesota's North Country Coffeehouse's organizers.[92] As discussed in chapter 1, the word "woman" could be code for lesbian, either intentionally or unintentionally. The finance committee of the Iowa City Women's Coffeehouse sent the collective a letter asking for clarification, stating that it "would like the collective to let them know if the coffeehouse is considered a women's space or a lesbian space."[93] The collective was evidently interested in exploring these questions because in the Iowa City Women's Coffeehouse archives, an article appeared multiple times about lesbian baiting and the tensions between lesbian and straight women within feminist movements.[94] To add more confusion, the language around lesbian coffeehouses focused on "women loving women." Where then, did bisexual women fit?

In December 1975, *Hera: A Philadelphia Feminist Publication* ran an anonymous article entitled "My Boyfriend Dropped Me Off at the Lesbian Coffeehouse," which explained the trouble that bisexual women faced in feminist women's spaces. Part of the reluctance to call lesbian spaces "lesbian" stemmed from the fear of the "lavender menace" and the fraught role of lesbians within some factions of the feminist movements. Furthermore, labelling themselves as "women's" instead of "lesbian" allowed coffeehouses to be a space for questioning women (women questioning their sexuality), as Flavia Rando explained when discussing the Women's Coffeehouse of New York City.[95] In 1974, the announcement for the opening of the Ann Arbor Women's Center and Coffeehouse said that it would be a "resource for women just coming out," meaning that women who attended might not yet have begun identifying as "lesbian," and calling it a "lesbian coffeehouse" could turn questioning women away.[96]

Furthermore, using the word "woman" instead of lesbian could be about safety. As Gail McArdle, one of the organizers of the Cup of Warmth Coffeehouse of Mankato, Minnesota, explained, if anyone reported that the teachers who attended the coffeehouse went to a "lesbian" event, the teachers could have been fired.[97] Feminist coffeehouses struggled to define what they meant by "women" because how they defined the word could expand or restrict their community and impact.

The term "woman" within coffeehouse titles was especially controversial when the coffeehouses were deciding whether they were open to transgender or transsexual women. A Woman's Coffeehouse of Minneapolis purported to want to encourage diversity, however, the collective integrated transphobic and gender-identity discrimination within its policies. On an index card, which was taped to the wall of the coffeehouse, the collective posted a notice to the community "To be re-evaluated Oct/ Nov '84 Temporary Policy on Transexuals—close vote, a decision was made that transexuals will not be welcome at the coffeehouse and will be asked to leave by a collective members. NOTE: not all members are willing to enforce this policy and are not required to do so."[98] While there were issues of lesbians being excluded by feminist organizations, lesbian and women's coffeehouses would also exclude other marginalized groups, particularly transsexual individuals by using the language "women-born-women." Lesbian feminist activists founded the Mountain Moving Coffeehouse for Womyn and Children of Chicago (1974–2005) as a "safe-space for womyn-born womyn and their young children."[99] Male children over the age of two and transsexual and transgender women were not allowed to attend. The womyn-born-womyn policy generated controversy beginning during the 1980s when pressure was put on the coffeehouse to allow admittance to men, as well as in the 1990s when transgender women contested it.[100] However, the organization staunchly defended the policy and never allowed admittance to men or to transgender women, preferring to close rather than broaden their membership. This kind of transphobia and idea of "women-born-women" was prevalent but not unanimously accepted across feminist coffeehouses. At A Woman's Coffeehouse of Minneapolis, the collective was divided.

In addition to the confusion of whether the coffeehouses were for lesbians or all women, including trans women, there were debates around whether they were separatist spaces and if so, what the implications were for mothers. After the finance committee of the Iowa City Women's Coffeehouse asked if the space was a women's space or a lesbian space, the committee's next question in the letter to the collective asked "IF it is considered a women's space what about boy children?"[101] While the feminist coffeehouses that called themselves "women's coffeehouses" were clear about banning men, boy children posed a difficult dilemma and the question over boy children was not unique to the Iowa City Women's Coffeehouse. When A Woman's Coffeehouse of Minneapolis sent its questionnaire to coffeehouse participants, the responses about boy children varied. As a result of the broad range of responses, the coffeehouse collective sent out a second questionnaire specifically focused on the place of children in the coffeehouse. This second questionnaire had twelve questions, inquiring about whether the individual filling out the survey was a mother herself, until what age should boys be allowed, if at all, and if women were interested in paying extra for childcare.[102] These anonymous surveys elicited strong emotional responses. One woman remarked,

> I feel very strongly about being able to bring my son to the coffeehouse. I would feel very UN-supported as a lesbian mother if I couldn't bring my son. I understand putting an age limit on male children—possibly twelve years old. It is very important that my son meet other children with lesbian

> mothers—so meeting other lesbian moms would be great. I can envision potluck lunches or suppers for lesbians and their children or some planned outings—sliding and hot chocolate, roller-skating and treats. In California, a group of lesbians rent a roller skating rink once a week for all lesbians and their children.[103]

Many women wrote such long responses that they drew arrows directing readers where to continue to read the rest of their responses on the back of the survey. The women who indicated that they had children wrote particularly long responses, indicating how important it was that they be able to bring their children. Banning children would mean that lesbian mothers would be restricted from attending the coffeehouse because finding a babysitter could be financially prohibitive. Another mother responded that she would drive one hundred miles to go to the coffeehouse and how much they needed it as a space to bring their kids. She continued, "Motherhood does not mean heterosexuality."[104] Furthermore, mothers argued that their children benefited from the experience of meeting other children of lesbians. Kids would face bullying at school for being the child of a lesbian mother. Meeting other children in a similar position helped them feel less isolated.

Lesbian mothers with sons felt that they faced additional hardships, both from society at large and within the lesbian community. In their responses to the questionnaires, lesbian mothers with sons expressed how other lesbians would refrain from socializing with them because they had boy children.[105] The divide seemed particularly apparent between mothers and non-mothers. While some women who did not have children wrote on their questionnaires that they recognized the importance of women being able to bring their children in order to participate, some women were less amenable. One respondent said that she was resentful of the attention given to mothers.[106] Another respondent went as far to say that the idea of children "makes me shudder," that "children should be given up for adoption," and concluded with the comment that she did not care about the age of boy children allowed at the coffeehouse because "children are children. Awake they are all disgusting."[107] This respondent was an outlier because even the majority of women who expressed that they wanted the coffeehouse to be for adult women only made clear that they were sympathetic to mothers. The antagonism between mothers and non-mothers was likely provoked due to a lack of communication about coffeehouse policies. During the open community meeting for A Woman's Coffeehouse, one participant asked why kids were running around on the dance floor because she thought the coffeehouse provided childcare, only to then be informed that the childcare was only provided during the pre-dance performance.[108] The topic of boy children and how mothers would feel welcomed as organizers and as attendees provoked strong emotions.

The question about boy children became more specific when coffeehouse members weighed in on how old the children should be if they were allowed to attend. Responding to the question about age, people typically stated that if children were allowed, boy children were only welcome until they reached puberty or became more "like men." The collective asked for recommendations for a specific age cutoff and bans were suggested on boys over the ages of five, eight, ten, eleven, and twelve.[109] By the tenth annual New Year's Eve party, which occurred shortly after this questionnaire was circulated, the collective announced that "all women, girls, and boys under ten welcome."[110] This debate about the age of boy children was not unique to A Woman's Coffeehouse. While the Minneapolis coffeehouse's archives provide a comprehensive record of these debates in their questionnaires, recorded community meeting, and in the collective's meeting minutes, it is evident that these kinds of discussions about boy children happened in feminist coffeehouse meetings across the United States. Event flyers would note "boy children allowed under twelve" and similar statements; the debate, however, would continue.[111]

Age

Age also divided coffeehouses. It was not that certain ages were banned, with the exception of boy children over a certain age, but rather there were divisions between generations. One respondent at community meeting for A Woman's Coffeehouse mentioned that she sometimes felt that she could not relate to some of the younger lesbians because she had grown up having different experiences. She had become accustomed to understanding lesbian relationship dynamics as butch and femme couples pairing off.[112] However, to her, the younger lesbians were rewriting the rules. She continued to say that one thing that could stop people from coming to the coffeehouse was "the power of the coffeehouse to define the structures of who we are as lesbians."[113] She added that some people found the definition of what it means to be a lesbian in the coffeehouse too narrow, and that this had to do with different values of what it meant to be a lesbian in 1983. She also found that by coming out before the founding of the women's community, she felt different from the ones who had come out after, especially with the differences in the rules of the relationships. She continued that "it feels lost to her" and that she felt that "she [had] lost her history."[114] What it meant to be lesbian differed between generations due to the different kinds of social conditions they had been raised in and come out into. One way that A Woman's Coffeehouse attempted to rectify age differences was to create special nights dedicated to specific age groups.

A Woman's Coffeehouse of Minneapolis had Old Dykes Nights, but community members also expressed that they thought socializing between the generations was important. According to a representative at the open meeting, many of the "old dykes" were not at the open meeting because it was the night of their Valentine's Day dance.

However, they had a strong community of women older than thirty-five and their friends that held monthly Old Dyke Nights. Another participant mentioned she knew that the coffeehouse had the Old Dyke group, but she wanted the opportunity to interact more with some of the women that were just coming out. The coffeehouse created a space for younger lesbians and women who were questioning their identities to discover themselves and find mentorship in older women of the community, at least in theory. Cliques, however, were a problem. Younger women who came to the coffeehouse would be labelled "jail bait," rather than welcomed. Participants at the meeting mentioned an issue with the music being played so loudly that it was hard to speak with women. If they wanted to hear others, they would be trapped in the front room with the smokers or crammed next to the pool table.[115] This meant it was harder for women of different generations to interact and to talk about their relationships. This desire to speak with each other was echoed when one participant mentioned that she would have come to the coffeehouse more if she could have talked to people and laughed with them, and that they needed one night of the weekend where dancing was not involved. She suggested that they could have tables set up and they could talk about friendships, art, ideas, and meet people.[116] This lack of communication between different groups within the community was especially clear when it came to matters of race.

Race

Unlike feminist restaurants and cafes, which were overwhelmingly run by white women, coffeehouses had greater racial diversity in their collectives; yet race remained a point of tension. On Christmas Day in 1974, the Las Hermanas Women's Cultural Center and Coffeehouse opened its doors in San Diego, California, offering a safe and welcoming space where women, particularly lesbians, could relax, enjoy homemade food, hear live music and poetry, and socialize.

The nonprofit coffeehouse was created by a group of mostly Latina women, including literature professor Dolores Valenzuela (a.k.a. "Mal Flora"), Carlota Hernandez, and Teresa Oyos.[117] Las Hermanas began as a seven-room collective house for women who were seeking refuge from abusive spouses. At its peak from 1975 to 1978, women packed the one-room space for "womyn's musical performances" by Meg Christian, Holly Near, Joan Armatrading, or Malvina Reynolds. The coffeehouse's popularity led to problems, especially as middle-class white women began to attend what had once been a primarily working-class Latina coffeehouse. One of the volunteers, Diane F. Germain, remarked in a recorded interview with the LAMBDA San Diego archives, "It was mostly working-class Latina women that (formed Las Hermanas). Then, as it started to take off and get bigger and more famous, there was kind of a set of middle-class women that came along and wanted to make it better, but their idea of making it better made working-class women feel not so good."[118] Working-class and middle-class white lesbians as well as straight feminists faced sexism, heterosexism, and classism, but maintained white privilege. In the case of Las Hermanas, white feminists who began to attend the coffeehouse usurped power and changed its dynamics, making the environment less friendly and inviting to the community that had formed it originally. These changes eventually led to the coffeehouse's closure. To be clear, this is not to say that all coffeehouses with predominantly white membership were oblivious to racial issues.

A Woman's Coffeehouse of Minneapolis had discussions around racial diversity.[119] During the meeting about the future of the coffeehouse, the organizers devoted twenty minutes to discussing race, stating "we need to make sure women of color are represented … and if not a woman of color on the collective we need outreach ongoing."[120] The collective knew that the question of race would not be solved in one meeting. One meeting attendant said that a large issue was that women of colour did not feel comfortable going there due to the overt racism they experienced.[121] Another participant restated what one of her friends, who was a Black woman, had once told her. She did not want to go to the coffeehouse because the white women in attendance looked at her like she was a sex object.[122] Additionally, she did not like the music and felt that the song selection catered to a specific demographic.

Not every participant was amenable to the discussion of race. One meeting attendee said, "I won't like everybody and might not like a woman of color but doesn't make me racist," Likewise, a participant, Paige, claimed that "when I go to women's festivals that there are so many committees and rules that I feel like if lesbians ran the world it would be a police state."[123] To counter that claim, one woman stated that she felt the opposite of "what Paige said about that police state bullshit." She continued to explain that the reason they were having this discussion about race in the open community meeting was because the collective was not trying to impose a set of rules on the coffeehouse from the top but instead wanted the community to work together to create a nourishing environment. Furthermore, she was offended by "all these white women saying that they know what Black women feel." She did not want people to guess what offends Black women. Another woman countered, "So they have to tell us all?" to which the original speaker replied, "No, we just shouldn't guess and use all of these analogies." Another participant had the last word when she responded, "the question should not be about whether or not racism was a problem—it was—as we are all racist."[124] The group needed to actively work on creating diversity.

A barrier to creating diversity was that racism was so ingrained within the community itself. They had a very narrow understanding of what it meant to be a lesbian and this could lead to cliques and feelings of exclusion. One respondent mentioned that even as a white woman who did not fit all the norms of what it meant to be a lesbian in the community, she could feel isolated, and so for women of colour it would be even harder to fit those norms. Another woman chimed in that while talking about race made her nervous, she appreciated that this discussion allowed her to finally discuss her concern that the coffeehouse did not represent different cultures. She believed that the coffeehouse had a narrow definition of what it meant to be a lesbian and this limited understanding of lesbian identity made the coffeehouse uncomfortable.[125] If the collective hoped to diversify membership, it was necessary for its members to examine the existing barriers to participation. The current requirements required intensive time commitments and a specific lifestyle and schedule. When hiring, the collective needed to advertise beyond the communities it typically contacted. Another participant added that racial issues would not be "solved by space, money, or just committees," and that the solution was "not just being friendly to a Black woman." Instead, the group needed to address the problem at "the core."[126] A Woman's Coffeehouse was determined to try.

A Woman's Coffeehouse collective created the following solutions through its discussions: it established a committee to address race and diversity; it dedicated funds to host anti-racism workshops; and it held new kinds of events. A member had suggested that women of colour could host women-of-colour-only nights, similar to the over thirty-five Old Dyke Nights. Although the Old Dyke Nights created an opportunity for a subsection of the coffeehouse community to organize around its specific needs, a racially specific night made some meeting attendees uncomfortable.[127] Women of colour also needed to be actively involved in this process and integrated into leadership roles. Another participant chimed in that the community needed to start doing workshops on racism because racism was not a problem restricted to the collective but to the entire community. A Woman's Coffeehouse created a committee on racism and race issues the following April because of these discussions. This committee created a report with a series of suggestions, including: the coffeehouse would develop a policy statement that all programming takes into consideration the needs and issues of all women of colour; 50 percent of performers would be women of colour; and 20 percent of Friday and

REGULAR EVENTS AT THE WOMEN'S COFFEEHOUSE

MONDAYS
SOUP SUPPERS, 5:30 - 7:30 PM, $1.50

THURSDAYS
BREAKFAST, 7:30 - 9:00 AM, Donations requested

FRIDAYS
5:00 R & R, 5:00 - 8:00 PM
Coffee & Tea provided - BYOB, Donation requested

* * * * * * * * * * * * * * * * SPECIAL EVENTS * * * * * * * * * * * * * * * *

SATURDAY - APRIL 3: SCENES FROM SCENES
An IC women's talent show on tape
Door opens at 7:30 PM
Videotape starts at 8:00 PM
$1.50

FRIDAY - APRIL 9: PASSOVER SEDER
Potluck (No leavening,eg.no bread or pasta)
7:00 PM

SUNDAY - APRIL 11: PINK TRIANGLES
A study of prejudice against lesbians & gay men
A film with discussion following
Door opens at 7:00 PM
Film starts at 7:30 PM
$1.00

SUNDAY - MAY 9: WE ALL HAVE OUR REASONS
A film about women and alcohol
Door opens at 7:00 PM
Film starts at 7:30 PM
Alcohol free/Chemical free night
Donation requested

For wheelchair accessibility contact a member of the Coffeehouse collective or the Women's Press (338 - 7022)
Non alcohol and chemical free events will be noted in the calendar
Volunteers are welcome - Stop in the Coffeehouse and sign up

Saturday night programming would be devoted to discussing issues (through non-performance presentations) specifically related to women of colour. The coffeehouse would try to involve other organizations in events, broaden their publicity tactics, and educate members about subtle racism.[128] As evidenced by later community calendars, A Woman's Coffeehouse then held a series of workshops about racism in the lesbian community.[129] Race remained a central issue for the last four years of the coffeehouse's existence: in a 1985 flyer, the collective announced "some of our main goals are to bridge the cultural gaps between white women and women of color and break down the walls of alienation that have been built up over the years."[130] While the solution was not perfect, the coffeehouse made significant efforts to address the racial divides in their community.

Accessibility

Coffeehouses primarily discussed issues of accessibility related to class consciousness. As the earlier section on finances made clear, feminist coffeehouse collectives prioritized making their spaces economically accessible by offering sliding scales for memberships, making event entrance fees by donation rather than a set fee, and by allowing

6.2 (OPPOSITE) *Although the Iowa City Women's Coffeehouse did not have a religious affiliation, the April Potluck was a Passover Seder. Since not all coffeehouse participants were Jewish, the poster mentions that no leavening can be used in food consumed during Passover. The poster notes the accessibility of the space and when events would be chemical free. This poster also provides insight into the types of movies coffeehouses would screen, such as documentaries about lesbian experiences and substance use issues. As can be seen on similar calendars of events, the Iowa Women's Coffeehouse also screened films about sexual assault, incest, and sexism. (Used with permission from the University of Iowa Library, Iowa Women's Archives, Jo Rabenold Papers, Box 4, IWA0191)* women to donate time and labour when money was tight. The members of A Woman's Coffeehouse also considered accessibility for disabled people with mobility impairments. At the church where the coffeehouse occurred, the collective wanted to add a ramp. Before the ramp was installed, coffeehouse members would have to carry their friends down the steps. Allegedly the church was interested in making the entire space accessible, but it was a slow-moving process.[131] As the collective only rented the space, it was limited to the kinds of changes they could make to the church itself, but collective members advocated for accessibility. This kind of consciousness around accessibility was also present in the Iowa City Women's Coffeehouse collective. On events calendars for the Women's Coffeehouse, a note at the bottom stated, "for wheelchair accessibility contact a member of the coffeehouse collective," followed by a telephone number.[132] However, when accessibility was discussed, coffeehouses typically referred to class, lesbian mothers with children, or substances.

Substance Issues: Disruptions over Drinking and Smoking

While food created an environment over which women could gather, drink could be divisive. In cities where a feminist or women's business (such as a bookstore, restaurant, or bar) already existed, feminist coffeehouses filled more specific community needs than just as a place for women to gather. Feminist coffeehouses existed as an alternative to the bar scene and it was in this mission that food and drink became particularly important. Mountain Moving Coffeehouse of Chicago advertised itself as a drug-free and alcohol-free space and an entertainment alternative to lesbian bars.[133] On a flyer advertising upcoming events, the collective of the Somerville, Massachusetts, Women's Coffeehouse reminded readers that it was also drug and alcohol free.[134] In a letter sent to the community to describe the financial difficulty they were facing in 1985, the collective of A Woman's Coffeehouse of Minneapolis reminded readers that "We feel strong[ly] that A Woman's Coffeehouse is vital to the Twin Cities Lesbian community. We know it is in the hearts of many, many women. We see the coffeehouse as an institution in Minneapolis, crucial for the culture and community it creates and nurtures. It is a place for women to come out, get support for sobriety."[135] The letter continued to state, "It is the only woman-only and chemically-free space in the [Twin] cities."[136] The Iowa City Women's Coffeehouse was substance free on some nights and would note these nights in their calendars.[137] However, collective meetings would happen over beers, as noted in the meeting minutes.[138] The establishment served all lesbians and women in the Iowa City area, not just the sober ones. When the coffeehouse had chemical-free days, it would ban drugs, alcohol, and tobacco.[139] On regular days, smokers were asked to consult with the women in the space if they could smoke, or if larger groups were around they were asked to go outside. In existing archival files, an old sign instructed smokers how to proceed and another sign indicated a table reserved for pot smokers.[140] To mitigate these tensions and to strive for greater accessibility, most coffeehouses emphasized coffee, tea, and juices. Food and drink were central to community building, yet coffeehouse organizers understood that the kind of refreshments provided would shape attendance.

While A Woman's Coffeehouse of Minneapolis greatly stressed that it was chemical free, the coffeehouse still retained floor-space for smokers. Smoking tobacco became a point of debate and a problem for multiple coffeehouses.[141] In the 1970s, there was a cultural and legal shift around smoking.[142] At the community meeting for A Woman's Coffeehouse, non-smokers were very verbal about how much they hated how the front room was used for smoking. Apparently, the smokers did not even like it.[143] A collective member responded that one reason they continued to allow smoking was because the collective did not want to define who lesbians were. There was some irony in this statement as the collective had already defined the space as chemical free. She continued that the collective "didn't want to say this isn't

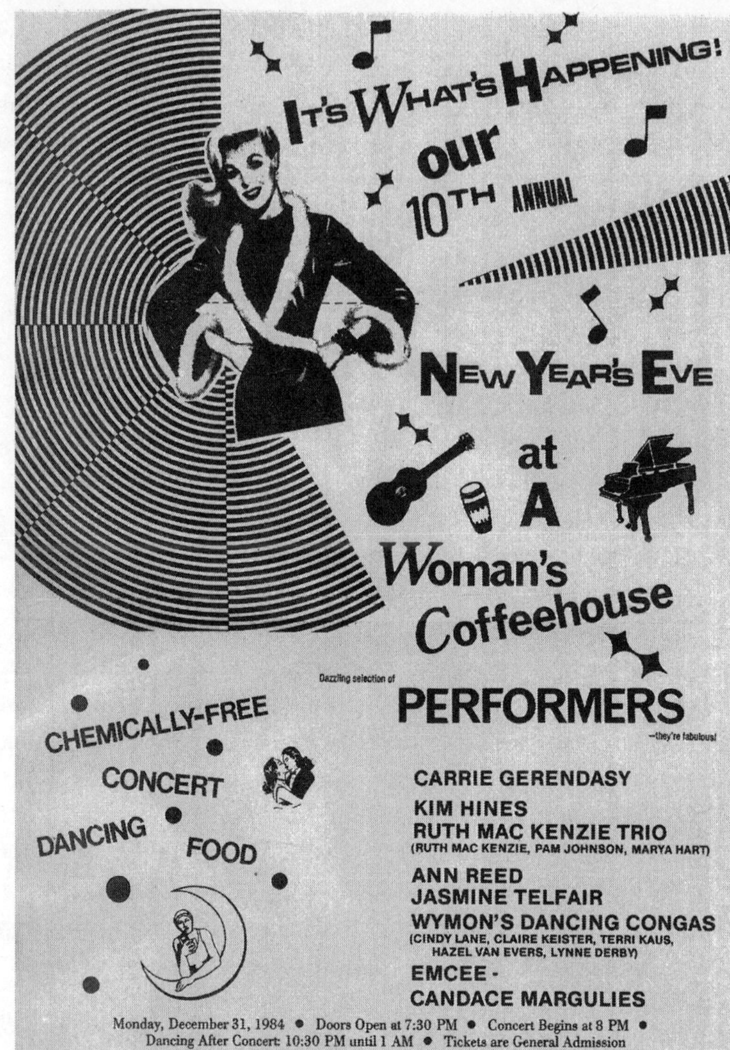

IT'S WHAT'S HAPPENING!
our
10TH ANNUAL
NEW YEAR'S EVE
at
A
Woman's
Coffeehouse
Dazzling selection of
PERFORMERS
—they're fabulous!
CHEMICALLY-FREE
CONCERT
DANCING
FOOD
CARRIE GERENDASY
KIM HINES
RUTH MAC KENZIE TRIO
(RUTH MAC KENZIE, PAM JOHNSON, MARYA HART)
ANN REED
JASMINE TELFAIR
WYMON'S DANCING CONGAS
(CINDY LANE, CLAIRE KEISTER, TERRI KAUS, HAZEL VAN EVERS, LYNNE DERBY)
EMCEE -
CANDACE MARGULIES

Monday, December 31, 1984 • Doors Open at 7:30 PM • Concert Begins at 8 PM •
Dancing After Concert: 10:30 PM until 1 AM • Tickets are General Admission
Sliding Scale: $7.00 - 12.00 • Admission After Concert: $4.00 •
Available at: Amazon Bookstore and A Woman's Coffeehouse •
Signed For Hearing Impaired • Wheelchair Accessible • For Childcare, Call Vesta at: 835-3552 •
For Work exchange, Call Candi at: 827-1067 or Jeanne at:729-9147

A WOMAN'S COFFEEHOUSE • ONE GROVELAND, MINNEAPOLIS, MN
(One Block North of Franklin, off Nicollet)

All Women, Girls, and Boys under 10 years welcome.

just a place for people who don't smoke."[144] Non-smokers were not satisfied with that explanation and they continued the discussion by mentioning their allergies and saying that they were concerned about their health and the venue's ventilation. Tensions continued around smoking, with some women citing the smoke as the reason they no longer wanted to attend the coffeehouse.

Sustainability and Attendance

Most of the suggestions are about how we can spend more money but how I feel is how most of the community is not supporting this place.[145]

A Woman's Coffeehouse of Minneapolis, open meeting recording

Changing cultural attitudes around feminism and lesbian identities made keeping a sustainable clientele difficult. Financial worries and concerns regarding diversity were intertwined with dwindling attendance. When A Woman's Coffeehouse of Minneapolis circulated a letter asking for donations, the collective noted "the coffeehouse has steadily lost money all year due to rising costs and declining attendance."[146] Dwindling attendance had pushed the coffeehouse to the

6.3 (OPPOSITE) *After much debate about whom the coffeehouse was for, this event flyer shows the compromises made within A Woman's Coffeehouse. The event welcomed (on the last line of the poster) "All Women, Girls, and Boys under 10 years" old. There are notes about accessibility with notes such as "signed for hearing impaired" and "wheelchair accessible." As New Year's Eve events were not covered by the membership pass, the entrance fee of $7 to $12 was a sliding scale and there was also the option for "work exchange" to increase class accessibility. The event was "chemically-free." The feminist bookstore Amazon sold tickets for the New Year's Eve celebration. (Courtesy of the Jean-Nickolaus Tretter Collection in GLBT Studies, University of Minnesota Libraries, A Woman's Coffeehouse Collective Records 1976–1985)* edge of bankruptcy and the collective emphasized, "IT IS URGENT THAT YOU SUPPORT THE COFFEEHOUSE THROUGH THIS CRISIS IN SPITE OF WHATEVER CHANGES YOU WISH FOR, SO THAT IT WILL CONTINUE TO BE HERE FOR ALL OF US."[147] Second to money and logistical matters, discussions during coffeehouse meetings focused on how to improve attendance.

A Woman's Coffeehouse was not the only one to struggle. Las Hermanas of San Diego, California, closed in 1980 over conflict, a lack of interest, and an increase in rent. A February 1980 article explained Las Hermanas' closure, stating that over the past five years conditions changed, "many new groups have formed, providing women with many choices for involving themselves politically, socially and culturally. Las Hermanas slowly and somewhat painfully declined in popularity and the nucleus of women nurturing it over the years have become exhausted."[148] One of the major draws of attendance was the cultural aspect of the feminist coffeehouses. In its July 10, 1980, meeting minutes the Iowa collective member Mary stated, "the problem is that no one comes here. Tess thinks it's the place. Vicki thinks it's not."[149] The collective came to the vague consensus that it needed entertainment every week, maybe twice a week, because changing spaces was not immediately feasible. For similar reasons, the Iowa City Women's Coffeehouse collective decided to add brunch every other Sunday. The group was going to encourage community member Mary Castern to do a film premiere at the coffeehouse.[150] Regardless of how innovative collective members were, financial troubles, the burnout of collective members, and declining membership caused feminist coffeehouses to eventually close.

While most feminist coffeehouses founded in the 1970s and 1980s in the United States closed by the 1990s, they played a meaningful role in women's lives. Former collective member and manager Candace Marguiles of A Woman's Coffeehouse in Minneapolis moved to New Haven, Connecticut, when her girlfriend left to attend

Yale University.[151] In a letter she sent to her former collective, she noted that without her coffeehouse community she had a hard time. Once she found Bloodroot Feminist Vegetarian Restaurant in nearby Bridgeport, Connecticut, she finally felt at home.[152] Feminist coffeehouses, like feminist restaurants, were important fixtures of the feminist community.

Conclusion

The phenomenon of feminist coffeehouses in the 1970s and 1980s in the United States expanded the possibilities of who could organize feminist space centred on food, drink, and socializing. Without high fixed costs, coffeehouses enabled women with less access to capital to create women-centred spaces that offered refreshments. While food bolstered community building, debates surrounding representation and inclusion/exclusion proved to be ongoing sources of conflict. Tensions were particularly high regarding issues of race, gender, sexual orientation, and age. Coffeehouse members disagreed about the inclusion of mothers and their children, the use of substances like alcohol, and how to make the space welcoming to new attendees. Trying to adapt to community needs was a difficult but important task for creating the kinds of places that organizers and attendees wanted, whether it was dancing, poetry, music, or just socializing.

Even when coffeehouse collectives endeavoured to make a space welcoming to all groups, such lofty goals were often out of reach. Although groups purported that their space was welcoming to all women, when women of colour were not centrally involved in organizing and creating a vision for the coffeehouses, mostly white women utilized the spaces. When only women without children created rules, mothers with sons faced barriers. It was not just about adding specific women to the location to create diversity but that women of diverse backgrounds needed to be involved in forming the entire structure.

Users seemed to want different things. As one participant at the open community meeting for A Woman's Coffeehouse of Minneapolis asked, "Is it possible to be open more to accommodate these differences? Like open another night like a weekday?"[153] Coffeehouses allowed for more flexibility and experimentation than feminist restaurants and cafes due to their lower overhead costs. Part of that experimentation enabled them to promote lesbian and feminist culture, as discussed in the next chapter.

CHAPTER 7

Coffeehouses and the Feminist Nexus

> Womon-identified culture is not a phase, or a fad, or a step along the path. It is the whole path beginning, middle, and end. It is both the vision and the real life of thousands who are building our existence on the solid foundation of our loyalty to wimmin. Out of this culture comes Sidney Spinster, a new Lesbian musician in a very old tradition. She sings songs of urgency, clarity, and love. IF you miss womon-identified music, don't miss this concert![1]
>
> *Sidney Spinster event flyer for Iowa City Women's Coffeehouse*

The above passage describing "womon-identified" culture comes from a flyer advertising Sidney Spinster's A Concert for Wimmin, a "chemical-free" show, hosted by the Iowa City Women's Coffeehouse sometime in the 1980s (exact date unknown).[2] This flyer speaks to the cultural contribution coffeehouses made. Feminist coffeehouses were social and cultural spaces utilized by touring musicians and authors. These coffeehouses served as performance spaces for professionals and fostered amateur artists developing their crafts in front of supportive communities. This chapter emphasizes the cultural and artistic contributions made by feminist coffeehouses and shows how the production of these cultural events was intertwined with the desire to create feminist social space.

As discussed in the last chapter, most coffeehouses functioned as nonprofit, alcohol-free, social environments. However, even for the

SIDNEY SPINSTER
A CONCERT
FOR WIMMIN
Womon-identified culture is not a phase, or a fad, or a step along the path. It is the whole path, beginning, middle and end. It is both the vision and the real life of the thousands who are building our existence on the solid foundation of our loyalty to wimmin.
Out of this culture comes Sidney Spinster, a new Lesbian musician in a very old tradition. She sings songs of urgency, clarity, and love. If you miss womon-identified music, don't miss this concert.
Sept. 10th, 8:30 p.m. / for women only
$2. donation / a chemically free performance
at the women's coffeehouse

The Women's Coffeehouse

7.1 In the archives of feminist restaurant, cafes, and coffeehouses it is not uncommon to find posters advertising Sidney Spinster, Holly Near, and Alix Dobkin concerts. These musicians toured between feminist and lesbian venues and connected women internationally. (Courtesy of University of Iowa Women's Archives Collection, Jo Rabenold Papers)

coffeehouses that served alcohol, the emphasis of these spaces was on producing cultural events over profits. As discussed in their collective meeting minutes, when the Iowa City Women's Coffeehouse moved to a larger location and needed to sponsor more activities to pay rental fees, the collective decided to host recurring events. There were Monday soup dinners for $1.50, Thursday breakfasts where patrons paid by donation, and they would open for free during the early evening on Fridays for rest and relaxation before concerts, poetry readings, film screenings, dances, and other events. At the evening events, donations were requested for the coffee and tea provided, but women were welcome to bring their own alcohol.[3] Coffeehouses would sponsor social coffee hours for women to chat and organize entertainment to enjoy.[4]

Coffeehouses were not the only spaces that supported feminist and lesbian culture. As explored in chapter 3, throughout the 1970s and 1980s women's centres, feminist restaurants and cafes, bookstores, and shops would host cultural and social events for women.[5] The feminist art space Diana's Place of Northampton, Massachusetts, held events such as the Witchy Song Night to celebrate an April full moon.[6] The 1982 calendar of Artemis Society Women's Café of San Francisco, California, showcased musical performances in its separate flyers for a 1984 ballroom dancing class and in 1986 a benefit concert for the San Francisco AIDS Foundation.[7] This chapter does not seek to create a dichotomy between feminist coffeehouses and other women's spaces as doing so would be historically inaccurate, especially as these operations were occasionally combined endeavours. The Full Moon was both a coffeehouse and a bookstore that likewise had a relationship with Old Wives' Tales Bookstore. Both institutes participated in the San Francisco feminist business nexus and advertised on the same flyers.[8] Sisterspirit Bookstore of San Jose, California, hosted coffeehouses.[9] A key distinction, however, is that coffeehouses prioritized cultural events. Feminist coffeehouses brought women together through music, dancing, art, politics, and socializing. Furthermore, coffeehouses connected to other businesses.

Music

Feminist coffeehouses served as music venues that provided a unique space for women, and especially lesbian performers. When lesbian country musician Willie Tyson was publicizing her show at A Woman's Coffeehouse in Minneapolis, Minnesota, she wrote on her flyer that, "the feminist concerts are a real high for me, the audience reception and support—you don't get that from many other places."

She continued to explain why performing at feminist coffeehouses was so valuable, stating that "my lyrics reach the people there because most of them have heads comparable to mine. The feminist concerts made me more aware of a spirit and support within the feminist community."[10] The coffeehouses were valuable to the entertainers and the community alike. Prominent female musicians, particularly lesbian ones, relied on recurring feminist coffeehouses when touring. In these spaces, lesbian performers were able to present their work without fear of homophobic harassment. Feminist entertainers would find themselves surrounded by like-minded and receptive audiences.

Prominent lesbian musicians would tour around North America, relying on feminist coffeehouses to provide the venues. Alix Dobkin performed, as her tour posters claimed, primarily for lesbian women.[11] Her music promoted lesbian culture, as evident from a selection of her song titles: "Lesbian Code," "Living with Lesbians," "A Woman's Love," and "The Lesbian Power Authority." Before a live performance of her song about the terms used by lesbians, "Lesbian Code," Dobkin reflected on the powerful role of touring musicians in spreading and sharing lesbian feminist culture. Dobkin particularly noted the reciprocal relationship between audiences and performers as vital for creating a shared understanding of lesbian identities.[12] One of Dobkin's performances was at a coffeehouse sponsored by the women's music distributor Ladyslipper in 1981 at the Community Church of Mason Farm in Chapel Hill, North Carolina. To increase audience participation, Ladyslipper also sponsored a potluck brunch with Dobkin the following Sunday with the time and location of the meal announced at the concert.[13] Even for recurring feminist coffeehouses, both examples demonstrate that feminist coffeehouse collectives would adapt their choice of venue based on the needs of the performer and available resources. Feminist coffeehouses did not inherently rely on a static location; instead, feminist coffeehouses created temporary feminist spaces that promoted touring women musicians.

Coffeehouses did not only showcase travelling entertainers but also provided a space for local musicians to perform. On a promotional flyer, the Somerville Women's Coffeehouse of Massachusetts noted it provided "space for local women performing artists to share their medium with Somerville women. This gives community women exposure to the performing arts and encourages local women artists to develop their talent. Creating this sense of community breaks down isolation among individual women. The coffeehouse gives women a sense of strength and creativity by drawing them into an atmosphere that brought an awareness of the resources available in their community and within themselves."[14] Local amateur and professional women musicians utilized feminist coffeehouse space. Depending on the city and time, coffeehouses were sometimes the only places where local feminists and especially lesbian performers could play or at least play music openly as lesbians.

According to the first issue of *Coffee Klatch*, A Woman's Coffeehouse of Minneapolis's 1976 newsletter, the coffeehouse began because the Minneapolis Lesbian Resource Center (LRC) was unable to provide a social and performance space for lesbian and non-lesbian women outside of local bars.[15] Initially the coffeehouse served as a fundraiser for the LRC. The organizers received a grant for one month's salary for a coordinator, and the LRC loaned the coffeehouse collective seed money for supplies to get the coffeehouse started. Originally, the coffeehouse was going to be in the basement of the LRC shared with Chrysalis, the Minneapolis Women's Center, but that plan was abandoned when it proved impossible to meet the fire regulations. Arrangements were made to use the Northeast Groveland facilities and the coffeehouse opened in December 1975, with the help of one woman who loaned the collective her stereo for several months. However, according to the collective, after a while it became clear that specific women were consistently committing themselves to showing up each week and generally responsible for keeping the coffeehouse going.[16] The collective members decided to formalize their collective structure and on February 28, 1975, they held their first meeting. The coffeehouse's relationship with the LRC became minimal by 1976. As its newsletter stated, the "LRC was not in touch with how much energy it takes to keep the coffeehouse going," so on July 31, 1976, members of the two collectives signed an agreement which said that the coffeehouse would donate $475 to the LRC but would otherwise be completely autonomous.[17] The need for social and performance space changed the relationship with the previously existing feminist and lesbian spaces in Minneapolis.

While the LRC and A Woman's Coffeehouse worked on creating a productive and positive relationship, the coffeehouse did not maintain smooth relationships with all Twin Cities women's organizations. As demonstrated in a letter sent in 1982, the collective of A Woman's Coffeehouse clashed with Terry of Persimmon's Event Organizing, who began to host concerts during hours when the coffeehouse was open in an adjacent location.[18] The collective members said that they had supported Terry's business by generally not scheduling performances at the coffeehouse on Persimmon's concert nights, by publicizing Persimmon's concerts in their coffeehouse calendar, by sponsoring annual, successful benefits for Persimmon's, and finally by providing space to Terry to sell tickets at the coffeehouse.[19] As the collective noted in their letter, "Put simply that will take away from our business. Also women may not realize that they are in the position of choosing between Persimmon's and supporting A Woman's Coffeehouse and will probably be misled to believe that we are producing your event (we know from experience that many lesbians assume that any woman-identified event at Plymouth Church is a coffeehouse event)."[20] Previously, Persimmon's programming had sufficiently differed from the coffeehouse's own events. However, when Terry began drawing from the same group of performers as the coffeehouse and hoped to reach basically the same audience, the coffeehouse's organizing collective felt threatened.[21] It noted that "it is equally

OCTOBER FULL MOON COFFEE-HOUSE FOR WOMEN
4416 18 ST. S.F.
TELEPHONE: 864-9274
closed mondays
TUESDAY HOURS: 4-11
WEDNESDAY 1 HOURS 4-11 PALMISTRY WORKSHOP 8 P.M.
THURSDAY 2 HOURS: 4-11 TERI BEI GUITAR+SONGS 8:30
FRIDAY 3 HOURS: 4-12 SUSAN GRIFFIN POETRY 8:30 $1 DONATION
SATURDAY 4 HOURS: 12-12 RUTH SCHOENBACH SONGS 8:30 $1 DONATION
SUNDAY 5 HOURS: 2-10
7
8 JUST US VIDEO "RAPE + SELF DEFENSE" DISCUSSION TO FOLLOW. 8:30
9 HONEY CREEK WOMEN'S BAND 7:30 $1 DONATION
10 "COMING INTO HER OWN" THEATRE PROD. (6 WOMEN) 8:30 $2 DONATION
11 WOMEN'S MUSIC OPEN STAGE NIGHT 8:30
12
14
15 CHRYSTOS POETRY 8 P.M.
16 CYNDI STRAUS 12 STRING GUITAR + SONGS 8:30
17 SHARON ISABELL author of "YESTERDAY'S LESSONS" 8:30 $1 DONATION
18 PARTY-MUSIC OPENING of THIS MONTH'S ART SHOW of "SAN DIEGO WOMEN'S MUSIC FESTIVAL" 7-12. ALL WOMEN WELCOME
19 BODY AWARENESS WORKSHOP 10 A.M.-4 CALL 552-2243 for DETAILS. FULL MOON CLOSED 'TIL 4 P.M.
21
22 WOMEN'S OPEN POETRY NIGHT 8:30
23
24 SATCHO SINGS AGAIN! 8:30 $1 DONATION
25 CAFÉ CONSUELO + CINDY 8:30
26 LESBIANS IN LAW: DISCUSS YOUR RIGHTS. 4 TO 6

7.2 The calendar for Full Moon Coffeehouse of San Francisco, California, is filled with almost nightly events. In addition to music and poetry, there are events about lesbians' legal rights, self defence, body awareness, and book readings. Events were free often with a $1 suggested donation. (Courtesy of the GLBT Historical Society. Full Moon Coffeehouse Folder, GLBT Ephemera Collection, Business Box)

possible that by duplicating our work you will lose money."[22] Terry's decision to compete with the coffeehouse felt like a betrayal because apparently Terry had recently asked the collective for information about space, sound equipment, and good women sound technicians, "which we (the collective) cooperatively, though perhaps naively, gave [her]."[23] From the perspective of A Woman's Coffeehouse collective, Terry then used this information against the interests of the coffeehouse. This conflict demonstrated that while music was important for building community, it could also create rifts. Furthermore, tensions such as the one above affected the performers.

Coffeehouses were oftentimes the only spaces for local women to perform, which could create problems. In the early 1980s, Sidney Spinster wrote an open letter to the women's community of the Twin Cities to address her concerns about the music scene at A Woman's Coffeehouse. In the letter, she remarked that because the coffeehouse was the only outlet for local performers, she felt like she was living in a company town, where the organizers of the coffeehouse had too much power over the entire music scene for feminist women. She also remarked that there appeared to be a hierarchy between local stars, non-stars, and stars from out of town, especially regarding pay. Feminist coffeehouses invited both local and touring performers to play, but maintaining equity between performers was a contested issue.

Tensions over money and business matters related to the music also led to prominent complaints. Coffeehouse collectives were caught between filling the needs of the community and the needs of managing a business. Spinster noted that "as bosses it is in your interests to keep our wages low and treat us in the most convenient and expedient ways for you. As lesbians it is in your interest to nourish and support Lesbian culture and the workers who create it. Sometimes these interests are mutually exclusive."[24] Spinster reminded readers that "Creating Lesbian Culture is very serious business. It is one of the most important tools that we have to transform this world into the healthy place for lesbians that we want it to be. I want the Coffeehouse to be more than a wimmin's space—I want the space to be filled with nourishing, empowering, Lesbian energy."[25] She said that the coffeehouse was not just an alternative to bars, as the collective had noted in its literature, "but something really new and different. It isn't living up to its potential. This is the responsibility of all of us, not just the collective."[26] She finished by remarking that the business model was hurting the performers. Spinster thought that the low entrance fees to the shows devalued women musicians. The irony was that she was also upset that the collective paid themselves, unlike at Mountain Moving Coffeehouse of Chicago, where she was apparently paid $100 to perform, more than four times what she would make at her hometown coffeehouse. The issue over paid versus unpaid labour plagued collectives. Deciding whether to pay the collective made that work accessible or inaccessible to different classes of women. The ability to pay organizers and performers stemmed from more issues than the low entrance fees, which were often offered at a sliding scale.

Audio Quality

Like the feminist restaurants that had difficulty surviving financially as businesses when they sold their food as inexpensively as possible (refer to chapter 5 on feminist food), the coffeehouses faced similar difficulties, leading to issues from the use of cheap sound equipment. As feminist restaurants tried to keep menu prices low so that women across classes could afford to eat there, coffeehouse collectives aimed to keep ticket prices low to make events accessible. However, low prices would mean that either the product would suffer or the business, and those who sought to maintain the business, would suffer. Feminist restaurants' owners typically accepted low profit margins to maintain the goal of their space without compromising on the quality of their food. As coffeehouse collectives usually worked on a volunteer basis or on low stipends, the only product that could be "cut" to keep costs low was usually the quality of the sound equipment. This complaint speaks to a dominant trend in both feminist coffeehouses and feminist restaurants and cafes—how could feminists work ethically? How could women pay and be paid in a way that aligned with their feminist ethics?

Sidney Spinster's open letter about the music situation at A Woman's Coffeehouse of Minneapolis was not just a complaint, though. She offered concrete suggestions, demanding for better pay, improved lighting, and better sound. The collective took the letter seriously and soon released its own document, outlining its new plans. It created legal contracts for performers with a set of regulations and schedules before every performance.[27] These matters were then put into effect and the women of the collective took measures to improve these events, including learning how to properly work the sound system—a great improvement from when A Woman's Coffeehouse relied on the borrowed stereo.[28] However, despite the measures the collective took to solve its sound quality problems, as one participant in its open community meeting remarked, the coffeehouse would always be limited by the acoustics of the space, which in its case was a church basement. No matter where the members hung the speakers the sound could never be of professional quality. As one meeting participant groaned, "there was nothing worse than a poor sound system at a loud volume."[29] The sound quality was never perfect, but it improved.

A Woman's Coffeehouse was not the only coffeehouse to have problems with audio quality. Every Woman's Coffeehouse of Richmond, Virginia, likewise faced sound issues. Music reviewer Robert Goldblum attended the Every Woman's Coffeehouse in 1983 to cover feminist musician Hunter Davis's blues show at the local Young Women's Christian Association, and the concert review seems typical in that it describes the artist's performance, vocal range, songs, and past albums.[30] However, Goldblum also singled out that "the coffeehouse is set in a smallish, second floor auditorium surrounded by large windows. As a result, much of the sound seemed to escape. A stage backdrop would have helped distribute the sound more evenly."[31] The spaces that held coffeehouses were not always ideal for producing a high level of sound quality. Financial pressures facing coffeehouses resulted in less-than-ideal performance spaces and audio quality. Music issues reached beyond sound quality; within feminist coffeehouses, there were debates about what kind of music would be played, especially when it came to DJing the dances.

Dancing and Visual Art

Dancing was a priority for some of the feminist coffeehouses, especially the ones that catered to a primarily lesbian feminist community. Women's dances could be fundraising events for coffeehouses to meet their overhead costs. The Iowa City Women's Coffeehouse advertised a women's dance as a special fundraising event.[32] Other coffeehouses included dances as a regular feature, especially substance-free or "chemical-free" coffeehouses that existed to provide a space in which lesbians could dance and cruise outside of the bar scene. A Woman's Coffeehouse had so many dances that the organizers sent a survey to users of the coffeehouse in 1985 asking if it would be okay to have nights without dancing as they dominated their typical programming. Holding dances was not controversial, but the choice over what music was played raised ire.

Decisions over the playlist for dances resulted in stress for the collectives. Playing music that met people's tastes could be difficult. At the open community meeting hosted by A Woman's Coffeehouse in 1985, the organizers devoted twenty-five minutes to the topic of music. Some women were upset that they were ignored when they made song suggestions. One collective member responded, "I think you have a very valid point, we don't have a policy to play everyone's request. If I don't know a song, but if someone requests something and I don't know it, and you have a lot of pressure and the floor clears," then everyone would blame the DJ.[33] The collective member who would DJ continued by stating, "I'm sympathetic. I like to hear the songs I like to hear, but we don't make a policy of playing all requests."[34] DJing an event could be stressful for the collective members that constantly had to deal with complaints. Former collective member and coffeehouse DJ Amy Lange reflected on how difficult navigating song requests could be, noting that "there was one woman ... that always wanted 'Native Dancer' by Chris Williamson, which does not even have a beat. And so it was always this dilemma 'cause we took requests like, am I going to play it? Am I not gonna play it? 'Cause it's such a downer because you couldn't really dance to it, but she wanted [it] every time."[35] The pressure to play the music that would meet everyone's expectations could be mitigated, as the Old Dyke Nights demonstrated.

An offshoot of A Woman's Coffeehouse, the Old Dyke Nights group of Minneapolis compromised by deciding to play a range of music, including country; however, the group's success at mitigating controversy over music was in deemphasizing the music itself. At each event members would play two getting-to-know-you games. One of the group's most popular games was hug tag and then the members would follow the games with a potluck. As stated in the letter from the Old Dyke Nights organizing group, which was read aloud at the open community meeting for A Woman's Coffeehouse, the "ritual has become vital to our evening together."[36] By playing the games and socializing, there was less pressure put on playing the right music. Additionally, the organizers would leave the lights up a little while dancing because "we like how we look and like to look at each other."[37] The event organizing committee members had a short, two-month term, one-month offset, so everyone could be involved with planning the events. The letter finished that "Simplicity is a key word here. We can't please everyone, but we can involve everyone. Change with the seasons. Change slow," but also experiment.[38] When the emphasis shifted away from dancing, the community relaxed more about the music. A Woman's Coffeehouse was not originally intended to be solely about dancing. However, its shift towards mostly dances led women to attend or not attend based on musical preferences. The collective members responded "that we are a business and a community service and tried to do programming" and it was hard to please everyone.[39] In addition to the open community meeting, the organizers had distributed a questionnaire and again the collective received a deluge of contradictory responses regarding the music.[40] Unlike coffeehouses that had less financial pressure and met less

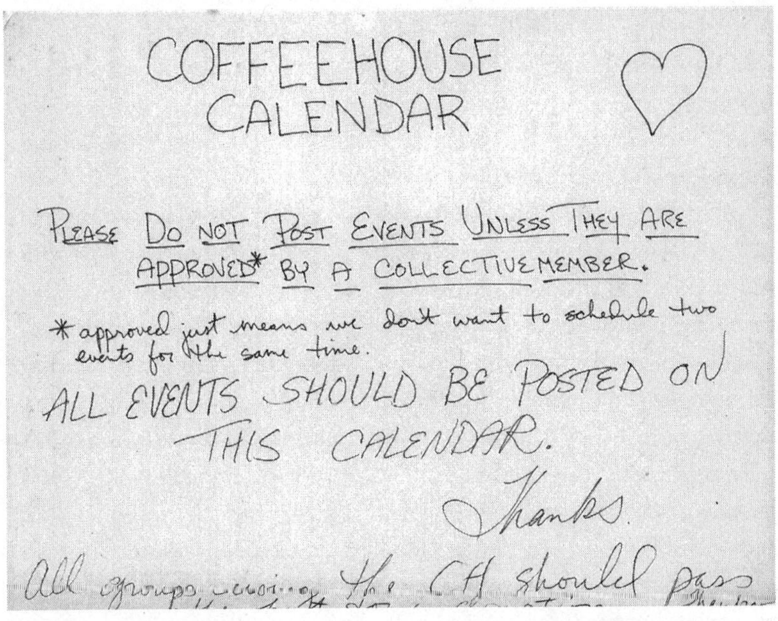

COFFEEHOUSE
CALENDAR
PLEASE DO NOT POST EVENTS UNLESS THEY ARE
APPROVED* BY A COLLECTIVE MEMBER.
* approved just means we don't want to schedule two
events for the same time.
ALL EVENTS SHOULD BE POSTED ON
THIS CALENDAR.
Thanks.

7.3 *Above the Iowa City Women's Coffeehouse events calendar was a note about how to get an event approved to be written on the event calendar. For November 1982, there were potlucks, poetry readings, and film screenings. Other months had workshops on repairing your own car, special meals, and members' vacation slideshows. (Courtesy of University of Iowa Library, Iowa Women's Archives, Jo Rabenold Papers, Box 4,* IWA0191*)*

often, the collective at A Woman's Coffeehouse felt immense stress. As a result of needing to appeal to a broader audience, issues around music became more important there than at other coffeehouses.

The collective of A Woman's Coffeehouse heard a range of suggestions at their open community meeting: some women wanted more top-forty music and some wanted less; some women thought the volume was too loud and others too soft; some wanted more women's music and others just wanted quiet; and another woman wanted waltzes and foxtrots. The collective relegated the decisions to the new music committee. Utilizing the talent in the community meant that they could buy discounted records from women who worked at record stores, or could get music at wholesale price, and find proper sound technicians.[41] Over the ten years of its existence, the services the coffeehouse provided became more and more technical and complicated and the coffeehouse needed to rely on a greater group within its community. One community member ended the discussions about music on a positive note, "Great blessings to the goddess to whip us into frenzy of dancing and wanting to come back again and again!"[42] Music was not the only form of art coffeehouses showcased and not the only medium that provoked controversy.

Coffeehouses displayed women's art on their walls. The Iowa City Women's Coffeehouse, in its June 1980 calendar, solicited headshots and portraits from local women for an upcoming art show. The Iowa City Women's Coffeehouse filled its calendar with feminist film screenings.[43] Some coffeehouses were more overt in their goal to display women's art. Wing Café Coffeehouse and Gallery of San Diego was a womyn's investment group project. As stated on its promotional materials, Wing Café and Gallery were women-owned-and-managed, serving the feminist and new age communities. Wing was especially "dedicated to the development and growth of women's culture and community."[44] Its organizers focused on displaying Southern Californian women's art. Showcasing art was a common practice of coffeehouses, yet controversy emerged over the care of the art. After Sidney Spinster's open letter regarding how the coffeehouse treated performers, A Woman's Coffeehouse of Minneapolis created a legal form informing artists that, while its insurance did not cover art damage, the organizers would "take care of it" as best they could.[45] Informal agreements and casual relationships around displaying art and playing music worked fine until an accident occurred. Conflict resulted when coffeehouses used similar legal forms and legal protections of the mainstream society. Controversies over payment and damages tested the lauded community of women and women's culture that this chapter describes. Facing these pressures, coffeehouses reverted to the legal protections and documents of American society at large.

Other Events and Building Skillsets

Feminist coffeehouses did not restrict their programming to musical and artistic performances. Mama Bears of the Bay Area in California was a bookstore, coffeehouse, and gallery. In September 1985, the organizers announced in their newsletter that they would be hosting an evening picnic and celebrating the autumn equinox.[46] Las Hermanas of San Diego, California, and the Iowa City Women's Coffeehouse were particularly innovative in their scheduling of events. The Iowa City Women's Coffeehouse collective organized pool tournaments and game nights. It held automotive maintenance classes to teach women to learn about their own cars and become more self-reliant.[47] In 1981, it also hosted a mermaid themed night.[48] A flyer from March 1981 advertised that the coffeehouse projected a slideshow about Ponape, a Pacific island in Micronesia. These events demonstrated the coffeehouse's desire to provide low cost educational opportunities, with the last event's entrance fee kept to a donation of $1.[49] Not every event was successful. A flyer announced relaxation and guided meditation classes every Monday evening at the Iowa City Women's Coffeehouse where women paid $2 if they made more than $10,000 a year or under $1 if they made less. However, it was "cancelled due to low attendance."[50] Endings did not necessarily equate to failure. All the coffeehouses likewise eventually ended, but they still made a meaningful contribution in their communities.

Las Hermanas of San Diego, California, hosted an event almost every day of the week. Beginning in 1975, the Las Hermanas collective produced a newsletter called *Feminist Communications*, which always included an event calendar. For the month of June 1975 alone it held rap groups on open relationships, an information session on setting up a women's land trust, "fat women's support" groups,

Alcoholics Anonymous meetings, a discussion for battered women, concerts, dances, picnics, and an event around the politics of childcare.[51] Its newsletter also included notes, event descriptions, and ads for local feminist businesses. The calendar noted when events had a fee. Childcare, when provided, was free, making the space more accessible for mothers. Food was served daily. The rest of the newsletter included articles, advertisements, and opinion pieces about feminist issues within San Diego and internationally. Las Hermanas demonstrates how feminist coffeehouses promoted and produced feminist culture.

Like the Iowa City Women's Coffeehouse, Las Hermanas' emphasis on education came through both in its programming and inadvertently through its hosting of events. The San Diego Lambda Archives volunteer Diane F. Germain, who learned about Las Hermanas after moving to San Diego from Los Angeles in 1976, said in a 2010 interview that, after a few visits to Las Hermanas for a $2 Sunday brunch, she began volunteering as a ticket-taker at the door.[52] She emphasized how the experience of volunteering at Las Hermanas gave many women valuable work skills that they carried into their professional careers, noting that "it's kind of hard to imagine now, but women weren't even carpenters." Germain explained that "women needed to know how to do lighting, and they needed to know how to do sound and put on a performance," adding that "sometimes we'd put on a concert and we couldn't find a woman to do the lighting, so we'd hire a guy and we would say, 'We'll pay you to do the lighting, but you have to have two women there and teach them while you're doing it.'"[53] As part of their feminist politics to empower the primarily working-class Latina women of their community, the organizers of Las Hermanas wanted to equip women with new skills. Even events that were not intended to be directly educational had an educational component. Las Hermanas was not alone in helping women explore their interests and develop professional skills as part of their operations.

Feminist coffeehouses acted as spaces in which women could pursue their interests and master new skills. The nonprofit Women's Coffeehouse in New York City began in 1973 after June Arnold, with her partner, donated ground-floor space on Abington Square. The idea behind the New York Women's Coffeehouse was to be "a separate women's space—a political space where women could bring their desires and dreams."[54] Now a women's studies and art history professor, Flavia Rando cooked at the New York Women's Coffeehouse from 1976 to 1977. She first became involved with the Women's Coffeehouse as a member of the Lesbian Art collective. This feminist art collective hosted shows and art discussions in the coffeehouse and presented slideshows. Initially the coffeehouse opened around four in the afternoon every day and served "nothing too exciting—coffee, tea, and snacks—maybe a cheese sandwich."[55] Rando believed that the women attending the coffeehouse deserved good food. Her plan was to cook one wonderful weekly meal that was offered for $3. Except for the first dinner when her sister helped, Rando would single-handedly cook between forty and sixty meals a night on a twenty-four-inch stove. As Rando proudly showed in her old journal, her first meal was lasagna served with whole wheat bread and butter. She used real mozzarella and the entire meal cost her $69.83 in supplies, which included the cost of transportation to pick up the supplies and olive oil.[56] The following week she hand-shucked fresh peas and also cooked pasta and spinach ricotta pie.[57] Rando emphasized that she was cooking "family meals" and that there were not too many adult men in these families but mostly women and children.[58] She made about $1.10 per hour, but the main reason she wanted to cook the meals was to provide people with special vegetarian food. The value of "food as respect" was something Rando wanted to share with the lesbian feminist community.[59] The Women's Coffeehouse of New York acted as a space where she could further develop these skills of art, cooking, and education, while living her politics.

Politics

While most coffeehouses were involved in fundraising for political events and hosted political rap sessions, feminist coffeehouses were inherently political whether or not they directly hosted political events. The Ann Arbor, Michigan, Women's Coffeehouse collective described the coffeehouse as a space where "the women also discuss other common problems experienced by many women in the Ann Arbor area such as childcare, health education, the lack of emergency housing and the need for a women's school to share skills."[60] For the women of the Ann Arbor Women's Coffeehouse, the act of creating a coffeehouse was political in and of itself. The coffeehouse additionally hosted political discussions.

By hosting political events, feminist coffeehouses made their politics apparent. A Woman's Coffeehouse of Minneapolis supported Take Back the Night events, as indicated on one of its fundraising flyers.[61] Las Hermanas of San Diego was particularly politically involved, as its newsletter engaged in both local and national feminist news and printed articles about the utility of separatism and problems with militantism.[62] The Iowa City Women's Coffeehouse held information sessions about the Equal Rights Amendment.[63] The coffeehouses also sometimes served as spaces for political groups to meet. In the summer of 1980, Lesbian Alliance members Jean and Jo wrote the Iowa City Women's Coffeehouse saying that they were planning their fall schedule and wanted to hold their meetings at the coffeehouse. The other program they were thinking about was lesbian rap sessions, stating that "presently what we have in mind is to have a different topic each month, have one or two or more women facilitate the meeting and to open the meetings to any lesbian who cares to participate. Topics would vary as interest shows."[64] Some of the topics they considered were "fat politics, black Lesbians, lesbians and money, and perhaps lighter topics if that is what women desire."[65] The Lesbian Alliance even offered to pay to use the space. Most of the overt politics involved money, either through fundraisers or renting out spaces to political groups. Most of the coffeehouses considered themselves as both political and not political: political in the sense that everything they did reflected their politics and not political in the sense that the coffeehouses were social and cultural spaces. Flavia Rando described the New York Women's Coffeehouse house as "basically a political meeting—a space that respected your ideas and who you were."[66] She remembered that many of the women who attended the coffeehouse were also involved in the organization Radicalesbians and other women's movement organizations.[67] Since so many of the women first entered feminist coffeehouses out of political motivations, the social was intertwined with the political.

Cultural Production: Newsletters

Coffeehouses also produced print culture. In addition to event flyers, feminist coffeehouses often produced newsletters with the events listed. Newsletters served the purpose of promoting events, asking for donations, and notifying the community of news. In the case of newsletters such as Las Hermanas' *Feminist Communications*, they also listed community events. Mama Bears coffeehouse of Oakland, California, produced *Mama Bear News*, which told readers about upcoming feminist events at both the Mama Bears bookstore and coffeehouse.[68] Newsletters could share information about coffeehouse events but also encourage community engagement.

Newsletters had the ability to create a sense of community by telling readers about the history of the coffeehouses and establishing transparency within the organization. Kay Lara Schoenwetter, editor of A Woman's Coffeehouse of Minneapolis's newsletter *Coffee Klatch*, explained, "this newsletter will be put out quarterly (or so) to publicize 'behind the scenes' information about how A Woman's Coffeehouse is run."[69] Announcements were still made from week to week at the coffeehouse; the collective had a public notebook with minutes of collective meetings, and the collective members encouraged patrons to talk with them, indicating that they that could be identified as the women at the food counter, the door, or the record player.[70] By making this information public, the coffeehouse collective hoped women would feel a greater connection to the institution and also be empathetic to some of the organizational difficulties that the collective encountered, such as insufficient funding. The Women's Coffeehouse of Cambridge, Massachusetts, in May 1988 began publishing *The Coffeehouse News*, stating, "We're delighted to present the very first edition of The Coffeehouse News—hot off the press! We've been looking for a way to keep in touch with new participants and veteran coffeehousers for updates and invitations."[71] In the issue, the writers also thanked their readers for their support for the past two years. They saw the newsletter as a way "to present a three-month schedule so you'll be sure not to miss any terrific events!"[72] The writers also emphasized that the coffeehouse was a nonprofit, volunteer-run women's collective organizing free feminist cultural events on Friday evenings at The Women's Center in Cambridge. Women who had never attended the coffeehouse but may have happened upon the letter would have also learned that "the coffeehouse is always free, is handicapped accessible and provides ASL [American Sign Language] interpretation at any event with two weeks' notice. As an experimental forum for creating and enjoying women's culture, we strive for relevance and community."[73] This periodical was also used to encourage new members to formally join the collective. Coffeehouses were not the only feminist businesses to have newsletters. Malaprop's feminist bookstore and cafe also had a newsletter in Ashville, North Carolina, announcing events.[74] Because coffeehouses typically sponsored so many events, distributing calendars that also served as newsletters became commonplace.

Feminist coffeehouses were also interconnected through literary culture by the feminist periodicals that wrote about them and ran advertisements of their businesses. The coffeehouses in turn would

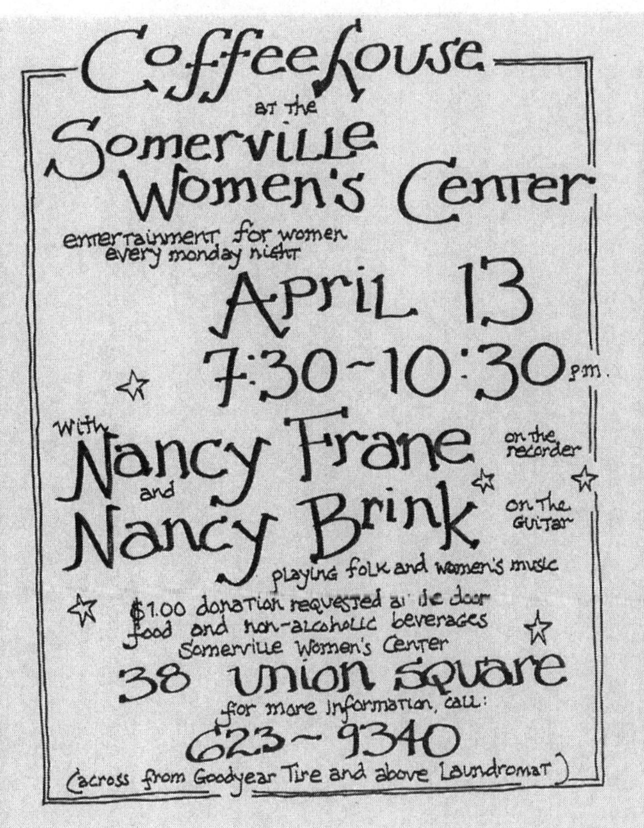

7.4 *The Somerville Coffeehouse of Somerville, Massachusetts, emphasized entertainment over educational events. (Courtesy of Northeastern University Archives, Somerville Women's Educational Center 1975–1983 (M26), Box 4 "Projects: Coffeehouse: Fliers and Notes")*

support feminist literary culture by hosting touring authors and by promoting and financially helping feminist periodicals. In 1977, the feminist periodical of the Twin Cities, *Goldflower*, recounted how the Women's Coffeehouse collective "generously made available the

Coffeehouse facilities [at The New Riverside Café] for *Goldflower*. Their time and help were much appreciated. As a result of the benefit, *Goldflower* made $157 in door donations and food sales."[75] These coffeehouses were also connected more directly.

Interconnected

Touring musicians connected feminist coffeehouses and, in addition, an informal support network existed between these coffeehouses. In trying to solve their problems, individual coffeehouses were not without guidance. In the Iowa City Women's Coffeehouse archives there is a letter written by Kimela in 1981 describing how the collective of A Woman's Coffeehouse of Minneapolis operated. Previously Kimela had offered "to answer any questions."[76] As a result, The Iowa City Women's Coffeehouse collective had explained to Kimela how it had managed its finances and sought her guidance in improving their organizational structure. It should be evident from the last two chapters that A Woman's Coffeehouse of Minneapolis was not without its own problems. However, after six years of operation, the Minneapolis collective members were able to lend support and offer advice about lessons learned through their own trial and error. A Woman's Coffeehouse collective also studied how other coffeehouses functioned. In its archives there is a flyer from the Mountain Moving Coffeehouse of Chicago. Furthermore, during collective meetings, as evidenced by members' handwritten meeting minutes, the Minneapolis collective discussed how Mountain Moving operated on a volunteer basis. In the Somerville Women's Coffeehouse archives' collective meeting minutes, the scribe noted that before members of the collective opened their own coffeehouse, they were looking into both currently operating and defunct coffeehouse/restaurants for advice.[77] They also decided that if the coffeehouse did not materialize they would donate whatever money remained to the women's community, as they saw themselves as part of a greater project of feminism and the creation of women's space.[78] Feminist coffeehouses actively supported each other and built a larger network of feminist cultural space.

Conclusion

After fifteen years of producing events, A Woman's Coffeehouse of Minneapolis ceased operations in September 1989. Infighting over matters of representation, inclusion, money, and programming became insurmountable. New feminist and lesbian organizations founded in the mid-1980s in the Twin Cities region began to produce events catering to the same demographic as A Woman's Coffeehouse. These new organizations were appealing, as they were not tied to the same contentious history of conflict as A Woman's Coffeehouse.[79] However, from 1975 to 1989, A Woman's Coffeehouse provided a meaningful space that supported lesbian and feminist culture. The unique value of the coffeehouse explained why women fought so hard to maintain it even when financial difficulties started to tear apart the organization in 1984. Ten years after its closure, the coffeehouse's pioneering members held one last event in the basement of the Plymouth Church, to celebrate the friendships, relationships, and programming that had been so significant in their lives and in the history of the Twin Cities.[80] Similarly when Mountain Moving Coffeehouse of Chicago ended after thirty-one years of operation in 2005, it was the oldest continuously operating "womyn-born womyn and girl-only feminist coffeehouse" in the United States. The coffeehouse had produced hundreds of concerts and social events for lesbians and feminists. However, it had excluded transgender women, thus fostering transphobic attitudes. A successor organization called the Kindred Hearts' Coffeehouse began offering a monthly event of women's music in its wake, trying to maintain Mountain Moving's cultural contribution.[81]

It was in part due to the success of women's coffeehouses increasing options for lesbian-feminist socializing that some lesbian feminists no longer felt the need for the coffeehouses to continue. One of the organizers of the Duluth, Minnesota's North County Coffeehouse, Kathy Heltzer, remarked that eventually a lot of the coffeehouse crowd started going to the women's hockey games together instead of coffeehouse nights.[82] Lesbian musician Ann Reed felt that she had more places to perform outside of the women's coffeehouse circuit.[83] Feminist coffeehouses, therefore, even after closing, continued to make an impact.

Feminist coffeehouses played a significant role in promoting feminist and lesbian culture and provided nonprofit temporary feminist social and political space. Coffeehouse events brought women together through music, dancing, art, politics, and socializing. These spaces provided a space for women to learn skills like business recordkeeping, sound and lighting design, and event coordination. In addition to providing women with training they could use in other aspects of their lives, coffeehouse collectives bolstered other existing feminist businesses and women entrepreneurs by creating a space in which these businesses and individuals could advertise and operate. Difficulties over money threatened coffeehouse collectives' abilities to create these cultural contributions. Not only was it difficult to raise enough capital to find space, provide refreshment, and compensate entertainers but coffeehouses' collectives had to maintain a precarious balance. The collectives were politically motivated to make events accessible across class lines while the coffeehouses also needed to meet operating costs, attempt to properly compensate artists, and provide economic and/or emotional support for the organizing committees. While these operations were not without conflict, the lower overhead costs of feminist coffeehouses allowed women of varying class and race backgrounds in the United States to create temporary spaces in which to play women's music, display women's art, and be in the company of other feminists and lesbians. Whether or not they served coffee, feminist coffeehouses created a buzz.

PART THREE

Conclusions and Legacies, 1989–2022

CHAPTER 8

Legacies, Conclusions, and New Futures

Feminist Restaurants, Cafes, and Coffeehouses beyond 1989

> Cafes have always been sites of resistance. What revolution wasn't planned in a coffee shop? We work hard to make ours a place where everyone feels comfortable, whether you're queer, trans, gender non-conforming, a person of color, of different ability (workin on a wheelchair plan, I promise), in need of a #socialistslidingscalesoup, elderly, newborn, etc. We're also here for people who have the privilege to be able to choose their variety of opposition to current societal norms: the vegans, the anarchists, feminists, freaks, garden variety weirdos, people who dress up as John Waters every Halloween, etc. It's deeply gratifying for me to work everyday with our staff on how we can try harder to be a place of refuge from the current, ah, situation. More than one member of our staff has told me that this is the first job they've ever had where they haven't been misgendered, and that makes me equal parts angry and proud. Anyway. Thank you for coming to Commissary! and getting what we're trying to do. I'm sorry it's so hard out there. We see you. We're here to support each other. — lagusta #zineoftheweek[1]
>
> *Lagusta's Commissary, Facebook post*

It has been fifty years since Dolores Alexander and Jill Ward founded the first feminist restaurant in the United States, Mother Courage of New York City. Despite serving as alternatives to hegemonic eatery culture, feminist restaurants, cafes, and coffeehouses were still vulnerable to mainstream economic patterns and governmental regulations, which ultimately curtailed some of their owners' dreams. Feminist restaurants, cafes, and coffeehouses fostered cultural, economic, and social communities that played an important role in the women's, feminist, and lesbian movements. Although this book focuses primarily on historical case studies within the United States from 1972 to 1989, the findings of this book elucidate important lessons for feminist organizations and businesses today. Contemporary feminist restaurants, cafes, and coffeehouses build upon the work of earlier generations; some owners of more recent feminist eateries even have a direct connection to the past. As the above quote from contemporary feminist cafe owner and vegan anarchist chocolatier Lagusta Yearwood's Facebook post demonstrates, the social, political, cultural, and dietary legacies of feminist restaurants and cafes founded during the 1970s and 1980s live on.

Endings for the Restaurants of the 1970s and 1980s

Most of the original founders of the restaurants, cafes, and coffeehouses examined in earlier chapters moved on with their lives or passed away by the late 1980s or early 1990s, with a few notable exceptions. Collectives formed in the 1970s and 1980s fizzled out due to infighting. Restaurant owners sold off their businesses because of financial problems, burnout, or loss of interest. When Jill Ward of Mother Courage could no longer continue with the daily grind of operating her business after six years, she sold the restaurant to Michael Safdia who transformed the location into a French bistro called the Black Sheep.[2] Her business partner and former romantic partner, Dolores Alexander, had left the business years earlier, citing disinterest.[3] Patricia Hynes of Bread and Roses Restaurant in Cambridge, Massachusetts, sold her space to the Ducky Haven Café Collective, which renamed the restaurant Amaranth. As its grand-opening posters claimed, Amaranth became an exclusively women's vegetarian restaurant with a focus on performances and art shows.[4] Afterwards,

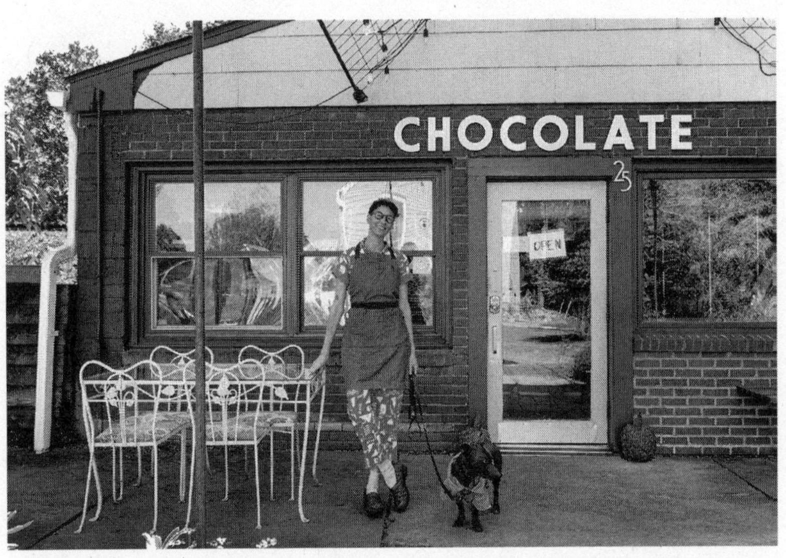

8.1 Lagusta Yearwood stands outside of Lagusta's Luscious of New Paltz, New York, selling feminist anarchist vegan chocolates. She shares her views on what it means to run on a feminist restaurant and chocolate shop on her many social media accounts. (Photo courtesy of Liz Clayman)

Hynes completed her graduate studies and became a renowned environmental activist, professor, and author.[5] Berkeley, California's Brick Hut, in its third iteration and after two moves, ultimately closed in 1997. Sharon Davenport of the Hut became an archivist-librarian living in Oakland, California. Joan Antonuccio currently works as a professional voice actor.[6] By the 1990s most of these spaces were gone or closing and feminist restaurants and cafes had largely become a thing of the past. By 2022, except for Bloodroot Feminist Restaurant and the Big Kitchen of San Diego, the feminist restaurants, cafes, and coffeehouses founded between 1972 and 1989 were nearly extinct. The world has changed, and feminist activism has changed with it; however, a new generation of feminist restaurants, cafes, and coffeehouses have followed in the wake of their predecessors.

New Generations and Connections with the Past

Feminism has evolved since the 1970s and 1980s and the needs of feminist communities have likewise transformed. Queer politics and postmodern theories of the body have shifted understandings of gender.[7] While many of the feminist restaurants of the 1970s and 1980s focused on women-only or women-centred spaces, there has since been a push for feminist spaces to be open to all genders beyond the gender binary. Queer politics and postmodernism have afforded men, non-binary, and transgender people a greater role in contemporary feminist eateries. Many of the community-level debates examined in this book's earlier chapters were issues that continued to evolve, growing into discussions of intersectional feminism, which consider the ways that race, class, gender, sexual orientation, age, disability, ethnicity, and immigration status impact one's experiences of oppression and marginalization. These issues importantly transformed feminist conversations.[8] Contemporary feminist restaurants, cafes, coffeehouses, and food businesses reflect these changes. For example, these changes are evident in the mission statement of Bluestockings Bookstore, Café, and Activist Center of New York, founded in 1999. The operating collective explains that Bluestockings "offers mutual aid, harm reduction support, non-judgmental resource research and a warming/cooling place that is radically inclusive of all genders, cultures, expansive sexualities and identities … Historically, we have served as a sanctuary for NYC's overlapping queer communities, and have evolved from a 'women's' bookstore to become a horizontalist feminist community center whose work is rooted in care and mutuality."[9] As Bluestockings's cooperative members note, feminist communities have transformed even in the past twenty years; therefore, it is unsurprising that there have been shifts in the ways that feminist restaurants, cafes, and coffeehouses have operated since the 1970s. Noting these differences does not seek to erase the revolutionary aspects of feminist restaurants, cafes, and coffeehouses founded in

8.2 The paint outside of Bluestockings original location in New York City (1999–2020) declares "Rad books / $1 coffee / stimulating events/ beautiful community" and "we are a safer space." (Courtesy of The Bluestockings Collective)

the 1970s and 1980s, such as the Brick Hut which, from its founding, aimed to welcome a broad diversity of people.[10] Rather, this chapter shows that contemporary feminist restaurants and cafes continue to grapple with similar challenges that plagued the restaurants founded between 1972 and 1989, while also reflecting the characteristics of feminist movements today. Despite generational differences, the human need for finding community spaces where one feels accepted and supported continues, and the desire to create spaces that reflect their founders' feminist values is as true today as it was in 1972.

The cultural production of feminist eateries of the 1970s and 1980s continues to influence new generations of feminist restaurant and cafe founders. In email correspondence, Lagusta Yearwood of Lagusta's Luscious, in New Paltz, New York (founded in 2003 with the brick-and-mortar location in 2011), reflected, "I bought a Bloodroot cookbook in college and fell in love with it. I wrote a fan letter to Noel and Selma and they wrote back, encouraging me to come visit."[11]

Yearwood later decided to cook at Bloodroot during her culinary school internship and then continued working there. Furthermore, she worked alongside Selma and Noel to produce some of their cookbooks. When asked about the impact of Bloodroot on her life, she replied, "Truly, it changed everything about how I wanted to live, and how I felt I could live. It opened up new worlds of possibility to me."[12] Noel Furie and Selma Miriam inspired her and mentored her. Even after Yearwood left Bloodroot, they continued to support her; they sell her chocolates at Bloodroot. Yearwood says that the influence of Bloodroot's proprietors is evident throughout her business. Even the name of her chocolate company and shop, Lagusta's Luscious, was the suggestion of Bloodroot's Noel Furie. Yearwood continued to bring lessons learned at Bloodroot with her as she went on to also found an additional three businesses: her vegan cafe, Commissary of New Paltz in 2016, The Confectionary of New York City, also co-founded in 2016 with vegan dessert maker Maresa Volante of Sweet Maresa's and, on February 8, 2022 she announced her newest venture, a CBD vegan candy company, Softpower Sweets.[13] This connection does not mean that there are not differences between the feminist restaurants, cafes, and coffeehouses of the 1970s and present, as Yearwood readily attests. However, there is both explicit and implicit interplay between generations.

The social and political landscapes of the United States have transformed since the 1970s and 1980s, but the historical narrative is not one of total progress. Despite shifts in some specific issues, sexism, classism, racism, heterosexism, and other forms of social injustice remain problems. As this book has demonstrated, feminist restaurants and cafes were never utopias. Patrons and collectives holding differing political opinions, combined with interpersonal conflicts, led to discord. While these institutions had their own flaws and problems, they provided the opportunity to navigate the world in new ways. Here we find parallels in contemporary feminist restaurants and cafes.

Parallels and Updates

SUSTAINABILITY, THE FEMINIST NEXUS, AND THE ARTS

When restaurant owners and operators face similar issues to proprietors of the past, they have explored similar solutions. Keeping their spaces operational—or even making a profit—continues to be a challenge. As chapter 3 explored, selling non-perishable goods such as books was a common practice used by feminist restaurants in the 1970s and 1980s to diversify income streams. The feminist restaurants of today, such as Lagusta's Commissary and Sweet Maresa's of Kingston, New York, do the same. In addition to food and drink, these establishments offer tote bags, merchandise, and goods from local artisans. For example, in April 2021, Lagusta's Commissary featured macramé terrariums and plant holders made by Two Buds and a Plant[14] and Sweet Maresa's sold dog biscuits.[15] Furthermore, these businesses sell of mix of freshly prepared foods that require immediate consumption and foods that can last longer, such as chocolates or canned goods. These feminist food businesses create space for smaller local businesses with shared values to grow their businesses, while trying to sustain their own.

On the other hand, it is important to remember that feminist bookstores would sell perishable goods such as food and drink in addition to their main inventory to foster community and create a space to linger. Many feminist bookstores of the 1970s and 1980s also functioned as cafes, or at least served coffee and tea, such as Sisterspirit Café and Bookstore of San Jose, California,[16] Three Birds Coffeeshop and Bookshop of Tampa, Florida, Pandora Womyn's Bookstore of Kalamazoo, Michigan, and A Place of Our Own Wimmin's Bookstore of Lincoln, Nebraska, to name just a few. This phenomenon continues today. For example, Cafe Con Libros in Brooklyn, New York, is an intersectional feminist bookstore and coffee shop. Founded in 2017, Cafe Con Libros states that "through our choice of books, programming and great coffee, we endeavor to create a vibrant community space where everyone,] specifically, female-identified folx, feel centered, affirmed and celebrated."[17] Firestorm Books and Coffee of Ashville, North Carolina, founded in 2008, and A Seat at the Table Books, Coffee, and Community of Elk Grove, California, whose physical space was founded in November 2021,[18] likewise feed bellies and minds with books and food. The technique of diversifying income streams enhances the stability of these feminist businesses. In the case of the feminist bookstore cafes, this strategy provides a dual purpose: fostering community and ensuring the longevity of their businesses.

The feminist restaurants, cafes, and coffeehouses of the 1970s and 1980s had an economic impact beyond the physical walls of their establishment. As discussed in chapters 4 and 7, these eateries were part of a larger nexus of feminist businesses. In addition to providing direct economic opportunities for the women who were employed by the restaurant, feminist restaurants and cafes promoted women-owned businesses and craftswomen. The owners of Bloodroot, Bread and Roses, and Wildrose sought to hire women plumbers, carpenters, and electricians. Common Women Café of Northampton, Massachusetts, worked with female real estate agents and lawyers. Feminist restaurants were not the only twentieth-century spaces in which the desire to hire from within a marginalized community happened in the United States; Black business movements were a key organizing strategy for some members of the civil rights movement and previous anti-racist organizing and community building, such as Booker T. Washington's National Negro Business League in 1900.[19] However, it was in the feminist businesses of the 1970s and 1980s in which an emphasis on gender was primary, a focus that continues today. Feminist restaurant owners' decisions to hire from within the lesbian-feminist and feminist communities and promote the products made by members of these communities are comparable to what has now become a call to action to support marginalized creators and businesses.

These calls span from where to buy products, to what businesses to frequent, and even to whom scholars should cite, such as the Twitter hashtag movements #WomenAlsoKnowHistory and #CiteBlackWomen. The circulation of lists of Black and Indigenous bookstores,[20] Black-owned businesses,[21] and mobile apps to help find Black-owned restaurants such as EatOkra, increased in response to the resurgence of the #BlackLivesMatter movement in 2020. Alongside these lists were those that highlighted Indigenous businesses,[22] LGBTQ+ businesses,[23] and feminist bookstores.[24] The promotion of these lists encourage shoppers to support businesses by and for marginalized communities.[25] They also indicate safety, listing places that are safer for members of these marginalized communities to frequent and work. These lists of businesses are reminiscent of the *Green Book* for Black travellers and the various gay and lesbian travel guides, which were key to researching this book.[26] Those guides were also important for connecting lesbian feminists and lesbian feminist business networks in the 1970s and 1980s, at home and abroad.

Contemporary feminist restaurants and cafes have carried forth the desire to support and amplify the businesses of other women. However, as intersectional feminism has highlighted the ways that oppressions such as sexism, racism, classism, and ableism are intertwined and perpetuated under heteropatriarchal capitalism, hiring and contracting protocols have expanded from women-only policies to include non-binary and transgender people. There is also a greater emphasis on working with and hiring people of colour. These policies are evident in the mission statement of feminist bookstore and cafe, Fulton Street of Tulsa, Oklahoma. Founded in 2019, Fulton Street centres the "narratives and lived experiences of people of color and marginalized communities" and at least 70 percent of the books they stock are written by or feature Black, brown, Indigenous, people of colour, and/or marginalized communities.[27] Cafe Con Libros has made similar decisions about their featured products. As part of the cafe's Feminist and Bookish Monthly Subscription, "books written by, about and for womxn and specifically, womxn of color" are prioritized.[28] The other contemporary feminist restaurants and cafes discussed in this chapter, likewise support the authors, creators, operators, and artists from their feminist communities and emphasize the importance of race, class, gender, and sexual orientation as informing their business decisions.

As discussed in chapters 4 and 7, feminist restaurants, cafes, and coffeehouses of the 1970s and 1980s were vital in the promotion of feminist literary culture, art, performance, and music. Like contemporary feminist bookstore cafes, they sold books. Touring musicians like Alix Dobkin and authors such as Adrienne Rich would visit. Wing Café and Art Gallery of San Diego held feminist art shows. Most feminist restaurants hung feminist art on their walls. They promoted other women's empowerment in their communities economically, socially, and politically. The feminist restaurants, cafes, and food businesses of today likewise continue this model. For example, Lagusta's Commissary hosts concerts and promotes a zine of the month.[29] Lagusta Yearwood covers her businesses' walls with art from local feminist artists.[30] The websites of Firestorm, Cafe Con Libros, and Bluestockings show a mix of in-person and virtual events that range from author readings, art shows, and even a performance of "Pirate Songs for Kids."[31] As a result of bringing together books, publications, performances, music, and art, the economic and cultural impact of these restaurants expanded beyond their single brick and mortar locations.

By frequenting these feminist restaurants and cafes, customers support an entire network of feminist businesses and creators. Buying a book by a feminist author at a major online retailer such as Amazon supports the author, but a multi-national corporation also profits. Purchasing a feminist book or pastry from a feminist restaurant or cafe means the author benefits, the feminist business benefits, and money circulates within feminist communities. In 2020, Kalima DeSuze of Cafe Con Libros, participated in the American Booksellers

8.3 Kalima DeSuze, owner of Cafe Con Libros in Brooklyn, New York, in front of the espresso machine. The awning of her business declares it is "Black, Feminist, and Bookish."

Association's Boxed Out campaign, in which she and the designers of ad agency DCX NYC transformed the façade of her cafe and bookstore to resemble the cardboard boxes ubiquitous with Amazon deliveries. They marked the boxes with slogans such as "Buy books from people who want to sell books, not colonize the moon" and "Don't let indie bookstores become a work of fiction."[32] The campaign was an effort to draw attention to how supporting small businesses with feminist initiatives has an important social, cultural, and economic impact in both feminist and local communities. As DeSuze remarked on the campaign, "The heart and soul of our industry is the spaces that we create in our communities—the spaces of learning, the spaces of action, community building, friendship building, exchanging of ideas that Amazon does not create … And we need folks to invest in us."[33] As economists have demonstrated, when money is spent in local communities, the money stays in the community, small businesses can thrive, and the impact is greater.[34] The impact of feminist restaurants and cafes extends beyond the feminist nexus.

CONTINUED LABOUR CHALLENGES: SEXISM IN PROFESSIONAL KITCHENS

The feminist restaurants, cafes, and coffeehouses founded in the 1970s and 1980s were formed in part as a response to sexist kitchens and restaurants, as discussed in chapter 2. They came into existence during a period when Americans dined outside the home at record-breaking numbers and acted as a response to sexual harassment and issues of capitalism. Feminist restaurants produced alternative work environments; they produced alternative economies within the restaurants, and the businesses they supported. However, the challenges of sexism and harassment in mainstream restaurants, particularly regarding the treatment of women chefs, cooks, and waitstaff continues. In the fall of 2017, in response to the preponderance of claims of sexual harassment within the restaurant industry, numerous articles were written about this gender imbalance. Notably chef Jen Agg's *New Yorker* piece, "A Harvey Weinstein Moment for the Restaurant Industry," and New York City–based chef Amanda Cohen's article for *Esquire*, "I've Worked in Food for 20 Years. Now You Finally Care About Female Chefs?: We Deserved Your Attention Long Before Sexual Harassment Made Headlines," drew attention to the ongoing sexism within the restaurant industry.[35] Feminist restaurants' response to the sexual harassment and gender inequity of the 1970s and 1980s continues to be relevant today.

Restaurant conditions in the twenty-first century are not the same as in 1972, when Mother Courage was first founded. More women are running their own restaurants than in the 1970s. In 2007, the Culinary Institute of America's Diversity Council recorded that female chefs and head cooks made up just 21 percent of professional kitchens, citing data from the US Bureau of Labor Statistics and National Restaurant Association (NRA).[36] In a December 2014 letter to congressional leaders, NRA president and CEO Dawn Sweeney stated that over half of American restaurants were owned or co-owned by women. According to this industry group, in the past decade, the number of women-owned restaurants has increased by 50 percent.[37] Despite women owning more restaurants than fifty years ago, women have continued to face barriers to success. Men owned and worked as chefs at most of the highest-ranking restaurants and most Michelin Star holders in the United States are male. All-male committees typically decide these rankings. During the 2017 San Pellegrino chef awards, only one woman was part of the judging for the entire contest.[38] While debates continue about the elitism behind the rankings, especially with cooking being judged against the French standard for fine cuisine, which pushes other cooking traditions to the peripheries, these rankings and awards have real ramifications. These rankings affect not only the elite status of restaurants but also the opportunities for the female chefs themselves and restaurant culture at large.

Building on the legacy of previous feminist restaurants, contemporary feminist restaurants and cafes work to tackle sexism, heterosexism, racism, and transphobia in their kitchens and dining rooms, for workers and customers alike. Kalima DeSuze of Cafe Con Libros says she wants her bookstore cafe to be an inclusive sanctuary of affirmation "for women and girls across race, class, gender, age, sexuality, sexual presentation."[39] This sentiment is echoed across the mission statements of the other contemporary feminist eateries such as in the quote opening this chapter. Feminist restaurants and cafes of the present, like those of the 1970s and 1980s, are not a cure-all for every problem in mainstream restaurant culture; rather, they offer new models of restaurants and eateries in which employees can be respected and where people from a variety of identity backgrounds can thrive.

COLLECTIVES OR INDIVIDUAL MANAGEMENT

Feminist restaurants and cafes vary in their operating and management structures; however, creating opportunities for employees or collective members to be able to work in a business that reflects their feminist values remains consistent. Chapters 2, 3, and 6 discussed how some feminist restaurants, cafes, and coffeehouses of the 1970s and 1980s were managed by collectives such as the Common Womon Club, A Woman's Coffeehouse, the Full Moon Coffeehouse, and the Brick Hut, whereas other establishments such as Bread and Roses and Ruby's were managed by one or two individuals. The tradition of collectives continues in feminist and restaurant cafes today. Firestorm functions on a collective, cooperative model. The members explain that "our co-operative operates without bosses or supervisors, relying instead on well-developed team structures. Decision making is achieved 'horizontally,' using a formal consensus process in which each participant has equal voice. This collaborative environment creates a more empowering and enjoyable workplace while strengthening the business itself."[40] Similarly, after twenty years of operating, Bluestockings became worker-owned and operated. The cafe, bookstore, and community centre is "led by a group of four queer and trans/gnc [gender non-conforming] people, five folks of color, three disabled and three mad people, three sex workers, survivors of sexual violence and a small number of co-conspirators."[41] Like Firestorm, Bluestockings cooperative members use a consensus-based decision-making structure and a horizontally shared decision-making model, they have transparent financial practices between members, and they work to establish their own living wages and/or sweat equity compensation.[42] As the dissolution of Northampton's Common Womon Club collective demonstrated, infighting and a lack of open communication could lead to a feminist business's demise in the 1970s and 1980s. However, the model of operating collectively is an attempt by enterprises such as Bluestockings to live out their feminist values. The cooperative notes that they do not think the model is "a cure-all for the immense violence of capitalism, but we feel this model best positions us to realize our goals, expand upon our mutual aid and care work, and achieve economic justice as workers."[43] For other feminist restaurants, other management structures have been more appealing.

Single or dual management models of feminist businesses existed in the 1970s and continue today. Lagusta Yearwood is the manager of her businesses because, as she admits, "I'm just not a collectivist, sadly. I'm a control freak with a strong vision for my business. I run it as collectively as possible these days, which is nice, though."[44] Since our initial 2015 correspondence, as Yearwood's businesses have expanded, she has spread work across other managers.[45] Despite relinquishing some control, Yearwood is not alone in her model of a single or dual owner and operator. Onikah Asamoa-Caesar founded Fulton Street Books & Coffee and continues to head the operation. Kalima DeSuze of Cafe Con Libros is a single operator as well. DeSuze commented on the challenges of a hierarchal management model in a feminist business, writing, "the humans who work with us are part of a team and will be regarded as such. While we do not deny there is hierarchy in the employee and employer relationship, we are committed to working hard to minimize the harmful impact of such relationships by remaining mindful, inclusive, and accountable to our values as well as to the larger Brooklyn, New York, and global communities."[46] Contemporary and past feminist restaurants and cafes shared this deep kind of reflection about the management models.

As evidenced throughout this book, feminist restaurant owners and operators experimented with management styles. Some feminist restaurants changed in their ownership structure. Some of the longer-running feminist restaurants founded the 1970s and 1980s shifted from collective ownership to single ownership. Collective members would lose interest, conflict would ensue, or new economic strategies were needed to survive. The Brick Hut collective narrowed to two. Wildrose's founding collective narrowed to one. Bloodroot moved from a collective model to being under Selma Miriam and

Noel Furie's leadership. It was these restaurants' adaptability to their circumstances that contributed to their longevity. While Bloodroot's success over forty-five years is unique for any restaurant, their adaptability to the changing nature of feminist communities and economic conditions has contributed to their sustainability. Like their namesake, the bloodroot flower whose rhizomes grow deep and form a network with their kin to help the community thrive, owners Selma Miriam and Noel Furie's passion for their restaurant and food spread throughout their community. Their efforts to connect and integrate with the larger neighbourhood led to their business being supported in return.

As contemporary feminist restaurants, cafes, and food businesses confront economic recessions, a global pandemic, and life under a climate crisis, they too may need to adapt to survive. Kalima DeSuze of Cafe Con Libros wrote, "we realize that we are a work in progress; continuously becoming. So, we value growth. We invite you to remain in community with us; tell us how we can be better."[47] The bookstore cafe has already had to innovate to survive COVID-19 pandemic lockdowns by creating feminist book subscriptions. Lagusta Yearwood has had to learn to delegate as her business expands.[48] Despite these challenges, Yearwood maintains that her businesses continue to operate "to be a community space of joy, safety, and peace; to use good ingredients and serve delicious things; to be sustainable and fun for the people who work [there]."[49] With changes in the global economy, labour conditions, and the influence of neoliberalism on ideology and lived reality, the new generation has taken the ideas of past feminist restaurant owners and altered them to fit current economic and social circumstances. In the future, as these feminist restaurants and cafes continue to operate, they too may rethink or reorganize their management styles.

Regardless of the management structure, the demographics of feminist restaurant and cafe founders and operators have changed since the twentieth century. Due to the confluence of limited credit opportunity, discrimination from living in a white supremacist society, and other barriers for participation, most feminist restaurants from 1972 to 1989 were founded by white women. As discussed in chapter 2, most founders identified as lesbians and a significant number of these women were Jewish. While there was more diversity within the management of feminist coffeehouses, in part due to the lower operating costs (as discussed in chapter 6), white women continued to be predominant. The owners and operators of contemporary feminist restaurants and cafes are a more racially diverse group. Kalima DeSuze identifies as an "Afro-Latinx feminist, social worker, activist, teacher, veteran, and new mother" from Crown Heights, New York.[50] Onikah Asamoa-Caesar is a Black woman, mother, former teacher, and policy advisor.[51] The collective of Bluestockings includes five people of colour. Diversity is not limited to race, however. While in the 1970s, most of the founders identified as lesbians, contemporary feminist restaurant and cafe owners, collective members, and employees identify as straight, lesbian, queer, and other sexual orientations.[52] Furthermore, while the feminist restaurants and cafes of the past were almost exclusively led and staffed by women, people of all genders including cisgender, transgender, non-binary, and gender non-conforming people work at Fulton Street and at Yearwood's multiple businesses. The Firestorm collective describes itself as a queer feminist group.[53] However, as in the past, women continue to be at the forefront of creating these spaces.

DOES CONTEMPORARY FEMINIST FOOD HAVE A NEW FLAVOUR?

Feminist restaurants' and cafes' menus have always reflected the managers' feminist politics. As chapter 5 discussed, the making of feminist food required the consideration of labour conditions, sourcing of products, cost for customers, the role of animal products, and the marketing of dishes. Most feminist restaurants and cafes of the 1970s and 1980s were vegetarian or at least had vegetarian items.

Over the course of Bloodroot's history, the menu transformed from a seasonal menu that once included fish, to an entirely vegetarian one, to then become more and more vegan as the years progressed. A major reason for the vegetarian menus of the 1970s and 1980s was because those feminist restaurant owners either linked the oppression of women and animals or acknowledged the deleterious environmental impact of industrially produced meat. In subsequent years, a growing awareness of the environmental impact of dairy (not to mention the impact on dairy-producing animals), has led more feminist eateries to focus on vegan menus. Lagusta Yearwood's businesses are completely vegan. Firestorm's pastries are vegan. Sweet Maresa's bakery is entirely vegan. Even though Fulton Street is not fully vegan—the menu includes a ham and cheese croissant—vegan options exist.[54] While vegan options are prevalent at contemporary feminist restaurants, cafes, and food businesses of today, there is more to feminist food than the inclusion or lack of animal products (as chapter 5 discussed).

Political and environmental considerations in the sourcing of the food has been an important component of feminist restaurants, cafes, and coffeehouses since the 1970s and 1980s. The owners of Brick Hut had wanted to source their eggs locally. The Bloodroot collective was so committed to sourcing seasonal produce that they wrote cookbooks organized by Connecticut's seasons. As many feminist restaurants and cafes thought critically about the role of labour within their businesses, they also examined how their ingredients were produced. Sourcing goods locally meant that they were better able to know their farmers and learn about labour practices.

Contemporary feminist restaurants continue this practice. Bolstered by the locavore movements that gained ground in the twenty-first century and by growing criticism of global food supply networks, the feminist restaurants and cafes of today show their commitment to local ingredients and products.[55] Maresa Volante of Sweet Maresa's supports the farm-to-table movement and works with local farmers whenever possible.[56] Firestorm's website announces that the business

8.4 Onikah Asamoa-Caesar, owner and operator of Fulton Street Books and Coffee of Tulsa, Oklahoma, stands with her child in the cafe section of the bookstore coffeeshop. By posing in an official business photo with her child, Asamoa-Caesar demonstrates the changing role of children in feminist restaurants, cafes, and coffeehouses. (Photo courtsey of James Parker and Onikah Asamoa-Caesar)

serves "organic and fairly-traded coffee, tea, and delicious vegan pastries made locally."[57] Cafe Con Libros's website likewise states the "our coffee is fair traded and pastries are locally baked."[58] The website continues to explain, "As emerging entrepreneurs, we recognize our role in the global commercial market as one that can either be complicit in exploitative practices or rooted in fairness and equality. Therefore, we have committed ourselves to pursuing business endeavors that honors the full worth of our partners."[59] For Cafe Con Libros and Firestorm this has meant using local products when it is possible and fair-trade products when it is not. Lagusta Yearwood's businesses' social media accounts regularly discuss her relationships with nearby farms.[60] Her website declares, "We want to live in a world where the people who produce our food get paid real prices for real labor and work under humane conditions."[61] For Yearwood, it is not enough that she creates fairer working conditions within her businesses; she thinks of the labour conditions throughout the chain of production. Her businesses depend on two products not produced in New Paltz, New York: chocolate and coffee. Yearwood has explained her approach to ethically sourcing these products in detail. For her, the fair trade and organic labels are limited due to the ways that the labels can be corrupted. Instead, her businesses "try to look at the whole picture and understand that the labels on packaging aren't often representative of the kind of world we want to live in, so we instead use ingredients we feel represent the values those labels are supposed to endorse but often don't."[62] Sourcing products often comes with compromises; however, these feminist restaurants and cafes think critically about where their ingredients come from. The owners want their businesses to support labour practices and companies that reflect similar values to their own. As Asamoa-Caesar of Fulton Street stated, "My goal with the bookstore and the cafe is to be able to tell the stories, narrative[s] and lived experiences of people of color and marginalized communities … Coffee is grown by people of color. I want to feature black and brown roasters and share their story."[63] The sourcing of these products is integral to the feminist identities of these businesses. Using high-quality, ethically produced ingredients and products can pose its own set of challenges.

PRICING AND BALANCE

Can a business give a crap about anything but money?[64]

Lagusta's Commissary website

Feminist restaurants and cafes founded after 1989 face similar challenges to the feminist restaurants of the past. How can a restaurant make sure to fairly pay workers, fairly compensate the producers of their ingredients, source high-quality ingredients, and sell food

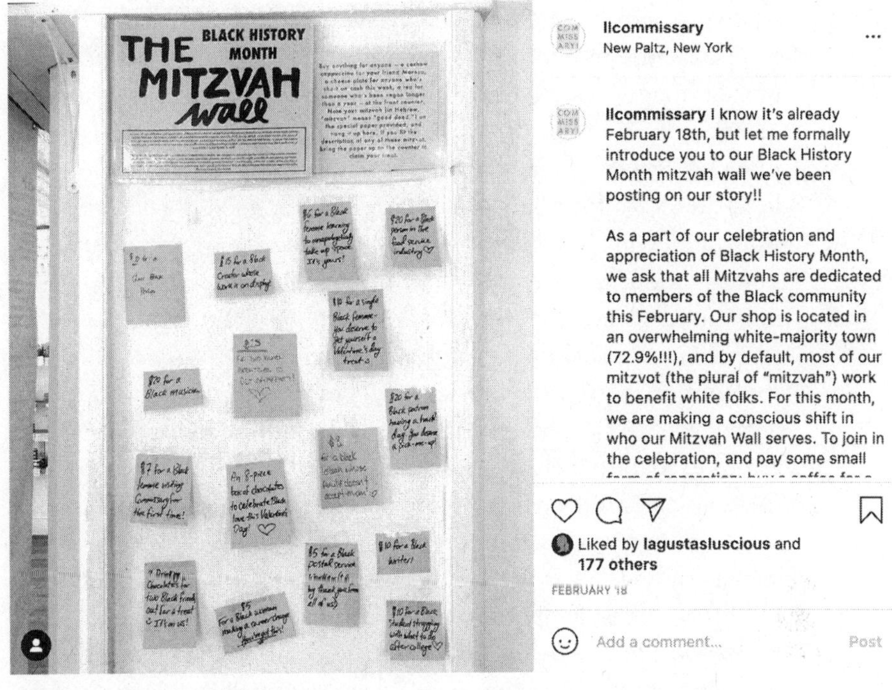

8.5 This screenshot of the February 18, 2021, Instagram post of Lagusta's Commissary of New Paltz, New York, is one of hundreds of grid posts and thousands of stories. The Mitzvah wall is ever changing. Social media enables feminist restaurant and cafe owners the ability to readily communicate their business decisions with their clientele. (Used with permission from Lagusta Yearwood. Lagusta Commissary, "Black History Month Mitzvah Wall," https://www.instagram.com/p/CLcxtvoD1d7/)

at accessible prices for customers from a variety of economic backgrounds? Lagusta Yearwood asks, "Can a business give a crap about anything but money?" On her website, she responds, "That's what Lagusta's Luscious has been attempting to figure out since 2003 … We try to walk the walk while ensuring everyone can have a great experience here, so we have sliding scale specials so if you're strapped this week you can still have a tasty meal—and if you're a fat cat you can pay a little more so it all evens out."[65] Similar to Bread and Roses of Cambridge, Massachusetts, in the 1970s, Yearwood offers a range of items at different prices. The sliding-scale soup has a suggested price but it is "pay what you can." Customers also are encouraged to leave mitzvahs for others. In Jewish culture, good deeds are "mitzvahs"—they are a fulfillment of Jewish law via an individual act of human kindness. In Lagusta's businesses, the mitzvah wall contains notes from customers pre-paying treats or menu items for other customers to redeem. Examples of notes include: "one coffee for someone trying to make ends meet," "20$ for someone who had an abortion," and "5$ for someone who lost someone to cancer."[66] Yearwood decided to include a mitzvah wall as a way for people to make the cafe and confectionary more accessible. The mitzvah wall also speaks to Yearwood's Jewish roots and her mother's lesson to try to perform a "mitzvah every day—preferably an anonymous one."[67] Like the feminist restaurants and cafes founded in the 1970s and 1980s, Yearwood's businesses are not alone in trying to make the space accessible to more customers, while standing by their feminist values.

Balancing prices to keep the space accessible is also a challenge at Cafe Con Libros. Kalima DeSuze explains why at her feminist bookstore cafe, the prices of both the coffee and the books are noticeably lower than the prices of most independently owned shops in New York. The markups are well below the suggested retail prices because, as she explains, "I have a strong commitment to keeping the price point at a place that's accessible to the community, to anyone who would like to come in and visit and patronize the space. I remain open to seeing what is possible, how I could do things a little differently without exploiting my community or isolating others."[68] She wants to make her business accessible to her local community. However, by choosing to lower retail markup, like feminist restaurants and cafes founded in the 1970s and 1980s, she risks the stability and potential sustainability of her establishment. By lowering her profit margins, she might be unable to continue working at the business. As this book has explored, choices around setting prices and paying workers and founders properly have been a challenge for feminist businesses since the 1970s. DeSeuze notes this phenomenon of forgoing maximum profit is gendered, stating, "I didn't go into this with the idea of making money, which is something I need to investigate internally, because I think that's a very gendered way of going about things. I think there is a way to go into a business endeavor saying that you want to make a profit but not exploiting communities in doing so. To not even consider profit is playing into the trope that women need to be sacrificial."[69] These challenges reflect the uncomfortable relationship between feminism and capitalism when these businesses function in a capitalist system. It also requires constant renegotiation. On July 1, 2021, Lagusta Yearwood announced on Facebook and Instagram that she would need to make the menu of Lagusta's Commissary smaller as her current restaurant model had become unsustainable if she wanted to continue to operate her businesses in a way that reflected her values.[70]

While Noel Furie and Selma Miriam have continued to operate their restaurant since 1977, they often do not bring home their cheques when money is tight at Bloodroot. However, Selma Miriam proclaimed, "We're going to keep going as long as we can, because a life worth living is to have new projects and things you want to do."[71] For fifty years feminist restaurants and cafe owners have had to rely on their passion to help their businesses survive. However, one cannot live on passion alone.

MARKETING AND PUBLISHING FOR COMMUNITY BUILDING

While feminist restaurants and cafes are businesses, they have always focused on building community as part of their missions. To build community and draw potential customers to their physical locations, the feminist restaurants, cafes, and coffeehouses of the 1970s and 1980s were deeply interconnected with feminist literary culture and communication networks. Written materials promoted their existence through guidebooks, periodicals, flyers, or business cards. Feminist restaurants also sold and distributed texts, hosted authors, and produced their own newsletters, advertisements, and ephemera. As much as feminist restaurants, cafes, and coffeehouses were about food, they also were spaces where attendees could find food for thought. Their writings, advertisements, and publications extended the feminist community beyond their physical locations as they helped share ideas about feminism. The connection of feminist establishments to greater feminist communication networks through books, art, and advertising remains as important after 1989 as it did before. However, the technologies of communication have shifted.

Feminist restaurants and cafes in the twenty-first century remain committed to feminist communication networks and publishing materials. While the production of physical materials such as books and interviews in newspapers continues, much of this feminist communication has moved online in spaces such as business websites and social media accounts. While Lagusta Yearwood published in 2019 a cookbook entitled *Sweet + Salty: The Art of Vegan Chocolates, Truffles, Caramels, and More from Lagusta's Luscious* and participates in interviews with traditional news outlets, she is actively involved in feminist digital communication networks. Yearwood and her employees often share five or more Instagram stories and at least one grid post a day on the accounts of each of her businesses. These stories include her views on the politics of feminist veganism, the sources of her ingredients, discussions of labour rights, and advertisements of upcoming events and new products. This social media work is bolstered by Yearwood's podcast *Thanks in Advance*, her blog *Resistance is Fertile*, a newsletter, and websites for each of her businesses.[72] As Yearwood demonstrates, digital media provides a space for the owners of feminist eateries to communicate with customers about how their menus and spaces reflect their feminist ideals within a multiplicity of feminisms: radical, radical lesbian, socialist, liberal, and anarchist.

While an in-depth discussion of how feminist restaurants and cafes use social media to promote their businesses, share feminist information, and build community is outside of the frame of this chapter,[73] it is important to understand how vital social media and the creation of a website has become in the digital age.

Feminist restaurants and cafes in 2022 must maintain a bold virtual presence. Like Lagusta's businesses, Cafe Con Libros, Firestorm, and Bluestockings all have Twitter feeds, Instagram accounts, Facebook pages, and websites. Even Bloodroot and Big Kitchen, feminist restaurants and cafes founded in the 1970s and 1980s, as part of surviving today, also maintain a virtual presence. Both businesses have websites, Instagram accounts, Facebook Pages, and Bloodroot has a weekly email newsletter that shares weekly menu specials and recipes.[74] Even still, other feminist restaurants that closed decades ago have grown an online presence with Facebook remembrance pages such as Remembering the Brick Hut Café.[75] These digital marketing and communication methods are part of a longer and more complicated lineage of feminist literary and communication culture around food. The technological affordances of social media and websites have not changed the fact that the founders of feminist food enterprises continue to communicate with customers and share their visions of feminism; the difference is that digital technologies mean these messages can more readily be shared with a global online community.

As Chapters 6 and 7 explained, feminist coffeehouses in the 1970s and 1980s enabled feminists with less access to capital to create temporary spaces for building feminist communities. Social media has enabled contemporary feminists without access to physical spaces to create feminist businesses and projects to engage feminists around food. The Instagram account and website of The Sweet Feminist are where self-taught baker Becca Rea-Holloway shares images of her feminist cakes, cookies, brownies, and pies. Since 2018 she has written feminist messages such as "Abortion is Healthcare" and "Decriminalize Sex Work" with frosting or dough on baked goods.[76] She sells merchandise such as buttons, stickers, patches, and postcards with images of her cakes through her website.[77] In 2022, she published a cookbook entitled *Baking By Feel*.[78] She is not alone; since 2016 Amy Larson has been sharing cake art and promoting the sale of her feminist foodie apparel and goods through her Instagram account and website, Overseasoned Amy.[79] She sells aprons, totes, and clothing with messages such as "Smash the Garlic and the Patriarchy" and "I Scream for Reproductive Justice," with illustrations of ice cream cones.[80] Feminist entrepreneurs can create feminist businesses around food without the higher cost of permanent physical space. Furthermore, while these digital spaces are not the same as a 1970s feminist coffeehouse in a church basement, they do enable feminists to find one another in the comment sections and connect. Both types of feminist community building were and are happening in physical and digital architecture not necessarily designed with feminists in mind: the church basement and the internet. However, feminists can temporarily transform spaces for their purposes. As was the case for feminist coffeehouses founded in the 1970s and 1980s, such as A Woman's Coffeehouse of Minneapolis, by not having full control of the space there would always be constraints. For A Woman's Coffeehouse this meant not being able to add a wheelchair ramp and having to try to convince the church to make the upgrades to the building. On social media in the 2020s this can mean being vulnerable to a platform's terms and conditions, which can be hostile to feminist politics.

Web-based feminist food businesses may not want a physical space and are satisfied by existing in the digital space. However, others use the digital space as a supplement or only one aspect of their businesses. Overseasoned Amy sold mini-cookbooks and aprons as part of an artisan fair.[81] In addition to their web store and social media presence, A Seat at the Table Books, Coffee, and Community has been running pop-up feminist book and coffee events since 2019 and opened a physical location in 2021.[82] By first introducing the business in an online space, these businesses can build up a clientele base, create interest in their future endeavours, and generate initial capital. Here, social media is reminiscent of the women's dances hosted by Common Womon prior to acquiring a permanent physical location in the 1970s. Social media enables an updated form of feminist community building and business making. However, social media has expanded digital and affective labour demands as the operators of current feminist eateries must produce feminist writings about food on multiple platforms simultaneously. Furthermore, the interactivity built into social media platforms means that while having to manage and respond to multiple audiences, operators of these accounts are also exposed to trolls and critics. Social media and the building of websites has a mixed impact on feminist eateries because it offers new possibilities for feminist communication, while being a challenge to sustain from a labour perspective.

SHARING BETWEEN GENERATIONS

There were other restaurants founded between the 1970s and 1980s that embodied similar principles as feminist restaurants but did not label themselves as such in the same specific or overt manner. Restaurants may instead identify themselves as socially conscious, as spaces of social justice, or as part of a food politics movement, or they may enact any of these principles without making them a conspicuous part of their identities.[83] However, this does not mean that marking a business as feminist is insignificant and feminist restaurants and cafes continue to be important. Reflecting on the impact of feminist restaurants, Lagusta Yearwood thinks these spaces hold "Immense value. Women-owned and women-focused spaces have so much value as standing proudly outside a patriarchal culture that still says they are rare and difficult to attain and, largely, useless, because 'feminism is over' because there is perfect parity between genders or because gender fluidity means they are not necessary."[84] One of the enduring legacies of feminist restaurants is how they changed the discussion about food, feminism, and social justice. Spaces like Bloodroot

8.6 Barbara Fried stands in front of the door of Bread and Roses of Cambridge, Massachusetts. She both closes the history on feminist restaurants of the past and opens the door to new feminist restaurant, cafe, and coffeehouse futures. (Courtesy of Barbara Fried and Patricia Hynes)

impacted the way that people within the food industry interacted with each other. Feminist restaurants and cafes worked to dismantle the patriarchal values of the food industry. They were designed with windows that allowed people to see the workers in their kitchens and most did without waitresses as they wanted to upend the hierarchical relationships between the patrons and the workers. Furthermore, they altered ideas about whom restaurants were for.

Feminist restaurants, cafes, and coffeehouses merit our attention because they provide a model for creating businesses that challenge workplace inequity. Studying these spaces combats the erasure of feminist and lesbian feminist culture and underscores the contributions that founders of feminist restaurants, cafes, and coffeehouses made to debates around food politics, community organizing, and labour rights, movements that continue today. But these spaces are valuable beyond history—they speak to larger efforts of feminists to combat the deleterious effects of heteropatriarchal white supremacist capitalism and the importance of community building. In the differences in their models and principles, they also speak to larger and broader understandings of feminism. As this book includes a history of the rise of these businesses, the disappearance of these spaces, and the creation of a new generation of feminist businesses, this text shows how women have adapted during changing political and economic climates to manage businesses.

Lessons Learned and Feminist Futures

In presenting the history of feminist restaurants, cafes, and coffeehouses in the United States as a case study of feminist organizations in a particular historical context, I have attempted to show that, despite the difficulty of creating a community based on shared values that is also open to a diverse constituency, such efforts are necessary. Feminism is a process of working towards a more socially just world. The history of feminist coffeehouses sheds light on the complexity of power relations within feminist organizations and underscores the need for ongoing reflection and adaptation within feminist enterprises. The lessons garnered from feminist restaurants, cafes, and coffeehouses provide guidance in resolving political friction around intragroup dynamics and division amongst feminists today. If these findings are not taken into account, present feminist businesses risk reproducing hierarchies of power across race, class, gender, and sexuality.

Feminist restaurants provided homes away from home. Though never utopic, for many women they were the first entrance to the world of feminism—a movement that offered a vision for a more equitable world. These restaurants, cafes, and coffeehouses were places where they could meet other women to build lasting friendships, engage in activism, and find purpose in their lives. For others, these spaces were places to meet lovers and explore their lesbian identities in a new way or in a first way. Their legacy persists because these places were more than restaurants; they were centres of community.

The history of these restaurants is notable beyond their owners' amalgamation of feminist values with food business; American feminist restaurants are significant because they have always been more than restaurants. Owners of feminist restaurants, cafes, and coffeehouses showed that despite economic, legal, and social barriers, creating the spaces of their dreams was indeed possible. Good luck to you in your search for that place you have always wanted to go but could never find! And if it does not exist yet, think back to Selma Miriam's reflective words about the founding of Bloodroot: "I had gone from being my father's daughter to my husband's wife and I had never thought of doing anything on my own."[85] But then she did!

ACKNOWLEDGEMENTS

Former co-owner of Berkeley, California's Brick Hut Café, Joan Antonuccio once told me, "the Brick Hut was the one place in my life where I had a strong sense of belonging. And that is what has helped me develop a much stronger sense of myself. And I am not the only one." Feminist restaurants, cafes, and coffeehouses have also changed my life. This book has been more than a decade in the making. Thank you to everyone who made this book possible.

The seeds for *Ingredients for Revolution* were sown in 2011, when I first began work on my undergraduate honours thesis at Wesleyan University. Thank you to my thesis advisors Courtney Fullilove and Lori Gruen who guided my early work on the intersections of feminist, food, and gender history. Thank you to Keiji Shinohara for supervising my independent studies of Japanese wood blocking, in which I created prints for that undergraduate thesis. Thank you to Jennifer Tucker who first planted the idea of writing a book on feminist restaurant history during a senior year advisory meeting. These Wesleyan professors, alongside Lorelle Semley and Javier Castro-Ibaseta, encouraged me to continue this research in graduate school.

Before even matriculating at McGill, Jarrett Rudy met with me for coffee to discuss the possibility of researching the history of Canadian feminist restaurants for my master's in history. I expanded the scope of that research during my PhD at McGill, under the supervision of Suzanne Morton and committee members Nathalie Cooke and Jarrett Rudy. While this book is not that dissertation, your mentorship and constructive comments enabled me to write this book. Thank you. I also want to acknowledge the ongoing support of Alanna Thain and Carrie Rentschler of the Institute for Gender, Sexuality, and Feminist Studies of McGill and Jason Opal from the Department of History. I am so grateful for the professors who supported this project and my academic career.

I grappled with questions surrounding the connections between feminist business, food, and community building through my writing in scholarly journals, zines, and blog posts. My 2016 article "Counter Culture: The Making of Feminist Food," published by *Cuizine: Journal of Canadian Food Studies*, is an early exploration of feminism and food. "Cooking the Books: Feminist Restaurant Owners' Relationships with Banks, Loans and Taxes," my 2019 article for the *Journal of Business History* grew into chapter 3. "All Are Welcome Here?" published by *Gender, Work, Organization* in 2020 was the initial work that guided chapter 6. In 2018, I pitched a practical guide bookette/zine on starting feminist restaurants based on my years of historical research and interviews and Microcosm Publishing responded enthusiastically in under an hour. Thank you to everyone at Microcosm for believing in this work; your support gave me the confidence to develop my dissertation work into subsequent publications for academic and trade audiences. I used the Historical Cooking Project website and blog to think through this project and share initial findings. Thank you to everyone who contributed, provided feedback, and/or interacted with these various projects.

I have been so fortunate to have worked with an editorial team that makes writing books fun. Thank you to Concordia University Press for supporting me in writing and publishing this book. It is my second time working with Ryan Van Huijstee, Geoffrey Little, and Meredith Carruthers. It is because of their professionalism, care, and commitment to accessible scholarship that I could not pass up the chance to work with them again. Thank you in particular to Ryan for acting as a developmental editor on this project; your belief in this project made writing during the COVID-19 pandemic far more feasible. Thank you to Garet Markvoort for the beautiful cover design. J. Naomi Linzer, it has been a pleasure to work with you on the index.

Over the past decade, this project has benefited from the material support of several grants. My doctoral research on feminist restaurants was funded by the Fonds de Recherche du Québec—Société et Culture under the Bourses de doctorat en recherché; McGill University's Department of History and Classical Studies under the Joseph Schull Fellowship in the Arts, the McCall MacBain Fellowship, the Yang and Schull Arts Fellowship; and McGill University's Institute of Gender, Sexuality, and Feminist Studies under the Shree Mulay Graduate Award. My original archival visits to the Sallie Bingham Center for Women's History and Culture at Duke University and the Schlesinger Library at Radliffe Institute of Harvard were funded by Wesleyan's Davenport and White Fellowships. My Social Sciences and Humanities Research Council of Canada Insight Grant (#435-2020-0228) and the Tri-Council COVID-19 Fund on open access and accessible scholarship funded my ability to experiment with the OA publishing of this text. Thank you also to the publications committee of the Awards to Scholarly Publications Program (ASPP) for the grant that further enabled this book's publication.

I want to thank my research assistants for reading through drafts, reformatting tables, and assisting with graphics and images. Thank you to Thai Hwang Judiesch, Kari Kuo, Sophie Ogilvie-Hanson for your feedback. Thank you also to Hyeyoon Cho, Amy Brant Edward, Hana Darling-Wolf, Dominique Grégoire, Charlene A Lewis-Sutherland, Astrid Mohr, Mohammed Odusanya, Meera Raman, Adi Sneg, Jacqueline Tam, and Zoe Tolon. It has been wonderful to collaborate with all of you and build the Just Feminist Tech and Scholarship Lab.

This project would not have been possible without the assistance of so many archivists. Thank you to the archivists at the Sallie Bingham Center for Women's History and Culture at Duke University, the Schlesinger Library on the History of Women in America of the

Radcliffe Institute at Harvard University, the Quebec Gay Archives (Les Archives Gaies du Québec), the Canadian Women's Movement Archives at the University of Ottawa, the University of Iowa Archives, the University of Minnesota Archives (and in particular, thank you Lisa Vecoli for your work on the Minnesota Lesbian Community Organizing Oral History Project at the Tretter Collection in GLBT Studies), the San Francisco GLBT Archives, the San Francisco Public Library Archives, Northeastern University Archives, Smith College Archives, New York University Fales Archives, New York University Archives of the Tamiment Libraries, John J. Wilcox Jr. Gay Archives at the William Way Center in Philadelphia, the San Diego LAMBDA Archives, the Lesbian Herstory Digital Archives, and Yale University Archives. As documents related to feminist restaurant histories are scattered across the United States and Canada, I also contacted every archive listed in the Lavender Legacies Guide produced by the Society of American Archivists to see if they had any unsorted materials not visible in their finding aids. I am grateful to the archivists who, in addition to recommending sources in their own collections, mentioned other resources that might be relevant. Thank you also to Joan Antonuccio, Mary Bahneman, Mary Bunch, Noel Furie, Bryher Herak, Patricia Hynes, Selma Miriam, Flavia Rando, Sarah Schulman, and Lagusta Yearwood for letting me interview them.

I appreciate the generous and constructive feedback of my peer reviewers. Thank you for taking the time to engage with this text. Thank you, Megan Elias and Bonnie J. Morris for your confidence in what this book could become.

My work would not be possible without the support of Kim Reany and Andrew Folco at the Institute for Gender, Sexuality, and Feminist Studies. Thank you both for all your help in processing paperwork, research assistant contracts, and so much more. Since 2018, I have been the Faculty Lecturer of the IGSF and have been the only full-time faculty member for the Gender, Sexuality, Feminist, and Social Justice Studies undergraduate program and the Women's and Gender

Studies Graduate Option. In this contingent role, each year I have taught three to four courses in the fall semester and three courses in the winter semester. Writing this book with such a heavy teaching load would not have been possible without the administrative support of Kim and Andrew. Thank you also to my fellow non-tenure-track colleagues at the IGSF including Dayna McLeod, Pascale Graham, Yolanda Muñoz, Vanessa Blais-Tremblay, Rachel Sandwell, D.J. Fraser, and Suzanne Kite. It has been a pleasure to work with you.

When you work on a project for more than a decade, the people who shape your life shape the project. Thank you to everyone (not already named above) who provided feedback on drafts of this work at various stages: Caitlin Aylward, Jenn Barrow, Michael Church Carson, Li Cornfeld, Laura Dunn, A. Finn Enke, Shanon Fitzpatrick, Felicia Francesca, Rachel Gallagher, Juawana Grant, Jeannette Greven, Kathleen Gudmundsson, Alais Hewes, Justin Irwin, Robert Jones, Brian Krug, Tamara Lees, BJ Lillis, Vinny Mazzeo, Cait McKinney, Carolynn McNally, Salim Moore, Firas Nassri, Fred Normandeau, Amanda Ricci, Jess Rose, Anna Sigrithur, Daniel Simeone, Ada Sinacore, Monique Ulysses, Darren Wagner, and David Wright.

It is my friends and family who have driven me to continue this project, metaphorically and literally. Thank you to Daniel Schniedewind for driving me to Bloodroot for the first time with a carload of friends, on the recommendation of our forager friend Zaac Chaves. Thank you to Pierre Faniel for your encouraging words. Thank you to Mariel Rowe-Heupler and Taylor Hughes for your friendship. Thank you to Stef Duguay for commiserating with me. Thank you to my parents Norgene and Dan for fostering my love of books and to my late godparents Ann and Jim Denison for sharing your love of learning. To my dogs Bubbles and Sprout, thank you for reminding me what is important: walks, good food, and cuddles.

I wrote the final manuscript of this book primarily while living in Tiohtià:ke (Montreal) on unceded Kanien'kehà:ka territory. These lands and waterways have also been a homeland and gathering place for many, including the Wendat, Abenaki, and Anishinaabeg peoples. I am grateful to the stewards of the land and waters from which I eat and drink. I also want to acknowledge and thank the people of the many lands that hold the servers enabling my research and writing, and the minerals that formed my technological devices. As this book seeks to draw attention to power relations that have been invisibilized, it is important to acknowledge both Canada's and the United States' long colonial histories and current political practices. Interwoven with this ongoing history of colonization is one of enslavement and racism. I wrote this book while employed by McGill University, a university whose namesake, James McGill, enslaved Black and Indigenous peoples. It was in part from the money he acquired through these violent acts that McGill University was founded. These histories and continued injustices inform the conversations within this text. Let us strive for respectful relationships with all the peoples of this land so that we can work towards collective healing and true reconciliation.

A special thanks to the wonderful people at Dispatch Café, where I spent so many hours working on this project (and then drinking their coffee from home during the pandemic). Chrissy Durcak, thank you for fostering such a wonderful LGBTQ+ friendly space.

The most important lesson I have taken away from my research on feminist restaurants, cafes, and coffeehouses is that the owners demonstrated radical hope. With a dream and a supportive community, you can create the kind of world you would like to see. Thank you to my community for every kindness you have bestowed upon me. Your support has allowed me to pursue my dreams.

Appendices

Methodological Usage

Visual and Spatial History

As noted in the introduction of this book, much of the initial sourcing and locating of feminist restaurants, cafes, and coffeehouses is the result of consulting editions of *Gaia's Guide*, which were comprised solely of a collection of listings. The physical object of a guidebook displayed the presence of women's communities, yet few books provided a visual representation of what these communities looked like. Women's, lesbian, and gay travel guides did not typically include maps. Further, these guides and directories included comments and hinted at experiences but did not speak about spatial awareness. A few of the regional guides, such as the lesbian guide to Washington, DC (1980s, exact date unlisted), did include a local street map, but this was a rare occurrence. However, with the development of geographic information system (GIS) mapping technologies, historians are no longer restricted to simply imagining what the landscape of feminist and lesbian socializing looked like across the United States at a particular time. It is now possible for us to make maps that speak to a kind of physicality, remembering that historical bodies have an actual form and moved through space.

While the spatial turn in history has begun, this subfield remains in its initial stages. One approach to understanding feminists in physical spaces is to mark where they gathered. In this way, it was the initial goal of this project to map out the locations of feminist restaurants and cafes within the United States beginning in 1972, a process which had previously never been completed. Each time a feminist restaurant, cafe, or coffeehouse was located, I entered the name of the business, address (if it was known), and any other elements of description into an Excel spreadsheet entitled the "Master Database." The information came from directories such as *Gaia's Guide*, *Gay Yellow Pages*, *Pink Pages*, and *Lavender Pages*, as well as from feminist periodicals, business cards, and event flyers. Additionally, I created a separate *Gaia's Guide* specific database to track changes over time within one guidebook. The collated information from the "Gaia's Guide Database" was also entered into the "Master Database." I then cleaned the data from the "Master Database" to create homogenized data sets, which could be utilized by GIS mapping programs. The rest of this appendix explains the multiple phases of developing these maps, the programs used, and why the chosen strategy was implemented.

To build my databases, I had to identify which restaurants in the United States were feminist and where they were specifically located. I located the restaurants through a variety of means. The first method is by locating the spaces from lesbian and feminist travel guides from the period.

In building my databases of restaurants, every mention of a feminist restaurant, cafe, or coffeehouse was useful; however, for the sake of consistency, I tracked every annual edition of *Gaia's Guide* from 1975 to 1991, except for the 1980, 1986, and 1987 editions as I could not locate a copy through any libraries, archives, booksellers, or private collections. Focusing on *Gaia's Guide* was useful for a variety of reasons. Compared to other guides from the period, I was able to access a more complete collection of *Gaia's Guide*. While the meaning of its star-rating system changed subtly over the years, from the earliest version *Gaia's Guide* noted if a space was feminist or not—a label that I took at its word because, as stated earlier, this book does not seek to define feminism but rather is interested in spaces that were marked intentionally as feminist. Although the star system was imperfect because it depended on feedback from users who were not evaluating every space relative to all of the others, but only speaking of their own experiences at one spot, having notes marking whether or not editors and researchers for the guide thought a space was feminist was particularly useful for my project.[1] Furthermore, there was a clear distinction between what kind of business the guide was discussing because under a location there were subheadings to indicate "restaurants," "bars," "bookstores," and more. No guidebook could ever have been perfect. As literature scholar and author of *The Lesbian Index: Pragmatism and Lesbian Subjectivity in the Twentieth Century* Kim Emery notes:

> Everyone knows that a club's clientele can change faster than any publication could hope to keep up with; that queer bars close, move and change ownership like some girls change hairstyles; that there's always some chance of meeting up with the stray lesbian-feminist at a men's leather bar. The sites of queer culture are neither homogenous nor stable. Like signs more generally, they are approximate; their meanings are shifting, always under negotiation. Hence the reliable market for updated editions. Hence, too, the big problem with this metaphor: *Gaia's Guide* and others like it are organized around a structuralist conceit—they attend to neither the material specificity nor the temporal dimension of the reality that they purport to describe. The representation of queer cultures that they offer—useful as it is—is an atemporal abstraction, a system of understanding unattached to actual time and actual space.[2]

This conceit does not render the methodology of consulting guidebooks useless. However, it is important to recognize the fluidity of the conditions that guidebooks sought to represent.

To supplement *Gaia's Guide*, I also looked at available copies of other lesbian and women's travel guides, *Gay Yellow Pages* and *Damron's Gay Guides*, various regional gay yellow pages/directories, as well as counterculture and alternative culture guidebooks and directories. According to Gina Gatta, the publisher of *Damron's Women's Traveller*, which was *Gaia's Guide*'s main competitor beginning in 1989, *Gaia's Guide* was the most popular travel guide in the 1970s and 1980s, but it was not the only guide on the market. Although exact publication numbers are unknown, Gatta thinks it is doubtful that *Gaia's Guide* published more than twenty thousand copies a year, a similar circulation to her own publication.[3] To put that number in perspective, *Damron's Men's Guide* (formerly called *Damron's Address Book*) peaked with the 1999 edition at sixty thousand copies that year, competing against *Spartacus.* The third major publisher of women's guides was Ferrari Publications, which released four women's guide series that mostly contained American listings: *Places for Women* (1984), *Places of Interest for Women* (1985, 1986) and later expanding to the international market from the mid-1990s with *Women's Travel in Your Pocket* and *Ferrari for Women: Worldwide Women's Guide* (1995), until Ferrari went out of business in the early 2000s. *Gaia's Guide*, from its inception, included international listings.[4] Unlike *Gaia's Guide*, which just focused on women's guides, both Ferrari and Damron began as publishers of gay male guides and expanded into the women's and lesbian travel market. Other independent national guides included *The Guide to Women's Resources* and *The New Woman's Survival Catalogue* (1973).

Often with low production quality, made on cheap paper with weak bindings, lesbians also created guides about their local areas. These smaller guides were more regionally focused, for example: *The Women's Yellow Pages of New England: The Original Source Book for Women* (1978) and *The Women's List for Greater Boston: The What and Where of Women's Action Groups* (1976); or focused on a smaller region like the Twin Cities; or focused on just a particular city, such as

The Women's Resource Guide to Ithaca, New York (1976), *San Francisco—East Bay Women's Yellow Pages* (1976), *The Women's Yellow Pages (New York)* (1978), and *Betty and Pansy's Severe Queer Review of San Francisco* (1994). For more local guides, lesbian and gay men oftentimes collaborated to create texts such as *A Gay Person's Guide to New England* (1976) and *New England Gay Community Guide* (1989). It is important to keep in mind the varying resources available to each community. As the focus became more local, there was more collaboration between the gay male and lesbian communities. For example, even in the women-focused guidebooks, gay male spaces were listed from time to time if women were invited to enter. This tradition of creating guidebooks has continued with the 1990 publication of *Shewolf's Directory of Wimmin's Lands and Lesbian Communities*; in 2012 they released a sixth edition.[5]

Other travel guides and resource guides from the 1970s and 1980s also listed feminist and lesbian restaurants, cafes, bookstores, and similar establishments. Alternative lifestyle telephone books such as *The People's Yellow Pages* (1971) and *The Philadelphia Whole City Catalogue* (1973) listed some of these spaces. I do not focus on these books, however, as women did not control them. As outsiders to the community produced those books, the political and social motivations were different for producing them than the guides by and for women; one type of guide was for the "alternative community" and the other for the women's community. Nonetheless, they do still provide researchers with a useful resource through which to study spaces in which feminists and lesbians gathered, collaborated, socialized, and did activism.

Feminist and lesbian periodicals functioned as guides. National feminist periodicals with a larger distribution occasionally published special issues focused on smaller regions, and in these publications (such as *Off Our Backs*, an American feminist periodical published between 1970 and 2008), there would be a section on some of the feminist businesses in that area. Regional feminist and lesbian journals published written guides to the local communities within their pages, such as *Las Hermanas Newsletter* of 1975 in San Diego, California, and *Hera's Journal* of 1978 in Philadelphia, Pennsylvania. In a similar manner, books focused on the needs of the lesbian community and/or women within a specific region often published lists of available resources in a directory format, including community spaces, such as in the final pages of *Our Right to Love* of 1978.[6]

In addition, I identified feminist restaurants in both the article section and in the advertisement sections in a variety of feminist and lesbian periodicals. The utility of periodicals for the purpose of this book is how they could function like micro-guidebooks, with information about specific areas as well as national advertisements. Periodicals worked like micro-guidebooks in three ways. First, periodicals occasionally printed explicit area guides to highlight either businesses in the area or to encourage out of town feminist readers to visit those spaces. For example, the writers of the *Amazon Quarterly* (1972–1975) published a guide for women and listed locations where lesbians and feminists could gather. It is important to remember that periodicals had a specific readership in mind for these guides. *Amazon Quarterly*'s guide did not focus on spaces that sold alcohol. As historian Martin Meeker wrote, "in distancing themselves and their work from the culture of lesbian bars, however, they also were removing those sites from a communication network that was designed to map a lesbian geography and from the list of options where lesbians might be able to meet other lesbians."[7] In doing so, the authors of *Amazon Quarterly* denoted their own class biases, distancing themselves from working-class lesbian bar culture. Furthermore, this bias reminds us that the women with access to the presses came out of specific class and racial groups. I am not arguing that all feminist presses were controlled by middle-class white women. Publications such as Iowa City's radical feminist *Ain't I a Woman* put racial and class issues at the forefront of most editions. The editors took their title from an 1851 speech by Sojourner Truth, the formerly enslaved African American abolitionist and women's rights activist. Apart from the literal guides feminist and lesbian periodicals published, their articles on local feminist businesses provided locations and other details about feminist restaurants, cafes, or coffeehouses, such as the article "In the Soup in New York City: Restauranters [sic] Compare Recipes for Success" in a 1975 issue of *Artemis: The Newsletter for Enterprising Women* on Mother Courage Feminist Restaurant in New York City. Furthermore, advertisement sections in periodicals, such as the Twin Cities' *Goldflower*, also provided addresses and descriptions of feminist restaurants.[8] Unlike my methodological approach to guidebooks (i.e., compiling a database of each edition of *Gaia's Guide* and supplementing it with additional guidebooks), for feminist and lesbian periodicals I did not seek out a dominant source. I consulted every available feminist and lesbian periodical housed at the archives I visited to see if there were any articles and/or advertisements about feminist restaurants, cafes, or coffeehouses. This required physically flipping through hundreds of periodicals and magazines.[9]

Flyers and business cards have survived in the archives and were useful in both the building of directories and in my case studies. These objects sometimes provided the only remaining piece of evidence of a feminist restaurant, cafe, or coffeehouse: a title and an address.[10] For this research project, I combed through thousands of flyers, the majority of which were photocopied, handwritten posters listing addresses, dates, and the price to see a performance or attend a special dinner. Knowing that a restaurant or cafe existed in a particular location encouraged me to contact archivists at the local lesbian, gay, queer, or social movement archives to seek further information about spaces that I would not have known existed otherwise. Additionally, I contacted every lesbian, gay, queer, and social movement archive in the United States listed on the Lavender Legacies of North America Directory produced by the Society of American Archivists: Diverse

Sexuality and Gender Section and asked if they had any information about feminist and lesbian restaurants, as these spaces would often not appear in finding aids but scant traces would exist in the fonds.[11]

My interviews with owners of restaurants that I had already identified led me to other restaurants that they knew about. Likewise, corresponding with archivists at some of the smaller lesbian and feminist archives yielded information beyond the archives' holdings. There were five occasions when librarians and archivists mentioned other regional businesses that did not house their records at the archive but had operated during the years of this study. With this information, I created databases that tracked the location of each restaurant and its years of existence, as well as any other available information.

An immediate benefit of quantitative mapping techniques is that they show the preponderance of these spaces. Based on my initial estimates I guessed that there were at most forty feminist restaurants, cafes, and coffeehouses in North America. In fact, the number of verified feminist restaurants, cafes, and coffeehouses is over 230 and, further, there are over 400 unverified spaces, but likely feminist spaces are included in this set. In 2013, I created *thefeministrestaurantproject.com* to showcase my findings and in commitment to open access and public dissemination of data. A colour-coded version of the database used to build the binary maps is publicly available on the website, and anyone can email me to suggest updates and edits. The reason behind making this information accessible to the public is manifold: so other scholars can use it, so people who may have attended, owned, or worked in these spaces can provide feedback, and so the information can be spread to the public, as most of the women interviewed for this project said that they wanted people to remember their legacy.

Once these databases were completed, I then went about building maps. Not only descriptive, these maps directly enabled my analysis. Importing Keyhole Markup Language (KML) data[12] or a file geodatabase (GDB)[13] mapping on economic figures and populations as layers within ArcGIS programs[14] can be useful, as researchers can then see links between poverty levels and locations of certain kinds of businesses.

However, one issue in the completion this project was a lack of consistency in the sources. *Gaia's Guide* and other travel guides were not always accurate in reporting when a space was still in business. A variance of one or two years would be less significant if this project studied a specific kind of business over a two-hundred-year period. However, as this study is focused only on a fifty-year period, having a standard deviation of a few years disrupts the utility of importing these figures. After experimenting with different strategies, I realized that the limitation of my data set's reliability on dates meant that layering other statistics, like income and population, would ultimately lead to inaccurate results. Despite this, creating the maps still enabled fruitful analysis.

For basic data plotting, Google's My Maps has proven far better than ArcGIS and QGIS. With a two-tiered, colour-coded system, it was possible to create one master map. Magenta bubbles represent verified feminist, lesbian, and women's restaurants, coffeehouses, and cafes. Blue circles mark unverified feminist restaurants and women-friendly establishments mentioned in the various women's travel guides and feminist and lesbian periodicals. These blue circles also marked women-owned (but not necessarily identified as feminist) spaces, establishments targeted at gay men that also welcomed lesbian women, or restaurants that advertised themselves as being spaces where women and lesbians were welcomed to eat alone or as a couple. This blue list is, at present, incomplete but provides a sample

9.1 (OVERLEAF, TOP) *The Feminist Restaurant Project website's homepage, thefeministrestaurantproject.com.*

9.2 (OVERLEAF, BOTTOM) *The map from The Feminist Restaurant Project of feminist restaurants, cafes, and coffeehouses that operated in the US and Canada between 1972 and 2021.*

The Feminist Restaurant Project

About Methodology Maps Directory Publications Bio Submissions

Maps

Display Data Map:

Below is the map of all of the feminist restaurants, cafes, and coffeehouses that I have found in my research. This map is useful to visualize the locations of these restaurants, cafes, and coffeehouses. If you visited the site prior to July 28, 2016 you only had access to the Beta Data Map.

Magenta bobbles represent verified feminist, lesbian, and women's restaurants, coffeehouses, and cafes. Blue circles mark women-friendly establishments mentioned in the various women's travel guides and feminist and lesbian periodicals (these include some establishments targeted towards gay men that also welcomed women). These spaces were women owned (but not identified as feminist) or advertised as being spaces where women and lesbians were welcome to eat alone or as a couple. The blue list is incomplete but provides a sample of the kinds of spaces women would use for socializing and that were advertised to women to socialize in that were not explicitly women's spaces/ feminist spaces/ lesbian spaces.

If the embedded map is glitchy, go to this link:

Feminist Restaurants, Cafes, and Coffeehouses in the USA a...

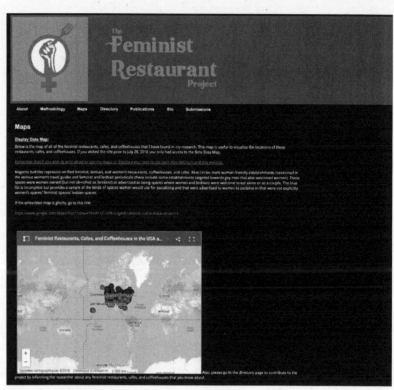

Also, please go to the directory page to contribute to the project by informing the researcher about any feminist restaurants, cafes, and coffeehouses that you know about.

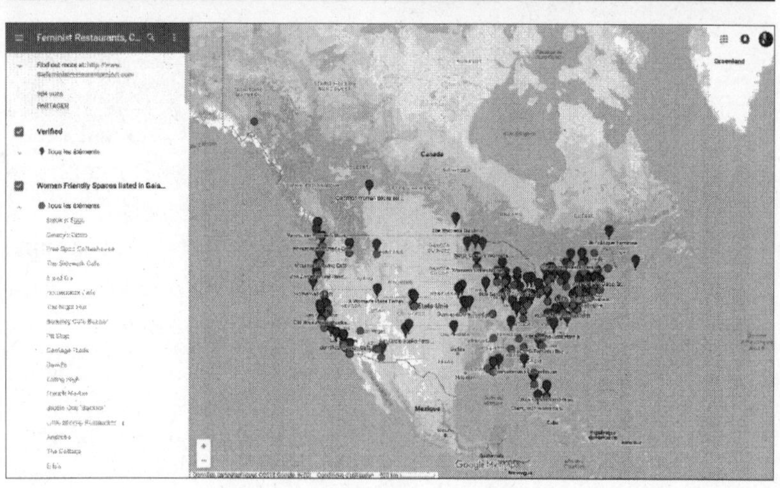

of the kinds of spaces that women used for socializing but were not explicitly verified as women's, lesbian, or feminist spaces. From this map it is possible to construct a sense of what the feminist and lesbian community in a particular space and time looked like. Maps can change our conceptualizations of the past.

Figure 9.2 shows the map of all the feminist restaurants, cafes, and coffeehouses that were located in the US and Canada as of May 2021, which is useful in visualizing their locations. This map is accurate only to the level of the cities and towns. Zooming in, therefore, will not reveal the exact address of the establishment, as addresses were not consistently listed in the guides.

Feminist Business Nexus of 1981 in Gaia's Guide

To understand the potential scope of mapping, below are three maps of the feminist nexus of businesses in 1981 in Tampa, Florida, Madison, Wisconsin, and Portland, Oregon based solely on one edition of *Gaia's Guide*. The three chosen cities span the United States in the South, the Midwest, and the Pacific Northwest, regions which have received little academic attention in regard to their contributions to the women's movements when compared with the predominance of studies of San Francisco, New York, and Washington, DC. However, these maps demonstrate that each of these locations indeed had feminist and lesbian business communities in 1981. In each of these cities, most of the lesbian and women-friendly spaces are concentrated in a single area, with the exception, somewhat, of Portland. While I wanted to choose cities with more than four businesses, I had quite a few options. I also wanted to use different examples than those used as case studies in the main body of this book. These maps are accurate down to the exact address whenever possible. However, if no address was listed in the guide, I located the site at the city's centre. These maps demonstrate the potential available to create a yearly map of each space and create a scrolling feature to view changes over time.

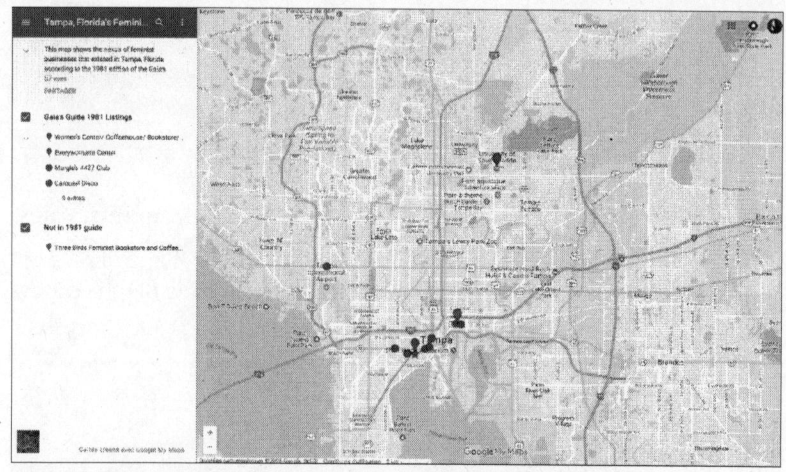

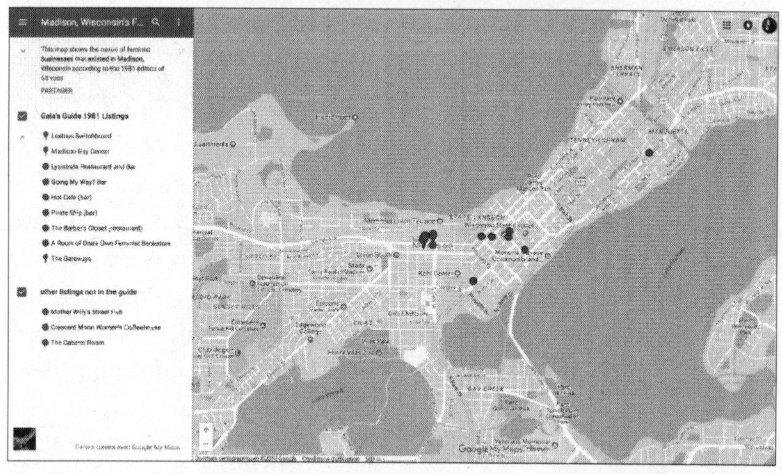

9.3 (TOP) *Map of Tampa, Florida, based on the 1981 edition of* Gaia's Guide *showing feminist restaurants, cafes, and coffeehouses, https://drive.google.com/open?id=1tLZ2PARqglnaKbFoYamIGllPfoQ&usp=sharing.*

9.4 (BOTTOM) *Map of Madison, Wisconsin, based on the 1981 edition of* Gaia's Guide *showing feminist restaurants, cafes, and coffeehouses, https://drive.google.com/open?id=1_BA1wghSQFeEHQirdtxrSKApL-8&usp=sharing.*

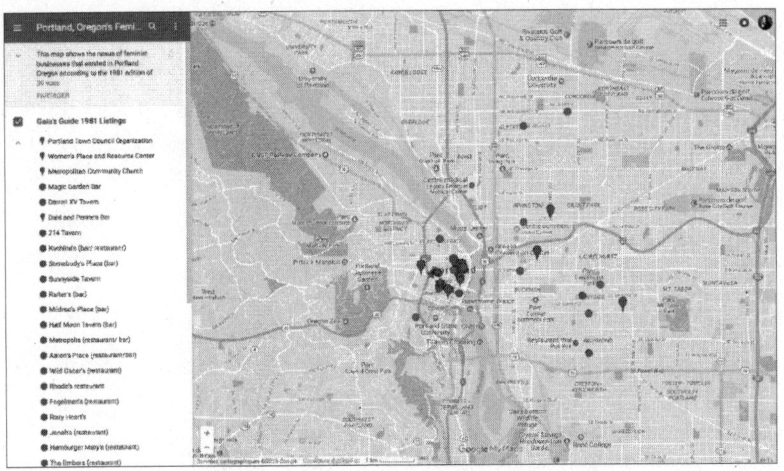

9.5 *Map of Portland, Oregon, based on the 1981 edition of* Gaia's Guide *showing feminist restaurants, cafes, and coffeehouses, https://drive.google.com/open?id=1xFqPz5UQIxJVTkcr8Q-bF9Xb2qA&usp=sharing.*

Based on population census data from 1980, Madison, Wisconsin, had 176,616 people, Tampa, Florida, had 271,523, and Portland, Oregon, had 366,383.[15] By 1981, their populations had not fluctuated significantly. As the larger feminist space map demonstrates, rural regions had some explicitly feminist businesses, but it was still necessary to have a large enough population to support such a business. This explains why in 1984 in Chattanooga, Tennessee, there was a bar named Alan Gold's where gay men and women congregated together because they did not have enough people to support two separate businesses. According to the entry in *Gaia's Guide*, "Gay women and men 'we basically stick together as a group.'"[16]

It is key to see and to understand that the feminist restaurants, cafes, and coffeehouses discussed in this book were not isolated but embedded in a feminist business nexus. The three maps below emphasize the arguments made in chapters four and seven, which show how feminist restaurants, cafes, and coffeehouses promoted women's culture and other feminist businesses. As discussed in chapter one, the choice to write about feminist restaurants throughout the United States makes this level of specificity impossible for every year of this project in every location. These three maps are presented, then, as a compromise.

The Public National Map

While this book demonstrates the importance of women's spaces and explores the political efficacy of separatism, another important motivation for this sort of research is to bring attention to the fact that these spaces existed. The maps for this project therefore serve multiple purposes. Some of the maps simply show the actual, physical location where these businesses existed, some show the variety of feminist businesses present in a single area during a single year based on the information presented in only one guidebook, and some are part of a larger public history project which not only takes information from interviewees but also provides a virtual space for continual community building through memory sharing. A large, public map served the purpose of drawing attention to the legacy of the women founders of feminist restaurants, cafes, and coffeehouses. These women indeed made this project feasible by making this information as publicly accessible as possible and by developing new forums in which former participants in feminist restaurants could expand their community during a time in which many women's spaces are closing or have closed.[17]

Controlling space is important to marginalized groups. Though identifying a space as queer may lead to gay bashing and danger, it is still important for community building.[18] Michel de Certeau has shown how those with little institutional power rely on tactics that allow them to gain advantage and to claim space for themselves and can, as a result, create pockets of power.[19] The creation of these maps allows not only for the creation of a record of communities but also for a continuation of those communities, furthering a sense of belonging by tying feminists, lesbians, and queer women to a history in particular locations.

Hope

My hope is that other scholars will build upon this project, particularly in regard to my technique of spatial history. While the methodologies I used to create my databases ultimately limited the full capabilities of GIS layering, there are many ways in which future researchers can build upon my methods. As the guidebooks relied on volunteered information, *Gaia's Guide* and other lesbian and women's travel guides were too inconsistent and therefore could not be trusted in regard to a location's existence in a particular year. Sometimes the directories published out-of-date material or offered few details. As this research becomes more public, I hope that I can confirm the exact operation dates of all spaces, not just those of the case studies included in this book. With more reliable data and using GIS software, it is possible to create and analyze maps by layering publicly available, government collected data about neighbourhood demographics and economic conditions under the points marking the locations of the restaurants. This technique allows researchers to draw broader conclusions about the demographic trends of these restaurants, cafes, and coffeehouses rather than relying solely on case studies and interviews.

In addition, it is my hope that future researchers will take my databases—which I have made publicly available on thefeminist restaurantproject.com and in the back of this book—and continue to enhance the project, perhaps widening it to include a study of all kinds of feminist and lesbian businesses. This kind of research would necessitate the collaboration of a team of researchers to best undertake the grueling task of collecting and inputting data. This sort of task would have been impossible for a single scholar, as the creation of the restaurant and cafe database alone required years of work. In this appendix, I included three sample maps of Tampa, Portland, and Madison in 1981 to demonstrate the enormous potential of this technique. Placing all these spaces on a map for a single year provides a sense of how feminist business networks interacted with each other. One day, perhaps a group of keen scholars might assemble to create such databases and maps, expanding the quantitative scope of this project. Likewise, this project could be extended to include feminist businesses outside North America, even by continuing the methodology of using editions of *Gaia's Guide*, as this series included European locations. For example, the feminist vegetarian restaurant Pulse, in Brighton, England, published its own cookbook and it was not the only European feminist restaurant.[20] Comparing feminist restaurants across continental boundaries could further enhance our understandings of feminist networks and the intellectual history of feminist ideas, which would in turn allow us to trace how these ideas spread and evolved.

The Directory of Feminist Restaurants, Cafes and Coffeehouses

In the list below, text set in roman font indicates verified feminist, lesbian, and women's restaurants, coffeehouses, and cafes. Italicized listings are possibly feminist restaurants but as-yet unverified. They were women-friendly establishments mentioned in the various women's travel guides and feminist and lesbian periodicals (these include some establishments targeted towards gay men that also welcomed women). These spaces were women owned (but not identified as feminist) or advertised as spaces where women and lesbians were welcome to eat alone or as a couple. The italicized list is incomplete but provides a sample of the kinds of spaces women would use for socializing and that were advertised to women to socialize in but were not explicitly women's spaces, feminist spaces, or lesbian spaces.

The dates refer to the first listed mention of a restaurant and the last listed mention. Occasionally *Gaia's Guide* would mention a business in their 1981 edition, skip it in the next edition, and re-mention the business two editions later. Even if the location was mentioned in *Gaia's*, if the dates listed do not come entirely from *Gaia's Guide* but from other sources such as periodicals, advertisements, or interviews, an asterisk (*) will be listed beside the dates. If the business is still in operation in 2022 an arrow symbol (→) will indicate this.

I tracked every annual edition of *Gaia's Guide*, except for the 1980, 1986, and 1987 editions as I could not locate a copy. The editor of *Gaia's Guide*, Sandy Horn, produced the last edition of the series in 1991. As a result, listings found only in the guides end in 1991.

Furthermore, as Horn solicited information from readers to create listings, her methodology could explain why in Ogunquit, Maine, every listing is shown in the 1977 edition and in Staten Island all three listings were in the 1982 edition. It is unlikely that all four businesses in Ogunquit or the three spaces in Staten Island began in the same year. Rather, it is more likely that a reader with knowledge about the local scene contacted Horn before that edition's publication. Also, as the guides were written in English and circulated amongst English-reading feminists, it is more likely that spaces catering to English speakers would be listed. Integrating references from periodicals, flyers, and ephemera into this directory works to compensate for the challenge of the guides' reliability.

State	*City*	*Verified/Unverified Feminist, Lesbian, Women's Restaurants*
Alabama	Birmingham	*Steak n Eggs* (1984–1985)
Arizona	Phoenix	*Free Spirit Coffeehouse* (sometimes held in individuals' homes) (1982)
		Ginzey's Oasis (1984)
	Tucson	Gay Woman's Liberation and Lesbian Coffeehouse/Desert Dykes Tucson (DDT) (1975)*
		The Sidewalk Café (1984)
California	Unknown	*Homemade Café* (1977)
	Albany	The Baachanal (1979–1982)
	Auburn	*E and G's* (1984)
	Berkeley	*Berkeley Café Bazaar* (1991)*
		Brick Hut Café (1975–1997)*
		Cheese and Coffee Center (1979–1985)/ The Cheese Board Collective (1967–)*→
		Kafeneo (restaurant) (1977–1979)
		The Old Mole (1984–1985)
		Vivoli's Ice Cream Parlor (1982–1985)
	Chico	Labrys Books sold coffee (1988–1989)
	Claremont	The Motley Coffeehouse (1974–)→

State	*City*	*Verified/Unverified Feminist, Lesbian, Women's Restaurants*
	Elk Grove	A Seat at the Table Books, Coffee, and Community (physical location, 2021)→
	Gardenia	*Pit Stop* (1977)
	Hayward	The Oracle Bookstore sold coffee (1978)*
	Hollywood and West Hollywood	*Carriage Trade* (1977–1988)*
		David's (1977–1982)
		Eating High (1979–1981)
		French Market (1981)
		Little Frida's Lesbian Café (1991–1999)*
		Studio One "Backlot" (women only Wednesdays) (1979)
		The Ultimate Feminist Restaurant: The Los Angeles Women's Saloon and Parlor (1974–1976)*
	Laguna Beach	*Andree's* (1977–1981)
		The Cottage (1977–1981)
		Eric's (1982)
		Little Shrimp Restaurant (1976–1995)*
	Los Angeles	*Bla-bla café* (1975–1981)
		The Blue Mouse Coffeehouse (1984)
		Bread and Roses Feminist Bookstore sold coffee and snacks (1989–1991)
		Catch One (1990–1991)
		Dolly's Dolphin Grill (1981)
		Fellini's (1984)
		Frog Pond (1984–1985)
		The Go-Between Coffeehouse (1983–1985)
		The Greenery Restaurant and 24 Hr Coffeeshop (1984)
		Identified Woman Café (1977–1978) transformed into Val's Café in the Women's Building (1979–1981)
		Jett's Café and Art Haus Coffeehouse (1982)
		The Last Drop Coffeehouse (1983)
		The Mainsail, closely connected with Womon Space (1982)

State	*City*	*Verified/Unverified Feminist, Lesbian, Women's Restaurants*
	Los Angeles (*continued*)	Marty's Restaurant (1983)
		New York Company Bar and Grill (1984–1985)
		On the Fringe Restaurant (1983)
		Rosalind's (woman-owned) (1985)
		Rose Tattoo (1984–1991)
		Wellington's Restaurant (1978)*
		Woman Space (1978–1982)*
		Yukon Mining Company (1982)
		Zoo Bar and Restaurant (1984)
	Long Beach	*Rusty's* (1984)
		Tee Cee's (1984)
	Menlo Park	Everywoman's Coffeehouse (1979)
	Monterey	*Café Balthazar* (1984)
		Tillie Gort's (1984)
	Nevada City	*Friar Tuck's Restaurant and Wine Bar* (1984)
	North Hollywood	*Brian's* (1977)
	Oakland	Bishop's Coffeehouse/ Womanspace (1976–1977)
		Grandma's House (1977)
		Mama Bears (1984–1991)
		Ollie's of Oakland Womyn's Restaurant (1982)
		A Woman's Place (1975)
	Pasadena	*Daily Double* (1981–1982)
	Redwood City	*Cruiser Restaurant* (1982)
	Sacramento	Earhart's Café Gallery (1979–1985)
		Lesbian Complex Private Club (1982)
		Mini Mouse Gay Coffeehouse (1976)
		Whistle Stop Feminist Coffeehoyse (1981–1984)
	San Diego	Amazon Sweet Shop (1981–1984)
		Boardwalk Café (1977)
		Big Kitchen (1979–)*→
		Jamie's Restaurant (1977)
		King Richard (1977)
		Las Hermanas Coffeehouse (1974–1981)*
		The Rendezvous (1982)
		Rose Canyon Café (1985–1989)

State	*City*	*Verified/Unverified Feminist, Lesbian, Women's Restaurants*
		Something Special Beach Fish and Salad Bar (woman owned) (1985)
		Wing Café (1980–1982)* Feminist Coffeehouse and Gallery
		Yogurt Express and Deli Ice Cream Shop (woman owned) (1985)
	San Francisco	1001 Nights Lesbian Bar and Restaurant (1972–1974)* (Former location of the Tortuga and Evonne's. It became the Royal Palace, Back Street, the Red Eye Saloon, the Deja Vu, and the Black Rose.)
		Artemis Society Women's Café (1977–1984)*
		The Baybrick Inn (1982–1987)*
		Breaking Bread Restaurant (woman owned) (1981–1982)
		Café Commons (1981–1988)
		Canary Island Restaurant (1982–1983)
		Casa de Cristal (1977)
		Clarion Coffeehouse (1981)
		Fanny's Super Club (1982)
		The Fickle Fox (1977)
		Full Moon Inc, Coffeehouse and Bookstore (1978–1979)*
		Klein's Deli and Restaurant (lesbian owned) (1984–1985)*
		Mary Midgett's Coffeehouse (1983–1984)*
		Maud's Restaurant (1966–1986)*
		The Neon Chicken (1979–1985)
		Nosheria Restaurant (woman owned and operated) (1984)
		Old Wives' Tales Bookstore (with tea and coffee) (1976–1996)*
		The P.S. (1977)
		Red Dora's Bearded Lady Café (1994)
		Tiffany's Restaurant (1973–1974)*
		Two Sisters Restaurant (1977)*

State	City	Verified/Unverified Feminist, Lesbian, Women's Restaurants
	San Francisco (*continued*)	Tuxedo Junction (1979–1981)*
		Valencia Rose (1984–1985)
	San Jose	*Interlude* (1985)
		Sisterspirit Café and Bookstore (1984–2010)* p
	San Louis Obispo	Dandelion Wine Book Company (lesbian and feminist bookstore with coffee and tea) (1981–1982)
		Women's Coffeehouse from the Dandelion Wine Book Company (1981–1982)
	San Rafael	*Ethel's* (1977)
		Rising Women Books Feminist Bookstore (sold coffee and tea) (1982)
	Santa Barbara	Beaudelaire's Coffeehouse (1983)
		Choices Book, Music, and Coffeehouse Feminist Bookstore (1989)
	Santa Cruz	Café Domenica (1983–1985)
		Two Sisters (1977–1978)
		Moonrise Café (1979–1982)
	Santa Rosa	Gertie's Café (1983)
	Sausalito	*Sausalito Inn* (1977)
		Two Turtles (1977)
		Zelda's (1977)
Colorado	Boulder	Boulder Lesbian Network Coffeehouse (1982)
		Carnival Café: Natural Foods (1977)
	Denver	*Alicia's Mexican Restaurant* (1977)
		Anywoman's Coffeehouse (1985)
		The Bellevue (1982)
		BJ's Carousel (1982–1988)
		Bway Café (1988)
		Café du Monde (1983)
		The Den (1988)
		Denver Waterworks (1988)
		Garbo's (1984–1988)
		Global Village (1977)
		Maxine's Place (1977)
		Women's Coffeehouse (1982)

State	*City*	*Verified/Unverified Feminist, Lesbian, Women's Restaurants*
Connecticut	Bridgeport	Black Rock Inn Restaurant (1976–1979)
		Bloodroot Feminist Vegetarian Restaurant (1977–)*→
	Danbury	The Answer Café (1978)*
	Greenwich	Homestead Inn
	Hartford	Reader's Feast Feminist Café and Bookstore (1985–1991)
		Sonya Weston's Books and Cheese (1982)
	New Britain	Edible Art Vegetarian Restaurant (1983–1984)
	New Haven	*La Machinetta Café/Coffeehouse* (1979)
		New Haven Women's Liberation Center (with a coffee house) (1978–1989)*
		The Pink Triangle Coffeehouse (1989)*
Delaware	Dewey Beach	*The Boat House* (1979)
	Wilmington	*Renaissance Gay Bar and Restaurant* (women only room) (1984–1991)
District of Columbia	Washington	*Hung Jury* (1980–2011)*
		JR's (1990–1991)
		Kalorama Café (1981–1982)
		Lil Sister (1990–1991)
		Lucy's Bar and Restaurant (1984)
		The Otherside Restaurant and Showbar (1981–1984)
		Paramount Steak House (1977)
		Phase One (1990–1991)
		Rising Women's Coffeehouse (1977)
		Suzanne's Wine Bar/Restaurant/Bakery/and Charcuterie (1990–1991)
		Town House (1977)
		Two Quail Restaurant (1990–1991)
		Washington Area Women's Center's Coffeehouse (1979)
		Zeigfield's (1990–1991)
Florida	Fort Lauderdale	Clever Bar/Women's Restaurant (1982)
		Shangri-La Disco Lounge and Restaurant (1985)

State	*City*	*Verified/Unverified Feminist, Lesbian, Women's Restaurants*
	Hallandale	Lou's Back Room (bar with sandwiches, snacks, and dancing) (1978)
		Sandy's Kitchen (1981)
	Key West	Claire (with women's only tea dance) (1984–1988)
	Miami	*The Courtyard Inn* (1982)
	Pinellas Park	Beaux Arts Coffeehouse and Art Gallery (1984–1991)
	Tallahassee	Everywoman's Coffeehouse (1985–1991)
	Tampa	*The Denny's at 102 Parker Street* (mostly gay clientele at night) (1977–1981)
		Feminist Connection Bookstore (served coffee and tea) (1978)*
		Three Birds Feminist Bookstore and Coffeeshop (1990–1991)
		The Women's Center Coffeehouse (1978)*
Georgia	Atlanta	*Gallus Restaurant and Bar* (1977)
		The Sportspage Restaurant and Bar (1984–1991)
Hawaii	Honolulu	*The Breeze Inn* (1985)
		The Godmother (1983–1989)
		Hamburger Mary's (1982–1989)
		The Tomato (1978)
	Maui	*Hamburger Mary's* (1983)
Illinois	Champaign	Lavender Prairie Collective (1978)*
	Chicago	Blue Gargoyle Coffeehouse (1975–1982)
		Gentry (1979–1984)
		Grandma's (1977)
		His N Hers (1979–1984)
		Jane Addams Bookstore and Coffeehouse (1981–1982)
		Karen's Kitchen (It really was her own kitchen) (1976)
		Mama Peaches (1975–1978)*
		Mountain Moving Coffeehouse (1974–2005)*

State	*City*	*Verified/Unverified Feminist, Lesbian, Women's Restaurants*
		My Brother's Place (1984)
		Paris Dance Restaurant and Bar (1989–1991)
		RSVP and Company Café, Bar, and Restaurant (1988)*
		Somewhere Coffeehouse (1983)
		Susan B's Feminist Restaurant (1975–1991)
		Up North (1977)
		Vittles (1977)
	Evanston	Kinehart Women's Center (served food) (1989–1991)
		Lesbian Coffeehouse at Women at Northwestern University (1978)*
Indiana	Bloomington	Mother Bear's Place (1977)
	Fort Wayne	Sisterspace Women's Coffeehouse (1989–1991)
Iowa	Iowa City	Grace and Rubies Feminist Social Club and Restaurant (1976–1978)*
		The Women's Coffeehouse (1979–1981)*
Kansas	Lawrence	Sister Kettle Café (1975–1979)*
		Womonspace Coffeehouse (as part of the women's center) (1977)
	Topeka	*Guys and Dolls* (food and dancing) (1978)*
Kentucky	Lexington	*The Bungalow Restaurant* (1983–1984)
		Montparnass (sic) Restaurant (1977)
	Louisville	Mother's Brew: A Coffeehouse for Women (1978)
Louisiana	Baton Rouge	*The Cock and Bull Restaurant and Bar* with separate women's room (1982–1983)
	New Orleans	Apple Barrel (1977–1982)
		Burgundy House (1977)
		Faubourg Marigny Gay Bookstore with coffee and tea (1982)
		Mas Cuiller Gras (1977)
		The Other Side Bar and Coffeehouse (1989)
		Tortilla Flats (1977–1989)

State	*City*	*Verified/Unverified Feminist, Lesbian, Women's Restaurants*
Maine	Ogunquit	Annabelle's (disco, brunch, dinner) (1977)
		Edelweiss Downtown (1977)
		The Fan Club (1977)
		The Trolley Stop (1977)
	Old Town	*Fig O My Heart Vegetarian Restaurant* (lesbian owned and operated) (1980)
Maryland	Bethesda	Community Café and Women's Bookstore (1983)
Massachusetts	Allston	Beetle's Lunch (1983–1984)*
		L'Odeon Macrobiotic Natural Foods (1985)
	Boston	*The Alternative Theater Restaurant* (1977)
		Crone's Harvest Radical Lesbian Feminist Coffeehouse
		Greystone's Restaurant and Bar (women owned) (1985)
		The Ideal, Women's Restaurant for Gay Women, Men, and Their Friends (1982–1984)
		The Iron Hose Coffeehouse (1982)
		Meetinghouse Coffeehouse (1976–1978)*
		Modern Times Café (1982–1988)
		Oasis Coffeehouse (1983)
		Somerville Women's Coffeehouse (1978–1980)*
	Cambridge	Amaranth (1978–1979)*
		Bread and Roses Feminist Restaurant (1974–1978)*
		Common Stock Restaurant (1981–1983)
		Indigo Women's Food and Bar (1990–1991)
		The Marquee (sponsors women athletes) (1985–1989)
	Greenfield	Green River Café (1981–1985)
	Northampton	Common Womon Club Restaurant (1976–1982)*
		Lesbian Gardens Coffeehouse and Bookstore
		Northstar Seafood Restaurant (1989–1991)

State	City	Verified/Unverified Feminist, Lesbian, Women's Restaurants
		The Women's Restaurant (probably referencing the Common Womon Club before it had its name) (1977)
	Provincetown	*Alice's* (1988)
		Hideaway (1977–1982)
		Lesbian Gardens Coffeehouse (1976–1992)*
		The Moors (1977)
		Pied Piper Restaurant (lesbian owned) (1979)
Michigan	Ann Arbor	Women's Coffeehouse (1974)*
	Detroit	Poor Woman's Paradise Coffeehouse (1974)
		The Underground Bar/Restaurant (1983–1989)
	Grand Rapids	Gaia Restaurant (1985)
	Kalamazoo	Pandora Womyn's Bookstore (sold coffee) (1985)
	Saugatuck	*Saugatuck Lodge* (1975–1977)
Minnesota	Duluth	North Country Women's Coffeehouse (1981–1988)*
	Minneapolis	Amazon Bookstore (sold coffee) (1981–1991)
		New French Café (1983)
		New Riverside Café (1975)*
		Park Rapids
		Prashad Kitchen Feminist Restaurant-International Vegetarian Cuisine (1977)
		Ruby's Café 1 (1985–1990)*
		Ruby's Café 2 (1990–)*
		Sister Wolf Bookstore and Café (1994–2015)*
		A Woman's Coffeehouse (1975–1989)*
		Women's Coffeehouse (1977–1991)
	Mankato	Cup of Warmth (1977–1979)*
	St. Paul	*Commonplace Restaurant and Vegetarian Cooperative* (1975–1977)*
Mississippi	Gulfport	Southern Wild Sisters Feminist Bookstore and Women's Resource Center (1978–1991)

State	*City*	*Verified/Unverified Feminist, Lesbian, Women's Restaurants*
Missouri	Kansas City	Kansas City Women's Liberation Union (served coffee) (1975–1984)
	St. Louis	*City Cousin* (1977–1979)
		Gay Coffeehouse (1976)
		Left Bank Books (sold coffee) (1982)
		The Sunshine Inn (women owned and operated vegetarian restaurant) (1976)
Montana	Helena	Northern Lights Café, Women's Collective (1983)
		Sweetgrass Bakery (woman owned) (1984–1985)
Nebraska	Lincoln	A Place of Our Own Wimmin's Bookstore (sold coffee and tea) (1982)
	Omaha	Common Womon Books (sold food and coffee) (1989)
Nevada	Los Vegas	*Le Café Restaurant* (1984)
New Hampshire	Portsmouth	*King's Wilde* (1977)
New Jersey	Atlantic City	*Lyle's Place Coffeeshop* (gay meeting place) (1977)
		Mama Mott's Restaurant (gay restaurant and gay waitresses) (1977–1983)
	Collinswood	*Chamomile's Woman Owned and Operated Restaurant* (1990–1991)
		Gatsby's (1990–1991)
	Fort Lee	*Tea and Symphony Coffeehouse* (1979–1981)
	Jersey City	*Pathway Lounge* (1984)
	Landing	*Hideaway Pizzeria* (woman owned) (1982)
	Newton	*Italian Kitchen* (1977–1979)
	Princeton	A Woman's Place (1988)*
	South River	A Place of One's Own Restaurant for Feminists and their Friends (1979–1981)
New Mexico	Albuquerque	Double Rainbow Bakery and Café (1985)
		Full Circle Books Feminist Bookstore (sold coffee) (1985)
	Santa Fe	Nifty Café Lesbian Coffeehouse (1989)

State	*City*	*Verified/Unverified Feminist, Lesbian, Women's Restaurants*
New York	Albany	Lilith Nonalcoholic Space (1981)
	Buffalo	Emma Feminist Bookstore (sold coffee) (1983–1988)
	East Hampton	The Attic Tea Dance (1983)
		Terrace Café (1982)
		Yoghurt Heaven (woman owned) (1977)
	Elmira	Mary's Grill (1978)*
	Ithaca	*Strange Paradise Café* (1988)
		Women's Coffeehouse at the Feminist Studio (1979–1982)
	Kingston	Sweet Maresa's (2011– , physical location began in 2019)* →
	Long Island	Women's Coffeehouse (1981–1984)
		Top of the Bay (1984)
	New Paltz	Lagusta's Commissary (2016–)*→
		Lagusta's Luscious Feminist Vegan Chocolate Shop Headquarters (2003– , physical location began in 2011)*→
		Oh Susanah, Inc, Café (1978)*
		Softer Power Sweets (2022–)*→
	New York City	*Applause* (1977)
		The Black Sheep (in former place as Mother Courage) (1977–1982)*
		Blue Skies (1984)
		Bluestockings Bookstore, Cafe, and Activist Center (1999–)*→
		Bonnie's Restaurant (women's half of Bonnie and Clyde's) (1976–1982)
		Brooklyn Women's Coffeehouse (1976–1979)
		Cafe Con Libros: An Intersectional Feminist Bookstore & Coffee Shop in Brooklyn (2017–)*→
		Company (1977–1979)
		The Confectionary (combined business between Lagusta's Luscious and Sweet Maresa's) (2016–)*→

State	*City*	*Verified/Unverified Feminist, Lesbian, Women's Restaurants*
	New York (*continued*)	*The Congress Restaurant* (1984)
		Cotton Patch (1977)
		Dapper Women's Restaurant (1981–1982)
		The Duchess Café Women's Restaurant (women-only) (1979–1984)
		La Fronde (1975–1982)
		La Papaya Women's Restaurant (1982)
		Les Pits (1977)
		Mother Courage Feminist Restaurant (first in the United States) (1972–1977)*
		One if By Land, Two if By Sea (1977)
		One Potato (1977)
		Peachstreet Dining Club for Women and their Friends (1981–1992), and becomes Peaches and Crème Bar-Restaurant (1984)
		The Pelican (1977)
		Pennyfeather (1989)
		Philippine Gardens Restaurant (women's night) (1982)
		Reno Sweekey's (1977)
		Reverse (1982)
		Shameira Huss Bookstore (sold coffee) (1979)
		Shescape Bar-Restaurant (1984)
		Uno's Café (1975–1981)
		Vegetaria (1976–1977)
		Vegetarian feminist restaurant (64 Charles Street)
		The Women's Coffee House (with sandwiches) (1975–1979)*
		WOW Theatre (had WOW Café) (1988–1990)
	Poughkeepsie	The Congress Restaurant (1984)
	Rochester	*Regular Restaurant* (1977)
		Snake Sister Café Women's Collective (1981–1984)
		Wild Seeds Feminist Bookstore and Café (1990–1991)

State	*City*	*Verified/Unverified Feminist, Lesbian, Women's Restaurants*
	Staten Island	*Beach Haven Restaurant and Bar* (1982)
		Brazil Bar and Restaurant (1982)
		Mother Earth Bar and Restaurant (1982)
	Woodstock	*Maverick Inn and Hotel Gourmet Restaurant* (1981)
		Sojourner's Women's Coffeehouse (1979–1991)
North Carolina	Ashville	Firestorm Books and Coffee (2008–)*→
		Malaprop's Bookstore and Café (1977–1984)*
	Charlotte	*Josh's Restaurant* (1977)
	Durham	Francesca's Gelato Café (1989–1991)
		Southern Sister's Feminist Bookstore (sold tea) (1990–1991)
North Dakota	Fargo	In 1989 there was a bar in Fargo
Ohio	Canton	Lesbian Activist Bureau (served coffee) (1978)*
	Cincinnati	*College Hill Coffee Co.* (lesbian-feminist owned) (2006–)→
		Flander's (1977)
		Greenwich Tavern (1977)
		Wild Iris Café/Crazy Ladies Bookstore (1994–1995)* (the bookstore 1979–2005, the cafe is still open)* →
	Cleveland	Genesis Feminist Vegetarian Restaurant and Bar (1977–1982)
		Gypsy's (1977–1982)
		The Mad Greek (1977–1982)
		Peabody's Café and Feminist Coffeehouse (1982)
	Columbus	Calico's Coffeehouse (1983–1988)
		Grapevine Café (women owned and operated) (1989–1991)
		Mel's Place (created by and for gay women) (1988–1989)
	Dayton	Iris Books Feminist Bookstore (sold coffee) (1990–1991)
	Painesville	*Rider's Tavern* (1977)

State	City	Verified/Unverified Feminist, Lesbian, Women's Restaurants
	Springfield	*Why Not Café* (1978)*
	Toledo	*Arlington* (1977)
		Nook N' Cranny (1977)
	Yellow Springs	Winds Café (feminist run restaurant) (1984)
Oklahoma	Oklahoma City	Herland Sister Resources Feminist Bookstore (sold coffee) (1985–1991)
	Tulsa	Fulton Street of Tulsa, Oklahoma (2019–)* →
Oregon	Eugene	*Book and Tea Shop* (1976–1982)
		Gertrude's Café (run by a women's collective) (1976–1985)
		Holding Together Coffeehouse (1976)
		Keystone Café (lesbian and gay counterculture café) (1984)
		Wild Iris Restaurant (1981–1982)
		Zoo Zoo's Natural Foods Restaurant (1979–1988)
	Myrtle Creek	Daphne and Judith's Tea Shop at Heritage Food Company (dates unknown)
		It's a Natural Foodstore (owned and operated by lesbians) (1988–1991)
	Portland	Bijou's Café (1970s)*
		Black Hawk Tavern (women's entertainment nights) (1982)
		Chez What? Lesbian Café (1982–1989)
		Cup and Saucer Café (now three outlets) (2007–)* →
		Hamburger Mary's (1976–1977)
		Hot Potata Café (gay run) (1984)
		Incredible Edibles (1977)
		Metropolis (under 21 allowed – many lesbians brought their teenage children here) (1982)
		Mountain Moving Café (1976–1979)
		Old Wives' Tales Restaurant and Women's Center (1980–2014)*

State	City	Verified/Unverified Feminist, Lesbian, Women's Restaurants
		Primary Domain Women's Restaurant (1985–1989)
		Wild Oscar's (1979–1982)
Pennsylvania	Erie	*Washington Grill* (1978)*
	Marietta	*The Railroad House* (gay owned and operated) (1984)
	New Hope	*The Baron* (formerly known as The Old Cartwheel) (1982–1984)
		The Raven (1984)
	Philadelphia	Amazon's Inc Coffeehouse (1978)*
		Astral Plane (1975)*
		Chamomile Women's Restaurant (1981–1982)
		Dee's Place (1975–1977)
		Dreamer's Café Women's Restaurant (1984)
		Giovanni's Room (1975)*
		Judy's Café (1975)*
		Mahogany Black Women's Club (1984)
		The Midway (1975)
		Philadelphia Gay Coffeehouse (1982)
		Philadelphia Lesbian Coffeehouse (1982)
		The Westbury (oldest gay establishment in Philadelphia) (1984)
		The Women's Book Connection Feminist Lesbian Bookstore (had coffee) (1984)
		Women's Space and Sisterhood (1981–1982)
	Pittsburgh	*Court Street Luncheonette* (1977)
		Gay Alternatives Coffeehouse at First Unitarian Church (1977)
		Home Circle Club (1977)
		Jackson's (gay restaurant) (1979–1984)
		Norreh Social Club (1982)
		Wild Sisters Restaurant and Bookstore (1982–1985)*
	State College	*The Left Bank* (1982)
		Seasons (1982)

State	*City*	*Verified/Unverified Feminist, Lesbian, Women's Restaurants*
Rhode Island	Providence	*Marantha Coffeehouse* (1976)
	Woonsocket	*High Street Café* (1978)*
South Carolina	Aiken	The Café: Feminist Bookstore and Café (1990–1991)
	Columbia	*MC B's Saloon* (1981–1982)
Tennessee	Chattanooga	*Alan Gold's* ("gay men and women basically stick together as a group here") (1984–1989)
	Memphis	*Terri's Townhouse* (1982)
	Nashville	Womankind Books (sold coffee) (1981–1989)
Texas	San Antonio	I've been told there were feminist restaurants there but have not found any
Utah	Salt Lake City	A Woman's Place Feminist Bookstore (sold coffee) (1989–1991)
Vermont	Brattleboro	*Common Ground Coffeehouse* (1982–1989)*
	Burlington	*The Fresh Ground Coffeehouse* (1977)
		Pearls Coffeehouse and Women's Restaurant (1984)
Virginia	Charlottesville	Muldowney's Women's Restaurant and Bar (1982)
	Norfolk	Shirley's Restaurant and Bar (1983–1984)
	Richmond	Every Woman's Coffeehouse (1981)*
	Roanoke	The Park Bar Restaurant Private Club (1981–1984)
Washington	Pullman	*Charity Corner* (1977)
		Fran Glors Creole Restaurant (1977)
		The Gertrude Stein/Alice B. Toklas Memorial Salon and Tea at the Lesbian Resource Center (1977–1979, in 1979 it is listed as Seattle though)
		Women's Coffee Coven (1977)
	Seattle	Innerspace Women's Coffeehouse (1981–1985)
		It's About Time Women's Bookcenter Feminist Bookstore (sold coffee) (1981–1985)

State	City	Verified/Unverified Feminist, Lesbian, Women's Restaurants
		Lesbian Separatist Potluck Brunches (1984)
		Mama Dot's (1981)
		Off Ramp Café (dates unknown)
		Sappho's (1983)
		A Special Place Womyn's Restaurant and Coffeehouse (1982–1988)
		Wildrose Tavern Women's Restaurant (1984–)* →
Wisconsin	Appleton	Doris's Super Bar (1978)
	Madison	*The Cabaret Room* (1979)
		Crescent Moon Women's Coffeehouse (1990–1991)
		Lysistrata Feminist Restaurant and Cultural Center (1979–1982)
		Mother Willy's Street Pub and Restaurant (1984–1985)
		A Room of One's Own Feminist Bookstore (sold coffee) (1981)
	Milwaukee	*The Beer Garden Bar and Restaurant (1984–1989)*
		Our Way (1977)*
		Sister Moon Feminist Bookstore sold coffee (1981)
		Sister Moon II (1981)

NOTES

CHAPTER ONE

1 Bloodroot Collective, "40 Year Anniversary Celebrations," March 2017, http://www.bloodroot.com/wp-content/uploads/Bloodroots-40th-Anniversary.pdf; Tejal Rao, "Mixing Food and Feminism, Bloodroot Is 40 and Still Cooking," *New York Times*, March 14, 2017, https://www.nytimes.com/2017/03/14/dining/bloodroot-feminist-restaurant.html?_r=0.

2 Joe Meyers, "Famed Bridgeport Vegetarian Restaurant Approaches 40th Anniversary," November 20, 2016, https://www.ctpost.com/living/article/Famed-Bridgeport-vegetarian-restaurant-approaches-10624322.php.

3 Morris, *The Disappearing L*, 2.

4 Wolfe, "Invisible Women in Invisible Places."

5 Podmore and Chamberland, "Entering the Urban Frame."

6 McFeely, *Can She Bake a Cherry Pie?* and Cowan, *More Work for Mother*.

7 Chenier, "Rethinking Class in Lesbian Bar Culture."

8 Chauncey, *Gay New York*.

9 Franzen, "Differences and Identities."

10 Boyd, *Wide Open Town*.

11 Kennedy and Davis, *Boots of Leather, Slippers of Gold*.

12 Jan Whitaker, "Women's Restaurants," Restauranting through History, last modified June 18, 2013, https://restaurantingthroughhistory.com/2013/06/18/womens-restaurants/.

13 Finnegan, *Selling Suffrage*. To be clear, there were other restaurants where women dined, as discussed in Andrew P. Haley, *Turning the*

Tables: Restaurants and the Rise of the American Middle Class, 1880–1920 (Chapel Hill: UNC Press Books, 2011).

14 *Hera: A Philadelphia Feminist Publication* 1, no. 2 (April/May 1975), back cover.

15 Nardi and Schneider, *Social Perspectives in Lesbian and Gay Studies*, 366–67.

16 In the late 2010s and early 2020s, "womxn" became a more popular term that within some feminist circles was meant to refute the patriarchal roots of the word "woman." However, there has been debate about whether the term is inclusive of trans women and some non-binary people.

17 Tandon, *Feminism*.

18 The word "queer" was reclaimed during the late 1980s in the United States during the midst of the AIDS epidemic. The activist organization Queer Nation, which sought to eradicate hate crime, explained its reasons for reclaiming the term in the pamphlet "Queers Read This," which the organization distributed during the 1990 New York Pride Parade. The pamphlet stated, "We've chosen to call ourselves queer. Using 'queer' is a way of reminding us how we are perceived by the rest of the world. It's a way of telling ourselves we don't have to be witty and charming people who keep our lives discreet and marginalized; we use queer as gay men loving lesbians and lesbians loving being queer. Queer, unlike GAY, doesn't mean MALE." However, the use of the word "queer" is still greatly contested within the lesbian, gay, bisexual, transexual, and transgender communities. The word "queer" is taken up more commonly by younger, white, college-educated individuals, but not exclusively so. Linguist Robin Brontsema traces the linguistic history of the word "queer" in the United States and delves deeply into the controversial employment of the term. In order to respect the self-identification of the owners of feminist restaurants, I have used the words that these owners used to self-describe. Robin Brontsema, "A Queer Revolution"; Queer Nation, "Queers Read This," 1990, http://www.qrd.org/qrd/misc/text/queers.read.this.

19 Nardi and Schneider, *Social Perspectives in Lesbian and Gay Studies*, 366–67. While it does not detract from the point, Olivia's website makes clear that while most guests are cis lesbians and queer women,

"non-binary and trans guests are and have always been welcome on Olivia trips." Oliva, "FAQ," November 15, 2021, https://www.olivia.com/faq-and-contact.

20 Jakobsen, *Working Alliances and the Politics of Difference*, 116.

21 Bunch, "Learning from Lesbian Separatism"; Radicalesbians, "The Woman-Identified Woman," in *Notes from the Third Year: Women's Liberation* (New York: Quadrangle, 1973), 240–45; Rudy, "Radical Feminism, Lesbian Separatism, and Queer Theory," 193; Shugar, *Separatism and Women's Community*; Lucia Valeska, "The Future of Female Separatism," *Quest* 2, no. 2 (Fall 1975): 2–16.

22 McGrath, "Living Feminist."

23 Taylor, Whittier, Morris, and Mueller, "Collective Identity in Social Movement Communities," 179.

24 Jang and Lee, "When Pop Music Meets a Political Issue"; Lewis, "Does Believing Homosexuality Is Innate Increase Support for Gay Rights?"

25 Selma Miriam and Noel Furie, "Bloodroot Interview 1," interview by Alex Ketchum, December 13, 2011.

26 Rebecca Jennings, "Practices of Intimacy in Australian Rural Lesbian-Separatist Communities in the 1970s and 1980s," conference presentation at Transnational Histories of Lesbian Migration, Rurality, and Politics in Australia and North America from the Berkshire Conference on the History of Women, University of Toronto, May 24, 2014.

27 This assertion was echoed in Penny House, "The New York Women's Coffee House," *Dyke: A Quarterly* 1 (September 1975), http://seesaw.typepad.com/dykeaquarterly/venue-ny-womens-coffee-house/.

28 Flavia Rando, "New York Feminist Food," interview by Alex Ketchum, March 7, 2015.

29 Julie Podmore, "Feminist Geographies," interview by Alex Ketchum, February 26, 2016.

30 Gilmore and Kaminski, "A Part and Apart."

31 Ross, *The House that Jill Built*.

32 Laughlin, Gallagher, Cobble, Boris, Nadasen, Gilmore, and Zarnow, "Is It Time to Jump Ship?," 82.

33 Meyerowitz, ed., *Not June Cleaver*.

34 Schwartz and Cook, "Archives, Records, and Power."

35 Cvetkovich, *An Archive of Feelings*, 167.

36 Scott, "The Evidence of Experience," 797.

37 The option of contributing to the map proved unpopular with site users. People preferred to email instead. As a result, I removed this map from the site in 2016.

38 Ingram, Bouthillette, and Retter, *Queers in Space*.

39 Nelson and Seager, eds., *A Companion to Feminist Geography*, 15.

40 Women and Geography Study Group of the IBG and Explorations in Feminism Collective of Great Britain, *Geography and Gender*, 20 and 43.

41 Madge, "Methods and Methodologies in Feminist Geographies," 6.

42 The editor of *Gaia's Guide* never purported to know everything about the listings and could make mistakes. In the 1977 edition's entry for Rising Woman Coffeehouse, the listing states, "Saturday nights only. Music, readings, games or some type of program. If you find out where it is please let Gaia know" (69).

43 Horn, *Gaia's Guide*. While these locations did not have a feminist restaurant, they were able to support some kind of women's, feminist, or lesbian center.

44 Ryan, *Feminism and the Women's Movement*.

45 Horn, *Gaia's Guide* (1984).

46 Depending on the study and depending on how "Jewish identity" is defined (whether the study includes being culturally Jewish but not practising the religion), Jewish Americans comprised between 1.5 to 2 percent of the population of the United States. US Census Bureau, "1980 U.S. Census," https://www.census.gov/library/publications/1980/compendia/statab/101ed.html.

47 Horn, *Gaia's Guide* (1984).

48 This literary culture made this book project possible by preserving records of the businesses during the period.

49 "Feminist Businesses," *Boston Herald: Special Women's Issue*, November 28, 1976, 8. For another example of a feminist nexus, Artemis Café and Women's Society (1977–1984), which was on Valencia Street in the Mission District of San Francisco, was just down the road from Old Wives Tales Bookstore (1976–1995).

50 Horn, *Gaia's Guide.*

51 "Mother Courage Restaurant: Mother Courage," title of periodical cut off, 176, Smith College Archives, Dolores Alexander Papers (unprocessed), Box 21, Folder 180, 39.

52 De Certeau, *The Practice of Everyday Life*, xix.

53 Agatha Beins, "Feminist Periodicals and the Locations of Feminism," unpublished conference presentation (used with permission) at A Revolutionary Moment: Women's Liberation in the late 1960s and early 1970s, a conference organized by the Women's, Gender, and Sexuality Studies Program at Boston University, March 27–29, 2014.

CHAPTER TWO

1 Patricia Hynes, "Business Prospectus of Bread and Roses," October 1974. Schlesinger Library at the Radcliffe Institute of Harvard University: Papers of Patricia Hynes, Box 1, Folder 3, 5–6.

2 "Women Working," *Country Women Magazine,* June 16, 1975, 4.

3 Perl and Abarbanell, *Guidelines to Feminist Consciousness Raising*, 3. According to the CR pamphlet, these sessions had "one basic purpose: it raises the woman's consciousness, increases her complete awareness, of her oppression in a sexist society. To do so, it helps her break through the conditioning all women have received, so that she can see and fully comprehend how society has deliberately trained and prepared her to play certain roles, accept certain situations, feel certain emotions, within the fabric of the culture; above all, how she is trained not to question, not to challenge, not to upset the way things are."

4 While the push for the Back to the Land movement originated from a leftist critique of capitalism and the imperial hegemonic context of the United States, other women decided to create women-only communes to additionally escape sexism. Despite the positive intent behind creating communes, there was disillusionment with these models. For more, refer to Mark Perlgutnov, "Communal Living: Adventure in Relating to Others," *New York Times*, November 28, 1971; Tetrault, "The Making of a Feminist Farm," 30.

5 Karen Lindsey, "Feminist Capitalism—Banks and Eateries," *Boston Phoenix*, May 7, 1974. The article was placed in the sexist-named "For

and About Women" section of the paper, implying that men would not be interested in news about women.

6 As legal scholar Laura Eckert argues, "In the early 1970s Congress investigated allegations of discriminatory credit practices. Congress focused on married women because financial institutions consistently required women to obtain their spouses' signatures in order to obtain credit. Congress sought to protect these women from discriminatory credit practices and to provide them with the opportunity to establish individual credit. To prohibit this type of credit discrimination, Congress passed the ECOA in 1974 and expanded the Act to its present scope in 1976 … Certain lending practices can pass this effects test, even though a creditor's practice results in a greater rejection of women and minorities. Creditors can use such criteria as 'income in excess of a certain amount' as long as there is a 'demonstrable relationship' between the criteria and creditworthiness for the level of credit involved. For example, requiring that applicants have a minimum income to qualify for an overdraft line of credit might negatively impact women and minority applicants at a higher rate than men and non-minority applicants. However, creditors may use this income standard if they can show a nexus between the income requirement and creditworthiness for the requested credit level." So even with the passage of the ECOA, lenders could still indirectly discriminate against women and people of colour. Furthermore, courts are not consistent in applying the ECOA to cases of discrimination on the basis of sexual orientation and as a result the ECOA does not protect lesbians from discriminatory loan practices. Eckert, "Inclusion of Sexual Orientation Discrimination in the Equal Credit Opportunity Act," 311.

7 Getting a loan was particularly difficult for marginalized, racialized communities in the 1970s and 1980s. As the United States Government Accountability Office shows, "Most studies suggest that discrimination may play a role in certain types of nonmortgage lending, but data limitations complicate efforts by researchers and regulators to better understand this issue. For example, available studies indicate that African-American-owned small businesses are denied loans more often or pay higher interest rates than white-owned businesses with similar risk characteristics." *Fair Lending: Race and Gender Data Are Limited for Nonmortgage*

Lending: Report to Congressional Requesters (Washington: US Government Accountability Office, 2008), https://www.gao.gov/new.items/d08698.pdf. Based on collating information from the studies on lending policy history in the United States, it appears that racial discrimination is more significant than gender discrimination in procuring loans in the United States. Marital status plays a role as single women are less likely to get loans than single men. Refer to Judith K. Robinson, "Race, Gender, and Familial Status: Discrimination in One US Mortgage Lending Market," *Feminist Economics* 8, no. 2 (2002): 63–85. There is not enough data available to speak to discriminatory lending policies related to lesbian and queer individuals. However, there was no ban on discrimination on the basis of sexual orientation under the Equal Credit Opportunity Act (ECOA) of 1974.

8 N. Jeanne Wertz, "Women Business Owners to Organize," *The Spokeswoman*, September 15, 1974, 3. It is possible to read Wertz's full "Statement on the Economic Problems Faced by Women in America" that she delivered to the Joint Economic Committee in 1973, regarding economic problems for American women. United States Congress Joint Economic Committee, "Economic Problems of Women: Hearings Before the Joint Economic Committee, Ninety-third Congress, First Session" (U.S. Government Printing Office, 1973), 565–79. Wertz had previously produced a 150-page report on behalf of the Small Business Association, "The SBA and Women" (March 1973).

9 Catherine Samuels of the Women's Action Alliance, "How to Make the Media Work for You" (New York: 1974) and Carol Shapiro of the Women's Action Alliance, "How to Organize a Multiservice Women's Center" (New York: 1973). Smith College Archives, Dolores Alexander Papers (unprocessed), Box 13.

10 Susan Schoch, Heidi Fiske, and Karen Zehring, "How to Start Your Own Business," Ms. Handbook of *Ms. Magazine*, April 1976, 106–9.

11 Schoch, Fiske, and Zehring, "How to Start Your Own Business."

12 Schoch, Fiske, and Zehring, "How to Start Your Own Business."

13 Schoch, Fiske, and Zehring, "How to Start Your Own Business."

14 Schoch, Fiske, and Zehring, "How to Start Your Own Business."

15 Many theoretical works trying to understand feminist business ethics settle on the idea of an ethics of care. Eva Feder Kittay's work on feminist ethics centers care as the solution. Rather than avoid ideas of dependency, an ethics of care acknowledges that all humans are interdependent and this understanding should influence how one conducts business. An ethics of care theoretically should permeate all aspects of a business such as the treatment of employees and customers, the kinds of products one sells and the source of their materials, and their relationships with other businesses. She positions this discussion within a reimagining of public policies like welfare reform, healthcare, and the changing of institutions to support the young, sick, and old. Other studies instead try to imagine what feminist ethics and feminist business practice could look like in a specific industry. For example, Laura Brown has written about how these ethics would work in therapy. While historians have done less research on feminist businesses, researchers from other fields have looked at feminist businesses, organizations, and collectives. Kittay, *Love's Labor*; Brown, "Ethics and Business Practice in Feminist Therapy."

16 Schoch, Fiske, and Zehring, "How to Start Your Own Business."

17 No first name exists in the historical records for Boulanger. Spang, *The Invention of the Restaurant*; and Coman, "Origins of First Restaurant Challenged," *Telegraph* (London, UK), September 3, 2000.

18 "There's a long tradition that goes back for centuries of assuming that the best chefs must be male, that men are the only ones who can operate on that very highest of culinary levels. Obviously, it makes a difference that they're getting paid large salaries, too. It also makes a difference that they're allowed to be creative [whereas] the woman who has to feed her four kids seven days of the week doesn't always have that opportunity." These discrepancies continue in present day. Sherrie Inness, "Interview with Dr. Sherrie A. Inness: New Research, Unexpected Sources," interview by Ashar Foley and Michelle Yost, *Aegis: The Otterbein Humanities Journal* (Spring 2005), https://digitalcommons.otterbein.edu/aegis_humanity/10/; Harris and Giuffre, *Taking the Heat*.

19 For more information on restaurant management, refer to Ketchum, "Restaurant Management."

20 Historian Dorothy Sue Cobble has traced the evolution of waitresses' attitudes towards feminist proposals such as the Equal Rights Amendment

and shown the way that waitresses have been engaged in activism over workers' rights throughout the twentieth century. Cobble, "'Practical Women.'"

21 According to economist Lisa Williamson at the US Bureau of Labor, detailed occupational employment estimates were first made available in 1972. There were considerably fewer detailed occupations in the classification system used for 1972 to 1982 than those used for more recent data (only about 150 occupations versus 535 in the 2010 Census classification). Many of the detailed occupations were of a miscellaneous or "all other" type. Lisa Williamson, "Data on Restaurant Employment by Sex/Gender," email correspondence with Alex Ketchum, February 26, 2018; US Bureau of Labor Statistics, "Employed Persons by Detailed Occupation by Sex and Race 1972–1982"; US Bureau of Labor Statistics, "Employed Persons by Detailed Occupation by Sex and Race 1983–2002."

22 US Bureau of Labor Statistics, "Employed Persons by Detailed Occupation, Sex, Race, and Hispanic or Latino Ethnicity," 2017, https://www.bls.gov/cps/cpsaat11.pdf.

23 Handwritten note on Gale Goldberg, "Feminism and Food: An Alternative to Restauranting" (Thesis, Massachusetts Institute of Technology, 1976), 1. Schlesinger Library at the Radcliffe Institute of Harvard University: Papers of Patricia Hynes, Box 1, Folder 3.

24 Patricia Hynes, "Business Prospectus of Bread and Roses," October 1974. Schlesinger Library at the Radcliffe Institute of Harvard University: Papers of Patricia Hynes, Box 1, Folder 3, 5–6.

25 Hynes, "Business Prospectus of Bread and Roses," 3.

26 Also in New York City, in 1973, the food editor of the *New York Daily*, Carol Brock, founded Les Dames d'Escoffier, an organization for women in the food, beverage, and hospitality industries, inspired by Boston's Les Dames des Amis d'Escoffier, a dining and philanthropic society formed in 1959 in response to the all-male Les Amis d'Escoffier. Memberships were available only by invitation. Since its founding, Les Dames d'Escoffier has spread throughout the United States, Canada, the United Kingdom, and Mexico and has over forty regional chapters and 2,300 members. The mandate of the organization is that members mentor other women in the food industry. In 2018, membership continues to

be offered only on an invitational basis. Les Dames d'Escoffier, "Our Complete History," 2016, http://www.ldei.org/index.php?com=pages&action=showpage&id=93.

27 "Fales Library and Special Collections Guide to the New York Women's Culinary Alliance Archive 1982–2010," Fales Library of New York University, MSS.279

28 Marjorie Parsons, "Coffeehouse Meeting," recorded presentation, 1979, Northeastern University Archives, AV2316, M120.

29 Lynne Cherry, "Grace and Rubies," *The Daily Iowan*, 1977, quoted within "Grace and Rubies Restaurant," *Lost Womyn's Space*, December 16, 2011, http://lostwomynsspace.blogspot.ca/2011/12/grace-and-rubies-restaurant.html. It was located at 309 North Linn Street.

30 Gloria Cole, "Bloodroots: A Dream on a Shoestring," *Fairpress*, March 16, 1977. Interestingly, the reviewer notes that "the food, the surroundings, and the ambiance will appeal to men as well." Such a comment reflects how Bloodroot is not a separatist women-only space but rather a woman-centred space.

31 Patricia Roth Schwartz, "Bloodroot: Not by Food Alone," *Hartford Advocate*, November 23, 1977, 27.

32 Goldberg, "Feminism and Food."

33 "Mother Courage," *Artemis* 3, November 1975, 3. In articles and documents, sometimes the former restaurant is spelled "Benny's" and sometimes "Bennie's."

34 "Mother Courage Restaurant: Mother Courage," title of periodical cut off, 176, Smith College Archives, Dolores Alexander Papers (unprocessed), Box 21, Folder 180, 39. However, there are contradictions in her narrative because in other papers she mentions that her father also helped them out. In interviews with magazine and newspaper reporters, there was a tendency for the feminist restaurant owners to emphasize the women's labour, which was impressive, but erase either the physical help of some male family members or financial support (and inheritance from fathers) that allowed them to buy these spaces.

35 "Mother Courage," *Artemis* 3.

36 "September 3," Day Planner, 1973, Smith College Archives, Dolores Alexander Papers (unprocessed), Box 13. For more on the use of feminist

calendars and day planners, refer to Yoken, "Transnational Transfers and Mainstream Mappings."

37 Syd Beiner, "The Feminist Gourmet Bill of Fare," Smith College Archives, Dolores Alexander Papers (unprocessed), Box 8.

38 Bryher Herak, "Wildrose," interview with Alex Ketchum, June 26, 2016.

39 Herak, "Wildrose."

40 Parsons, "Coffeehouse Meeting."

41 Gloria Cole, "Bloodroot: A Dream on a Shoestring," *Fairpress,* March 16, 1977. Selma Miriam was referred to as "Ms. Bunks," her married name, in this interview.

42 Cole, "Bloodroot."

43 Jo Ann Passariello, "Feminist Movement Creates Small Business," *New England Business Journal*, February 1975, 9.

44 Cole, "Bloodroot."

45 Parsons, "Coffeehouse Meeting."

46 Parsons, "Coffeehouse Meeting."

47 She continued, "So we made a conscious decision, we would buy a place with windows, we were going to buy a place with light and we were going to buy a place that has a kitchen." Herak, "Wildrose."

48 Herak, "Wildrose."

49 Levin, *In the Pink*; Ingram, Bouthillette, and Retter, *Queers in Space.*

50 Joan Antonuccio, "Brick Hut," email correspondence with Alex Ketchum, June 9, 2015.

51 Antonuccio, "Brick Hut," email correspondence with Ketchum.

52 Crime was not restricted to interactions with community outsiders. In a 1975 article on the New York Women's Coffeehouse, it was revealed that occasionally women would sneak into shows without paying and once someone stole cash out of the cash box during an event. Penny House, "The New York Women's Coffee House," *Dyke: A Quarterly* 1 (September 1975), http://seesaw.typepad.com/dykeaquarterly/venue-ny-womens-coffee-house/.

53 Antonuccio, "Brick Hut," email correspondence with Ketchum.

54 Antonuccio, "Brick Hut," email correspondence with Ketchum.

55 Herak, "Wildrose."

56 Selma Miriam and Noel Furie, "Bloodroot Interview 1," interview by Alex Ketchum, December 13, 2011. Selma Miriam's mother's warning

speaks to the cost that could come with identifying one's business as feminist. While there were advantages such as drawing in a like-minded clientele, there was the financial risk of serving too niche of a market. The word "feminist" drew ire from critics and sometimes violence. Furthermore, labelling a business as "feminist" opened its owners up for critique from within feminist communities as feminist business practices were debated.

57 "Letters to Bloodroot," personal papers of Noel Furie and Selma Miriam shared with Alex Ketchum.

58 Richard Weitzel, "Review of the Second Seasonal Political Palate," *The Boston Sunday Globe*, September 13, 1998, 27. "I probably should have been worried about scaring away men, and it probably wasn't very practical. Everyone, even my mother, was saying, you mustn't do this. She said, go ahead and open up a restaurant if you like, but you must not put up the word feminist, you will scare away customers."

59 "Womanwise," *Connecticut Post*, July 21, 1998.

60 "Womanwise," *Connecticut Post*.

61 Sharon Davenport, "LGBT Pride: Remembering the Brick Hut Café—Part 1," *Bay Area Bites*, June 23, 2011, http://ww2.kqed.org/bayareabites/2011/06/23/lgbt-pride-remembering-the-brick-hut-café-part-1/.

62 Jim Miller and Kelly Mayhew, "The Self Appointed Mayor of Golden Hill Holds Court in Big Kitchen," *San Diego Free Press*, May 20, 2013, https://sandiegofreepress.org/2013/05/the-self-appointed-mayor-of-golden-hill-holds-court-in-the-big-kitchen/.

63 Miller and Mayhew, "The Self Appointed Mayor of Golden Hill Holds Court in Big Kitchen."

64 LAMBDA Archives, "Big Kitchen: Food for Thought," http://www.lambdaarchives.us/2010_honorees/food_for_thought.htm.

65 Miller and Mayhew, "The Self Appointed Mayor of Golden Hill Holds Court in Big Kitchen."

66 You can listen to the musical's soundtrack at music director and composer Bob Schleeter's website. Bob Schleeter, "Big Kitchen: A Counter Culture Musical Playlist," November 8, 2021, https://www.bobschleeter.com/big-kitchen.

67 Paul Hormick, "Someone's in the Kitchen with Judy: 35 Years of the Big Kitchen," *San Diego Troubadour*, November 2015, https://sandiegotroubadour.com/2015/11/someones-in-the-kitchen-with-judy-35-years-of-the-big-kitchen/.

68 Anonymous, "Remembering Big Kitchen," Big Kitchen Facebook Page, July 2013. This appreciation of The Big Kitchen's contribution to the neighbourhood was echoed in a July 2013 Facebook post to The Big Kitchen's page, when a poster published a family photo with the caption that "Judy the Beauty and the Big Kitchen were an integral part to raising my kids in Golden Hill. She opened up the kitchen for Spaghetti nights for our Mom's group so we could build a better community. She held an initial fundraiser for the tot lot on Cedar and 28th because we needed a nice place for our toddlers to play. And she started a little art program at Brooklyn elementary to make sure the kids in the community had a little art and beauty for the start. Well … years later my little toddler just graduated from UCLA School of Design and Media Arts. Thank you Judy for celebrating with us and being part of our community experience!"

69 The award cites her role in creating after-school programs and her good influence on the neighbourhood. The award noted how The Big Kitchen helped with benefits and spaghetti/spinach lasagna dinners for baseball teams and also catered for hospital meetings, church events, funerals, Balboa Park Museums, and political events. The award goes on to state, "While managing her restaurant, Judy has been extremely active in her community, participating in events such as the Grass Roots Cultural Center, which was next door to the Big Kitchen; and she is a major contributor to the Woman's History Museum" and "The Big Kitchen has been a community center for so many people, and the lively community spirit is exemplified by the art work and pictures throughout the restaurant, featuring customers, friends, and family." California Legislature Assembly, "Woman of the Year," 2005, http://bigkitchencafé.com/wp/awards/woman-of-the-year/.

70 Esther Rubio-Sheffrey, "Heroes, Pioneers and Trailblazers 2010 Honoree: Judy Forman," *San Diego Gay Lesbian News*, February 15, 2010, http://sdgln.com/news/2010/02/25/heroes-pioneers-and-trailblazers-2010-honoree-judy-forman.

71 Mary Bahneman, "Ruby's," interview by Alex Ketchum, October 15, 2015.

72 Bahneman, "Ruby's."

73 Herak, "Wildrose."

74 "Mother Courage Restaurant: Mother Courage," 176.

75 Irene Backalenik, "Feminist Food for Thought," *New York Times*, June 26, 1977.

76 Antonnucio, "Brick Hut."

77 Antonnucio, "Brick Hut."

78 Parsons, "Coffeehouse Meeting."

79 Miriam and Furie, "Bloodroot Interview 1."

80 Bahneman, "Ruby's."

81 Hormick, "Someone's in the Kitchen with Judy."

82 Hormick, "Someone's in the Kitchen with Judy."

83 Robin Nicole Whiting, "Bloodroot, a Feminist Outpost on the Sound," April 27, 1996, title of publication cut off, Yale University Archives, Bloodroot Collective Records, MS 1955, Box 10.

84 Whiting, "Bloodroot, a Feminist Outpost on the Sound."

85 Parsons, "Coffeehouse Meeting."

86 Antonuccio, "Brick Hut."

87 Herak, "Wildrose."

88 Antonuccio, "LGBT Pride: Remembering the Brick Hut Café—Part 2."

89 Dolores Alexander and Jill Ward, "Mother Courage History," Smith College Archives, Dolores Alexander Papers (unprocessed), Box 13.

90 Sharon Johnson, "In Los Angeles Saloon Women Get the Red Carpet," *Lakeland Ledger* (Florida), June 16, 1976, https://news.google.com/newspapers?id=d4ksAAAAIBAJ&sjid=2PoDAAAAIBAJ&pg=7132%2C4566266.

91 Goldberg, "Feminism and Food."

92 Johnson, "In Los Angeles Saloon Women Get the Red Carpet."

93 In addition to a federal minimum wage, states set their own minimum wage. State of California Department of Industrial Relations, "History of the Minimum Wage," CA.Gov, https://www.dir.ca.gov/iwc/minimumwagehistory.htm.

94 Johnson, "In Los Angeles Saloon Women Get the Red Carpet."

95 Goldberg, "Feminism and Food," 9.
96 Schwartz, "Bloodroot."
97 Johnson, "In Los Angeles Saloon Women Get the Red Carpet."
98 Parsons, "Coffeehouse Meeting."
99 Parsons, "Coffeehouse Meeting."
100 Parsons, "Coffeehouse Meeting."
101 Johnson, "In Los Angeles Saloon Women Get the Red Carpet."
102 Parsons, "Coffeehouse Meeting."
103 Striving to make a living wage was highlighted in interviews with the press. Ruth Bayard Smith, "Feminists Operate Club," *The Sumter Daily*, September 11, 1978.
104 Antonuccio, "Brick Hut."
105 Parsons, "Coffeehouse Meeting."
106 Parsons, "Coffeehouse Meeting."
107 Parsons, "Coffeehouse Meeting."
108 Parsons, "Coffeehouse Meeting."
109 Smith, "Feminists Operate Club." As Smith explained, "From the outset, the women have been committed to what they call 'alternative economies.' As often as possible, they buy from food cooperatives."
110 Parsons, "Coffeehouse Meeting."
111 Parsons, "Coffeehouse Meeting."
112 Elizabeth Kent, "A Journey through 'Lesbian Mecca': Northampton LGBTQ History Walking Tour," September 14, 2014. Script provided by Elizabeth Kent to Alex Ketchum on request.
113 Parsons, "Coffeehouse Meeting."
114 The restaurant opened at 11:00 a.m. and served lunch. The atmosphere included a quiet afternoon shift and a dinner shift and bar scene at night.
115 Herak, "Wildrose."
116 Antonuccio, "Brick Hut," email correspondence with Ketchum.
117 Herak, "Wildrose."
118 "Employee Manual," San Francisco Public Library Archives, Bay Brick Inn Records 1982–1987, Collection 194-23, Box 1, Folder 3.
119 Mary Blume, "The Food's Bad But the Ideology Is Strong," *International Herald Tribune*, (exact date unknown), 1974, 18–19.
120 Blume, "The Food's Bad But the Ideology Is Strong."

121 Blume, "The Food's Bad But the Ideology Is Strong."
122 Miriam and Furie, "Bloodroot Interview 1."
123 "Women Working," *Country Women Magazine.*
124 "Women Working," *Country Women Magazine.*
125 "More than Just a Restaurant," *Fairfield Count Advocate*, September 8, 197?, date cut off. Yale University Archives, Bloodroot Collective Records, MS 1955, Box 10.
126 Emily Ferrar, "Following Someone Else's Pattern is Anathema: A Portrait of Selma Miriam," *Ways of Knowing*, December 5, 1998, 6.
127 Ferrar, "Following Someone Else's Pattern is Anathema."
128 "Five Feminist Run Bloodroot Gourmet Vegetarian Eatery," *Black Rock News*, June 28, 1989.
129 "Five Feminist Run Bloodroot Gourmet Vegetarian Eatery."
130 Ferrar, "Following Someone Else's Pattern is Anathema."
131 "Mother Courage Restaurant: Mother Courage," 176.
132 Dolores Alexander and Jill Ward, "Food," Smith College Archives, Dolores Alexander Papers (unprocessed), Box 21.
133 Alexander and Ward, "Food."

CHAPTER THREE

1 Marjorie Parsons, "Coffeehouse Meeting," recorded presentation, 1979, Northeastern University Archives, AV2316, M120.
2 Robin Nicole Whiting, "Bloodroot, a Feminist Outpost on the Sound," April 27, 1996, title of publication cut off, Yale University Archives, Bloodroot Collective Records, MS 1955, Box 10.
3 Whiting, "Bloodroot, a Feminist Outpost on the Sound."
4 Whiting, "Bloodroot, a Feminist Outpost on the Sound."
5 *Lesbians: The Invisible Minority*, KGO-TV Special, 1981, posted by the San Francisco Public Library to https://www.youtube.com/watch?v=XgfjIMAAwvQ.
6 More attention has been given to the way that social enterprises (and specifically social enterprises run by women for women) or social enterprises run for or by Black, Indigenous, and social entrepreneurs of colour, have always been outside the scope of male commercial banking. For example, in her book *Collective Courage* Jessica Gordon Nembhard shows the

role played by worker- or consumer-owned businesses as alternatives to finance networks dominated by white Americans. In *Black Business in the New South*, historian Walter B. Weare draws attention to Black Wall Street of Tulsa, Oklahoma, in which Black commerce by and for the Black community thrived. However, the role of feminist restaurants and cafes within feminist business networks is largely absent in the existing literature.

7 The historiography emphasizes the hard work and compromises necessary to create these businesses. Refer to Davis, "To Serve the 'Other'"; Halkias and Adendorff, *Governance in Immigrant Family Businesses*; Coe, *Chop Suey*; Light, *Ethnic Enterprise in America*; and Pearce, "Today's Immigrant Woman Entrepreneur."

8 As founder of New York City's Mother Courage Dolores Alexander remarked when asked what a "feminist" restaurant meant to her, "Well, a woman's space. There was no such thing … There was Schrafft's, the Tea Rooms … that kind of thing. But we didn't want to be a tea room. We wanted to be a space for strong, independent women who would be hopefully involved in the women's movement, and that did happen." Kelly Anderson, "Dolores Alexander Interview," *Voices of Feminism Oral History Project of Smith College*, March 20, 2004 and October 22, 2005, https://www.smith.edu/libraries/libs/ssc/vof/transcripts/Alexander.pdf.

9 US Bureau of Labor Statistics, "Employed Persons by Detailed Occupation by Sex and Race 1972–1982"; US Bureau of Labor Statistics, "Employed Persons by Detailed Occupation by Sex and Race 1983–2002."

10 Historian Heather Murray discusses the impact that this philosophy had on women-owned businesses in more detail. Refer to Murray, "Free for All Lesbians."

11 Gloria Cole, "Bloodroots: A Dream on a Shoestring," *Fairpress*, March 16, 1977.

12 Cole, "Bloodroots."

13 Deborah Emin, "For the Love of Food and Women: Two Bridgeport, Connecticut, Lesbians Reflect on Nearly Three Decades of a Feminist Space," *Gay City News* 4, no. 22 (June 2–8, 2005), http://gaycitynews.nyc/gcn_422/fortheloveoffood.html.

14 Parsons, "Coffeehouse Meeting."

15 Parsons, "Coffeehouse Meeting."

16 This type of law was not the specialty of the collective's lawyer.

17 United States Consumer Financial Protection Bureau 6500, 1974, https://www.fdic.gov/regulations/laws/rules/6500-1200.html.

18 Mary Bahneman, "Ruby's," interview by Alex Ketchum, October 15, 2015.

19 Bahneman, "Ruby's."

20 The Cheese Board opened as a small cheese store in 1967. In 1971, the two original owners sold their business to their employees and created a 100 percent worker-owned business. The new owners shared a belief that the collective process would organically create a truly democratic society. Cheese Board, "About Us," December 2017, http://cheeseboardcollective.coop/about-us/about-main.

21 Joan Antonuccio, "Remembering the Brick Hut Café, Part 2," *Bay Area Bites*, June 23, 2011, https://ww2.kqed.org/bayareabites/2011/06/23/lgbt-pride-remembering-the-brick-hut-café-part-2. It was located at 3222 Adeline Street.

22 Despite being ambitious the collective had to bring its rates down. The collective initially thought that it could pay off $150 a month between sales and rents, but it had to lower it to $75 a month due to the initial operating expenses. Parsons, "Coffeehouse Meeting."

23 Parsons, "Coffeehouse Meeting."

24 Dolores Alexander and Jill Ward, "Mother Courage History," Smith College Archives, Dolores Alexander Papers (unprocessed), Box 13.

25 Richard Weitzel, "Review of the Second Seasonal Political Palate," *The Boston Sunday Globe*, September 13, 1998, 27. She added, "and my mother helped too."

26 Bryher Herak, "Wildrose," interview with Alex Ketchum, June 26, 2016.

27 Parsons, "Coffeehouse Meeting."

28 One woman gave $500, while another provided a few thousand dollars. Some women in the collective did not put in any money. The promissory notes differed from ownership in that they were six-year notes with the highest interest possible. Parsons would then donate her interest back into the process of supporting the restaurant, so her note in 1979 was worth $1,500. Parsons, "Coffeehouse Meeting."

29 Parsons, "Coffeehouse Meeting."

30 Parsons, "Coffeehouse Meeting."

31 Alexander and Ward, "Mother Courage History," Smith College Archives, Dolores Alexander Papers (unprocessed), Box 13.

32 "Mother Courage Restaurant: Mother Courage," title of periodical cut off, 176, Smith College Archives, Dolores Alexander Papers (unprocessed), Box 21, Folder 180, 39.

33 Mark Mittlestadt, "Grace and Rubies 'Not Private,'" *The Daily Iowan: Iowa's Alternative Newspaper* 108, no. 158, February 27, 1977, http://dailyiowan.lib.uiowa.edu/DI/1976/di1976-02-27.pdf.

34 Herak, "Wildrose."

35 Herak, "Wildrose."

36 Herak, "Wildrose."

37 Parsons, "Coffeehouse Meeting."

38 Parsons, "Coffeehouse Meeting."

39 Alexander and Ward, "Mother Courage History."

40 Anderson, "Dolores Alexander Interview."

41 Parsons, "Coffeehouse Meeting."

42 Parsons, "Coffeehouse Meeting."

43 Valley Women's History Collective (Northampton, Massachusetts), "The Valley Women's Movement: A Herstorical Chronology 1968–1988," 2016, http://www.vwhc.org/timeline3.html.

44 "Mother Courage," *Artemis*, November 1975, 3.

45 Parsons, "Coffeehouse Meeting."

46 The Valley Women's History Collective published a timeline that included the Common Womon Club's fundraising efforts and events. Valley Women's History Collective, "The Valley Women's Movement: A Herstorical Chronology 1968–1988."

47 Parsons believed that potential funders' trust was harder to earn because the Common Womon Club refused to sell stock because the collective wanted to retain all decision-making ability. Parsons, "Coffeehouse Meeting."

48 Parsons, "Coffeehouse Meeting."

49 Parsons, "Coffeehouse Meeting."

50 Smith, "Feminists Operate Club."

51 Parsons, "Coffeehouse Meeting."
52 Mittlestadt, "Grace and Rubies 'Not Private."
53 Georgina Hickey, "Tuxedo Junction and Calico Club," email correspondence with Alex Ketchum, May 14, 2015.
54 Horn, *Gaia's Guide* (1981), 62.
55 Parsons, "Coffeehouse Meeting."
56 Ceres Incorporated was allegedly created for women interested in exploring women in business. Even though the collective had the goal of operating a restaurant, they wrote their corporation plans about "women in business" more generally so that the members had flexibility. The collective discussed the ideas it had with the bank but tried to keep the particulars about the restaurant among itself. The members sold their project as an educational research centre with food service. They assumed that approaching the bank to start a feminist restaurant would appear less stable. Also, by becoming a corporation the collective members protected themselves as individuals. To retain its nonprofit status, the collective of the Common Womon Club could not allow it to appear that corporate members had bought in, and thus the collective needed to delineate their corporation from the business by only including some members' names on the corporate papers. Ceres Incorporated owned the company. Parsons, "Coffeehouse Meeting."
57 Elizabeth Kent, "A Journey through 'Lesbian Mecca': Northampton LGBTQ History Walking Tour," September 14, 2014. Elizabeth Kent provided the script to Alex Ketchum, on request.
58 Ceres Incorporated owned the building that it rented out to the Common Womon Club collective. In total, the restaurant was paying Ceres Incorporated $325 a month. Seventy-five dollars of that figure was for the rented equipment (to compensate for the equipment's depreciation over time) and the rent helped cover the mortgage. Ceres Incorporated charged the Common Womon Club a "low rent" of $275 a month. The rental fee covered the large glass front porch, a large dining room, two small dining areas, a bathroom, and a large kitchen. In addition, the Common Womon Club had an office upstairs and use of the basement. Parsons, "Coffeehouse Meeting."
59 Kent, "A Journey through 'Lesbian Mecca.'"

60 Parsons, "Coffeehouse Meeting."

61 To continue to argue that its nonprofit was about education, the members also rented the storefront to the women's karate dojo, which was a nonprofit, and the space was later taken over by a bookstore. The papers of Ceres Incorporated were written such that they supported women in business, so any women's business they allowed to use the building was under their corporation papers, and through this method they could declare their tax-exempt status. The collective presented the Common Womon to the government in legal terms as a club for exploring vegetarianism and feminism with the food service component secondary to the club. Ruth Bayard Smith, "Feminists Operate Club," *The Sumter Daily*, September 11, 1978.

62 Parsons, "Coffeehouse Meeting."

63 Reflecting on the transition, Parsons wished she could have written an actual guide to make the switch smoother, but she did not have the time. Parsons, "Coffeehouse Meeting."

64 The next group running the space was able to learn from the mistakes of the first collective. Parsons, "Coffeehouse Meeting."

65 Parsons, "Coffeehouse Meeting."

66 Parsons, "Coffeehouse Meeting."

67 Horn, *Gaia's Guide*, various editions.

68 Bloodroot Collective, *Political Palate*; Bloodroot Collective, *The Second Seasonal Political Palate*; Bloodroot Collective, *The Perennial Palate*.

69 Horn, *Gaia's Guide*, various editions.

70 One might wonder why the collective did not just work the fair circuit, as it was more financially lucrative than the restaurant. However, financial success was not the motivation for creating the Common Womon Club. Creating a women-only space for socializing and political organizing was the goal. Parsons, "Coffeehouse Meeting."

71 Parsons, "Coffeehouse Meeting."

72 Lynne Cherry, "Grace and Rubies," *The Daily Iowan*, 1977, quoted within "Grace and Rubies Restaurant," *Lost Womyn's Space*, December 16, 2011, http://lostwomynsspace.blogspot.ca/2011/12/grace-and-rubies-restaurant.html.

73 Alexander and Ward, "Mother Courage History."

74 "Mother Courage," *Artemis* 3.

75 Even when restaurants did serve alcohol, the restaurant owners often tried to market their business as an alternative to bar culture. Sara Lewinstein, owner of San Francisco's Artemis Women's Café (1977–1984) stated, "the reason that I had started the Artemis was for women having an alternative space to go to rather than just going to the bars. We're a women's community. It doesn't matter whether you are gay or whether you are straight. This is a women's community. And there needs to be alternative spaces where you can feel free enough to come in and not be hassled by men—to have a glass of wine and not be picked up—and believe me I've been in that scene a long time and I know it happens." *Lesbians: The Invisible Minority* KGO-TV Special, 1981.

76 Murray, "Free for All Lesbians"; Davis and Kennedy, *Boots of Leather, Slippers of Gold*.

77 Parsons, "Coffeehouse Meeting."

78 Parsons, "Coffeehouse Meeting."

79 Parsons, "Coffeehouse Meeting."

80 Parsons, "Coffeehouse Meeting."

81 Parsons, "Coffeehouse Meeting."

82 Herak, "Wildrose."

83 Alexander and Ward, "Mother Courage History."

84 Anderson, "Dolores Alexander Interview."

85 "Women's Lib Takes the Plunge—Into Business," *Newsday*, 1972.

86 Alexander and Ward, "Mother Courage History."

87 "Securities Act," Securities and Exchange Commission, August 5, 1963, https://www.sec.gov/news/digest/1963/dig080563.pdf.

88 Alexander and Ward, "Mother Courage History."

89 Alexander explained that it was not in a business account because the bank would not let them open a business account without an EA form and that you cannot get one until you are incorporated, which they could not do as they were still at the initial stage of the process of creating their business. This explanation does not entirely make sense. EA forms are filled in by the employer for filing annual income tax returns of the employees from private sector companies. EC Forms are the equivalent for public sector companies. The EA or EC Form is generated at the end of the year and contains information on the personal details of the

employee, his or her earnings for the year, and the amount deducted and remitted under the Schedular Tax Deduction (STD) scheme. Perhaps she misspoke and meant that she needed an Employment Identification Number (EIN) or her Articles of Incorporation, as both would have been necessary to open a business account.

90 Anderson, "Dolores Alexander Interview."

91 Alexander and Ward, "Mother Courage History."

92 "Final Rule: Non-public Offering Exemption: Release 33-4552," US Securities and Exchange Commission, November 6, 1962, https://www.sec.gov/rules/final/33-4552.htm.

93 Anderson, "Dolores Alexander Interview."

94 Anderson, "Dolores Alexander Interview."

95 Alexander and Ward, "Mother Courage History."

96 Alexander and Ward, "Mother Courage History."

97 Alexander and Ward, "Mother Courage History."

98 Alexander and Ward, "Mother Courage History."

99 Alexander and Ward, "Mother Courage History."

100 "Correspondents and Ads," *Dyke: A Quarterly* 2, 86, http://seesaw.typepad.com/dykeaquarterly/issue-2/. Additionally, the Iowa City Public Library maintains a vertical file of materials documenting the legal struggles of Grace and Rubies. Eventually, the commission ruled in the favour of Grace and Rubies.

101 T.C. Boyle, "The Women's Restaurant," *Penthouse Magazine*, May 1977.

102 Parsons, "Coffeehouse Meeting."

103 Parsons, "Coffeehouse Meeting."

104 Parsons, "Coffeehouse Meeting."

105 Smith, "Feminists Operate Club"; and Parsons, "Coffeehouse Meeting."

106 Parsons, "Coffeehouse Meeting."

107 Chapter 11 status is a form of bankruptcy in which the owners propose a plan of reorganization to keep the business alive and pay creditors over time.

108 Antonuccio, "Remembering the Brick Hut Café, Part 2."

109 Bloodroot Collective, "Letter to Marge," personal papers lent to author.

110 Tejal Rao, "Mixing Food and Feminism, Bloodroot Is 40 and Still Cooking," *New York Times*, March 14, 2017, https://www.nytimes.com/2017/03/14/dining/bloodroot-feminist-restaurant.html?_r=0.

111 For more discussion of these themes, refer to Ferree and Martin, "Doing the Work of the Movement: Feminist Organizations," in *Feminist Organizations*, ed. Ferree and Martin, 4; Eastland, *Communication, Organization, and Change within a Feminist Context*; Staggenborg, "The Survival of the Women's Movement"; Woehrle, "Claims-Making and Consensus in Collective Group Processes"; Waring, *Counting for Nothing*; Hochschild and Machung, *The Second Shift*.
112 Parsons, "Coffeehouse Meeting."
113 Parsons, "Coffeehouse Meeting."
114 Parsons, "Coffeehouse Meeting."
115 Parsons, "Coffeehouse Meeting."
116 "Mother Courage Restaurant: Mother Courage," 176.
117 Parsons, "Coffeehouse Meeting."
118 Jurate Kazickas, "Doing Very Well, Thank You, Says First Women's Restaurant," *The Capital Times*, May 21, 1975.
119 Kazickas, "Doing Very Well, Thank You, Says First Women's Restaurant."
120 Kazickas, "Doing Very Well, Thank You, Says First Women's Restaurant."
121 Mary Blume, "The Food's Bad But the Ideology Is Strong," *International Herald Tribune,* (exact date unknown) 1974, 18–19.
122 "Mother Courage Restaurant: Mother Courage," 176.
123 Parsons, "Coffeehouse Meeting;"
124 Parsons, "Coffeehouse Meeting;"
125 Parsons, "Coffeehouse Meeting."
126 Parsons, "Coffeehouse Meeting."
127 Blume, "The Food's Bad But the Ideology Is Strong."
128 Blume, "The Food's Bad But the Ideology Is Strong."
129 Blume, "The Food's Bad But the Ideology Is Strong."

CHAPTER FOUR

1 Bonnie Carr, "New Feminist Eatery Aims to 'Warm Belly and Mind,'" *Bridgeport Sunday Post*, March 27, 1977.
2 Carr, "New Feminist Eatery Aims to 'Warm Belly and Mind.'"
3 Joan Antonuccio, "Brick Hut," email correspondence with Alex Ketchum, June 9, 2015.

4 Bryher Herak, "Wildrose," interview with Alex Ketchum, June 26, 2016.

5 Sturgis, "Ladyslipper," 38.

6 Loe, "Feminism for Sale."

7 Hogan, "Reading at Feminist Bookstores."

8 McDowell, *Gender, Identity and Place*.

9 "Feminist Businesses," *Boston Herald: Special Women's Issue,* November 28, 1976, 8.

10 Ruby's had two locations. The first Ruby's was on a major thoroughfare, 28th and Hennepin, and the second one was near Lorne Park. Ruby's owner remarked that Lorne was a very gay park, where Gay Pride would happen. Mary Bahneman, "Ruby's," interview by Alex Ketchum, October 15, 2015.

11 Bahneman, "Ruby's."

12 Sharon Davenport, "Remembering the Brick Hut Café, Part 1," *Bay Area Bites,* June 23, 2011, https://ww2.kqed.org/bayareabites/2011/06/23/lgbt-pride-remembering-the-brick-hut-café-part-1/.

13 Marjorie Parsons, "Coffeehouse Meeting," recorded interview, 1979, Northeastern University Archives, AV2316, M120.

14 In 2018, Bloodroot sells the chocolate of feminist vegan chocolate maker, Lagusta Yearwood, in their store. This principle of supporting other feminist businesses and women-focused small businesses has continued from the 1970s.

15 US Bureau of Labor Statistics, "Employed Persons by Detailed Occupation, Sex, Race, and Hispanic or Latino Ethnicity," 2017, https://www.bls.gov/cps/cpsaat11.pdf. In 2017, 19.7 percent of head chefs were women. Prior to 1976, the bureau did not distinguish between cooks and executive chefs. In 1976, the American Culinary Federation lobbied to elevate the position of the executive chef from service status to the professional category in the US Department of Labor's Dictionary of Official Titles. "History of the ACF," American Culinary Federation: San Diego, http://www.cdcefsandiego.org/american-culinary-foundation.html. For more qualitative information regarding the gender disparity in the kitchen, refer to Amanda Cohen, "I've Worked in Restaurants for 20 Years. Now You Finally Care about Female Chefs," *Esquire,* November 6, 2017, http://www.esquire.com/food-drink/restaurants/a13134079/sexual-harassment-sexism-food-industry/.

16 Davenport, "Remembering the Brick Hut Café, Part 1."
17 Joan Antonuccio, "Remembering the Brick Hut Café, Part 2," *Bay Area Bites*, June 23, 2011, https://ww2.kqed.org/bayareabites/2011/06/23/lgbt-pride-remembering-the-brick-hut-café-part-2/.
18 At the time the restaurant opened, some of the collective members were on government assistance. Parsons, "Coffeehouse Meeting."
19 "Letter to Marge," Bloodroot Personal Papers privately loaned to Alex Ketchum by Noel Furie and Selma Miriam.
20 Herak, "Wildrose."
21 Jim Jerome, "Feminists Hail a Restaurant Where the Piece de Resistance Is an Attitude, Not a Dish," *People Magazine*, June 2, 1975.
22 Jerome, "Feminists Hail a Restaurant Where the Piece de Resistance Is an Attitude, Not a Dish."
23 Parsons, "Coffeehouse Meeting."
24 Parsons, "Coffeehouse Meeting."
25 Parsons, "Coffeehouse Meeting."
26 Parsons, "Coffeehouse Meeting."
27 Jo Ann Passariello, "Feminist Movement Creates Small Business," *New England Business Journal*, February 1975, 9.
28 Susan Schoch, Heidi Fiske, and Karen Zehring, "How to Start Your Own Business," *Ms. Handbook* of *Ms. Magazine*, April 1976, 106–9.
29 Schoch, Fiske, and Zehring, "How to Start Your Own Business."
30 Joan Antonuccio, "Brick Hut," email correspondence with Alex Ketchum, June 9, 2015.
31 Patricia Hynes, "Bread and Roses," interview by Alex Ketchum, May 9, 2012.
32 Selma Miriam and Noel Furie, "Bloodroot Interview 1," interview by Alex Ketchum, December 13, 2011.
33 Antonuccio, "Brick Hut," email correspondence with Ketchum.
34 Bryher Herak, "Wildrose," interview with Alex Ketchum, June 26, 2016.
35 Herak, "Wildrose."
36 Levin, *In the Pink*.
37 Herak, "Wildrose."
38 Herak, "Wildrose."
39 Davenport, "Remembering the Brick Hut Café, Part 1."

40 Antonuccio, "Brick Hut," email correspondence with Ketchum.
41 Parsons, "Coffeehouse Meeting."
42 Sexist social values and educational practices dissuaded women from working in the trades. Beginning as early as divisions in high school with boys taking shop class and women funneled into home economics, the trades remained dominated by men during the 1970s and 1980s. Blau, Simpson, and Anderson, "Continuing Progress?"; Cruickshank, "The Participation of Women Employed in Traditionally Male Dominated Occupations including Plumbing: 1975–2013."
43 Carr, "New Feminist Eatery Aims to 'Warm Belly and Mind.'"
44 Levin, *In the Pink*.
45 Dolores Alexander, Smith College Special Collections and Archives, Dolores Alexander Papers (unprocessed), Tracy Young Howard Smith Scenes. Box 180, Folder 39, 176.
46 Thornton, *Club Cultures*.
47 Davenport, "Remembering the Brick Hut Café, Part 1."
48 Petersen, "An Investigation into Women-Identified Music in the United States," 208.
49 Antonnucio, "Remembering the Brick Hut Café, Part 2."
50 Mary Watkins and Pat Parker, "The Brick Hut" (song) on *Something Moving* (album) (Olivia Records: 1979).
51 Antonnucio, "Remembering the Brick Hut Café, Part 2."
52 "Feminist Restaurant," *Pittsburgh Post-Gazette*, July 27, 1982. It was located at 27th and Jane streets.
53 "Feminist Restaurant," *Pittsburgh Post-Gazette*.
54 Bahneman, "Ruby's."
55 Alison Bechdel, "Frivolous and Aimless Queries," *Dykes to Watch Out For*, July 26, 2021, https://dykestowatchoutfor.com/frivolous-aimless-queries/.
56 Bechdel, *The Essential Dykes to Watch Out For*, 46 and 78.
57 Bahneman, "Ruby's."
58 Herak, "Wildrose."
59 Herak, "Wildrose."
60 Horn, *Gaia's Guide* (1976). It was located on 532 Southeast 39th Street.
61 Vida, *Our Right to Love*.

62 Horn, *Gaia's Guide* (1979). It was located at 134 Hampshire Street.
63 "Wing Café Flyer," LAMBDA San Diego Archives, Folder: Businesses-Cafés.
64 Klein, "The Ritual Body as Pedagogical Tool," 220.
65 Wolverton, "Introduction," 32.
66 Dolores Alexander, "Letter from Dolores Alexander to New York Magazine Asking for a Review," Smith College Special Collections and Archives, The Dolores Alexander Papers (unprocessed), Tracy Young Howard Smith Scenes, Box 180, Folder 39.
67 Chrystos, "Letter to Noel Furie," private letter shared with the author.
68 Aleegra, "Letter to Bloodroot," private letter shared with the author. September 10, 1984.
69 It was located at 120 Harvard Avenue.
70 Irene Backalenik, "Feminist Food for Thought," *New York Times,* June 26, 1977, http://www.nytimes.com/1977/06/26/archives/long-island-opinion-feminist-food-for-thought-this-must-be-a-place.html?_r=0.
71 Smith College Special Collections and Archives, Joan Biren Papers, MS587.
72 Judy Syfers, "I Want a Wife," *Ms. Magazine,* December 1971.
73 Horn, *Gaia's Guide* (1984 and 1985).
74 Jerome, "Feminists Hail a Restaurant."
75 Jerome, "Feminists Hail a Restaurant." Renowned photographer, Mary Ellen Mark, captured the event for the article. Mary Ellen Mark Library, "People," October 2021, https://www.maryellenmark.com/bibliography/magazines/article/people/feminists-hail-a-restaurant-where-the-piece-de-resistance-is-an-attitude-not-a-dish-637521256092033589/P.
76 Alexander, "Letter from Dolores Alexander to New York Magazine Asking for a Review."
77 Antonuccio, "Brick Hut," email correspondence with Ketchum.
78 Horn, *Gaia's Guide* (1982).
79 Herak, "Wildrose."
80 Davenport, "Remembering the Brick Hut Café, Part 1."
81 Herak, "Wildrose."
82 "Wing Café of San Diego Flyer," LAMBDA San Diego Archives.
83 Herak, "Wildrose."

84 Bloodroot Collective, *The Political Palate*, xx–xxi. "Her death, like nine million others between the fourteenth and seventeenth centuries, was an act of woman hating … Andrea Dworkin has said in reference of the genocide of witches: 'A lot of knowledge disappears with nine million people.' The G. Knapp Historical Society is an attempt to remind women that such knowledge must not disappear again."

85 Davenport, "Remembering the Brick Hut Café, Part 1."

86 Antonuccio, "Brick Hut," email correspondence with Ketchum.

87 "I met a young man who had just gotten off the bus from Salt Lake City. The first place he went was the Brick Hut because a friend had told him he would be safe there. He told me his story. I bought him breakfast to welcome him. A few short years later, wracked by AIDS, his friends carried him into the Hut and sat him in a booth. He quietly ordered a blueberry waffle, was able to eat only one bite, but it made him smile. After a while, his friends carried him back home, where he passed away." Antonuccio, email correspondence with Ketchum.

88 Davenport, "Remembering the Brick Hut Café, Part 1."

89 Antonuccio, "Brick Hut," email correspondence with Ketchum.

90 Anonymous, "Softball," *Ain't I a Woman* 1, no. 16 (June 4, 1971).

91 Antonuccio, "Brick Hut," email correspondence with Ketchum.

92 Horn, *Gaia's Guide* (1990).

93 Jim Provenzano, "BARchive: Homo Base," Bay Area Report, March 21, 2011, https://www.ebar.com/bartab/nightlife//116978.

94 "Letter at the One Year Mark: Letter to Stockholders," October 1975, Schlesinger Library at the Radcliffe Institute of Harvard University, Patricia Hynes Papers, Box 1, Folder 1.

95 Herak, "Wildrose."

96 The idea of space as being important for community building is not new. In 1989, sociologist Ray Oldenburg argued that third spaces such as cafes, churches, and public parks were important for civil society, democracy, civic engagement, and establishing feelings of a sense of place. By his definition, home is the "first place," and the workplace is the "second place." Oldenburg, *The Great Good Place*.

97 Jerome, "Feminists Hail a Restaurant."

CHAPTER FIVE

1 Selma Miriam, email message to Alex Ketchum, June 28, 2016.

2 The National Restaurant Association of the United States defines the restaurant industry as "that which encompasses all meals and snacks prepared away from home, including all takeout meals and beverages." According to this association, over the past fifty years, when taking inflation into account, Americans spent the most amount of money on exterior dining from 1972 to 1978.

3 The program was so successful that by the end of the year, the Black Panther Party developed kitchens in cities across the United States, feeding over ten thousand children every day before they went to school. Geographer Nik Heynen argues that the breakfast program was significant because it "was imperative for the social reproduction of many inner-city communities and that it was both the model for, and impetus behind, all federally funded school breakfast programs currently in existence within the United States." Heynen, "Bending the Bars of Empire from Every Ghetto for Survival," 406.

4 Turner, *From Counterculture to Cyberculture*.

5 Scholar of intentional communities Timothy Miller states that this number is highly disputed. He claims that in 1970, the *New York Times* published an article which stated two thousand communes existed without clear evidence and after that piece came out, other sources continued to cite it. In fact, the author of the article, Bill Kovach, states that the methodology used to produce the number could be improved. Bill Kovach, "Communes Spread as the Young Reject Old Values," *New York Times*, December 17, 1970, http://www.nytimes.com/1970/12/17/archives/communes-spread-as-the-young-reject-old-values-communes-are-a-way.html. Refer also to Miller, *The 60s Communes*, xviiii.

6 Waters and Duane, *Edible Schoolyard*.

7 While it is difficult to find the exact numbers of how many people were vegetarian in the United States in the 1970s and 1980s, studies tend to estimate between 3 to 7 percent of the population. Refer to Dietz, Frisch, Kalof, Stern, and Guagnano, "Values and Vegetarianism." This study claims that in the 1990s, 7 percent of the United States' population was vegetarian.

8 Clark, "The Raw and the Rotten."

9 Jabs, Devine, and Sobal, "Maintaining Vegetarian Diets: Personal Factors, Social Networks and Environmental Resources."

10 Spencer, *The Heretic's Feast.*

11 Kopp, *American Countercultures*, 73.

12 Iacobbo and Iacobbo, *Vegetarian America.*

13 Patricia Roth Schwartz, "Bloodroot: Not by Food Alone" *Hartford Advocate*, 23 November 1977, 27

14 The Bloodroot Collective, *The Political Palate*, xi.

15 Gaard, "Vegetarian Ecofeminism," 117.

16 Bloodroot Collective, *The Perennial Political Palate*, 3.

17 Selma Miriam, email message to author, June 28, 2016.

18 For more on the history of lesbian and queer cookbooks, refer to Alex Ketchum, "What's the Recipe for a Queer Cookbook? Digitized Exhibit," *The Historical Cooking Project*, August 15, 2021, http://www.historicalcookingproject.com/2021/08/digitized-whats-recipe-for-queer.html.

19 Peter Singer's 1975 text *Animal Liberation: A New Ethics for Our Treatment of Animals* reflected the belief of other vegetarians in the 1970s that eating some kinds of seafood was permissible. This specific vegetarian belief framework was based around the idea of pain.

20 Selma Miriam and Noel Furie, "Bloodroot Interview 2," interviewed by Alex Ketchum, May 2012.

21 Lisa Pierce, "A Vegetarian Spot Where Feminism Is a Main Course," *The New York Times*, November 16, 2002; Bloodroot Collective, *The Political Palate*; Bloodroot Collective, *The Second Political Palate*; Bloodroot Collective, *The Perennial Palate*. To give a sense of the kinds of foods offered, some of these dishes included a shiitake mushroom with soba noodles soup, pappardelle pasta with butternut squash sauce, apple slices, sage, and walnuts, and the chocolate "devastation" cake.

22 Inness, *Dinner Roles*, 87–91.

23 Alice Kennedy, "This Consciousness Raising Café Wants You to Eat like a Feminist," *Munchies: Vice*, July 20, 2015, http://munchies.vice.com/articles/this-consciousness-raising-cafe-wants-you-to-eat-like-a-feminist.

24 Marjorie Parsons, "Coffeehouse Meeting," recorded interview, 1979, Northeastern University Archives, AV2316, M120.

25 Marjorie Childers, "Working in the CWC Collective," *From Wicked to Wedded: Northampton's LGBTQ History*, November 15, 2019: https://fromwickedtowedded.com/2019/11/15/working-in-the-cwc-collective/

26 Parsons, "Coffeehouse Meeting."

27 Kaymarion Raymond, "The Wimmin's Restaurant Project," *From Wicked to Wedded: Northampton's LGBTQ History*, October 16, 2019, https://fromwickedtowedded.com/2019/10/16/the-wimmins-restaurant-project/.

28 Horn, *Gaia's Guide* (1981).

29 Horn, *Gaia's Guide* (1978).

30 Horn, *Gaia's Guide* (1981).

31 The dish is so popular that Carol Graham has discussed the recipe on CT Public Radio, accessed September 15, 2020, https://www.ctpublic.org/recipes/bloodroots-jamaican-jerk-chicken/.

32 Weichselbaumer and Winter-Ebmer, "A Meta-analysis of the International Gender Wage Gap."

33 Patricia Hynes, "Business Prospectus of Bread and Roses," October 1974, 2, Schlesinger Library at the Radcliffe Institute of Harvard University, Papers of Patricia Hynes, Box 1, Folder 3.

34 Hynes, "Business Prospectus of Bread and Roses."

35 Jan Whitacker, "Women's Restaurants," Restauranting Through History, June 18, 2013, https://restaurantingthroughhistory.com/2013/06/18/womens-restaurants/. The menu reflects feminist positions. There are no diet drinks or low-calorie specials because the restaurant did not want to offend its overweight women clients. Sharon Johnson, "In Los Angeles Saloon Women Get the Red Carpet," *Lakeland Ledger* (Florida), June 16, 1976, 4D, https://news.google.com/newspapers?nid=rwEhk56xNqMC&dat=19760616&printsec=frontpage&hl=en.

36 McGrath, "Living Feminist," 203.

37 See the directory in this book's appendix.

38 Horn, *Gaia's Guide* (1980).

39 Sarah Schulman, interview by Alex Ketchum, August 11, 2016.

40 "Susan B's," *Chicago Magazine*, July 1975. For more information on Susan B's, refer to Enke, *Finding the Movement*.

41 Hochschild, "Emotion Work, Feeling Rules, and Social Structure.".

42 Parsons, “Coffeehouse Meeting.”

43 Parsons, “Coffeehouse Meeting.”

44 Miriam, interview by Ketchum, April 5, 2011.

45 Joan Antonuccio, “Brick Hut,” email correspondence with Alex Ketchum, June 9, 2015.

46 Sharon Davenport, “LGBT Pride: Remembering the Brick Hut Café, Part 1,” *Bay Area Bites*, June 23, 2011, http://ww2.kqed.org/bayareabites/2011/06/23/lgbt-pride-remembering-the-brick-hut-café-part-1/.

47 Antonuccio, “Brick Hut,” email correspondence with Alex Ketchum.

48 Antonuccio, “Brick Hut,” email correspondence with Alex Ketchum.

49 Berkeley, California, and the greater Bay Area, which includes San Francisco, was a centre of countercultural food movements. Turner, *From Counterculture to Cyberculture*.

50 Noel Furie and Selma Miriam, “Bloodroot Interview,” in conversation with the author, December 13, 2011.

51 Whitacker, “Women’s Restaurants”; “Los Angeles Women’s Saloon and Parlor,” Lost Womyn’s Space, April 22, 2012, http://lostwomynsspace.blogspot.ca/2012/04/los-angeles-womens-saloon-and-parlor.html; Faderman and Timmons, *Gay LA*, 188–89 and 206.

52 Flavia Rando, “New York Feminist Food,” interview by Alex Ketchum, March 7, 2015.

53 Rando, “New York Feminist Food.”

54 Dozens of restaurant reviews of Bloodroot challenged the misconception that vegetarian food was bland and stated that Bloodroot served delicious food. One example is Joan Cook, “Feminists Publish a Cookbook,” *New York Times*, June 13, 1982.

55 Cook, “Feminists Publish a Cookbook.”

56 LAMBDA Archives, “Big Kitchen: Food for Thought,” http://www.lambdaarchives.us/2010_honorees/food_for_thought.htm.

57 LAMBDA Archives, “Big Kitchen.”

58 Linda Wolfe, “Among Friends,” *New York Magazine*, May 14, 1973.

59 Bahneman, in conversation with Ketchum.

60 Bahneman, in conversation with Ketchum.

61 Anonymous comment on Ruby’s Café Minneapolis History’s Facebook page, June 29, 2014.

62 Bahneman, in conversation with Ketchum.

63 Joan Antonnucio, "Remembering the Brick Hut Café, Part 2," *Bay Area Bites,* June 23, 2011, https://ww2.kqed.org/bayareabites/2011/06/23/lgbt-pride-remembering-the-brick-hut-café-part-2/.

64 Echols, *Daring to Be Bad.*

65 Haber, "Cooking with Joy," 23.

66 *Amazon News*, 1978; and *Ain't I a Woman* 1, no. 7.

CHAPTER SIX

1 "Women's Coffeehouse: Community Letter," University of Iowa Women's Archives Collection, Jill Jack Papers (IWA0519), Activism Series 2, Box 1, The Women's Coffeehouse Histories, Policies, and Finances, 1981–1982 and undated.

2 "Women's Coffeehouse: Community Letter." The new address was 529 South Gilbert Street. Beginning on December 12, the new location would be able to accommodate more women and events than the former space.

3 Emphasis in the original document. The comment about roller skating not only placed the coffeehouse within the context of the early 1980s and contemporary popular recreational activities but also speaks to the coffeehouse collective's desire to stay abreast of current trends to broaden its appeal.

4 "Coffeehouse Calendar," undated, University of Iowa Women's Archives Collection, Jill Jack Papers (IWA0519), Activism Series 2, Box 1, Women's Coffeehouse: Calendar pages, 1981–1983 and "Calendars," University of Iowa Women's Archives Collection, Jo Rabenold Papers (IWA0191), Series 5: Organizations, Box 4, Women's Coffeehouse: Women's Coffeehouse: Signs, Flyers, and Calendars, 1975–1982.

5 "Letter from the Pledge Committee," University of Iowa Women's Archives Collection, Jo Rabenold Papers (IWA0191), Series 5: Organizations, Box 4, Women's Coffeehouse: Organizational History and Pledge Drives, 1981–1982.

6 "Women's Coffeehouse: Community Letter."

7 The $10 figure was based on a percentage of the past operating expenses.

8 "Women's Coffeehouse: Community Letter."

9 Ingram, Bouthillette, and Retter, *Queers in Space*.

10 Podmore, "Lesbians in the Crowd."

11 Oldenburg, *The Great Good Place*.

12 Reno, "Women's Coffeehouse."

13 Betsy Zelchin, "Coffeehouse Meeting," recorded presentation, 1979," Northeastern University Archives. AV2318, M120.

14 "Meeting Minutes October 28, 1978," Northeastern University Archives, Somerville Women's Educational Center 1975–1983 (M26), Box 4 "Projects: Coffeehouse: Fliers and Notes," Folder 65: Philosophy and Notes.

15 Interview with Candace Margulies by Lisa Vecoli, Minnesota Lesbian Community Organizing Oral History Project at the Tretter Collection in GLBT Studies, 2019.

16 *The People's Yellow Pages of Massachusetts*, Sophia Smith College Archives, Women's Liberation Collection, Series II: United States, Catalogues, Directories, Guides, Box 6.

17 Reno, "Women's Coffeehouse."

18 This decision was on the advice of Allegra Productions that a concert could pose a financial risk. "Meeting Minutes October 28, 1978."

19 "Meeting Minutes October 28, 1978."

20 "Women's Coffeehouse: Community Letter."

21 "Flyer from August 25, 1981," University of Iowa Women's Archives Collection, Jo Rabenold Papers (IWA0191), Series 5: Organizations, Box 4, Women's Coffeehouse: Women's Coffeehouse: Signs, Flyers, and Calendars, 1975–1982.

22 "June 30 Meeting Minutes," University of Iowa Women's Archives Collection, Jo Rabenold Papers (IWA0191), Series 5: Organizations, Box 4, Women's Coffeehouse: Minutes, 1980–1981.

23 "June 30 Meeting Minutes."

24 "Flyer Handwritten on Orange Paper," Northeastern University Archives, Somerville Women's Educational Center 1975–1983 (M26), Box 4 "Projects: Coffeehouse: Fliers and Notes," Folder 65: Philosophy and Notes.

25 "Meeting Minutes Journal," Northeastern University Archives, Women's Coffeehouse Records (M120), Box 1, Folder: Meeting Minutes 1978–1980.

26 A Woman's Coffeehouse Community, "Open Community Meeting Tapes," Jean Nickolaus Tretter Collection in GLBT Studies of the University of Minneapolis Libraries and Archives, A Woman's Coffeehouse Collective Records 1976–1985, Box 1, A Woman's Coffeehouse Meeting Cassette Tapes, 1983.

27 The goal was to make women feel more invested in the space. A Woman's Coffeehouse Community, "Open Community Meeting Tapes."

28 "New Year's Eve Party Flyer," Jean Nickolaus Tretter Collection in GLBT Studies of the University of Minneapolis Libraries and Archives, A Woman's Coffeehouse Collective Records 1976–1985, Box 1, Miscellaneous and AWC Poster, 1984–1985. Amazon Bookstore also sold tickets for the coffeehouse's New Year's Eve Party.

29 As historian Heather Murray has argued, the relationship that lesbian feminists had with money in the 1970s was fraught. She demonstrates that not only did lesbian feminist businesses have to contend with a poorer clientele but also the idea of making money was seen as exploitative. For example, Murray says "the lesbian national newsletter *Lesbian Connection* [started in the early 1970s in East Lansing, Michigan] had to recognize that its lesbian readership and in turn the lesbian market could be quite poor as well … As a general stance, the *Lesbian Connection*, which was 'free for all lesbians,' characterized its readership as financially pinched. In a letter to the editor called 'Lesbianism on a Budget,' a lesbian living in Pittsburgh explained her view that much of 'lesbian oppression is directly economic—low wages, etc. … We live in a high pressure advertising environment, especially in a city … very little in our lives but sheer necessity teaches us to use money wisely. I try to spend what money I have to spare (after rent and food and light and household expenses) in a way that's good for me and for the lesbians of Pittsburgh.' Accordingly, advertising encouraged lesbians to practice the same kind of monetary exchange that this Pittsburgh lesbian advocated. If lesbians must buy at all, they should buy from other lesbians, a kind of strategy for ethical consumption that had been taken up earlier in the twentieth century by African American communities, for example." Murray added that "For these lesbian producers, asking for a lot of money and perhaps even making a living from writing, special skills, or art rendered that product

less poignant and themselves exploiters rather than supporters of the lesbian community." Heather Murray, "Free for All Lesbians: Lesbian Cultural Production and Consumption in the United States during the 1970s," *Journal of the History of Sexuality* 16, no. 2 (2007): 251–75.

30 "September 4, 1980 Meeting Minutes," University of Iowa Women's Archives Collection, Jo Rabenold Papers (IWA0191), Series 5: Organizations, Box 4, Women's Coffeehouse: Minutes, 1980–1981.

31 "December 5, 1984 Meeting Minutes," Jean Nickolaus Tretter Collection in GLBT Studies of the University of Minneapolis Libraries and Archives, A Woman's Coffeehouse Collective Records 1976–1985, Box 1.

32 Voltz, "Sister Moon."

33 A Woman's Coffeehouse Community, "Open Community Meeting Tapes."

34 A Woman's Coffeehouse Community, "Open Community Meeting Tapes."

35 A Woman's Coffeehouse Community, "Open Community Meeting Tapes."

36 Horn, *Gaia's Guide*, various editions.

37 Interview with Gail McArdle by Lisa Vecoli, Minnesota Lesbian Community Organizing Oral History Project at the Tretter Collection in GLBT Studies, March 11, 2020.

38 Interview with Candace Margulies by Lisa Vecoli, Minnesota Lesbian Community Organizing Oral History Project at the Tretter Collection in GLBT Studies, 2019 and Interview with Amy Lange by Lisa Vecoli, Minnesota Lesbian Community Organizing Oral History Project at the Tretter Collection in GLBT Studies, September 27, 2019.

39 A Woman's Coffeehouse Community, "Open Community Meeting Tapes."

40 A Woman's Coffeehouse Community, "Open Community Meeting Tapes."

41 A Woman's Coffeehouse Community, "Open Community Meeting Tapes."

42 Kay Lara Schoenwetter, "A Woman's Coffeehouse History," *Coffee Klatch* 1 (1976), Jean Nickolaus Tretter Collection in GLBT Studies of the University of Minneapolis Libraries and Archives, A Woman's Coffeehouse Collective Records 1976–1985, Box 1.

43 Interview with Toni McNaron by Lisa Vecoli, Minnesota Lesbian Community Organizing Oral History Project at the Tretter Collection in GLBT Studies, May 21, 2019.

44 "November 1985 Letter," Jean Nickolaus Tretter Collection in GLBT Studies of the University of Minneapolis Libraries and Archives, A

Woman's Coffeehouse Collective Records 1976–1985, Box 1, A Woman's Coffeehouse Letters.

45 A Woman's Coffeehouse Community, "Open Community Meeting Tapes."

46 Zelchin, "Coffeehouse Meeting."

47 "Meeting Minutes October 28, 1978."

48 "July 10, 1980 Meeting Minutes," University of Iowa Women's Archives Collection, Jo Rabenold Papers (IWA0191), Series 5: Organizations, Box 4, Women's Coffeehouse: Minutes, 1980–1981.

49 "July 10, 1980 Meeting Minutes."

50 "Attention Women: Chuck," University of Iowa Women's Archives Collection, Jill Jack Papers (IWA0519), Activism Series 2, Box 1, Women's Coffeehouse: Flyers posted, 1981–1982.

51 "July 10, 1980 Meeting Minutes."

52 "July 10, 1980 Meeting Minutes."

53 "Guidelines for Using the Coffeehouse Letter," University of Iowa Women's Archives Collection, Jill Jack Papers (IWA0519), Activism Series 2, Box 1, The Woman's Coffeehouse Histories, Policies, and Finances, 1981–1982 and undated.

54 There are feminist coffeehouses where I only know their name and location. As such, I cannot claim that all feminist coffeehouses operated on the nonprofit model.

55 Zelchin explained that once they wrote the organizational bylaws, the process would be quite simple and take about two months. Zelchin, "Coffeehouse Meeting."

56 In the United States, the structure of tax exemption granted to the charitable and voluntary sector outlined in the United States the Tax Code was developed through legislation enacted between 1894 and 1969. According to Internal Revenue Service, which regulates American taxes, over that seventy-five year period, Congress established the basic principles and requirements of tax exemption, identified business activities of tax-exempt organizations that were subject to taxation, and defined and regulated private foundations as a subset of tax-exempt organizations. For a timeline and breakdown of the history of tax-exempt status, refer to Paul Arnsberger, Melissa Ludlum, Margaret Riley, and Mark Stanton, "A History of the Tax-exempt Sector: An SOI Perspective," Statistics of

Income Bulletin, Winter 2008, 105–35, https://www.irs.gov/pub/irs-soi/tehistory.pdf.

57 Zelchin, "Coffeehouse Meeting."

58 Zelchin, "Coffeehouse Meeting."

59 Zelchin, "Coffeehouse Meeting."

60 Zelchin, "Coffeehouse Meeting."

61 "Lest We Begin to Oink," *Ain't I a Woman?* (September 25, 1970), 4.

62 "Lest We Begin to Oink."

63 Kanter, *Commitment and Community*, 66.

64 Kanter, *Commitment and Community*, 66. Emphasis in the original text.

65 Kanter, *Commitment and Community*, 66. "Men" underlined in the original text.

66 "Collective Member Application," Jean Nickolaus Tretter Collection in GLBT Studies of the University of Minneapolis Libraries and Archives, A Woman's Coffeehouse Collective Records 1976–1985, Box 1.

67 "Full Moon Open Community Letter," GLBT Historical Society of San Francisco Archives, Full Moon Coffee House Reunion records (#1992-13), 1974–1988.

68 "Collective Member Application."

69 "Collective Member Application."

70 A Woman's Coffeehouse Community, "Open Community Meeting Tapes."

71 "June 1982 Letter," University of Iowa Women's Archives Collection, Jo Rabenold Papers (IWA0191), Series 5: Organizations, Box 4, Women's Coffeehouse: Organizational History and Pledge Drives, 1981–1982.

72 A Woman's Coffeehouse Community, "Open Community Meeting Tapes."

73 A Woman's Coffeehouse Community, "Open Community Meeting Tapes."

74 A Woman's Coffeehouse Community, "Open Community Meeting Tapes."

75 A Woman's Coffeehouse Community, "Open Community Meeting Tapes."

76 A Woman's Coffeehouse Community, "Open Community Meeting Tapes."

77 A Woman's Coffeehouse Community, "Open Community Meeting Tapes."

78 A Woman's Coffeehouse Community, "Open Community Meeting Tapes."

79 A Woman's Coffeehouse Community, "Open Community Meeting Tapes."

80 The letter was circulated on April 10, 1975. "Full Moon Open Community Letter."

81 "Full Moon Open Community Letter."

82 "Full Moon Open Community Letter."

83 In the meeting notes of Iowa City Women's Coffeehouse collective member Laura Kate Rotifer, she described "lots of bickering" over how to word a sign, yet most collective members just would "chuckle into their beer." On August 21, 1980, she recorded, "Vicki suggests we all go out to dinner. Christie says in three months" when they would not be as busy organizing. "August 21, 1980 Meeting Minutes," University of Iowa Women's Archives Collection, Jo Rabenold Papers (IWA0191), Series 5: Organizations, Box 4, Women's Coffeehouse: Minutes, 1980–1981.

84 "Maybe Christie will make out with Pat instead of Vicki … Christie tells Mary to drop dead. Mary says she loves it." "August 21, 1980, Meeting Minutes."

85 Reno, "Women's Coffeehouse."

86 Reno, "Women's Coffeehouse."

87 "Thank You!," University of Iowa Women's Archives Collection, Jo Rabenold Papers (IWA0191), Series 5: Organizations, Box 4, Women's Coffeehouse: Signs, Flyers, and Calendars, 1975–1982. December 12, 1981, was the date the coffeehouse re-opened at the new location.

88 "Meeting Minutes 1979," Northeastern University Archives, Somerville Women's Educational Center 1975–1983 (M26), Box 4 "Projects: Coffeehouse: Fliers and Notes," Folder 65: Philosophy and Notes.

89 "Meeting Minutes 1979."

90 "Transexual" was the more commonly used word during the 1970s and 1980s. "Transgender" has become the more common terminology since the late 1980s.

91 A Woman's Coffeehouse Community, "Open Community Meeting Tapes."

92 Interview with Kathy Heltzer by Lisa Vecoli, Minnesota Lesbian Community Organizing Oral History Project at the Tretter Collection in GLBT Studies, October 18, 2019.

93 "Letter from the Finance Committee," University of Iowa Women's Archives Collection, Jo Rabenold Papers (IWA0191), Series 5: Organizations, Box 4, Women's Coffeehouse: Organizational History and Pledge Drives, 1981–1982.

94 "Lesbian Baiting," University of Iowa Women's Archives Collection, Jo Rabenold Papers (IWA0191), Series 5: Organizations, Box 4, in multiple files.

95 Flavia Rando, "New York Feminist Food," interview by Alex Ketchum, March 7, 2015.

96 Gibson, "Ann Arbor Women's Center and Coffeehouse."

97 Interview with Gail McArdle by Lisa Vecoli, Minnesota Lesbian Community Organizing Oral History Project at the Tretter Collection in GLBT Studies, March 11, 2020.

98 "Policy on Transexuals 1984," Jean Nickolaus Tretter Collection in GLBT Studies of the University of Minneapolis Libraries and Archives, A Woman's Coffeehouse Collective Records 1976–1985, Box 1, Policy on Transexuals.

99 Bergquist and McDonald, *A Field Guide to Gay and Lesbian Chicago*, 183. Their policy of exclusion of transgender women was also challenged in the 1990s by a local gay male journalist.

100 Bergquist and McDonald, *A Field Guide to Gay and Lesbian Chicago*, 183.

101 "Letter from the Finance Committee."

102 "Second Questionnaire," Jean Nickolaus Tretter Collection in GLBT Studies of the University of Minneapolis Libraries and Archives, A Woman's Coffeehouse Collective Records 1976–1985, Box 1, Questionnaires.

103 "Anonymous Questionnaire Responses," Jean Nickolaus Tretter Collection in GLBT Studies of the University of Minneapolis Libraries and Archives, A Woman's Coffeehouse Collective Records 1976–1985, Box 1, Questionnaires.

104 "Anonymous Questionnaire Responses."

105 "Anonymous Questionnaire Responses."

106 "Anonymous Questionnaire Responses."

107 "Anonymous Questionnaire Responses."

108 A Woman's Coffeehouse Community, "Open Community Meeting Tapes."

109 "Anonymous Questionnaire Responses."

110 "New Year's Eve Party Flyer."

111 GLBT Historical Society of San Francisco Archives, San Francisco LGBT Business Ephemera Collection (#BUS EPH).

112 A Woman's Coffeehouse Community, "Open Community Meeting Tapes."

113 A Woman's Coffeehouse Community, "Open Community Meeting Tapes."

114 A Woman's Coffeehouse Community, "Open Community Meeting Tapes."

115 A Woman's Coffeehouse Community, "Open Community Meeting Tapes."

116 A Woman's Coffeehouse Community, "Open Community Meeting Tapes."

117 Pat Sherman, "A Moment in Time: Las Hermanas (The Sisters)," *Gay San Diego*, December 9, 2010, https://gay-sd.com/moments-in-time-las-hermanas-the-sisters/. It was located at 4003 Wabash Avenue.

118 Sherman, "A Moment in Time: Las Hermanas (The Sisters)."

119 The following section pulls exclusively from a recording of a meeting of A Woman's Coffeehouse in Minneapolis, Minnesota. I found it important to my argument to cite so heavily from this source as the recording demonstrates the tension in discussions over race in coffeehouse communities. This coffeehouse, with primarily white members, sought to address the lack of racial diversity in their space. These tapes show the way that members suggested solutions, how those solutions were problematized and debated, and then how the group continues to explore the topic in new ways.

120 A Woman's Coffeehouse Community, "Open Community Meeting Tapes."

121 A Woman's Coffeehouse Community, "Open Community Meeting Tapes."

122 A Woman's Coffeehouse Community, "Open Community Meeting Tapes."

123 A Woman's Coffeehouse Community, "Open Community Meeting Tapes."

124 A Woman's Coffeehouse Community, "Open Community Meeting Tapes."

125 A Woman's Coffeehouse Community, "Open Community Meeting Tapes."

126 A Woman's Coffeehouse Community, "Open Community Meeting Tapes."

127 One participant asked if this division was "like apartheid." A Woman's Coffeehouse Community, "Open Community Meeting Tapes."

128 "Policy Statement," Jean Nickolaus Tretter Collection in GLBT Studies of the University of Minneapolis Libraries and Archives, A Woman's Coffeehouse Collective Records 1976–1985, Box 1, Committees (CH).

129 "Calendars," Jean Nickolaus Tretter Collection in GLBT Studies of the University of Minneapolis Libraries and Archives, A Woman's Coffeehouse Collective Records 1976–1985, Box 1, Mailing, undated.

130 Shelley Anderson, "Coffeehouse Makes Changes," *Equal Times*, December 18, 1985, 9.

131 A Woman's Coffeehouse Community, "Open Community Meeting Tapes."

132 "June Coffeehouse Calendar," University of Iowa Women's Archives Collection, Jill Jack Papers (IWA0519), Activism Series 2, Box 1, Women's Coffeehouse: Calendar Pages, 1981–1983.

133 Kathie Bergquist and Robert McDonald, *A Field Guide to Gay and Lesbian Chicago*, 183.

134 "Flyer handwritten on Orange Paper."

135 "Community Letter 1985," Jean Nickolaus Tretter Collection in GLBT Studies of the University of Minneapolis Libraries and Archives, A Woman's Coffeehouse Collective Records 1976–1985, Box 1, Letters.

136 "Community Letter 1985."

137 "Assorted Calendars," University of Iowa Women's Archives Collection, Jill Jack Papers (IWA0519), Activism Series 2, Box 1, Women's Coffeehouse: Calendar Pages, 1981–1983 and "Calendars," University of Iowa Women's Archives Collection, Jo Rabenold Papers (IWA0191), Series 5: Organizations, Box 4, Women's Coffeehouse: Women's Coffeehouse: Signs, Flyers, and Calendars, 1975–1982.

138 "Assorted Meeting Minutes," University of Iowa Women's Archives Collection, Jill Jack Papers (IWA0519), Activism Series 2, Box 1, The Women's Coffeehouse Histories, Policies, and Finances, 1981–1982 and undated.

139 "Guidelines for Using the Coffeehouse Letter."

140 "Smokers," University of Iowa Women's Archives Collection, Jo Rabenold Papers (IWA0191), Series 5: Organizations, Box 4, Women's Coffeehouse: Signs, Flyers, and Calendars, 1975–1982 and "This Table is Reserved for Pot-Smokers Only with Fondest Regards Judy," University of Iowa Women's Archives Collection, Jo Rabenold Papers (IWA0191), Series 5: Organizations, Box 4, Women's Coffeehouse: Signs, Flyers, and Calendars, 1975–1982.

141 "Collective Member Application." For example, the application to become a collective member of A Woman's Coffeehouse in Minneapolis had multiple questions about substances, including "What does chemically free space mean to you?"

142 Graham, "Smoking, Stigma and Social Class"; and Bell, Salmon, Bowers, Bell, and McCullough, "Smoking, Stigma and Tobacco 'Denormalization.'"

143 A Woman's Coffeehouse Community, "Open Community Meeting Tapes."
144 A Woman's Coffeehouse Community, "Open Community Meeting Tapes."
145 A Woman's Coffeehouse Community, "Open Community Meeting Tapes."
146 "Community Letter 1985," Jean Nickolaus Tretter Collection in GLBT Studies of the University of Minneapolis Libraries and Archives, A Woman's Coffeehouse Collective Records 1976–1985, Box 1, Letters.
147 Emphasis is in the document. "Community Letter 1985."
148 Pat Sherman, "A Moment in Time: Las Hermanas (The Sisters)."
149 "July 10, 1980 Meeting Minutes," University of Iowa Women's Archives Collection, Jill Jack Papers (IWA0519), Activism Series 2, Box 1, The Woman's Coffeehouse Histories, Policies, and Finances, 1981–1982 and undated.
150 "July 10, 1980 Meeting Minutes."
151 Interview with Candace Margulies by Lisa Vecoli, Minnesota Lesbian Community Organizing Oral History Project at the Tretter Collection in GLBT Studies, 2019.
152 "Letter from Candace on December 6, 1981," Jean Nickolaus Tretter Collection in GLBT Studies of the University of Minneapolis Libraries and Archives, A Woman's Coffeehouse Collective Records 1976–1985, Box 1, Letters.
153 A Woman's Coffeehouse Community, "Open Community Meeting Tapes."

CHAPTER SEVEN

1 "Sidney Spinster Event Flyer," University of Iowa Women's Archives Collection, Jill Jack Papers (IWA0519), Activism Series 2, Box 1, Women's Coffeehouse: Calendar pages, 1981–1983.
2 "Sidney Spinster Event Flyer."
3 "June Coffeehouse Calendar," University of Iowa Women's Archives Collection, Jill Jack Papers (IWA0519), Activism Series 2, Box 1, Women's Coffeehouse: Calendar pages, 1981–1983.
4 By 1985, at A Woman's Coffeehouse of Minneapolis, Minnesota, music and dancing grew to eclipse the social conversation hours. However, at an open community meeting, the participants expressed that they longed for more social time, especially once the disagreements over the cultural and artistic events threatened to tear apart the community. A Woman's Coffeehouse Community, "Open Community Meeting," Jean Nickolaus

Tretter Collection in GLBT Studies of the University of Minneapolis Libraries and Archives, A Woman's Coffeehouse Collective Records 1976–1985, Box 1, A Woman's Coffeehouse Meeting Cassette Tapes, 1983.

5 Examples include Southern Wild Sisters Feminist Bookstore of Gulfport, Mississippi (1978), Common Woman Books of Omaha, Nebraska (1989), Mama Bears of Oakland, California, and Pandora Womyn's Bookstore of Kalamazoo, Michigan (1985). Horn, *Gaia's Guide*, various editions.

6 "Witchy Song Nights at Diana's Place," Sophia Smith College Archives, Diana Davies Papers (MS 390), 1960s–1996.

7 "June 21 Benefit Concert," GLBT Historical Society of San Francisco Archives, San Francisco LGBT Business Ephemera Collection (#BUS EPH).

8 "Full Moon and Old Wives Tales," San Francisco Public Library Archives, Flyers 1976, Box 2, Old Wives Tales, 95-24.

9 On Sisterspirit's December 1991 calendar the owners publicized appearances by writer Pat Califia and folk guitarist Tret Fure. "Sisterspirit 1991 Calendar," GLBT Historical Society of San Francisco Archives, San Francisco LGBT Business Ephemera Collection (#BUS EPH).

10 "Willie Tyson Flyer," Jean Nickolaus Tretter Collection in GLBT Studies of the University of Minneapolis Libraries and Archives, A Woman's Coffeehouse Collective Records 1976–1985, Box 1, Letters.

11 "Alix Dobkin Flyer for April 23, 1975 Concert," Canadian Women's Movement Archives, Three of Cups, Box 105, Folder 2.

12 Alix Dobkin, "Lesbian Code," recorded for *Yahoo Australia! Alix Live from Sydney*, 2010 album, Youtube video, accessed February 2022, https://www.youtube.com/watch?v=cwn7VjoKIqo.

13 "Alix Dobkin for Ladyslipper," Sophia Smith College Archives, Women's Liberation Collection, Joan E. Biren Papers, Box 55, Location 63 E.

14 "Flyer handwritten on Orange Paper," Northeastern University Archives, Somerville Women's Educational Center 1975–1983 (M26), Box 4 "Projects: Coffeehouse: Fliers and Notes," Folder 65: Philosophy and Notes.

15 Kay Lara Schoenwetter, "A Woman's Coffeehouse History," *Coffee Klatch* 1 (1976), Jean Nickolaus Tretter Collection in GLBT Studies of the University of Minneapolis Libraries and Archives, A Woman's Coffeehouse Collective Records 1976–1985, Box 1.

16 Schoenwetter, "Women's Coffeehouse History."

17 Schoenwetter, "Women's Coffeehouse History." The collective, ever the prudent record keepers, made clear that a copy of the agreement was in their public notebook for anyone who wished to read it.

18 Frederique Delacoste, "Letter to Terry of Persimmons on April 21, 1982," Jean Nickolaus Tretter Collection in GLBT Studies of the University of Minneapolis Libraries and Archives, A Woman's Coffeehouse Collective Records 1976–1985, Box 1, Letters. She was only referred to as Terry in the letter.

19 Delacoste, "Letter to Terry of Persimmons on April 21, 1982."

20 Delacoste, "Letter to Terry of Persimmons on April 21, 1982."

21 A Woman's Coffeehouse collective continued in the letter by stating, "In addition to threatening our financial stability this sets up a situation where two local lesbian performers have to compete for an audience … we recognize that the lesbians in our community have limited money and deserve a variety of programming." They noted that "this community is big enough to support a wide variety of women's businesses but not two of thc same."

22 Delacoste, "Letter to Terry of Persimmons on April 21, 1982."

23 Delacoste, "Letter to Terry of Persimmons on April 21, 1982."

24 Sidney Spinster, "Open Letter to the Community," Jean Nickolaus Tretter Collection in GLBT Studies of the University of Minneapolis Libraries and Archives, A Woman's Coffeehouse Collective Records 1976–1985, Box 1, Letters.

25 Spinster, "Open Letter to the Community."

26 Spinster, "Open Letter to the Community."

27 "Blank Contracts for Musical Performers," Jean Nickolaus Tretter Collection in GLBT Studies of the University of Minneapolis Libraries and Archives, A Woman's Coffeehouse Collective Records 1976–1985, Box 1, Contracts.

28 Schoenwetter, "Women's Coffeehouse History."

29 A Woman's Coffeehouse Community, "Open Community Meeting Tapes."

30 Robert Goldblum, "Hunter Davis Concert Review," *Richmond Times Dispatch* 133, no. 231, August 19, 1983.

31 Goldblum, "Hunter Davis Concert Review."

32 Three of Cups, "Dance Flyer," Canadian Women's Movement Archives, Three of Cups, Box 105, Folder 2.

33 A Woman's Coffeehouse Community, "Open Community Meeting Tapes."

34 A Woman's Coffeehouse Community, "Open Community Meeting Tapes."

35 Interview with Amy Lange by Lisa Vecoli, Minnesota Lesbian Community Organizing Oral History Project at the Tretter Collection in GLBT Studies, September 27, 2019.

36 The letter was also provided in written form. "Old Dyke Night Notes for The Open Community Meeting," Jean Nickolaus Tretter Collection in GLBT Studies of the University of Minneapolis Libraries and Archives, A Woman's Coffeehouse Collective Records 1976–1985, Box 1, Letters.

37 "Old Dyke Night Notes for The Open Community Meeting."

38 "Old Dyke Night Notes for The Open Community Meeting."

39 A Woman's Coffeehouse Community, "Open Community Meeting Tapes."

40 "Questionnaire," Jean Nickolaus Tretter Collection in GLBT Studies of the University of Minneapolis Libraries and Archives, A Woman's Coffeehouse Collective Records 1976–1985, Box 1, Questionnaires

41 A Woman's Coffeehouse Community, "Open Community Meeting Tapes."

42 A Woman's Coffeehouse Community, "Open Community Meeting Tapes."

43 "June Coffeehouse Calendar."

44 "Wing Café Flyer," LAMBDA San Diego Archives, Wing Café, 1980–1982.

45 "Art Policy," Jean Nickolaus Tretter Collection in GLBT Studies of the University of Minneapolis Libraries and Archives, A Woman's Coffeehouse Collective Records 1976–1985, Box 1, Policy.

46 *Mama Bears Newsletter* 2, no. 4 (September 1985).

47 "Event Flyer: Cars," University of Iowa Women's Archives Collection, Jo Rabenold Papers (IWA0191), Series 5: Organizations, Box 4, Women's Coffeehouse: Women's Coffeehouse: Signs, Flyers, and Calendars, 1975–1982.

48 "Event Flyer: Mermaid Night," University of Iowa Women's Archives Collection, Jo Rabenold Papers (IWA0191), Series 5: Organizations, Box 4, Women's Coffeehouse: Women's Coffeehouse: Signs, Flyers, and Calendars, 1975–1982.

49 "Event Flyer: Ponape," University of Iowa Women's Archives Collection, Jo Rabenold Papers (IWA0191), Series 5: Organizations, Box 4, Women's Coffeehouse: Women's Coffeehouse: Signs, Flyers, and Calendars, 1975–1982.

50 "Assorted Calendars," University of Iowa Women's Archives Collection, Jo Rabenold Papers (IWA0191), Series 5: Organizations, Box 4, Women's Coffeehouse: Women's Coffeehouse: Signs, Flyers, and Calendars, 1975–1982.

51 Las Hermanas Coffeehouse, *Feminist Communications* (June 1975), LAMBDA Archives of San Diego, Las Hermanas Box.

52 Pat Sherman, "A Moment in Time: Las Hermanas (The Sisters)," *Gay San Diego*, December 9, 2010, https://gay-sd.com/moments-in-time-las-hermanas-the-sisters/.

53 Sherman, "A Moment in Time: Las Hermanas (The Sisters)."

54 Flavia Rando emphasized that she wanted this statement directly quoted. Flavia Rando, "New York Feminist Food," interview by Alex Ketchum, March 7, 2015.

55 Rando, "New York Feminist Food" interview by Ketchum.

56 Flavia Rando, "Journal," personal papers shared with Alex Ketchum.

57 Flavia Rando, "Menu," personal papers shared with Alex Ketchum.

58 Rando, "New York Feminist Food" interview by Ketchum.

59 Rando, "New York Feminist Food" interview by Ketchum.

60 Reno, "Women's Coffeehouse."

61 "Take Back the Night Flyer," Jean Nickolaus Tretter Collection in GLBT Studies of the University of Minneapolis Libraries and Archives, A Woman's Coffeehouse Collective Records 1976–1985, Box 1, Flyers.

62 Las Hermanas Coffeehouse, "Issue with Militant Separatism," *Feminist Communications* 3, no. 12 (December 1977), LAMBDA Archives of San Diego, Las Hermanas.

63 "ERA," University of Iowa Women's Archives Collection, Jo Rabenold Papers (IWA0191), Series 5: Organizations, Box 4, Women's Coffeehouse: Women's Coffeehouse: Signs, Flyers, and Calendars, 1975–1982.

64 Jean and Jo of the Lesbian Alliance, "Letter to The Women's Coffeehouse," University of Iowa Women's Archives Collection, Jo Rabenold Papers (IWA0191), Series 5: Organizations, Box 4, Women's Coffeehouse.

65 Jean and Jo of the Lesbian Alliance, "Letter to The Women's Coffeehouse."

66 Rando, "New York Feminist Food" interview by Ketchum.

67 Radicalesbians was a radical lesbian activist organization based in New York City in 1970. It began in reaction to Betty Friedan calling lesbians "the lavender menace."

68 Mama Bear Coffeehouse, *Mama Bear News*, GLBT Historical Society of San Francisco Archives, San Francisco LGBT Business Ephemera Collection (#BUS EPH).

69 Schoenwetter, "A Woman's Coffeehouse History."

70 Schoenwetter, "A Woman's Coffeehouse History."

71 The Women's Coffeehouse of Cambridge, Massachusetts, "About," *The Coffeehouse News* (May 1988).

72 Women's Coffeehouse of Cambridge, Massachusetts, "About."

73 Women's Coffeehouse of Cambridge, Massachusetts, "About."

74 Malaprop's, *Malaprop's Newsletter*, GLBT Historical Society of San Francisco Archives, San Francisco LGBT Business Ephemera Collection (#BUS EPH).

75 "Benefit," *Goldflower* 5, no. 2 (January 1977).

76 "Kimela's Letter to Iowa's Women's Coffeehouse," University of Iowa Women's Archives Collection, Jo Rabenold Papers (IWA0191), Series 5: Organizations, Box 4, Women's Coffeehouse: Organizational History and Pledge Drives, 1981–1982.

77 "Meeting Minutes October 28, 1978," Northeastern University Archives, Somerville Women's Educational Center 1975–1983 (M26), Box 4 "Projects: Coffeehouse: Fliers and Notes," Folder 65: Philosophy and Notes.

78 Their contribution to the Northeastern Archives of their tapes of Marjorie Parsons's presentation greatly aided this project.

79 Archivist Stewart Van Cleve believes that the contentious environment of the coffeehouse led to its demise. He argues that several lesbian bars and alternative social organizations (such as Out to Brunch) organized and opened in the mid-1980s and actively competed with the coffeehouse's once-unique status as a social venue for women in the Twin Cities because the new spaces "offered an easygoing alternative to the contention of regular meetings. Thus, the majority of women who just came to dance went elsewhere." As a result, membership dwindled, and the organization

closed in September 1989. Stewart Van Cleve, "From the Archives: A Woman's Coffeehouse," *The Column*, August 31, 2010, http://thecolu.mn/4505/from-the-archives-a-womans-coffeehouse; Peg Dryer and Trina Porte, "The Coffeehouse: A Final Accounting," *Equal Time News* (August 1990), 4.

80 Plymouth Church's basement was the location of the coffeehouse during its fifteen years of operation. This event was marked with a commemorative coffee cup that was donated to the Tretter Collection at the University of Minnesota with an explanatory note. Stewart Van Cleve, personal correspondence with Alex Ketchum, February 21, 2018.

81 Bergquist and McDonald, *A Field Guide to Gay and Lesbian Chicago*, 183.

82 Interview with Kathy Heltzer by Lisa Vecoli, Minnesota Lesbian Community Organizing Oral History Project at the Tretter Collection in GLBT Studies, October 18, 2019.

83 Interview with Ann Reed by Lisa Vecoli and Kit Hadley, Minnesota Lesbian Community Organizing Oral History Project at the Tretter Collection in GLBT Studies, October 2, 2019.

CHAPTER EIGHT

1 Lagusta's Luscious Commissary, "Cafés have always been sites of resistance …" Facebook post, October 23, 2018, 9:12 PM, https://www.facebook.com/LLCommissary/photos/a.170481903973999/2136540906567808.

2 Dolores Alexander, interview by Kelly Anderson, March 20, 2004 and October 22, 2005, https://www.smith.edu/libraries/libs/ssc/vof/transcripts/Alexander.pdf.

3 Alexander, interview by Anderson.

4 "Amaranth: The Women's Restaurant Poster," Lesbian Herstory Digital Archives,http://cdm16694.contentdm.oclc.org/cdm/singleitem/collection/p274401coll1/id/781/rec/31.

5 Patricia Hynes, "Bread and Roses," interview by Alex Ketchum, May 9, 2012.

6 Joan Antonuccio, "Remembering the Brick Hut Café, Part 2," *Bay Area Bites*, June 23, 2011, https://ww2.kqed.org/bayareabites/2011/06/23/lgbt-pride-remembering-the-brick-hut-café-part-2/.

7 Changes in feminist politics with the rise of postmodernism, the development of queer theory, and critiques of radical separatist feminism has shifted how communities operate and how members of queer communities choose to spend time. The rise of postmodernism and poststructuralism has also changed the landscape of what it means to operate lesbian spaces. The rise of queer theory's prominence in the late 1980s and the subsequent move away from identity politics has made it that some of these spaces no longer seem useful. Michel Foucault's poststructuralist writings influenced theorists such as Judith Butler to challenge essentialist ideas about gender and sexuality. Queer theory, furthermore, challenged ideas of fixed identities. These writings influenced the ways in which activists have decided to organize their politics, moving away from a politics built on identity towards one built on affinity. The push for queer space has meant that younger lesbians, in particular, socialize in all gendered spaces, yet gay male bars continue to flourish.

8 Kimberle Crenshaw coined the term in 1989 but women of colour had been working with intersectional feminism for decades. Crenshaw, "Mapping the Margins."

9 Bluestockings Cooperative (website), "About Us," accessed on April 24, 2021, https://bluestockings.com/?q=p.about_us.

10 As the Brick Hut Café co-owner Sharon Davenport remarked on her cafe, "We welcomed everyone who was an ally in our common cause of social justice and inclusion. The weekend crowds spilled out into the street even after we built a backyard patio where we served a limited menu of blueberry muffins, coffee, and tea. We were a haven for lesbians and gay men, an information center for LGBT activists, an anchor for a diverse community that included working girls, bad-boys, suburban queens, transmen and transwomen. We were the Dyke Diner: the Lesbian Luncheonette: the Chick Hut: the Brick Hut. When AIDS hit a group of customers affectionately named the Shattuck Street Fairies (SSF) we became a refuge and an information outlet for AIDS awareness. Sometimes we were the last stop: as when Ron, one of the SSF housemates, was lovingly carried in on the arms of his friends for his last Brick Hut meal. We worked to maintain The Brick Hut as a viable business in spite of threats and intimidations. We invited all our customers to cross the demoralizing barriers of class, race, and gender differences, and join

us at the community table." Davenport, "Remembering the Brick Hut Café, Part 1."

11 Yearwood, personal communication with author, April 16, 2015.

12 Yearwood, personal communication with author, April 16, 2015.

13 Softpower Sweets (@softpowersweets), Instagram post, February 8, 2022, https://www.instagram.com/p/CZsZqgnru72/?utm_medium=copy_link.

14 Lagusta's Luscious Commissary (@llcommissary), Instagram post, April 24, 2021, https://www.instagram.com/p/COD6TLmjxOE/.

15 Sweet Maresa's Bakery (website), "Dog Biscuits," accessed April 24, 2021, https://sweetmaresa.com/dog-biscuits/.

16 Eileen Reynolds, "A Bookstore of Our Own," *The New Yorker*, September 1, 2010, https://www.newyorker.com/books/page-turner/a-bookstore-of-our-own.

17 "Cafe Con Libros" (homepage), Cafe Con Libros, accessed April 24, 2021, https://www.cafeconlibrosbk.com.

18 A Seat at the Table Books (@aseatatthetablebooks), Instagram profile, accessed April 24, 2021, https://www.instagram.com/aseatatthetablebooks/?hl=en. The cafe opened in November 2021. "Please Welcome," Instagram post, September 28, 2021: https://www.instagram.com/p/CUWB_u8MmF-/.

19 Refer to Nembhard, *Collective Courage* and Weare, *Black Business in the New South*. The National Negro Business League organized a business service to promote advertising in African American newspapers and magazines. In addition, this service also encouraged national advertisers to use African American publications to reach this audience with growing purchasing power.

20 "Black- and Indigenous-owned Bookstores in Canada and the USA," Second Story Press, June 12, 2020, https://secondstorypress.ca/wavemaker/2020/6/12/black-and-indigenous-owned-bookstores-in-canada-and-the-usa.

21 Lauren Steele, "How to Find and Support Black-Owned Businesses, Wherever You Are," *Fast Company*, June 5, 2020, https://www.fastcompany.com/90512942/how-to-find-and-support-black-owned-businesses-wherever-you-are.

22 "Indigenous Business Directory: An Online Directory that Allows Procurement Officers and the Private Sector to Identify Indigenous

Businesses," Government of Canada, modified December 19, 2020, http://www.ic.gc.ca/eic/site/ccc_bt-rec_ec.nsf/eng/h_00011.html.

23 "USA," The Pink Pages Directory, accessed April 20, 2021, https://thepinkpagesdirectory.com/listings/usa/. This digital version of the pink pages harkens back to the physical pink pages directories used for the research of this book.

24 "List of Feminist Bookstores," Charis Books and More, accessed February 8, 2022, https://www.charisbooksandmore.com/list-feminist-bookstores.

25 The contemporary circulation of these lists has even enabled me to write this chapter. Charis Books' list of feminist bookstores helped me locate feminist restaurants that also function as cafes and coffee shops. "List of Feminist Bookstores," Charis Books and More (website).

26 Ketchum, "Say 'Hi' from Gaia."

27 "Fulton Street Books & Coffee" (homepage), Fulton Street Books & Coffee, accessed April 26, 2021, https://www.fultonstreet918.com/.

28 "Feminist & Bookish Monthly Book Subscription FAQ," Café Con Libros, accessed April 24, 2021, https://www.cafeconlibrosbk.com/feminist-bookish-faq.

29 "Zine of the Month," Lagusta's Luscious Commissary, accessed April 25, 2021, https://llcommissary.square.site/zine-of-the-month.

30 Lagusta's Luscious Commissary (@llcommissary), Instagram, post, July 16, 2020, https://www.instagram.com/p/CCtdFX9DPvX/.

31 During the COVID-19 pandemic in 2020 and 2021, more events moved online.

32 Jackson Ferrari Ibelle, "Brooklyn's Café Con Libros Boxes Out Amazon in Support of Indie Bookstores," Featured News, *BK Reader*, October 21, 2020, https://www.bkreader.com/2020/10/21/brooklyns-cafe-con-libros-boxes-out-amazon-in-support-of-indie-bookstores/.

33 Ibid.

34 Judith D. Schwartz, "Buying Local: How It Boosts the Economy," *Time*, June 11, 2009, http://content.time.com/time/business/article/0,8599,1903632,00.html; George J. Mailath, Andrew Postlewaite and Larry Samuelson, "Buying Locally," *International Economic Review* 57, no. 4 (November 2016): 1,179–1,200, https://doi-org.proxy3.library.mcgill.ca/10.1111/iere.12194.

35 Jen Agg, "A Harvey Weinstein Moment for the Restaurant Industry," *The New Yorker*, October 26, 2017, https://www.newyorker.com/culture/annals-of-gastronomy/a-harvey-weinstein-moment-for-the-restaurant-industry; Amanda Cohen, "I've Worked in Food for 20 Years. Now You Finally Care About Female Chefs?: We Deserved Your Attention Long Before Sexual Harassment Made Headlines," *Esquire,* November 6, 2017; and Sarah Henry, "Girl Talk: Top Chefs on Why Women Don't Get the Respect They Deserve in the Kitchen," *Edible San Francisco,* January 26, 2016, http://ediblesanfrancisco.ediblecommunities.com/girl-talk-why-women-dont-get-respect-in-kitchens#.VqqHSsXXN9Q.twitter.

36 Office of Consumer Affairs (OCA), "Chapter 9. Consumer Spending," Innovation, Science, and Economic Development Canada, May 4, 2011, https://www.ic.gc.ca/eic/site/oca-bc.nsf/eng/ca02117.html#a95.

37 "Restaurant Industry Forecast," National Restaurant Association, 2014, http://www.restaurant.org/Downloads/PDFs/News-Research/research/RestaurantIndustryForecast2014.pdf.

38 Cara Water, "Where Are the Women Chefs?" *The Sydney Morning Herald,* September 13, 2017, http://www.smh.com.au/small-business/trends/where-are-the-women-chefs-san-pellegrino-competitions-gender-problem-20170912-gyfiyg.html.

39 Lisa Mullins and Serena McMahon, "As Local Bookstores Fight to Stay Afloat, One Brooklyn Shop Persists Through Strategy, Resilience," Here & Now, *wbur,* October 23, 2020, https://www.wbur.org/hereandnow/2020/10/23/local-bookstores-amazon-coronavirus.

40 "About Us," Firestorm Co-op, accessed April 22, 2021, https://firestorm.coop/about.html.

41 "Mad" is a reclaimed term used by activists and scholars who may identify as mad, mentally ill, psychiatric survivors, consumers, service users, patients, neurodiverse, and disabled.

42 "About Us," Bluestockings Cooperative, accessed April 26, 2021, https://bluestockings.com/?q=p.about_us.

43 "About Us," Bluestockings Cooperative.

44 Lagusta Yearwood, personal communication with author, April 16, 2015.

45 Lagusta's Luscious Commissary, "No #rammissary This week! Ram ram is hopping on a biweekly schedule because wintery chocolate production

at @lagustasluscious is HEaTiNG Up!!! and dividing myself in half …" Facebook post, September 25, 2017, 8:54 PM EST, https://www.facebook.com/LLCommissary/posts/no-rammissary-this-week-ram-ram-is-hopping-on-a-biweekly-schedule-because-winter/1929359273952640/.

46 "Our Story," Cafe Con Libros, accessed April 20, 2021, https://www.cafeconlibrosbk.com/our-story.

47 "Our Story," Cafe Con Libros.

48 Julia Tausch, "What the World Needs Now Is Anarcha-Feminist Vegan Chocolates," *Medium*, October 14, 2019, https://tenderly.medium.com/what-the-world-needs-now-is-anarcha-feminist-vegan-chocolates-14a657a0b4e3.

49 Lagusta's Luscious Commissary (@llcommissary), Instagram post, October 24, 2021, https://www.instagram.com/p/CVaQhcDgRu-/.

50 Former Agent, "Badass Women: Kalima DeSuze, founder of feminist bookstore, Cafe con Libros," *Nooklyn,* accessed April 19, 2021, https://nooklyn.com/stories/badass-women-kalima-desuze-founder-of-feminist-bookstore-cafe-con-libros.

51 Victor Luckerson, "Linking Allies to Action in the Heart of the Black-Bookstore Boom," *The New Yorker,* August 27, 2020, https://www.newyorker.com/news/dispatch/linking-allies-to-action-in-the-heart-of-the-black-bookstore-boom.

52 Since the reclamation of the word "queer" beginning in 1989, this umbrella term has become more popular, especially over the past ten years. The term provides flexibility and the ability to build solidarity and alliances across non-heterosexual sexual orientations and non-cisgender gender identities.

53 Firestorm Books & Coffee (@firestormcoop), Instagram profile, accessed April 26, 2021, https://www.instagram.com/firestormcoop/.

54 "Menu," Fulton Street Books & Coffee, accessed April 23, 2021, https://www.fultonstreet918.com/menu.

55 Locavore movements focus on eating locally. The goals are to connect food producers and consumers in the same geographic region, to develop more self-reliant and resilient food networks, and to have a beneficial effect on a community's health, environment, and local economy.

56 Molly Marquand, "Sweet Maresa: A Vegan Bakery on the Path to Indulgence," *Edible Hudson Valley*, March 15, 2014, https://ediblehudsonvalley.ediblecommunities.com/eat/sweet-maresa-vegan-bakery-path-indulgence.

57 "About Us," Firestorm Co-op, accessed April 22, 2021, https://firestorm.coop/about.html.

58 "Our Story," Café Con Libros, accessed April 20, 2021, https://www.cafeconlibrosbk.com/our-story.

59 "Our Story," Café Con Libros.

60 Lagusta's Luscious Commissary (@llcommissary), Instagram post, June 13, 2019, https://www.instagram.com/p/ByplNY6gRXS/.

61 "Our Values and Us," Lagusta's Luscious Commissary, accessed April 25, 2021, https://lagustasluscious.com/our-values-and-us/.

62 "Our Values and Us," Lagusta's Luscious Commissary. She also recommends the book by Carol Off, *Bitter Chocolate* (Toronto: Random House Canada, 2006). She furthermore discusses these issues in detail in her book: Lagusta Yearwood, *Sweet + Salty: The Art of Vegan Chocolates, Truffles, Caramels, and More from Lagusta's Luscious* (Boston: Da Capo Lifelong Books, 2019).

63 Craig Batory, "Black Coffee, Lives and Literature at Fulton Street Books & Coffee in Tulsa," Daily Coffee News, *Roast Magazine*, November 9, 2020, https://dailycoffeenews.com/2020/11/09/black-coffee-lives-and-literature-at-fulton-street-books-coffee-in-tulsa/.

64 "Our Values," Commissary, accessed April 20, 2021, https://llcommissary.square.site/values.

65 "Our Values," Commissary.

66 Lagusta Yearwood, "best of 2020," Lagusta's Luscious (blog), December 31, 2020, https://lagustasluscious.wordpress.com/2020/12/31/best-of-2020/.

67 Caroline Lagnado, "Chocolate as Mitzvah: The Kindness of Strangers' Chocolates," *JW Food and Wine*, March 13, 2017, https://jwfoodandwine.com/article/2017/03/13/chocolate-mitzvah. Yearwood's Mitzvah wall has also inspired Bluestockings to create a Give & Take Wall, which in turn has inspired a Solidarity Section in the gift shop at the Eugene V. Debs Museum. Raquel Espasande of Bluestockings, personal correspondence with Alex Ketchum, October 11, 2021.

68 Former Agent, "Badass Women."

69 Former Agent, "Badass Women."

70 Lagusta Yearwood, "We're Not Closing We're Changing," Facebook post, July 1, 2021, https://www.facebook.com/LLCommissary/photos/pcb.2845613672327191/2845613492327209.

71 Molly McDonough, "A Woman's Place," *TuftsNow,* June 16, 2020, https://now.tufts.edu/articles/woman-s-place.

72 Lagusta Yearwood, Lagusta's Luscious Blog (homepage), accessed April 18, 2021, Wayback Machine, https://web.archive.org/web/20210125224325/https://blog.lagusta.com/.

73 For more discussion of this subject, refer to Alex Ketchum, "The Surprisingly Long History of Feminist Eateries on Instagram," in *Food and Instagram: Identity, Influence, and Negotiation*, ed. Emily J.H. Contois and Zenia Kish (Champlain: University of Illinois Press, 2022).

74 "Big Kitchen Café" (homepage), Big Kitchen Café, accessed April 22, 2021, http://judysbigkitchen.com/; Judy's Big Kitchen (@thebigkitchen), Instagram, profile, accessed April 22, 2021, https://www.instagram.com/thebigkitchen/; The Big Kitchen, Facebook profile, accessed April 22, 2021, https://www.facebook.com/BigKitchenCafe/; "Bloodroot (homepage)," Bloodroot, accessed April 22, 2021, https://www.bloodroot.com/; Bloodroot Restaurant (@bloodrootrestaurant), Instagram profile, accessed April 22, 2021, https://www.instagram.com/bloodrootrestaurant/.

75 Ketchum, "Memory Has Added Seasoning."

76 Becca Rea-Holloway(@thesweetfeminist), Instagram profile, accessed April 27, 2021, https://www.instagram.com/thesweetfeminist/.

77 "The Sweet Feminist" (homepage), The Sweet Feminist, accessed April 24, 2021, https://www.thesweetfeminist.com/shop.

78 "The Face of Someone Who Turned in Their Manuscript Today," The Sweet Feminist, Instagram post, September 27, 2021, https://www.instagram.com/p/CUS6l-2JRJJ/.

79 Amy Larson (@overseasoned_amy), Instagram profile, accessed April 20, 2021, https://www.instagram.com/overseasoned_amy/.

80 "Shop," Overseasoned, accessed April 19, 2021, https://overseasoned.com/shop.

81 Amy Larson (@overseasoned_amy), Instagram post, July 9, 2017, https://www.instagram.com/p/BWVygnujYtM/.

82 The physical location opened in November 2021 at 9257 Laguna Springs, Suite 130. The space has a bookstore, coffee shop, community space, quiet room, and play area. "FAQ," A Seat at the Table Books, May 5, 2021, https://aseatatthetablebooks.org/faq-events/faq.

83 Clark, "The Raw and the Rotten." There are, however, a handful of new feminist restaurants in the United States and Canada.

84 Yearwood, personal communication, April 16, 2015.

85 *Lesbiana: A Parallel Revolution*, directed by Myriam Fougère (Women Make Movies, 2012).

APPENDIX: METHODOLOGICAL USAGE: VISUAL AND SPATIAL HISTORY

1 For more on the history of *Gaia's Guide*, refer to Ketchum, "Say 'Hi' From Gaia."

2 Emery, *The Lesbian Index*, 1.

3 "I think my largest run of the *Damron's Women's Traveller* was twenty thousand in the late 90s." Gina Gatta, "On Travel Guides," email to Alex Ketchum, August 18, 2014.

4 Jeffreys, *The Lesbian Heresy*, dedication page.

5 Wimminland Collective, *Shewolf's Directory of Wimmin's Lands and Lesbian Communities*.

6 Vida, *Our Right to Love*.

7 Meeker, *Contacts Desired*, 248.

8 "In the Soup in New York City: Restauranters (sic) Compare Recipes for Success," *Artemis: The Newsletter for Enterprising Women* 3 (1975), 3–4.

9 For the full list, refer to the periodical section of the bibliography.

10 The GLBT Historical Society San Francisco Archives, in particular, has an extensive ephemera collection with the San Francisco LGBT Business Ephemera Collection (#BUS EPH) holding twelve and a half linear feet of microfiche and the San Francisco LGBT General Subjects Ephemera Collection (#SUB EPH) holding fifteen and a half linear feet, both ranging from 1960 to 2010.

11 "Lavender Legacies Guide," Society of American Archvists: Diverse Sexuality and Gender Section, 2012, https://www2.archivists.org/groups/diverse-sexuality-and-gender-section/lavender-legacies-guide.

12 Keyhole Markup Language (KML) is an XML notation for expressing geographic annotation and visualization within internet-based, two-dimensional maps and three-dimensional Earth browsers. KML was developed for use with Google Earth, which was originally named Keyhole Earth Viewer.

13 A file geodatabase is a collection of files in a folder on disk that can store, query, and manage both spatial and nonspatial data. You create a file geodatabase in ArcGIS. The geodatabase is the native data structure for ArcGIS and is the primary data format used for editing and data management. While ArcGIS works with geographic information in numerous geographic information system (GIS) file formats, it is designed to work with and leverage the capabilities of the geodatabase.

14 It is impossible for ArcGIS to use raw KML files. First you must convert the KML file into a personal geodatabase (.gdb) using a tool provided within ArcGIS called KML2Layer. The only way to actually view a KML file natively in ArcGIS without having to convert it is to purchase the ArcGIS Data Interoperability extension, which allows ArcGIS to directly view more than 100 different GIS file formats.

15 City of Madison Planning Documents, http://www.cityofmadison.com/dpced/planning/documents/v1c1.pdf; US Department of Commerce, Bureau of the Census, "1980 census of population: Characteristics of the population. General Social and Economic Characteristics of Florida," (1983); Portland, Oregon Demographic Data, https://www.portlandoregon.gov/oni/56507.

16 Horn, *Gaia's Guide* (1984).

17 Greggor Mattson, "Lesbian Bar Closures," Who Needs Gay Bars, August 5, 2016, https://greggormattson.com/2016/08/05/lesbian-bar-closures-lost-womyns-space/.

18 Ingram, Bouthillette, and Retter, *Queers in Space*, 35.

19 De Certeau, *The Practice of Everyday Life*, xix.

20 Pulse Collective, *How Many Beans Make Pulse*.

BIBLIOGRAPHY

ARCHIVES AND COLLECTIONS

Bloodroot Archives, Yale University Archives, New Haven
Boxed Newspaper Collection, Taiment Library, New York University, New York
Canadian Women's Movement Archives, Ottawa
Chez Nous (Box 509-512)
Clementine's Café (Toronto, ON) 1974–1976
Fales Library and Special Collections of New York University, New York
New York Women's Culinary Alliance Archive 1982–2010 (MSS 279)
GLBT Historical Society of San Francisco Archives, San Francisco
Full Moon Coffee House Reunion Records, 1974–1988 (1992-13)
San Francisco LGBT Business Ephemera Collection (BUS EPH)
Women's Press/Up Press (GLC 31)
Jean Nickolaus Tretter Collection in GLBT Studies of the University of Minneapolis Libraries and Archives, Minneapolis
A Woman's Coffeehouse Collective Records, 1976–1985 (162)
Minnesota Lesbian Community Organizing Oral History Project
John J. Wilcox Jr. Gay Archives at the William Way Center, Philadelphia
Periodicals Collection
LAMBDA San Diego Archives, San Diego
Folder: Businesses-Cafés
Las Hermanas
Lesbian Herstory Digital Archives, New York
http://lesbianherstoryarchives.org

Northeastern University Archives, Boston
"Coffeehouse Meeting," Tapes (AV2316, M120 and AV2318, M120)
Somerville Women's Educational Center, 1975–1983 (M26)
Quebec Gay Archives (Les Archives gaies du Québec), Montreal
Miscellaneous Ephemera (unprocessed)
Sallie Bingham Center for Women's History and Culture of Duke University, Durham
Atlanta Lesbian Feminist Alliance Archives, 1972–1994 (ALFA)
San Francisco Public Library Archives, San Francisco
Barbara Grier/Naiad Press collection (GLC 30)
Feminist Bookstore News Records (GLC 105)
Old Wives' Tales Records (GLC 18)
Schlesinger Library at the Radcliffe Institute of Harvard University, Cambridge
Patricia Hynes Papers
Sophia Smith College Archives, Northampton
Diana Davies Papers (MS 390)
Dolores Alexander Papers (unprocessed)
Joan Biren Papers (MS587)
Women's Liberation Collection (MS 408)
University of Iowa Women's Archives Collection, Iowa City
Jill Jack Papers (IWA0519)
Jo Rabenold Papers (IWA0191)

PERIODICALS

I utilized every available feminist and lesbian periodical housed at the archives I visited to see if there were any articles and/or advertisements about feminist restaurants, cafes, or coffeehouses. This required physically flipping through hundreds of periodicals and magazines. I went through every edition of Iowa City's *Ain't I a Woman* by Iowa City Women's Liberation Front Publications Collective (1970); *Amazon of Milwaukee: A Midwest Journal for Women* (1971); *Ca s'attrape* of Montreal (1982); *Country Women* (1973–1980); *Feminist Communications: Las Hermanas Coffeehouse Newsletter* (1976–) in San Diego, California; *Goldflower: A Twin Cities Guide for*

Women (1972–1975); *Hera's Journal: A Philadelphia Feminist Publication* (1978); *It Ain't Me Babe: Women's Liberation* of Berkeley, California (1970); and *Les Sourcieres* of Quebec (1980s).

However, for some periodicals I could not locate every single edition and if a date is not specified below, it is because the dates were uncertain or not known. I still utilized all of the copies that I could find of the following periodicals: *Amazon Quarterly* (1972–1975); *Artemis* (1977); *Canadian Feminist Periodicals/Periodiques Feministes du Canada* (1989); *Commu-nique'Elles* (Quebec, 1980s); *Diversity*; *Dyke: A Quarterly* of New York City (1975–1978); *L'Evidente Lesbienne* of Quebec; *The Feminist Voice*; *The Fourth World*; *Furies* of Washington, DC (1972–1973); *Herizons* of Winnipeg, Manitoba (1979–1992); *Hysteria* (1971); *Lavender Woman* of Chicago (1971–1976); *Lavender Woman: A Lesbian Newspaper* (1971); *The Lesbian Calendar* (1988–); *Lesbian Connection of Michigan* (1974–); *Lesbian Ethics* (1984); *Lesbian Newspaper* of Ann Arbor, Michigan (1975); *Lesbian News* of Los Angeles (1975–); *The Lesbian Rag* (1988); *Ms. Magazine* (1971–); *New York Woman Tribune*; *Northern Women's Journal* (1979); *Off Our Backs: A Women's Liberation Biweekly* (1970–2008, looked at every edition until 1990); *Open Road* (1976); RAT (1970); *Rites* (1987); *Sapphire* of San Francisco (1973); *Sinister Wisdom: A Multicultural Journal by and for Lesbians*, published in Charlotte, North Carolina, Berkeley and Oakland, California, at various points, (1972–2012); *Small Arms of Springfield Massachusetts* (date unlisted); *Through the Looking Glass* (1971); *Valley Women's Voice* (1979); *Wicce* of Philadelphia (1973–1974); *WomaNews* (1985); *Woman's World* (1971); *Women's Collective Press*; *Whole Woman Catalogue* (1971); *Women's Newspaper* (1971); *Women and Revolution*; *Women's Undercurrents*; *Women United*; *Women's Way*; and the *Wree View* (1977). In addition to *Feminist Communications*, by the feminist coffeehouse Las Hermanas of San Diego, I also looked through three other publications, *Malaprop's Feminist Bookstore and Café Newsletter*; *Mama Bears News and Notes* of Oakland, California (1983–1986); *New Words' Bookstore's News and Notes* (1979), were linked to a feminist café that sold books. Although most of the editions I read through were published between 1970 and 1989, I also read copies of the editions that were also published in the early 1990s. I found them relevant to search through as feminist restaurants such as Bloodroot and Brick Hut that were founded during the period of study continued to be listed in feminist periodicals in the early 1990s.

There were useful collections of periodicals at the Sallie Bingham Center for Women's History and Culture at Duke University, the Schlesinger Library on the History of Women in America of the Radcliffe Institute at Harvard University, the Gay Archives of Quebec (Les Archives gaies du Québec), the Canadian Women's Movement Archives at the University of Ottawa, the San Francisco GLBT Archives, the San Francisco Public Library Archives, Northeastern University Archives, John J. Wilcox Jr. Gay Archives at the William Way Center in Philadelphia, the San Diego LAMBDA Archives, and the Yale University Archives. However, the Smith College Archives and the New York University (NYU) Archives housed extensive collections. NYU's Tamiment Library's collection of feminist periodicals, in particular, provided access to more than half of the above listed periodicals. Although collections such as *Ms. Magazine* have been digitized, most of these feminist and lesbian periodicals are only accessible in physical form, scattered around the United States and Canada in incomplete collections.

BOOKS AND JOURNAL ARTICLES

Adam, Barry D. *The Rise of a Gay and Lesbian Movement.* New York: Simon and Schuster Macmillan, 1995.

Adams, Carol J., ed. *Ecofeminism and the Sacred.* New York: Continuum, 1993.

Adams, Carol J. *The Sexual Politics of Meat: A Feminist-Vegetarian Critical Theory*. New York: Continuum Press, 1990.

Adams, Carol J., and Lori Gruen, eds. *Ecofeminism: Feminist Intersections with Other Animals and the Earth*. New York: Bloomsbury Publishing USA, 2014.

Adams, Kate. "Built Out of Books: Lesbian Energy and Feminist Ideology in Alternative Publishing." *Journal of Homosexuality* 34, no. 3 (1998): 113–41.

Alaimo, Stacy. "Ecofeminism without Nature? Questioning the Relationship between Feminism and Environmentalism." *International Feminist Journal of Politics* 10, no. 3 (2008): 299–304.

Alonso, Harriet Hyman. *Peace as a Women's Issue: A History of the US Movement for World Peace and Women's Rights*. New York: Syracuse University Press, 1993.

Anderson, Benedict. *Imagined Communities: Reflections on the Origin and Spread of Nationalism*. New York: Verso Books, 2006.

Avakian, Arlene Voski, and Barbara Haber, eds. *From Betty Crocker to Feminist Food Studies: Critical Perspectives on Women and Food*. Liverpool: Liverpool University Press, 2005.

Barrett, Michele. *Women's Oppression Today: Problems in Marxist-Feminist Analysis*. New York: Verso, 1981.

Baxandall, Rosalyn, and Linda Gordon, eds. *Dear Sisters: Dispatches from the Women's Liberation Movement*. New York: Basic Books, 2000.

Bechdel, Alison. *The Essential Dykes to Watch Out For*. Boston: Houghton Mifflin Harcourt, 2008.

Belasco, Warren James. *Appetite for Change: How the Counterculture Took on the Food Industry*. New York: Cornell University Press, 2007.

Bell, Kirsten, Amy Salmon, Michele Bowers, Jennifer Bell, and Lucy McCullough. "Smoking, Stigma and Tobacco 'Denormalization': Further Reflections on the Use of Stigma as a Public Health Tool. A Commentary on Social Science and Medicine's Stigma, Prejudice, Discrimination and Health Special Issue." *Social Science and Medicine* 70, no. 6 (2010): 795–99.

"Benefit." *Goldflower* 5, no. 2 (January 1977).

Bennett, Judith. "Feminism and History." *Gender and History* 1, no. 3 (Autumn 1989): 251–72.

Bennett, Judith. "'Lesbian-Like' and the Social History of Lesbianism." *Journal of the History of Sexuality* 9, no. 1 (January–April 2000): 1–24.

Bergquist, Kathie, and Robert McDonald. *A Field Guide to Gay and Lesbian Chicago*. Chicago: Lake Claremont Press, 2006.

Blau, Francine D., Patricia Simpson, and Deborah Anderson. "Continuing Progress? Trends in Occupational Segregation in the United States over the 1970s and 1980s." *Feminist Economics* 4, no. 3 (1998): 29–71.

Bloodroot Collective. *The Perennial Political Palate: The Third Feminist Vegetarian Cookbook*. Bridgeport: Sanguinaria Publishing, 1993.

Bloodroot Collective. *The Political Palate: A Feminist Vegetarian Cookbook*. Bridgeport: Sanguinaria Publishing, 1980.

Bloodroot Collective. *The Second Seasonal Palate: A Feminist Vegetarian Cookbook*. Bridgeport: Sanguinaria Publishing, 1984.

Borgerson, Janet L. "On the Harmony of Feminist Ethics and Business Ethics." *Business and Society Review* 112, no. 4 (2007): 477–509.

Bourdieu, Pierre. *Distinction: A Social Critique of the Judgement of Taste*. Cambridge, Massachusetts: Harvard University Press, 1984.

Boyd, Nan Alamilla. *Wide-Open Town: A History of Queer San Francisco to 1965*. Berkeley: University of California Press, 2003.

Brontsema, Robin. "A Queer Revolution: Reconceptualizing the Debate Over Linguistic Reclamation." *Colorado Research in Linguistics* 17, no. 1 (2004): 1–17.

Brown, Laura S. "Ethics and Business Practice in Feminist Therapy." In *Handbook of Feminist Therapy: Women's Issues in Psychotherapy*, edited by Lynne Bravo Rosewater and Lenore E. Walker, 297–304. New York: Springer Publishing Company, 1985.

Bunch, Charlotte. "Learning from Lesbian Separatism." In *Lavender Culture*, edited by Karla Jay and Allen Young, 433–44. New York: Jove Books, 1978.

Burnett, Gary, Michele Besant, and Elfreda A. Chatman. "Small Worlds: Normative Behavior in Virtual Communities and Feminist Bookselling." *Journal of the Association for Information Science and Technology* 52, no. 7 (2001): 536–47.

Butler, Judith. *Gender Trouble: Feminism and the Subversion of Identity*. New York: Routledge, 1990.

Canning, Kathleen. "Feminist History after the Linguistic Turn: Historicizing Discourse and Experience." *Signs* 19, no. 2 (Winter 1994): 368–404.

Chauncey, George. *Gay New York: Gender, Urban Culture, and the Making of the Gay Male World, 1890–1940*. New York: Basic Books, 1994.

Chenier, Elise. "Rethinking Class in Lesbian Bar Culture: Living the Gay Life in Toronto, 1955–1965." *Left History* 9, no. 2 (2004): 85–118.

Clark, Dylan. "The Raw and the Rotten: Punk Cuisine." *Ethnology* 43, no. 1 (2004): 19–31.

Cloke, Paul J., and Jo Little, eds. *Contested Countryside Cultures: Otherness, Marginalisation, and Rurality*. New York: Psychology Press, 1997.

Coate, John. "Cyberspace Innkeeping: Building Online Community." In *Reinventing Technology, Rediscovering Community: Critical Explorations of Computing as a Social Practice*. Santa Barbara: Greenwood Publishing Group, 1997.

Cobble, Dorothy Sue. *The Other Women's Movement: Workplace Justice and Social Rights in Modern America*. Princeton: Princeton University Press, 2005.

Cobble, Dorothy Sue. "'Practical Women': Waitress Unionists and the Controversies over Gender Roles in the Food Service Industry, 1900–1980." *Labor History* 29, no. 1 (1988): 5–31.

Coe, Andrew. *Chop Suey: A Cultural History of Chinese Food in the United States.* New York: Oxford University Press, 2009.

Cohen, Marcia. *The Sisterhood: The True Story of the Women Who Changed the World.* New York: Simon and Schuster, 1988.

Cole, Nicki Lisa, and Alison Dahl Crossley. "On Feminism in the Age of Consumption." *Consumers Commodities and Consumption* 11, no. 1 (2009), https://csrn.camden.rutgers.edu/newsletters/11-1/cole_crossley.htm.

Collins, Patricia Hill. *Black Feminist Thought*. New York: Routledge, 1991.

Coontz, Stephanie. *The Way We Never Were: American Families and the Nostalgia Trap*. New York: Basic Books, 1993.

Counihan, Carole, and Penny Van Esterik, eds. *Food and Culture: A Reader*. New York: Routledge, 2012.

Cowan, Ruth Schwartz. *More Work for Mother: The Ironies of Household Technology from the Open Hearth to the Microwave*. New York: Basic Books, 1983.

Crenshaw, Kimberle. "Mapping the Margins: Intersectionality, Identity Politics, and Violence Against Women of Color." *Stanford Law Review* (1991): 1241–99.

Cruickshank, Garry. "The Participation of Women Employed in Traditionally Male Dominated Occupations including Plumbing: 1975–2013." PhD Thesis, Auckland, New Zealand: Unitec Institute of Technology, 2015.

Cvetkovich, Ann. *An Archive of Feelings: Trauma, Sexuality, and Lesbian Public Cultures.* Durham: Duke University Press, 2003.

Cvetkovich, Ann, and Selena Wahng. "Don't Stop the Music: Roundtable Discussion with Workers from the Michigan Womyn's Music Festival." *GLQ: A Journal of Lesbian and Gay Studies* 7, no. 1 (2001): 131–51.

Daly, Mary. *Gyn/Ecology: The Metaethics of Radical Feminism.* Boston: Beacon Press, 1978.

Davis, Netta. "To Serve the 'Other': Chinese-American Immigrants in the Restaurant Business." *Journal for the Study of Food and Society* 6, no. 1 (2002): 70–81.

Davy, Kate. *Lady Dicks and Lesbian Brothers: Staging the Unimaginable at the WOW Café Theatre*. Ann Arbor: University of Michigan Press, 2010.

De Certeau, Michel. *The Practice of Everyday Life*, trans. Steven Rendall. Oakland: University of California Press, 1984.

D'Emilio, John. *Sexual Politics, Sexual Communities: The Making of a Homosexual Minority in the United States, 1940–1970*. Chicago: University of Chicago, 1983.

Derry, Robbin. "Feminist Theory and Business Ethics." In *A Companion to Business Ethics*, edited by Robert E. Frederick, 81–87. Hoboken, NJ: Wiley, 1999.

Dietz, Thomas, Ann Stirling Frisch, Linda Kalof, Paul C. Stern, and Gregory A. Guagnano. "Values and Vegetarianism: An Exploratory Analysis." *Rural Sociology* 60, no. 3 (1995): 533–42.

Driver, Elizabeth. "Cookbooks as Primary Sources for Writing History, a Bibliographer's View." *Food, Culture, and Society: An International Journal of Multidisciplinary Research* 12, no. 3 (2009): 257–74.

Dubois, Ellen, and Vicki Ruiz, eds. *Unequal Sisters: A Multicultural Reader in U.S. Women's History*, 3rd edition. New York: Routledge, 2000.

Eastland, Lynette J. *Communication, Organization, and Change within a Feminist Context: A Participant Observation of a Feminist Collective*. Lewiston: Edwin Mellen Press, 1991.

Echols, Alice. *Daring to Be Bad: Radical Feminism in America, 1967–1975*. Minneapolis: University of Minnesota Press, 1989.

Eckert, Laura. "Inclusion of Sexual Orientation Discrimination in the Equal Credit Opportunity Act." *Commercial Law Journal* 103, no. 3 (1998): 311–35.

Emery, Kim. *The Lesbian Index: Pragmatism and Lesbian Subjectivity in the Twentieth Century.* New York: SUNY Press, 2001.

Enke, Anne (A. Finn). *Finding the Movement: Sexuality, Contested Space, and Feminist Activism*. Durham: Duke University Press, 2007.

Epstein, Barbara. *Political Protest and Cultural Revolution: Nonviolent Direct Action in the 1970s and 1980s*. Oakland: University of California Press, 1993.

Evans, Sara Margaret. *Personal Politics: The Roots of Women's Liberation in the Civil Rights Movement and the New Left*. New York: Random House, 1979.

Faderman, Lillian. *Odd Girls and Twilight Lovers: A History of Lesbian Life in Twentieth Century America*. New York: Columbia University, 1991.

Faderman, Lillian, and Stuart Timmons. *Gay LA: A History of Sexual Outlaws, Power Politics, and Lipstick Lesbians*. Oakland: University of California Press, 2009.

Faludi, Susan. *Backlash: The Undeclared War Against American Women*. New York: Crown Publishers, 1991.

Ferree, Myra Marx, and Patricia Yancey Martin. *Feminist Organizations: Harvest of the New Women's Movement*. Philadelphia: Temple University Press, 1995.

Finnegan, Margaret. *Selling Suffrage: Consumer Culture and Votes for Women*. New York: Columbia University Press, 1999.

Firestone, Shulamith. *The Dialectic of Sex: The Case for Feminist Revolution*. New York: Batam Books, 1970.

Fortin, Nicole M., and Michael Huberman. "Occupational Gender Segregation and Women's Wages in Canada: An Historical Perspective." *Canadian Public Policy* (2002): 11–39.

Foucault, Michel. *The Foucault Reader*. New York: Pantheon, 1984.

Franzen, Trisha. "Differences and Identities: Feminism and the Albuquerque Lesbian Community." *Signs* 18, no. 4 (1993): 891–906.

Fraser, Nancy. *Fortunes of Feminism: From State-Managed Capitalism to Neoliberal Crisis*. New York: Verso Books, 2013.

Freedman, Estelle. *No Turning Back*. New York: Ballantine Books, 2002.

Freeman, Elizabeth. *Time Binds: Queer Temporalities, Queer Histories.* Durham: Duke University Press, 2010.

Friedan, Betty. *The Feminine Mystique*. New York: W.W. Norton & Company, 1963.

Gaard, Greta. "Toward a Queer Ecofeminism." *Hypatia* 12, no. 1 (1997): 114–37.

Gaard, Greta Claire. "Vegetarian Ecofeminism: A Review Essay." *Frontiers: A Journal of Women Studies* 23, no. 3 (2002): 117–46.

Gallo, Marcia M. *Different Daughters: A History of the Daughters of Bilitis and the Rise of the Lesbian Rights Movement.* New York: Carroll and Graf Publishers, 2006.

Geschwender, James A., ed. *The Black Revolt: The Civil Rights Movement, Ghetto Uprisings, and Separatism.* Englewood Cliffs: Prentice Hall, 1971.

Gibson, Judy. "Ann Arbor Women's Center and Coffeehouse." *Ain't I a Woman* 3, no. 7, December 1974.

Gilmore, Stephanie, and Elizabeth Kaminski. "A Part and Apart: Lesbian and Straight Feminist Activists Negotiate Identity in a Second-wave Organization." *Journal of the History of Sexuality* 16, no. 1 (2007): 95–113.

Godard, Barbara. "Feminist Periodicals and the Production of Cultural Value: The Canadian Context." *Women's Studies International Forum* 25, no. 2 (2002): 209–23.

Godard, Barbara. "Theorizing Feminist Discourse/Translation." In *Translation, History and Culture*, 42–53. London: Pinter, 1990.

Goldberg, Gale. "Feminism and Food: An Alternative to Restauranting." MA Thesis: Massachusetts Institute of Technology, 1976.

Graham, Hilary. "Smoking, Stigma and Social Class." *Journal of Social Policy* 41, no. 1 (2012): 83–99.

Haber, Barbara. "Cooking with Joy." *The Women's Review of Books* 21, no. 1 (October 2003).

Haber, Barbara. *From Hardtack to Home Fries: An Uncommon History of American Cooks and Meals*. New York: Free Press, 2002.

Halkias, Daphne, and Christian Adendorff. *Governance in Immigrant Family Businesses: Enterprise, Ethnicity and Family Dynamics*. London: Routledge, 2016.

Harding, Sandra. *Feminism and Methodology*. Bloomington: Indiana University Press, 1987.

Harris, Deborah A., and Patti Giuffre. *Taking the Heat: Women Chefs and Gender Inequality in the Professional Kitchen*. New Brunswick, NJ: Rutgers University Press, 2015.

Hartmann, Heidi I. "The Unhappy Marriage of Marxism and Feminism: Towards a More Progressive Union." *Capital and Class* 3, no. 2 (1979): 1–33.

Hawkesworth, Mary. *Feminist Inquiry: From Political Conviction to Methodological Innovation*. New Brunswick, NJ: Rutgers University Press, 2006.

Haywood, Leslie, and Jennifer Drake, eds. *Third-Wave Agenda: Being Feminist, Doing Feminism*. Minneapolis: University of Minnesota Press, 1997.

Hewitt, Nancy A. *No Permanent Waves: Recasting Histories of US Feminism*. New Brunswick, NJ: Rutgers University Press, 2010.

Higginbotham, Evelyn Brooks. "African American Women's History and the Metalanguage of Race." *Signs* 17, no. 2 (1992): 251–74.

Heynen, Nik. "Bending the Bars of Empire from Every Ghetto for Survival: The Black Panther Party's Radical Antihunger Politics of Social Reproduction and Scale." *Annals of the Association of American Geographers* 99, no. 2 (2009): 406–22.

Hochschild, Arlie, and Anne Machung, *The Second Shift: Working Families and the Revolution at Home*. New York: Penguin, 2012.

Hochschild, Arlie Russell. "Emotion Work, Feeling Rules, and Social Structure." *American Journal of Sociology* (1979): 551–75.

Hoff, Joan. "Gender as a Postmodern Category of Paralysis." *Women's History Review* 3, no. 2 (June 1994): 149–68.

Hogan, Kristen. *The Feminist Bookstore Movement: Lesbian Antiracism and Feminist Accountability*. Durham: Duke University Press, 2016.

Hogan, Kristen. "Women's Studies in Feminist Bookstores: 'All the Women's Studies Women Would Come In.'" *Signs* 33, no. 3 (2008): 595–621.

Hogan, Kristen Amber. "Reading at Feminist Bookstores: Women's Literature, Women's Studies, and the Feminist Bookstore Network." PhD dissertation: The University of Texas at Austin, 2006.

Horn, Sandy, *Gaia's Guide*. San Francisco: Women's Up Press, 1976–1991 editions.

Iacobbo, Karen, and Michael Iacobbo. *Vegetarian America: A History*. Santa Barbara: Greenwood Publishing Group, 2004.

Iacovetta, Franca, Valerie Korinek, and Marlene Epp, eds. *Edible Histories, Cultural Politics: Towards a Canadian Food History*. Toronto: University of Toronto Press, 2012.

Ingram, Gordon Brent, Anne Bouthillette, and Yolanda Retter. *Queers in Space: Communities, Public Places, Sites of Resistance*. Seattle: Bay Press, 1997.

Inness, Sherrie A. *Dinner Roles: American Women and Culinary Culture*. Iowa City: University of Iowa Press, 2001.

Inness, Sherrie A. *Secret Ingredients: Race, Gender, and Class at the Dinner Table*. New York: Palgrave Macmillan, 2006.

Jabs, Jennifer, Carol M. Devine, and Jeffrey Sobal. "Maintaining Vegetarian Diets: Personal Factors, Social Networks and Environmental Resources." *Canadian Journal of Dietetic Practice and Research* 59, no. 4 (1998): 183–93.

Jackson, Sherman A. *Islam and the Blackamerican: Looking toward the Third Resurrection*. New York: Oxford University Press, 2005.

Jakobsen, Janet R. *Working Alliances and the Politics of Difference: Diversity and Feminist Ethics*. Bloomington: Indiana University Press, 1998.

Jang, S. Mo, and Hoon Lee. "When Pop Music Meets a Political Issue: Examining How 'Born This Way' Influences Attitudes toward Gays and Gay Rights Policies." *Journal of Broadcasting and Electronic Media* 58, no. 1 (2014): 114–30.

Jeffreys, Sheila. *The Lesbian Heresy: A Feminist Perspective on the Lesbian Sexual Revolution*. North Geelong, Australia: Spinifex Press, 1993.

Jenkins, Betty Lanier, and Susan Phillis. *Black Separatism*. Westport, Connecticut: Greenwood Press, 1976.

Johnston, Jill. *Lesbian Nation: The Feminist Solution*. New York: Simon and Schuster, 1973.

Jo Kim, Amy. *Community Building on the Web: Secret Strategies for Successful Online Communities*. Boston: Addison-Wesley Longman Publishing, 2000.

Josephy, Alvin M., Jr. *Red Power: The American Indian's Fight for Freedom.* New York: American Heritage Press, 1971.

Julier, Alice P. "Hiding Gender and Race in the Discourse of Commercial Food Consumption." In *From Betty Crocker to Feminist Food Studies: Critical Perspectives on Women and Food*, edited by Arlene Voski Avakian and Barbara Haber, 163–84. Amherst: University of Massachusetts Press, 2005.

Kahn, Richard, and Douglas Kellner. "Internet Subcultures and Oppositional Politics." *The Post-Subcultures Reader* (2003): 299–314.

Kamp, David. *The United States of Arugula: How We Became a Gourmet Nation*. New York: Clarkson Potter, 2006.

Kanter, Rosabeth Moss. *Commitment and Community: Communes and Utopias in Sociological Perspective*. Cambridge: Harvard University Press, 1972.

Kauffman, Linda S., ed. *American Feminist Thought at Century's End: A Reader*. Oxford: Blackwell, 1993.

Kennedy, Elizabeth Lapovsky, and Madeline D. Davis. *Boots of Leather, Slippers of Gold: The History of a Lesbian Community*. New York: Routledge, 2014.

Ketchum, Alex. "Memory Has Added Seasoning: The Legacy of Feminist Restaurants in the United States and Canada." *Anthropology of Food* (2018), http://journals.openedition.org/aof/9904.

Ketchum, Alex. "Restaurant Management." In *The SAGE Encyclopedia of Food Issues*, vol. 1, edited by Ken Albala, 1204–1206. Stockton: SAGE and University of the Pacific Press, 2015.

Ketchum, Alexandra Diva. "Say 'Hi' from Gaia: Women's Travel Guides and Lesbian Feminist Community Formation in the Pre-internet Era (1975–1992)." *Feminist Media Studies* (2019): 1–17. ttps://doi.org/10.1080/14680777.2019.1665569.

Kheel, Marti. "Ecofeminism and Deep Ecology: Reflections on Identity and Difference." *Trumpeter* 8, no. 2 (1991): 55–63.

Kittay, Eva Feder. *Love's Labor: Essays on Women, Equality, and Dependency*. New York: Routledge, 1999.

Klein, Jennie. "The Ritual Body as Pedagogical Tool: The Performance of Art in The Women's Building." In *From Site to Vision: The Women's*

Building in Contemporary Culture, edited by Sondra Hale and Terry Wolverton, 192–227. Los Angeles: Otis College of Art and Design, 2011.

Kopp, James J. *American Countercultures: An Encyclopedia of Nonconformists, Alternative Lifestyles, and Radical Ideas in US History*. New York: Routledge, 2015.

Koshar, Rudy. "'What Ought to Be Seen': Tourists' Guidebooks and National Identities in Modern Germany and Europe." *Journal of Contemporary History* 33, no. 3 (1998): 323–40.

Laughlin, Kathleen A., Julie Gallagher, Dorothy Sue Cobble, Eileen Boris, Premilla Nadasen, Stephanie Gilmore, and Leandra Zarnow. "Is It Time to Jump Ship? Historians Rethink the Waves Metaphor." *Feminist Formations* 22, no. 1 (2010): 76–135.

Leclair, Louise, and Sheila Gilhooly. "Canada's Oldest Women's Centre Plans Change." *Upstream* 2, May 1978.

Lee, Martha F. *The Nation of Islam: An American Millenarian Movement*. New York: The Edwin Mellen Press, 1988.

Lesbian History Group. *Not a Passing Phase*. London: The Women's Press, 1989.

Lévi-Strauss, Claude. "The Culinary Triangle." In *Food and Culture: A Reader*. New York: Routledge, 1997.

Levin, Sue. *In the Pink: The Making of Successful Gay and Lesbian Owned Businesses*. New York: The Haworth Press, 1999.

Levine, Philippa. "The Humanising Influences of Five O'Clock Tea: Victorian Feminist Periodicals." *Victorian Studies* 33, no. 2 (1990): 293–306.

Lewin, Ellen, ed. *Inventing Lesbian Cultures in America*. Boston: Beacon Press, 1996.

Lewis, Gregory B. "Does Believing Homosexuality Is Innate Increase Support for Gay Rights?" *Policy Studies Journal* 37, no. 4 (2009): 669–93.

Liddle, Kathleen. "More Than a Bookstore: The Continuing Relevance of Feminist Bookstores for the Lesbian Community." *Journal of Lesbian Studies* 9 (2005): 145–59.

Liedtka, Jeanne. "Feminist Morality and Competitive Reality: A Role for an Ethic of Care." *Business Ethics Quarterly* (1996): 179–200.

Light, Ivan Hubert. *Ethnic Enterprise in America: Business and Welfare among Chinese, Japanese, and Blacks*. Oakland: University of California Press, 1972.

Loe, Meika. "Feminism for Sale: A Case Study of a Pro-Sex Feminist Business." *Gender and Society* 13, no. 6 (1999): 705–32.

Luxton, Meg. *More Than a Labour of Love: Three Generations of Women's Work in the Home*. Toronto: The Women's Press, 1980.

Luxton, Meg, Harriet Rosenberg, and Sedef Arat-Koç. *Through the Kitchen Window: The Politics of Home and Family.* Toronto: Garamond Press, 1990.

Lyon, Phyllis, and Del Martin. *Lesbian/Woman.* New York: Bantam Books, 1972.

MacKenzie, John M. "Empires of Travel: British Guidebooks and Cultural Imperialism in the 19th and 20th Centuries." *Histories of Tourism: Representation, Identity and Conflict* 6 (2005): 19–38.

Madge, Clare. "Methods and Methodologies in Feminist Geographies: Politics, Practice and Power." *Feminist Geographies: Explorations in Diversity and Difference* (1997): 86–111.

Mainardi, Patricia. "The Politics of Housework." *Redstockings* (1970).

Marcus, Sara. *Girls to the Front: The True Story of the Riot Grrrl Revolution*. New York: Harper Collins, 2010.

Maroney, Heather Jon, and Meg Luxton. "Gender at Work: Canadian Feminist Political Economy Since 1988." In *Understanding Canada: Building on the New Canadian Political Economy* (1997): 85–117.

Marsh, Clifton E. *From Black Muslims to Muslims: The Transition from Separatism to Islam, 1930–1980*. Metuchen: The Scarecrow Press, 1984.

Marx Ferree, Myra, and Patricia Yancey Martin. *Feminist Organizations: Harvest of the New Women's Movement*. Philadelphia: Temple University Press, 1995.

Mather, Anne. "A History of Feminist Periodicals, Part I." *Journalism History* 1, no. 3 (1974): 82–100.

Mather, Anne. "A History of Feminist Periodicals, Part II." *Journalism History* 1, no. 4 (1974): 108–20.

McDowell, Linda. *Gender, Identity and Place: Understanding Feminist Geographies*. Minneapolis: University of Minnesota Press, 1999.

McFeely, Mary Drake. *Can She Bake a Cherry Pie?: American Women and the Kitchen in the Twentieth Century*. Amherst: University of Massachusetts Press, 2001.

McGrath, Maria. "Living Feminist: The Liberation and Limits of Countercultural Business and Radical Lesbian Ethics at Bloodroot Restaurant." *The Sixties* 9, no. 2 (2016): 189–217.

McIntosh, Elaine N. *American Food Habits in Historical Perspective*. Westport: Praeger, 1995.

McKinney, Cait. "'Finding the Lines to My People': Media History and Queer Bibliographic Encounter." *GLQ: A Journal of Lesbian and Gay Studies* 24, no. 1 (2018): 55–83.

McKinney, Caitlin J. "Feminist Information Activism: Newsletters, Index Cards and the 21st Century Archive." PhD dissertation: York University, 2015.

McRobbie, Angela. "Notes on Postfeminism and Popular Culture: Bridget Jones and the New Gender Regime." In *All About the Girl: Culture, Power and Identity*, edited by Anita Harris, 3–14. New York: Routledge, 2004.

Meeker, Martin. *Contacts Desired: Gay and Lesbian Communications and Community, 1940s–1970s*. Chicago: University of Chicago Press, 2006.

Meyerowitz, Joanne Jay, ed. *Not June Cleaver: Women and Gender in Postwar America, 1945–1960*. Philadelphia: Temple University Press, 1994.

Miller, Timothy. *The 60s Communes: Hippies and Beyond*. New York: Syracuse University Press, 1999.

Miner, Valerie. *Competition: A Feminist Taboo?* New York: Feminist Press, 1987.

Mitchell, Juliet. *Women: The Longest Revolution*. New York: Vintage, 1984.

Montanari, Massimo. *Food Is Culture*. New York: Columbia University Press, 2006.

Morgan, Robin, ed. *Sisterhood is Powerful: An Anthology of Writings from the Women's Liberation Movement*. New York: Random House, 1970.

Morris, Bonnie J. *The Disappearing L: Erasure of Lesbian Spaces and Culture*. New York: SUNY Press, 2016.

Murray, Heather. "Free for All Lesbians: Lesbian Cultural Production and Consumption in the United States During the 1970s." *Journal of the History of Sexuality* 16, no. 2 (2008): 251–75.

Murthy, Dhiraj. "Digital Ethnography: An Examination of the Use of New Technologies for Social Research." *Sociology* 42, no. 5 (2008): 837–55.

"My Boyfriend Dropped Me Off at the Lesbian Coffeehouse." *Hera: A Philadelphia Feminist Publication* 1, no. 5 (December 1975): 7.

Nardi, Peter M., and Beth E. Schneider, eds. *Social Perspectives in Lesbian and Gay Studies: A Reader*. New York: Routledge, 2013.

Nelson, Lise, and Joni Seager, eds. *A Companion to Feminist Geography*. Hoboken: John Wiley & Sons, 2008.

Nembhard, Jessica Gordon. *Collective Courage: A History of African American Cooperative Economic Thought and Practice*. University Park, Pennsylvania: Penn State University Press, 2014.

Oldenburg, Ray. *The Great Good Place: Café, Coffee Shops, Community Centers, Beauty Parlors, General Stores, Bars, Hangouts, and How They Get You Through the Day*. St. Paul: Paragon House Publishers, 1989.

Onosaka, Junko. *Feminist Revolution in Literacy: Women's Bookstores in the United States*. New York: Routledge, 2013.

Parkin, Katherine J. *Food Is Love: Food Advertising and Gender Roles in Modern America*. Philadelphia: University of Pennsylvania Press, 2006.

Parr, Joy. *Domestic Goods: The Material, the Moral, and the Economic in the Postwar Years*. Toronto: University of Toronto Press, 1999.

Pearce, Susan C. "Today's Immigrant Woman Entrepreneur." *The Diversity Factor* 13, no. 3 (2005): 23–29.

Perl, Harriet, and Gay Abarbanell, *Guidelines to Feminist Consciousness Raising*. Los Angeles: National Task Force on Consciousness Raising of the National Organization for Women, 1976.

Petersen, Karen E. "An Investigation into Women-identified Music in the United States." In *Women and Music in Cross-cultural Perspective*, edited by Ellen Koskoff, 203–12. Champaign: University of Illinois Press, 1987.

Podmore, Julie. "Lesbians in the Crowd: Gender, Sexuality and Visibility along Montreal's Boul. St-Laurent." *Gender, Place, and Culture* 8, no. 4 (2001): 333–55.

Podmore, Julie A., and Line Chamberland. "Entering the Urban Frame: Early Lesbian Activism and Public Space in Montréal." *Journal of Lesbian Studies* 19, no. 2 (2015): 192–211.

Pulse Collective. *How Many Beans Make Pulse: Trade Secrets, The Pulse Cookbook*. Brighton, England: Brighton Resource Center Publication, 1970s (exact date unknown).

Reno, Molly. "Women's Coffeehouse." *Herself: Women's Community Journal* 3, no. 4 (August 1974).

Rentschler, Carrie A. *Second Wounds: Victims' Rights and the Media in the U.S.* Durham: Duke University Press, 2011.

Roberts, John Anthony George. *China to Chinatown: Chinese Food in the West*. Islington, United Kingdom: Reaktion Books, 2004.

Rodgers, Daniel T. *Age of Fracture.* Cambridge: Harvard University Press, 2011.

Rome, Adam. *The Genius of Earth Day: How a 1970 Teach-In Unexpectedly Made the First Green Generation.* New York: Hill and Wang, 2013.

Rosen, Ruth. *The World Split Open: How the Modern Women's Movement Changed America*. Old Saybrook: Tantor, 2013.

Ross, Becki. *The House that Jill Built: A Lesbian Nation in Formation*. Toronto: University of Toronto Press, 1995.

Roth, Benita. *Separate Roads to Feminism: Black, Chicana, and White Feminist Movements in America's Second Wave*. Cambridge: Cambridge University Press, 2004.

Rothblum, Esther, and Penny Sablove, eds. *Lesbian Communities: Festivals, RVs, and the Internet.* Binghamton: The Haworth Press, 2005.

Rudy, Kathy. "Radical Feminism, Lesbian Separatism, and Queer Theory." *Feminist Studies* 27, no. 1 (2001): 191–222.

Ryan, Barbara. *Feminism and the Women's Movement: Dynamics of Change in Social Movement Ideology and Activism*. New York: Routledge, 2013.

Sandilands, Catriona. "Lesbian Separatist Communities and the Experience of Nature Toward a Queer Ecology." *Organization & Environment* 15, no. 2 (2002).

Schenone, Laura. *A Thousand Years Over a Hot Stove: A History of American Women Told through Food, Recipes, and Remembrances*. New York: W.W. Norton, 2003.

Schulman, Sarah. *Stagestruck: Theater, AIDS, and the Marketing of Gay America.* Durham: Duke University Press, 1998.

Schwartz, Joan M., and Terry Cook. "Archives, Records, and Power: The Making of Modern Memory." *Archival Science* 2, no. 1 (2002): 1–19.

Scott, Joan. "The Evidence of Experience." *Critical Inquiry* 17, no. 4 (1991): 773–97.

Scott, Joan. *Gender and the Politics of History*. Revised Edition. New York: Columbia University Press, 1999.

Scraton, Sheila, and Beccy Watson. "Gendered Cities: Women and Public Leisure Space in the 'Postmodern City.'" *Leisure Studies* 17, no. 2 (1998): 123–37.

Shapiro, Laura. *Perfection Salad: Women and Cooking at the Turn of the Century*. New York: Modern Library, 2001.

Shapiro, Laura. *Something from the Oven: Reinventing Dinner in 1950s America*. New York: Viking Press, 2004.

Shreve, Bradley G. *Red Power Rising: The National Indian Youth Council and the Origins of Native Activism.* Norman: University of Oklahoma Press, 2011.

Shugar, Dana R. *Separatism and Women's Community.* Lincoln: University of Nebraska Press, 1995.

Singer, Peter. *Animal Liberation: A New Ethics for Our Treatment of Animals*. New York: HarperCollins, 1975.

Smart, Josephine. "Ethnic Entrepreneurship, Transmigration, and Social Integration: An Ethnographic Study of Chinese Restaurant Owners in Rural Western Canada." *Urban Anthropology and Studies of Cultural Systems and World Economic Development* 32, no. 3/4 (Fall–Winter 2003): 311–42.

Spang, Rebecca L. *The Invention of the Restaurant: Paris and Modern Gastronomic Culture*. Cambridge: Harvard University Press, 2001.

Spencer, Colin. *The Heretic's Feast: A History of Vegetarianism*. Lebanon: University Press of New England, 1996.

Staggenborg, Suzanne. "The Survival of the Women's Movement: Turnover and Continuity in Bloomington, Indiana." *Mobilization: An International Quarterly* 1, no. 2 (1996): 143–58.

Stewart, Matthew D. *Metropolitan Community Church: A Perfectly Queer Reading of the Bible*. Gainesville: University of South Florida Press, 2008.

Strasser, Susan. *Satisfaction Guaranteed: The Making of the American Mass Market*. New York: Pantheon Books, 1989.

Stuckey, Sterling. *The Ideological Origins of Black Nationalism.* Boston: Beacon Press, 1972.

Sturgis, Susanna J. "Ladyslipper: Meeting the Challenges of Feminist Business." *Hot Wire: Journal of Women's Music and Culture* (1985): 38–60.

Tandon, Neeru. *Feminism: A Paradigm Shift*. Halifax: Atlantic Publishers and Distributers, 2008.

Tannahill, Reay. *Food in History.* New York: Crown Publishers, 1989.

Taylor, Verta, Nancy Whittier, A.D. Morris, and C.M. Mueller. "Collective Identity in Social Movement Communities: Lesbian Feminist Mobilization." In *Social Perspectives in Lesbian and Gay Studies: A Reader*, edited by Peter M. Nardi and Beth E. Schneider, 349–65. New York: Routledge, 1998.

Tetrault, Jeanne. "The Making of a Feminist Farm." *Country Women* 1, no. 5 (March 1973).

Thornton, Sarah. *Club Cultures: Music, Media, and Subcultural Capital*. Middletown: Wesleyan University Press, 1996.

Travers, Ann. "Parallel Subaltern Feminist Counterpublics in Cyberspace." *Sociological Perspectives* 46, no. 2 (2003): 223–37.

Turner, Fred. *From Counterculture to Cyberculture: Stewart Brand, the Whole Earth Network, and the Rise of Digital Utopianism*. Chicago: University of Chicago Press, 2010.

Uneke, Okori. "Ethnicity and Small Business Ownership: Contrasts Between Blacks and Chinese in Toronto." *Work, Employment and Society* 10, no. 3 (1996): 529–48.

Van Cleve, Stewart. *Land of 10,000 Loves: A History of Queer Minnesota*. Minneapolis: University of Minnesota Press, 2012.

VanDeburg, William L. *New Day in Babylon: The Black Power Movement and American Culture, 1965–1975*. Chicago: The University of Chicago Press, 1992.

Vida, Ginny, ed. *Our Right to Love: A Lesbian Resource Book*. Englewood Cliffs, New Jersey: Prentice Hall, 1978.

Visser, Margaret. *Much Depends on Dinner: The Extraordinary History and Mythology, Allure and Obsessions, Perils and Taboos, of an Ordinary Meal.* New York: Grove Press, 1986.

Voltz, Karen. "Sister Moon." *Amazon: A Midwest Journal for Women* 7, no. 2 (April/May 1978).

Vronwode, Catherine. "Garden of Joy Blues." *Country Women: Homesteading* 1, March 1973.

Walker, Dennis. *Islam and the Search for African-American Nationhood: Elijah Muhammad, Louis Farrakhan and the Nation of Islam*. Atlanta, Georgia: Clarity Press, 2005.

Waring, Marilyn. *Counting for Nothing: What Men Value and What Women Are Worth*. Toronto: University of Toronto Press, 1999.

Warner, Michael. *Publics and Counterpublics*. New York: Zone Books, 2005.

Warner, Michael. "Publics and Counter Publics." *Public Culture* 14, no. 1 (2002): 49–90.

Warren, Karen, and Nisvan Erkal, eds. *Ecofeminism: Women, Culture, Nature*. Bloomington: Indiana University Press, 1997.

Waters, Alice, and Daniel Duane. *Edible Schoolyard*. San Francisco: Chronicle Books, 2008.

Weare, Walter B. *Black Business in the New South: A Social History of the NC Mutual Life Insurance Company*. Durham: Duke University Press, 1993.

Weichselbaumer, Doris, and Rudolf Winter-Ebmer. "A Meta-Analysis of the International Gender Wage Gap." *Journal of Economic Surveys* 19, no. 3 (2005): 479–511.

Wheaton, Barbara. "Finding Real Life in Cookbooks: The Adventures of a Culinary Historian." *Humanities Research Group Working Papers* 7 (1998). https://scholar.uwindsor.ca/hrg-working-papers/7.

Whittier, Nancy. "From the Second to the Third Wave: Continuity and Change in Grassroots Feminism." In *The US Women's Movement in Global Perspective*, edited by Lee Ann Banaszak, 45–67. Lanham: Rowman and Littlefield, 2006.

Wimminland Collective. *Shewolf's Directory of Wimmin's Lands and Lesbian Communities*. Womonworld: Shewolf Self Published, 2012.

Woehrle, Lynne M. "Claims-Making and Consensus in Collective Group Processes." *Research in Social Movements, Conflicts and Change* 24 (2002): 3–30.

Wolf, Deborah Goleman. *The Lesbian Community*. Oakland: University of California Press, 1980.

Wolfe, Maxine. "Invisible Women in Invisible Places: The Production of Social Space in Lesbian Bars." In *Queers in Space: Communities, Public Spaces, Sites of Resistance*, edited by Gordon Brent Ingram, Anne Bouthillette, and Yolanda Retter, 301–24. Seattle: Bay Press, 1997.

Wolverton, Terry. "Introduction." In *From Site to Vision: The Women's Building in Contemporary Culture*, edited by Sondra Hale and Terry Wolverton, 18–38. Los Angeles: Otis College of Art and Design, 2011.

Women and Geography Study Group of the IBG and Explorations in Feminism Collective of Great Britain. *Geography and Gender: An Introduction to Feminist Geography*. Toronto: Random House of Canada Limited, 1984.

Yoken, Hannah. "Transnational Transfers and Mainstream Mappings: Women's Liberation Calendars of the 1970s and 1980s." In *Translating Feminism: Interdisciplinary Approaches to Text, Place, and Agency*, edited by Maude Anne Bracke, Julia C. Bullock, Penelope Morris, and Kristina Schulz, 117–46. New York: Palgrave Macmillan, 2021.

INDEX

Page numbers in italic indicate figures and illustrations.